AMERICAN

SUGA

KINGDOM

AMERICAN

SUGAR

KINGDOM

The Plantation
Economy of the
Spanish Caribbean,
1898–1934

César J. Ayala

The University of North Carolina Press

Chapel Hill and London

Designed by Heidi Perov
Set in Monotype Garamond
by Keystone Typesetting, Inc.
Manufactured in the United States of America

The paper in this book meets the guidelines for permanence and
durability of the Committee on Production Guidelines for Book
Longevity of the Council on Library Resources.

Library of Congress Cataloging-in-Publication Data
Ayala, César J.
American sugar kingdom : the plantation economy of the
Spanish Caribbean, 1898–1934 / by César J. Ayala.
p. cm.
Includes bibliographical references and index.
ISBN 0-8078-2506-9 (cloth : alk. paper)
ISBN 0-8078-4788-7 (pbk.: alk. paper)
1. Sugar trade—Cuba—History—20th century. 2. Sugar trade—
Puerto Rico—History—20th century. 3. Sugar trade—Dominican
Republic—History—20th century. 4. Sugar trade—
United States—History—20th century. I. Title.
HD9114.C89A96   1999
382'.41361'0973—dc21   99-17349
                                                    CIP

03 02 01 00 99   5 4 3 2 1

Contents

Tables

Figures and Maps

Figures

Maps

Acknowledgments

This book owes a great debt to many individuals, none of whom is responsible for its shortcomings.

The idea for this research project emerged out of common work with my friend Félix Córdova Iturregui of Guaynabo, Puerto Rico, when we started examining the listings of the directors of Puerto Rico's sugar companies in the Firestone Library of Princeton University more than a decade ago. Rafael Bernabe, of Trujillo Alto, Puerto Rico, has helped me at all stages of this project.

Many librarians and archivists have helped me at different times in my research: Nelly Cruz, director of the Archivo General de Puerto Rico, Tomás Fernández Robaina and Zoila Lapique of the Biblioteca Nacional José Martí in Havana, Rachelle Moore of Binghamton University Library, Amilcar Tirado of the Centro de Estudios Puertorriqueños in Hunter College, the late Olga Torres Seda of Lehman College's library, and Carl Van Ness of the University of Florida Archives. I would like to thank the anonymous librarians of the Mudd Manuscript Library in New Haven, the New York Public Library, the Firestone Library at Princeton University, Binghamton University Library, and the Albert R. Mann Library of the College of Agriculture and Life Sciences at Cornell University.

Joseph Dorsey of Hamilton College introduced me to the Cuban National Archives, where I would have never been able to do any research except for the generous guiding hand of Fe Iglesias García of the Instituto de Historia de Cuba, who in addition pointed out many sources in the Biblioteca Nacional José Martí, shared her own primary research, and allowed me to read the manuscript of her forthcoming book *Del ingenio al central*. Oscar Zanetti of the Instituto de Historia de Cuba likewise shared his primary research on U.S. ownership of Cuban sugar mills. Alfredo Menéndez of the Instituto de Historia de Cuba shared many stories on the nationalization of Cuban sugar mills in the 1960s and provided firsthand knowledge of the Cuban sugar industry and the labor movement.

Nancy Herzig Shannon, Muriel McAvoy Weissman, and Emilio Zamora shared their research or directed me to important sources. Samuel Farber, James Geschwender, Juan Giusti, the late Terence Hopkins, Erick Pérez Velasco, James Petras,

Charles Post, and José Luis Rénique read parts or all of the manuscript and provided invaluable commentary. Martin Murray and Dale Tomich of Binghamton University read more drafts of the manuscript than I would like to admit. Their enduring dedication to their students, even after graduation, is beyond the call of duty.

Two Professional Staff Congress–City University of New York grants supported research trips to Havana. Ramón Bosque, Juan Flores, Gabriel Haslip Viera, and Antonio Lauria, of the Centro de Estudios Puertorriqueños, enabled me to have two semesters of residence at the University of Puerto Rico through the City University of New York–University of Puerto Rico Exchange Program. María Dolores Luque of the Centro de Investigaciones Históricas, and Aarón Ramos and Félix Ojeda of the Instituto de Estudios del Caribe, University of Puerto Rico, hospitably welcomed me to the resources of their institutions. Benjamin Bernier offered essential computer assistance at the University of Puerto Rico. I would like to thank Deborah Pacini Hernández and Frank Moya Pons for their hospitality during a research trip to Gainesville. My friend and colleague Héctor Cordero Guzmán of the New School for Social Research provided indispensable assistance in the use of the Statistical Package for the Social Sciences.

I would like to thank Francisco Scarano of the University of Wisconsin at Madison for a close reading of the manuscript and for his encouraging remarks. Professor Maurice Zeitlin, of the University of California at Los Angeles, read the manuscript and provided immensely helpful and detailed commentary. I would like to thank my editor, Elaine Maisner of the University of North Carolina Press, for her encouragement and support. Last but not least, thanks to Jennifer McCormick for her cheerful companionship and inspiring support.

This book is dedicated to my son, Miguel Tomás Ayala Grady.

AMERICAN

SUGAR

KINGDOM

Introduction

In the Spanish-American War of 1898 the United States seized Cuba and Puerto Rico. In 1905 it seized the customs of the Dominican Republic, and it occupied that country from 1916 to 1924. Cuba became an independent state in 1902, under the tutelage of the United States and under the shadow of the Platt Amendment. Puerto Rico became a formal colony. The Dominican Republic saw its independence progressively curtailed, and U.S. influence remained paramount even after the withdrawal of U.S. troops in 1924. Thus the United States became an imperial power controlling the economic life of the three nations, and the Spanish Caribbean as a whole became a sphere for U.S. direct investment, a colonial region dominated by the decisions of U.S. capitalists. Although U.S. capital flowed into all economic sectors, sugar production became the primary locus of investment, the premier economic activity of the islands. Sugar was the principal export. This book is about the social and economic structure of the three islands during the high period of sugar monoculture dominated by U.S. capital in the first three and a half decades of the twentieth century.

The influence of the economically vibrant United States transformed the social and economic structure of the three nations. The transfer of the Spanish colonies of Cuba and Puerto Rico and of the independent Dominican Republic into the sphere of influence of the United States represented a landmark phenomenon that was totally new in the life of the islands. The new imperialism, however, appeared at first merely to have strengthened old institutions. Sugar plantations were not new to the Caribbean. In one way or another, all of the islands of the Spanish, British, and French Caribbean experienced plantation booms at some point in their histories since the initial European conquest of the archipelago. The place of the islands in the history of the world economy since the time of the conquest lies in its plantation-based sugar production. Monocultural dependence on one export product, lack of internal diversification of the economy, metropolitan absentee ownership, metropolitan control of shipping and currency, and pauperization of the labor force have all been persistent features of plantation systems in the Caribbean since the time of the conquest and a source of persistent underdevelopment for the region as a whole. On the surface, then, it would seem that U.S. imperialism merely reproduced old patterns of economic organization associated with the previous European colonizers in the region—new wine in old casks, as it were.

This book argues, to the contrary, that a radical social and economic transformation took place in the islands of the Caribbean as a result of U.S. imperial expansion. It is an argument against an analysis that emphasizes continuity in plantation systems, which in the Caribbean is associated with the so-called plantation school. The plantation school is a Caribbean version of dependency theory which argues, in essence, that the persistence of plantations in the region is the cause of economic underdevelopment. Although it would be hard to take issue with such an argument, a debate formulated on the terms of the plantation school obscures the historical specificities of twentieth-century Caribbean plantations and capitalist underdevelopment. Beneath the surface of economic continuity, vast changes swept the islands, economic relations were radically transformed, and a new form of underdevelopment took hold based on capitalist relations of production instead of the persistence of noncapitalist relations.

Despite appearances of continuity, the persistence of underdevelopment in the Caribbean in our century is not the product of the survival of precapitalist relations of production. On the contrary, a new form of underdevelopment, based on the spread of wage labor and the introduction of the most modern forms of economic organization, plagued the islands. Poverty and inequality were not the product of the survival of forms of extraeconomic coercion of the labor force or of antiquated methods of production, much less of isolation from the transformative influences of the world market or of lack of capital investment. To the contrary, in the case of the Spanish Caribbean in the early twentieth century, the development of a free labor market, the introduction of the latest technological advances in the sugar mills, and fast-paced economic integration to the U.S.

economy are to be blamed for the persistence of poverty and underdevelopment. The paradox of this form of "development," which is actually a form of under-development, is the subject of this book. What we have cannot be described accurately as new wine in old casks. A more appropriate metaphor would be to say that not only the barrels were new—made of Kentucky white oak—but that even the distilled product was entirely different—new rum in new barrels, as it were.

The focus of this book is therefore what was new in the plantations. It aims at locating the historical specificity of the social and economic transformation of the islands under U.S. influence by examining the patterns of organization of capitalist enterprise, the interaction between the new colonial masters and the social struc-ture they found in place in each region of the Sugar Kingdom, and the transforma-tion of the class structure. In short, the focus is on the discontinuities in plantation development. The starting point is corporate organization. The sugar refiners who eventually acquired control of a large share of the sugar produced in the plantations were at the forefront of the transformation of American industry in the late nineteenth century. They were among the pioneers of the "industrial trusts" of the late nineteenth century and of the modern corporation as we now know it. The refiners consolidated horizontally, by merging their refineries into a single enterprise to restrict output and raise prices, before the Spanish-American War and the U.S. acquisition of colonies in the Caribbean. When the United States finally settled its decades-long contest with the British over supremacy in the Caribbean and seized the Spanish islands, the refiners were fully armed with the latest organizational means to expand economically. Through a system of holding companies, they assembled an empire of plantations without precedent in the history of the Caribbean archipelago.

In the islands, the refiners confronted a variety of local conditions, diverse land tenure structures, and variable availability of workers. These conditions were a product of an incomplete and uneven transition that had been taking place in the islands since the abolition of slavery. With different degrees of success, planters in the islands had been busy reconstructing cane agriculture after abolition, using contract farmers and wage workers, merely surviving in some places and thriving in others. The transition to the corporate-owned plantation was highly uneven. In regions where the new sugar barons encountered established plantation systems, the transition was complex and the resulting product was a hybrid system in which the descendants of the old planter class became independent contract farmers delivering cane to the mills and the descendants of the slaves became a permanent agricultural proletariat. In virgin zones previously untouched by the phenomenon of sugar monoculture—notably eastern Cuba—the corporate plantations achieved nearly universal control of land resources and, lacking a resident agricultural proletariat, they resorted to the importation of immigrant workers at harvest time.

Everywhere, however, sugar was king. Yet the phenomenon of twentieth-century sugar monoculture has escaped the comparative, Caribbean-wide scrutiny it deserves. Plagued by the ubiquitous problems associated with nation building, historians and social scientists in the islands have devoted considerable energies to the island-by-island study of sugar monoculture and underdevelopment but little effort to the common, comparative study of the region as a whole. What the Spanish once called their Antillas became, to nineteenth-century Caribbean revolutionaries such as Ramón Emeterio Betances, Gregorio Luperón, Eugenio María de Hostos, and José Martí the possible locus of a utopia they called the Confederacy of the Antilles. In the twentieth century, U.S. imperial officers circulated throughout the islands, and the Bureau of Insular Affairs held some notion of the historical unity of the region. Once the dream of Cuba Libre was shattered in the Spanish-American War of 1898, the utopia of a unified Caribbean faded, to the point that the study of the Spanish Caribbean as a historical region has become a quasi-heretical proposition. This book is a study of the dynamics of capitalist underdevelopment in a colonial region where the dream of national liberation was shattered in the defeat of the Cuban revolution of 1895 by the imperial project initiated in the Spanish-American War. For the peoples of the islands, the possibilities lost were replaced by the reality of a world turned upside down and the development, on the ashes of a great utopian project, of the American Sugar Kingdom in the Caribbean.

A Caribbean Plantation System

Sugar plantations have been central institutions in the economic development of the Caribbean for the last five hundred years. All the islands of the Antilles experienced the growth of plantation agriculture. The comparative study of plantation societies has provided important insights into the development of economy and society in this region. This book is a study of the plantation economy of the Spanish Caribbean between the Spanish-American War of 1898 and the crisis that shook the foundations of the sugar industry of Cuba, Puerto Rico, and the Dominican Republic in 1933–34. The colonial transfer of the islands of Cuba and Puerto Rico from Spain to the United States in 1898 and the U.S. occupation of the Dominican Republic in 1916–24 opened the way for massive U.S. investments in sugar plantations. The combined sugar production of the three islands doubled from 433,000 tons in 1900 to 1,127,000 tons in 1902. Sugar output then doubled again between 1902 and 1910, reaching 2,470,000 tons. Between 1910 and 1919, production doubled once more and reached 5,033,000 tons.

At the end of World War I the three islands produced close to one-third of the sugar sold in the world market. Production continued to increase until 1925 (6,753,000 tons) and fell thereafter because of a series of restrictive policies, first on the part of the Cuban government and then on the part of the United States, aimed at reducing overproduction and restoring prices. This expansion accentuated Cuba's traditional dependence on sugar exports, replaced coffee as the main export of Puerto Rico, and elevated sugar to first rank among the Dominican Republic's export crops. Large parts of the islands were converted to cane agriculture, and the livelihood of millions of people became dependent on the international price of sugar. No region of the world ever experienced a process of expansion of sugarcane plantation agriculture comparable in scope and depth to that which took place in the Spanish Caribbean in the first three decades of this century.

An examination of the expansion of sugar plantations in this region in the twentieth century necessarily calls forth an inquiry into its specific features and how they compare to previous systems of plantation agriculture in the Caribbean. The persistence of plantations in the Antillean archipelago throughout the centuries has attracted the attention of scholars who have pondered their importance not only for the Caribbean but for the development of the world economy as a whole throughout its different stages since the formation of a world market in the early sixteenth century. This book borrows its title from Eric Williams, whose scholarship is probably the best-known English-language synthesis of the development of plantation agriculture in the Caribbean from a world-historical perspective.[1] The appropriation of the term "American Sugar Kingdom" from a scholar whose main interest was the development of plantations based on slavery implies a comparative study of plantation agriculture across different historical epochs. Indeed, many of the questions raised in this book revolve around problems of continuity and discontinuity in plantation development. Boldly put, the question can be raised as follows: if the American Sugar Kingdom was indeed a plantation economy, how did it differ from previous plantation systems based on coerced labor in the history of the Caribbean? Conversely, what did this plantation system have in common with the Cuban slave plantations of the nineteenth century, the Haitian plantations of the eighteenth, the Barbadian plantations of the seventeenth, or even with the plantations of Hispaniola in the sixteenth century? Can a concept that encompasses phenomena so distant in time and so different in nature contribute to our understanding of twentieth-century sugar monoculture?

Plantations in the Caribbean have been viewed in one of three ways. The dependency and world-system approaches to the problem have emphasized the continuity of the large agricultural estates producing for the world market throughout the history of the Caribbean, while downplaying somewhat the differences between the diverse forms of labor that have typified different plantation systems.[2] In opposition to this view, "productionist" writers have emphasized local relations of production and overlooked external, metropolis-satellite relations. The plantation school, which is a Caribbean version of dependency theory, has developed a concept of plantation economy that implies continuity in the external, metropolis-satellite relations, as well as in the internal aspects of the plantation economy. The internal relations of production of plantation economies have elements of continuity, according to this view. The problems of conceptualization reflect wider differences of conception about the capitalist world economy and its evolution through the centuries. The problems raised by the different conceptions of plantation economy inform the questions raised in this book, which is intended as a dialogue with other social scientists and historians who have used it to try to understand the development of the Caribbean as a specific region of the capitalist world economy.

The Circulationist School

To this day the debates on modernization and north-south relations feel the impact of the pioneering studies of André Gunder Frank, whose work developed in conflict with the prevailing dualist conceptions of modernization theory. According to modernization theory, societies move from "traditional" to "modern" stages as they develop. Contact with the European world economy is the driving force of a transformation that steadily replaces "backward" or "traditional" social forms by "modern" ones. It would seem, according to this perspective, that underdevelopment is coextensive with lack of contact with the world market or the Western world. In the perspective of modernization theory, societies move from a "universal original state" to a "universal end state." Methodologically, the study of underdevelopment becomes a search for the specific location of a country or area in the continuum leading from the "traditional" to the "modern." Frank, in an apt phrase, labeled modernization theory the "comparative statics of polar ideal types."[3] Alain de Janvry has pointed out that under the "modernization" approach, "development is reduced to a process of diffusion of innovations. The history and specificity of the less-developed countries are thus effectively negated, and their only possible future is predetermined by the history of the more-developed countries."[4]

Frank's attack on modernization theory in the Latin American context pointed out that seemingly "feudal" forms of production had been established in Latin America as part of the expansion of European capitalism and that the most isolated and seemingly most "traditional" areas of the continent were really the product of the decay of former boom areas previously linked to the world market.[5] Underdevelopment, therefore, is not a surviving atavism from a traditional past of isolation from the world market. It is not a state characterized by isolation from the world market or an original point of departure but is instead relational, that is, it involves the articulation of the economy of a region with the wider European world economy. In other words, underdevelopment is the product of the expansion of the European-dominated world economy. It is not asynchronic with European development in the sense of occupying an "early" position in the continuum from "traditional" to "modernity." Instead, underdevelopment is simultaneous in historical time with development, and both are aspects of an integrated whole: the capitalist world economy.

Retrospectively, the paradigm of modernization theory seems to be based on a curious historical trompe l'oeil which is easier to accept in continental Latin America than in the Caribbean. The existence of areas of the continent with claims of continuity with ancient pre-Columbian civilizations, large peasantries, and surviving pre-Columbian languages (the central Andes, Guatemala, Mexico) lends plausibility to the notion of a traditional society relatively untouched by European civilization. In the plantation Caribbean, by contrast, this mirage was never possible. There is very little that can be characterized as "traditional" in the Caribbean.[6] The native Arawak populations of the archipelago were almost totally exterminated in the course of the sixteenth century.[7] Subsequent Caribbean development took place entirely by human populations transplanted from Europe, Africa, and Asia across the sea-lanes of a developing world economy, for the purpose of producing plantation crops for the world market.

In Latin America, the autarchic hacienda emerged out of a process of involution associated with the decline of the mining centers. The contrast with the plantations is revealing. As Ida C. Greaves put it, "The fact that the plantations were in their origins and subsequent development exporting enterprises explains many of the differences now to be found between them and the hacienda. The latter produced mainly for the domestic market because in the Spanish colonies the dominant export interest was in precious metals, not in agricultural products."[8] Once the suppliers of food to the mining centers, the haciendas imploded when these mining centers decayed. The social structure that emerged out of this involution resembled in many ways the European feudal patterns, and the idea of a Latin American feudalism thus emerged. The historical involution leading to the autarchic hacienda erased its own tracks. Its origins in an earlier, world-market-oriented era had subsequently to be rediscovered.[9] At first sight, the hacienda seemed to have always been there, its origins not related to the world market. By comparison, the plantation Caribbean always had a more transparent history. The mirage of traditionalism, of backwardness as an atavism, did not apply. In the words of Raymond T. Smith, the bipolar opposition between tradition and modernity "does not capture the essence of the Caribbean experience."[10] In the Caribbean the typical social institution—the plantation—remained linked to the world market, inserted in a world division of labor producing staples for the metropolitan countries. The criteria used to identify a Latin American "feudalism"— autarchic productive units, isolation from the market—were absent in the Caribbean. If anything, the illusion generated by Caribbean development tended to be the opposite. Sugar was the most important commodity in the world market in the seventeenth century,[11] and, according to Sidney Mintz, world sugar "shows the most remarkable upward production curve of any major food on the world market over the course of several centuries, and it is continuing upwards still."[12] Combined with the complex industrial processes required for its manufacture, the large capital outlays required, and the fact that, according to Smith, "plantations were among the first industrial organizations in which the workers were separated from the means of production and subjected to something like factory discipline,"[13] the permanent insertion of plantations within the world economy produced the illusion that a capitalist economy had existed from the beginning.[14]

As a result, notions of a "traditional" society of the type suggested by modernization theory never took hold in the Caribbean.[15] Gunder Frank's contribution to the study of underdevelopment did not surprise students of the Caribbean. To the contrary, his critique seemed a logical outflow of the history of the region. For much the same reasons, arguments for the existence of some variant of feudalism were out of the question. In the Caribbean, the real problem centered on how to understand the combination of uninterrupted production for the world market on the one hand and the diversity of precapitalist and capitalist relations of production on the other. In the twentieth century, with its modern plantations run by wage labor, the identification of underdevelopment with the persistence of precapitalist relations of production became untenable. It became necessary to acknowledge the existence of a form of underdevelopment not based on the persistence of precapitalist relations of production and to explain it.[16] Caribbean plantations used native and then European indentured labor at the beginning, then African slaves. Asian indentured labor replaced African slaves after abolition of slavery in the British Caribbean in the nineteenth century. *Agregados*, *colonos*, and transitional forms between sharecropping and wage labor characterized the plantations of the Spanish Caribbean after abolition. The corporate plantations of the American Sugar Kingdom in the twentieth century used primarily wage workers.

The persistence of plantations has strengthened notions of continuity in the world market over time.[17] Whereas the involution of the haciendas in continental Latin America produced notions of clearly demarcated feudal and capitalist stages, in the plantation Caribbean the sequential development of different plantation systems—all linked to the world market—generated the notion of a smooth flow interrupted only by labor problems. It is this peculiarity that accounts for the difficulties of the concept "plantation." For, when one reads that the plantation has been the central institution of Caribbean development (or underdevelopment) one is surely making abstraction of the differences, for example, between the early twentieth-century estates and mills of the South Porto Rico Sugar Company (SPRSC) in Puerto Rico and the Dominican Republic, on the one hand, and the Barbadian plantations of the seventeenth century, on the other. The "circulationist" approach, that is, the approach that defines capitalism as the production and circulation of commodities for the world market, is thus useful in pointing to the persistence of the large agricultural estate producing raw materials for the world market but is limited in allowing us to see the differences among very different types of so-called plantation.

The Plantation School

The illusion of continuity has generated conceptual problems. At one extreme is the notion, I think best exemplified by André Gunder Frank, that the plantation Caribbean has been capitalist since the Europeans created it in the sixteenth century. This theoretical school bases its conclusions on the correct observation of features that are common to all Caribbean plantation systems. These include the global division of labor into which plantations are inserted, the uninterrupted linkages of plantations to the world market, the tendency toward monoculture, and, coupled with the latter, the internal disarticulation of the productive forces because of the lack of horizontal linkages.[18] While correctly pointing to the features that are common to all plantation systems, this theoretical approach obliterates distinctions among plantation systems by overlooking differences in production relations.

At the other extreme, but based on the same premise of uninterrupted linkage to the world market, lies the plantation school of thought. This school argues that there exists a plantation economy whose features can be mapped at the level of international circulation of capital, commodities, and profits, as well as internally as a set of production relations. Notwithstanding the differences among them, I would classify Lloyd Best, George Beckford, and Jay Mandle as belonging to this school.[19] According to Best, a plantation economy is first of all a "hinterland economy" and falls within the wider category of "externally propelled economies." There are three kinds of "hinterland economy": the "hinterlands of conquest," the "hinterlands of settlement," and the "hinterlands of exploitation." Examples of the first are the Andes and Mexico in the epoch of the conquest and during the Spanish silver age. Examples of the second are the European colonial settlements of New England and the Southern Cone of South America. An example of the third is the plantation Caribbean. Thus the plantation economy is not only a hinterland economy but more specifically a hinterland of exploitation.[20] Best's hinterlands resemble Charles Wagley's "culture spheres." According to Wagley, the Americas can be divided into three regions or "culture spheres." These are "Indo-America" (Best's hinterlands of conquest); "Euro-America" (Best's hinterlands of settlement); and "Plantation-America" (Best's hinterlands of exploitation).[21]

In Best's conception, the "general institutional framework" of plantation economies has five components. First, a plantation economy is an exclusive sphere of influence of a metropolis with "limited external intercourse." Second, a plantation economy is limited to the production of raw materials or terminal activities that concentrate little "value added." This feature Best calls *Muscovado Bias*. Third, there is the overarching influence of the metropolitan financial system, what Best calls the *Metropolitan Exchange Standard*. Fourth, there is metropolitan control of all shipping, which Best calls the *Navigation Provision*. And finally, there is *Imperial Preference* for the products of the plantation economy. These five conditions define Best's concept of plantation economy.[22] All five conditions refer to metropolis-satellite relations. None refers to internal relations of production of the plantation economy. All five conditions are perfectly applicable to the American Sugar Kingdom in the twentieth century.

Best further defines plantations as "total economic institutions." This concept is also considered important by George Beckford. According to Beckford, the concept "plantation economy" is applicable to "those countries where the internal and external dimensions of the plantation system dominate the country's economic, social, and political structure and its relations with the rest of the world."[23] Beckford analyzes the plantations from the time of the conquest, when they were institutions of settlement, to contemporary times and includes an extended and fascinating analysis of modern, plantation-based corporations such as Tate & Lyle, Unilever, the United Fruit Company, and the Firestone Company. In his analysis the term "plantation economy" is flexible enough to accommodate the slave-run *ingenios* together with twentieth-century corporate enterprises. Internally, all plantations are "total economic institutions." The plantation regulates all aspects of the life of its labor force and in this sense can be considered, together with prisons and concentration camps, "total."[24] Lloyd Best and George Beckford both argue, therefore, that the internal social organization of plantations displays continuity over time. The common elements of the internal social organization of plantations can be grouped under the notion "total economic institution."

More recently, Jay Mandle placed the debate on plantations in explicit relation to the debates on the transition to capitalism in Europe, linking the concept of plantation to broader discussions of the origins and nature of the capitalist world economy itself.[25] For Mandle, the social relations that "inhere" in the plantation indicate that the plantation economy is not a capitalist economy, its essential mechanism being the use of extraeconomic coercion against the labor force. The different forms of this extraeconomic coercion are not as important as the fact that extraeconomic coercion is present in all kinds of plantations:

> What therefore seems to be essential to a plantation society is not the form of the non-market mechanism by which labor is mobilized in large numbers for low-productivity agricultural work, but simply that some such non-market mechanism exists. Slavery, indentured immigration, share-cropping, or the artificial maintenance of monocultural plantation production, can all serve to guarantee the labor force requirements of the plantation system and all do so in the absence of a viable labor market mechanism, an essential aspect of a functioning capitalist economy.[26]

This approach conflates all precapitalist forms of labor exploitation under the rubric "extraeconomic coercion." Since all precapitalist forms of labor exploitation are extraeconomic, the approach impedes the study of what is specific to each one.[27] A careful reading of Mandle shows, further, that "the artificial maintenance of monocultural plantation production" refers to the different postemancipation labor arrangements in plantations, including wage labor. In Mandle's conception plantation wage labor is artificial because it is also characterized by extraeconomic coercion. Mandle extends the concept "extra-economic coercion" to include plantation wage labor to show the internal social continuity of the plantation and extends the argument for internal social continuity throughout the history of plantations by developing the idea of a "plantation mode of production." Unlike the capitalist mode of production, which generates economic growth, the plantation mode of production is essentially stagnant and actually hampers economic development.[28] Its defining features are as follows:

First, large-scale export-oriented agriculture dominates the society. Second, the labor force requirements of the agricultural sector are greater than can be supplied through the functioning of a domestic labor market. Third, as a result, a non-market mechanism of mobilizing and allocating labor is present and this mechanism is dominant in defining the class relations of society. Finally, a specific culture both emerges and reinforces the class relations which are articulated in this way.[29]

To demonstrate that such a mode of production exists, Mandle attempts to show that wage labor in plantations involves fundamental extraeconomic coercion. After emancipation, extraeconomic coercion (to Mandle, the "non-market mechanisms" of labor recruitment) took the form of lack of access to land. Thus emancipated slaves who had no land remained on the plantations. Mandle refers to this condition as the "artificial maintenance" of the plantation economy:

> Land policy was the key to alternative employment opportunities. For if land had been made available to the former slaves, its availability would have represented precisely the alternative which would have doomed the plantations. As a result, throughout the region planters struggled to ensure that land was not made available to former slaves. To the extent that they were successful in this blocking effort the planters succeeded in insulating themselves from the need to compete for a labor force.[30]

I will argue to the contrary that lack of access to land after emancipation increased the pressures toward proletarianization for the freed slaves. Instead of a "non-market mechanism" of allocating labor, the successful efforts of the planters to prevent the former slaves from having access to land initiated a process of proletarianization and contributed to the creation of a labor market in the Spanish Caribbean. Separation of the direct producers from access to land is the defining process of formation of capitalist agriculture everywhere. It is the sine qua non of agrarian capitalist production. Lack of access to land in the transition that took place after emancipation did not "block" the development of a free labor market. Rather, it created a free labor market. The characterization of plantation wage labor as one more instance of extraeconomic coercion makes it possible to conceptualize the twentieth-century corporate plantation staffed with wage workers as an accretion of the precapitalist plantations based on coerced labor. It is also essential to the notion of a plantation mode of production insofar as it helps to differentiate it from the capitalist mode of production. Some of the questions raised in this book revolve around the degree to which the twentieth-century plantations in the Spanish Caribbean displayed fundamental continuity with previous plantation systems along the lines suggested by theorists of the plantation school.

The search for internal social continuity in the plantation economy leads thus from "total economic institution" (Best, Beckford, Smith) to "extraeconomic coercion" (Mandle, 1972) to, finally, a "plantation mode of production" (Mandle, 1982). Like the circulationist or world-system approaches, the theorists of the so-called plantation economy attempt to find common elements across time in all Caribbean plantation systems, but they do so by compressing different relations of production sequentially under the category "total economic institution" or by associating twentieth-century wage labor with extraeconomic coercion based on nonmarket mechanisms of allocation of labor.

The attempt to identify the common features of plantation economies has not always led to the conclusion that there is internal social continuity in plantation development. The North American anthropologist Sidney Mintz, for example, defined plantations as "a capitalist type of agricultural organization in which a considerable number of unfree laborers were employed under the unified direction and control in the production of a staple crop." He further specified four distinguishing characteristics: the sharp separation of worker and employer classes, the aim of continuous commercial agriculture, monocrop specialization, and the capitalist nature of the enterprise, with the planter as businessman not farmer. Reflecting on the relation between twentieth-century corporate plantations and precapitalist plantations, Mintz argued that "if the term 'unfree' be struck from the above definition, it becomes a thoroughly applicable preliminary characterization of modern plantations."[31] Mintz distinguished continuous from discontinuous elements in twentieth-century plantation agriculture and placed free labor among the latter.

Similarly, Clive Thomas provides insightful criticisms of the plantation school in a study on the plantation economy of Guyana by focusing on the differences between coerced and free labor. Thomas draws a distinction between the "colonial-slave mode of production"[32] and modern plantations operated by transnational corporations on the basis of wage labor. According to Thomas, the focus on the plantation as an institutional form leaves too many questions unanswered.[33] To define a plantation economy or a plantation mode of production on the basis of formal similarities is like attempting to define fully developed capitalism solely on the basis of the joint stock corporation, which existed for centuries before it evolved but became the principal organizational form of capital only in the twentieth century.[34] Mapping out what is specific to twentieth-century plantations allows the researcher to study the transformation of plantation agriculture. Otherwise, the history of the Caribbean and the struggle for economic development become one long, uniform, tautological struggle against the plantation, a uniform enemy invariant through time.

The Long Lineage of the Plantation

The problems in conceptualizing plantations are a product of the long historical lineage of the plantation and more specifically of sugarcane cultivation.[35] Before arriving in the New World in a voyage of Christopher Columbus in 1493, sugarcane had been produced in the littoral areas of the Mediterranean. It had arrived to the coasts of the Mediterranean via Persia and forms part of the "Arab Agricultural Revolution" of A.D. 700–1100. Sugar reached the economy of the Mediterranean together with at least another sixteen crops introduced by the Arabs, mostly from India, and hitherto unknown to the Europeans: rice, sorghum, hard wheat, cotton, watermelons, eggplants, spinach, artichokes, colocasia, sour oranges, lemons, limes, bananas, plantains, mangoes, and coconut plants.[36] For almost a thousand years until the sixteenth century, North Africa, the Middle East, and Europe received their supply of sugar from an industry located around the shores of the Mediterranean.[37] At that point, the industry's center was displaced to plantations in the Atlantic—to the coast of Africa, to the Caribbean, and to Brazil. Although, for natural reasons, tropical America provided a better habitat to the sugarcane than the Mediterranean lands (which are the northernmost place of sugar cultivation), the displacement of the sugar industry across the Atlantic is part of a wider shift of economic activity from the Mediterranean to the Atlantic. According to J. H. Galloway, "By the end of the seventeenth century cotton, rice and sugar had largely disappeared as crops from the Mediterranean basin, where they had once been so important; these crops, long ago introduced to the Islamic world as import substitutes, had in turn been replaced by imports. Their disappearance is part of the general economic decline of the Mediterranean basin in this period."[38] Galloway and Charles Verlinden state that the precursor of the plantation economies of the New World was the irrigated Mediterranean sugar industry of southern Iberia. Sugar was grown commercially in Palestine, Egypt, Sicily, Cyprus, and Crete, in addition to North Africa.[39] In Cyprus and Morocco plantations used slaves.[40] Elsewhere it seems that sugar mills used mostly sharecropping systems. The extension into the Atlantic of these Mediterranean "plantations" give, according to Verlinden, a definite continuity to the process of colonization from the Middle Ages through the epoch of the Great Discoveries. The most likely precursors of the New World plantations are probably the Portuguese plantations in the island of São Tomé, off the coast of Africa.[41]

The European processes of conquest and colonization extended the plantation to Hispaniola,[42] Brazil,[43] and the British West Indies.[44] On the eve of the French Revolution, French Saint Domingue was the principal sugar producer of the New World.[45] Caribbean plantations generated immense wealth for the European planters who owned them and contributed to the accumulation of wealth which enabled the transition to capitalism in Europe. Richard Sheridan argues that the "plantation revolution" of the seventeenth century contributed to the industrial revolution of the eighteenth: "Britain's industrial development was in no small way a process of diversification around her export-base in the Caribbean plantations."[46] European observers were aware of the central role of the Caribbean plantation economies in the development of the European-dominated world economy. Abbé Raynal wrote: "The labours of the people settled in those islands, are the sole basis of the African trade: they extend the fisheries and cultures of North America, afford a good market for the manufactures of Asia, and double, perhaps treble, the activity of all Europe. They may be considered the principal cause of the rapid motion which now agitates the universe."[47]

Cuba, a hitherto undeveloped Spanish possession, became the principal plantation economy of the Caribbean after the Haitian Revolution of 1791–1804. Eric Williams described it: "The slave revolution in Saint Domingue and the annihilation of its sugar industry provided the immediate stimulus to Cuba sugar production. The country forged rapidly ahead, until it became the centre of gravity of the Caribbean in the nineteenth century, as Hispaniola, Barbados, Jamaica, and Saint Domingue had been in their day."[48] The still less developed island of Puerto Rico also experienced a sugar boom from 1800 to 1850 as a result of the international changes in sugar supply generated by the Haitian revolution.[49] In neighboring Santo Domingo, the Haitian invasion of 1822 had the opposite effect of eliminating plantation slavery forever.

Both Cuba and Puerto Rico experienced a belated expansion of plantation agriculture in the nineteenth century.[50] Whereas in the British and French Caribbean the nineteenth century was the century of abolition, in the Spanish Caribbean it was the golden age of slavery. Slavery was abolished in the British Empire in 1833, but Britain and the world economy continued to consume the products of slave plantations located outside the empire. Williams contends that "British capitalism had destroyed West-Indian slavery, but it continued to thrive on Brazilian, Cuban, and American slavery."[51] The spread of the factory system and industrial capitalism in Britain, western Europe, and the North of the United

States increased demand for colonial raw materials such as cotton and sugar. The slave regime actually expanded in Cuba, the South of the United States, and Brazil. This "second slavery"[52] of the nineteenth century was characterized by articulation between the regions producing raw materials with slave labor with the industrializing regions of the world, whose economies now consumed raw materials more voraciously. It was also characterized by the introduction to the plantations of some of the technologies of the industrial revolution, such as the steam engine. The increase in cane-grinding capacity accentuated the need for agricultural labor and increased the Atlantic demand for slave labor.

The industrial revolution also shattered the mercantilist system and reoriented the trade of the new producers of sugar in the Caribbean toward the United States. The principal consumer of the sugars of Cuba and Puerto Rico in the nineteenth century was the United States, not Spain, the ruling metropolitan power. Industrialization caused dramatic changes in the diet of the rising industrial conurbations of the metropolitan economies. Sugar ceased to be a luxury accessible only to the rich and became a fundamental dietary requirement of the working class. Sugar consumption evolved, from use as a "spice" in minute quantities and selling at an extremely high price, into an article of consumption for the rich, and finally into a basic component of the daily caloric intake of the working class. Sidney Mintz has traced the evolution of sugar consumption in relation to the rise of the English working class: "The biggest sucrose consumers, especially after 1850, came to be the poor, whereas before 1750 they had been the rich. . . . Cheap sugar, the single most important addition to the British working class diet during the nineteenth century, now became paramount, even calorically. By 1900, it was contributing on average nearly one sixth of per-capita caloric intake."[53] In the United States industrialization increased the demand for cotton and, through a dietetic revolution similar to the one taking place in Britain, sugar consumption rose dramatically, from 12.5 to 65 pounds per capita between 1830 and 1900. The slave plantation economies of Cuba and Puerto Rico in the nineteenth century developed outside the mercantilist framework desired by Spain and abhorred by local planters in the islands. Meanwhile, Spanish colonialism in the two islands survived until the end of the century, conditioned by the deadlocked struggle between Great Britain and the United States for supremacy in the Caribbean.[54]

The transfer of Cuba and Puerto Rico to the United States in 1898 removed the political control of Spain, one of the most backward European nations at the turn of the century, and placed the islands under the political and economic influence of the most dynamic industrial power of the time. In 1900 the United States was not as industrialized as Britain relative to its population, but its industrial output was already greater than Great Britain's in absolute terms. The extension of U.S. power over the Dominican Republic in the customs receivership of 1905 and the occupation of 1916–24 consolidated U.S. colonial power in the region. For the first time, a Caribbean plantation economy developed under the auspices of a non-European colonizer. The economic organization of the emerging sugar plantations reflected the immense gap between the economic power of the United States and that of Spain. The political reorientation of the islands also signified an economic leap directed by immensely powerful industrial and financial groups in the United States.

Metropolitan Capital, Industrial Organization, Class Structure

The questions posed in this book are largely a dialogue with the plantation school. I have attempted to locate just where the plantation economy of the Spanish Caribbean in the early twentieth century fits the model of plantation economy developed largely by social scientists from the British West Indies, and just where it does not. While the questions raised are mostly inspired by the queries of scholars who have studied plantations comparatively, the answers provided are often at odds with those of the plantation school. Instead of broad generalization about the Caribbean's "insertion" into the global economy, I attempt to look at the historical specificity of Caribbean underdevelopment, that is, at the historical process through which underdevelopment was constructed. I begin with an attempt to understand those aspects of the industrial evolution of the United States in the last decades of the nineteenth century most closely associated with the colonial economy of the Spanish Caribbean after 1898. In Chapter 2, I explore the development of the sugar refining industry of the United States in the last decades of the nineteenth century, the period of the so-called second industrial revolution. The emergence of oligopoly in the sugar refining industry serves as the background for the expansion of the investments of U.S. sugar refiners in colonial plantations after 1898. The horizontal consolidation in the sugar refining industry in the United States was part of the corporate revolution that changed the structure of capitalist enterprise in that country, and in all advanced industrialized nations, at the turn of the century. This transformation was not an automatic response to technological transformations or to market demands. It involved a struggle between different sectors of capital in the metropolitan economy and a redefinition on the part of the metropolitan state of the concept of the corporation and indeed of the very idea of private property of the industrial means of production.[55] The emergence of the holding company capable of controlling the stock of other corporations provided a formidable mechanism of industrial consolidation. Sugar refining was a pioneering industry in this respect. The process of horizontal consolidation and the emergence of holding companies provided the platform from which the U.S. sugar refining industrialists built an empire of sugar plantations in the Caribbean after 1898.

In Chapter 3, I explore the development of the tariff system as it concerns the sugar industry. In an attempt to understand the basis for the colonial division of labor which emerged, I examine the specific class segments that lobbied the state and benefited from tariff protection. Protectionist beet and cane farmers in the United States were able to block the establishment of colonial free trade with Cuba in 1903, while Puerto Rico, by contrast, was incorporated into the U.S. customs area, with immense consequences for the development of the sugar industry in both islands. In plantation school terminology, this chapter studies "imperial preference" and "muscovado bias," two of the defining features of a plantation economy. But in contrast to the plantation school formulation, in which the imposition of a colonial division of labor is a sort of abstract quality of the metropolis-satellite relation, I examine which sectors of the metropolitan economy gained and which lost from the imperial tariff system and the evolution of that system over time. Far from being static, tariff policies changed drastically between 1898 and 1934 in response to the demands of continental sugar producers to overproduction and falling prices.

Chapter 4 is a study of the industrial organization of metropolitan capital in the colonial economies. Many seemingly independent U.S. sugar corporations in Cuba, the Dominican Republic, and Puerto Rico were actually owned by capitalists from the sugar refining business in highly centralized clusters of enterprises that were vertically integrated with the sugar refineries of the United States. Foreign capital has played a prominent role in the development of plantations in the Caribbean throughout the centuries. Even though the transnational organization of capital is actually one of the oldest features of the world economy in general and of its plantation sector in particular, the extent of centralization of ownership and the scope of the phenomenon of vertical integration in the American Sugar Kingdom are unprecedented. This, in turn, is an expression of the profound transformation in industrial organization wrought by the corporate revolution. Chapter 4 is at the center of the arguments concerning plantation economy. While the "circulationist" or "world systems" perspectives on the world economy emphasize core-periphery relations and the "productionist" or "class analysis" approach focuses mostly on local relations of production, I believe a proper understanding of the plantation needs to integrate analysis of local relations of production with that of the transnational organization of capital. The plantations of the Caribbean were part of a larger structure encompassing the metropolitan refining industry, and the transformation of local relations of production cannot be understood outside the metropolitan refining/colonial plantation complex. Instead of a dualist conception of the world economy which juxtaposes development and underdevelopment as two separate poles, I view the American Sugar Kingdom as an integrated yet differentiated whole subject to a single dynamic of capital accumulation encompassing metropolitan and colonial economies. This integration does not in the least mean an end to the hierarchical organization of industrial production or the end of unequal development. Subordinate integration is instead at the root of unequal development in the world economy.

Chapters 5 and 6 concern the class structure of the American Sugar Kingdom. The development of a class of capitalist cane farmers who delivered cane to the mills is explored in Chapter 5. Some of the cane of the American Sugar Kingdom was grown under the administration of the sugar mills. Most of the cane, however, was grown by local capitalist farmers, although there was a numerically strong group of small farmers who worked the land themselves and with family labor. Although metropolitan capital controlled the industrial process of milling the cane and processing it into unrefined sugar, local capitalist farmers employed the majority of agricultural workers of the American Sugar Kingdom. The local class structure of the American Sugar Kingdom was characterized by the preponderance of local capitalist farmers and wage laborers, not by the survival of precapitalist relations.

Contrary to the claims of the plantation school, the emergence of a class of wage laborers was not based on the continuation of extraeconomic coercion. Instead, the process of emergence of this class, the process of proletarianization, was based on the classic model of separation of the direct producers from access to the means of production and the elimination of extraeconomic bonds. The uneven process of proletarianization across the islands is explored in Chapter 6. In some regions, there had been a transition to wage labor after the abolition of slavery. This transition was partial in that some of the former slaves had been able to escape proletarianization and acquired land, principally in eastern Cuba. Regional differences in land tenure are in turn critical determinants of the patterns of labor migration which emerged in the twentieth century. Inherited local differences in patterns of agrarian settlement, land tenure, and class structure, which were in turn a product of the evolution of class relations after abolition, meant that the availability of wage workers for the cane farms varied considerably across the islands. In Cuba, labor power was as abundant in the west as it was scarce in the east. In the twentieth century, mills and farms in areas with a scarce supply of labor power in Cuba and the Dominican Republic imported migrant workers from Haiti, Jamaica, and the eastern Caribbean and initiated an inter-Caribbean flow of migrants that is without precedent in the region. The analysis in these chapters diverges sharply from the views of the plantation school, which identify under-development with the persistence of noncapitalist mechanisms of labor alloca-tion. Instead, the example of the American Sugar Kingdom shows an integrated yet differentiated core-periphery structure characterized by the dominance of capitalist relations of production and specifically the prevalence of wage labor, both in the metropolitan refining industry and in the colonial plantations.

Chapter 7 examines the transition from the plantations of the slave regime to the corporate plantations of the twentieth century. There were two distinct pro-cesses of transition. Between the abolition of slavery and the Spanish-American War, the transition to wage labor took place simultaneously with the emergence of central sugar mills characterized by the separation of the industrial process of milling and processing the cane from the agrarian processes of planting and harvesting it. Central sugar mills and independent colonos (cane farmers) who hired wage labor replaced the unitary ingenios of the epoch of slavery. Whereas during the slave economy mill and farm were integrated under the same owner-ship and management, under the system of *centrales* these two processes were typically under separate ownership. The process of separation of milling from cane farming was successfully developed in the Cuban sugar industry before 1898 and had allowed that island to expand sugar output immediately after abolition. In Puerto Rico and the Dominican Republic the process was less successful and the plantation economy languished. After 1898, however, gigantic, U.S.-owned sugar mills invaded all the islands, transforming the scale and the organization of cane agriculture and sugar production everywhere. The new colossal U.S. mills were unitary enterprises that controlled the milling operations and the cane lands in what became veritable company towns in the Caribbean countryside.

Chapter 8 examines briefly the sudden collapse of sugar prices during the Great Depression of the 1930s, the social explosions the crisis caused, and the imperial attempts to regulate the sugar industry through a system of sugar quotas.

Throughout the book, I have kept in mind the notion that the Spanish Carib-bean does have a certain historical unity that makes it amenable to study as a specific region of the world economy, with certain unifying tendencies. For rea-sons that are rooted in the specific colonial histories of the islands, most social scientists still study the Spanish Caribbean as a fragmented collection of national and colonial economies, not as a greater unit of analysis. I have heretically chosen to look at the region as a whole instead of carrying out a study of a specific island. While this approach surely misses some of the complexities of the insular economies, I believe it captures the central social and economic reality of the region in the early twentieth century.

The Horizontal Consolidation of the U.S. Sugar Refining Industry

The invasion of Cuba and Puerto Rico in 1898 took place at a time when capitalist enterprise in the United States was undergoing a momentous transformation into its modern, corporate structure. The wave of mergers and consolidations of 1898–1904 firmly established the limited liability, joint stock corporation with ability to hold the stock of other corporations (holding company) as the essential unit of capitalist industrial enterprise in the United States. While the corporate form and a market for securities had existed in railroads since the 1870s, the transformation of industry and the development of a market for industrial securities took place essentially after 1898. Thus the emergence of the United States as an imperial power in the Caribbean coincided with a historical transformation in the structure of capitalist property. How did these changes in the structure of capitalist enterprise affect the industrial organization of the sugar refining industry of the United States and its subsequent expansion into the production of raw sugar in colonial plantations? Did the concentration and centralization of production in the metropolitan refining industry have any effect on the structure of capitalist property in the sugar plantations of the Caribbean after 1898? Did it condition the economic relation between the colonial power and its colonies? Did the process of horizontal consolidation of the sugar refiners affect the purchase and construction of plantations to supply raw sugar for the refineries? What was the property structure of the refinery/plantation complexes that emerged? Were native mill owners in the colonies displaced by metropolitan capital? In short, how was the colonial bond organized economically?

The economic structure of U.S. colonial enterprise in the Caribbean was immensely influenced by the industrial transformation of the sugar refining industry. Sugar refining was a pathbreaking industry in that it had been one of the earliest to consolidate as a "trust" and among the first to use the New Jersey holding company as a mechanism of industrial consolidation. In contrast to the majority of the consolidations in 1898–1904, which took place after the basic legal framework for the modern corporation was established, sugar refining was responsible for the epochal transformation in corporate law implied by the decision in *United States v. E. C. Knight Co.*, which laid the legal framework determining what kind of corporate entities could exist and what their powers were.[1] After 1898 U.S. sugar refining corporations established and operated vertically integrated sugar plantations in the Caribbean. To understand the specific form of industrial organization of these colonial plantations it is necessary first to examine the process of horizontal consolidation of the metropolitan sugar refining industry in the United States. This chapter examines that process in the last decades of the nineteenth century, the formation of the Sugar Trust, and the eventual development of oligopoly in the sugar refining industry. This examination lays the groundwork for understanding how metropolitan capital expanded into the Spanish Caribbean once it became a colonial region dominated by the United States.

Colonial intervention and metropolitan investment turned the Spanish Caribbean into a region of sugar monoculture whose principal market was the United States. As in other contemporary colonial empires, the trade of the islands was oriented toward the industrialized cities of the ruling metropolis, and the banking and currencies of the colonial territories were linked to those of the metropolitan economy. Most of the sugar of the islands was purchased by United States enterprises, principally by sugar refineries or their subsidiary enterprises. After 1898 metropolitan capital undertook the direct organization of production of raw sugar in the colonies, revolutionizing the technological base of those areas of the colonial economies that were complementary to those of the metropolitan economy, while leaving other areas of production untouched, producing sharp patterns of uneven development. Metropolitan capital also participated in the establishment of the essential infrastructure, building ports and railroads to support the production of agricultural raw materials for the export economy. U.S. corporations directly involved in the production of sugar in the islands of the Caribbean typified the new economic role of metropolitan capital in the colonies. The vertically integrated structure of the sugar companies emerged in part as a mechanism to strengthen the power of horizontally consolidated metropolitan sugar refiners seeking to crush industrial competitors.

The reorganization of the sugar industry forms part of a broader phenomenon called the second industrial revolution, which recast the technological base of production and transformed the social structures of the metropolitan economies of western Europe, the United States, and Japan. The introduction of the electric motor, the invention of Bessemer steel, transatlantic steam navigation, refrigerated railroad and sea transport, the launching of telephone and wireless communication, the internal combustion engine, electric lighting, and the modern chemical industry all form part of this revolution.[2] This revolution had many social effects. Internationally, the second industrial revolution signaled the end of Britain's monopoly of industrial production in the world market and the rise of new, industrializing nations. The United States experienced a remarkable industrial revolution after the conclusion of its Civil War in 1865. After processes of revolution from above, both Germany and Japan underwent rapid industrialization at an accelerated pace starting in the 1870s. Japan launched a program of industrialization after the Meiji Restoration of 1868.[3] World trade increased dramatically with the improvements in navigation. In the seas, warfare capabilities were augmented by the introduction of steel-plated ships and of cannon designed to pierce steel plate. On land, the new industrial revolution featured the introduction of repetitive firepower, extensively used in colonial conquest and subjugation.[4] In its breadth and scope, the second industrial revolution had a greater impact on the world economy than the first industrial revolution initiated in England.[5]

The social effects of this industrial transformation were no less momentous. The industrial working class grew, the peasantries or farming communities declined in numbers and political importance, and capitalist enterprise was transformed from an individual to a collective endeavor through the creation of joint stock companies, the new typical form of organization of business enterprise. The developing technologies required outlays of capital much in excess of what individuals or families could command. Industrial plants grew in size, and the capital outlays required to launch them increased. Concentration of production in one industrial branch after another caused a decrease in the number of competing firms. Increased barriers to entry allowed established industrialists to create monopolistic horizontal combinations through the creation of trusts and later holding companies, which socialized the property of the capitalist class. Technology was determinant in the sense that the increased size of investments and consequently the increased barriers to entry into an industrial branch permitted the

creation of monopolistic combinations.[6] The specific process through which capitalist property evolved from the family-owned firm of the nineteenth century into
its modern corporate form was not, however, an automatic response to technological change. It required a struggle to redefine the corporation, which was
originally a chartered public institution to which the state granted some privileges
and transferred some of its sovereign functions in the interest of fulfilling some
function related to the public good. Through a tortuous process involving many
contingencies, this quasi-statal institution eventually evolved into the quintessen-
tial form of capitalist private property in the twentieth century.[7] The joint stock
corporation became the principal means of centralizing capital to launch and
sustain new concerns of increased size, employing many more workers, and requiring much greater outlays of capital.

According to one view, the secular trend of increasing productivity caused such
an expansion of production that in certain branches of industry the supply of
colonial raw materials lagged behind the demand created by the more voracious,
technologically revamped factories of the metropolitan economies. The pressure
thus generated propelled metropolitan capitalists to invest directly in the colonial
economies, where raw materials production was revolutionized through the introduction of enterprises based on some of the same technologies unleashed in the
metropolis.[8] Although no doubt productivity increased and with it the demand for
raw materials, the leap by the sugar refiners into production of raw sugar in the
colonies was not an automatic response to increased productivity. It was instead
conditioned by capitalist competition in which control over raw materials offered
advantages over oligopolistic competitors.

Metropolitan capital organized the production of these raw materials in the
underdeveloped regions of the world, often, although not always, under the tutelage of direct colonial rule by metropolitan states, often in enclaves or plantations.[9] In the specific case of the American Sugar Kingdom, the transformation of
the sugar refining industry of the United States in the last three decades of the
nineteenth century determined the increased drive on the part of metropolitan
sugar refiners to control sugar plantations in the colonies, and it conditioned the
way they went about organizing colonial enterprises. The Spanish-American War
of 1898 gave the refiners a new political framework within which these new,
expansive economic forces could be unleashed.

Innovative technologies and increases in the scale of production radically transformed the business of sugar refining. Industrial concentration advanced as sugar
refineries became more productive, much larger, employed more workers, and

consumed increasing amounts of raw sugar. The technological advances propelling the transformation of sugar refining were many: steam power, vacuum pans, centrifugal machines, chemical advances to purify the sugar. The increase in the scale of production of the average sugar refinery in the United States was accompanied by a reduction of the number of enterprises capable of profitably producing sugar using the new technologies.

The accumulation of technological advances throughout the nineteenth century helped to transform the industry. Steam power was introduced to the sugar refineries in 1833 and was in widespread use by 1838.[10] The vacuum pan, a device that permitted the boiling of molasses at low temperatures, was introduced in 1855. Animal charcoal (bone black through which liquid sugar is passed to remove impurities) began to be used at around the same date as the vacuum pan. The centrifugal machine was introduced around 1860.

Under conditions of industrial competition, technological improvements translated into falling price margins between refined and raw sugar. The cost of refining sugar decreased significantly and the consumption of refined sugar in the United States increased very rapidly, especially after the Civil War. The increase in the productivity of sugar refining was offset by the increasing demand for refined sugars. The destruction of the Louisiana sugar industry—which produced a semi-refined sugar—during the Civil War contributed to consumers' shift toward refined sugar. The dramatic process of industrialization in the United States from 1865 to 1900 transformed the country into the foremost industrial producer in the world and contributed to the increase in the per capita consumption of sugar. The combined effect of the use of steam, the vacuum pan, animal charcoal, and the centrifugal machine reduced the time of refining raw into white sugar from three weeks to sixteen hours.[11] The technological improvements made in refining outstripped the increases in consumption and demand.

Sugar had been a colonial commodity since the formation of the world market in the sixteenth century. In the nineteenth century, the abolition of slavery in one country after another created crisis in the cane industry. From 1870 to 1900, sugar produced from beet overtook the production of cane sugar in the world market. In 1870, world beet sugar production amounted to 952,000 tons while sugar from cane outpaced it at 1,771,000 tons. In 1880, on the eve of the abolition of slavery in Cuba, cane and beet sugar were produced in approximately equal amounts: 1,857,000 tons of beet sugar and 1,975,000 tons of cane sugar. By 1890 sugar beet had overcome cane as the principal source of sugar in the world market (3,463,000 tons versus 2,253,000 tons of cane sugar). In 1900, the primacy of beet reached a peak, accounting for 65 percent of the sugar produced in the world market.

In 1900, however, the trend was reversed. A new wave of metropolitan invest-ments in colonial sugar industries augmented the output of the cane regions drastically. The principal centers of the twentieth-century expansion of sugar production were the Dutch East Indies and Cuba.[12] The destruction of European beet crops between 1914 and 1919 restored the primary position of cane, reversing the domination of beet sugar in the world market in the period 1870–1900. The 2,200,000 hectares planted in sugar beet in Europe in 1913 shrank to 1,279,346 in 1920–21. Beet sugar production, which had reached 8,891,000 tons in 1912–13, shrank to 3,883,000 in 1918–19. After 1922, beet sugar production recovered, but it was not able to overtake cane sugar production in the world market. When the Great Depression began in 1929, world cane sugar production was 15,888,000 tons while beet sugar production amounted to 9,579,000. Beet sugar production was protected from its tropical competitor by tariffs in most metropolitan countries.

The importance of sugar increased as industrialization advanced. Sugar was refined in the metropolitan countries and had many industrial uses. It served as a preservative in the canning industries and in other food industries as well and in the production of alcohol for human consumption and industrial purposes. Be-cause industrialization caused increasing urbanization and urbanization entailed shifting patterns of food consumption, sugar acquired increasing importance in the dietary intake of urban populations. Its importance increased as its share in the caloric intake of the average metropolitan citizen advanced.[13] In the United States per capita annual sugar consumption increased from 29 to 54 pounds between 1867 and 1890, and total consumption of sugar tripled in the same period, from 467,268 tons in 1867 to 1,522,731 in 1890.[14] Thereafter, per capita consumption continued to increase until it reached a peak in 1930. Total consumption of sugar grew at an even faster pace, reflecting the combination of increasing per capita consumption and swift population increase. Per capita consumption of sugar increased 211 percent in the period 1870–1930, whereas total sugar consumption increased by 1,009 percent in the same period.

Technological changes and deepening and broadening demand under condi-tions of competition generated a process of industrial concentration. Once the firms acquired a certain size, competition was transformed into a battle among a reduced number of refiners who individually had more at stake. The increase in the investment required to build a sugar refinery increased barriers to entry. In this sense, technological development enabled the restriction of competition, which the refiners could have contemplated but not achieved in an earlier age. Refineries grew in size, decreased in number, and employed more workers. By the late 1880s, the refining industry was made up of a relatively small number of large refineries.

Competition among these enterprises meant that, in case of business failure, the capitals paralyzed were ever larger. Refiners with very large investments in the business began to search for ways to reduce competition in the industry.

Falling price margins between raw and refined sugar indicate that increases in productivity were passed on to the consumer in the form of lower prices and increased consumption. Before the Civil War, the price margin between refined and raw sugar had been approximately 5 cents a pound; by 1869 it had fallen to 3.59 cents, and it continued to fall in the following decade. Technological improvements and falling prices were accompanied by a process of competitive expropriation in the refining industry. The smaller refineries went out of business and in their place there arose fewer, although larger, refineries employing more machinery. The period 1870–87 was characterized by the failure of small plants and the survival of large refining companies.[15] Between 1870 and 1887, the number of sugar refineries declined from twenty-eight to twelve in New York, from twenty to twelve in Philadelphia. In Boston, the number of refineries remained stable at five during this period.[16] By 1870 sugar refining had become New York's most important industry. In 1872, 59 percent of the raw sugar imported from abroad was processed in New York; and in 1887, the year of the formation of the Sugar Trust, New York refined 68 percent of the sugar consumed in the United States.[17] The process of competitive expropriation had been most severe in New York, where only 43 percent of the refineries survived the years 1870–87, compared to 60 percent in Philadelphia and 100 percent in Boston.

The industrial concentration and increasing market shares by fewer firms were evident in the sugar refining industry even before the formation of the trust. The industry was concentrated in relatively few plants in New York, Boston, and Philadelphia. As the output and capital invested in individual sugar refining firms increased, a critical point was reached. The refiners in the business were all survivors from the previous decade of competitive expropriation. The competitive process that lay ahead appeared ominous. For even though competition would henceforth pit a smaller number of contenders against each other, each represented a larger capital investment. The stakes were much higher for both the potential winners and the potential losers. The larger refiners were faced with the choice of crushing out competition in what looked like a long and bitter battle or developing a price-fixing combination to limit production, control prices, and share profits.[18] They chose the latter road.

To be sure, the refiners themselves did not present the forthcoming struggle in a positive light, that is, as a struggle for additional market share driven by a desire for increased profits. They expressed their dilemma as a reaction to excessive

Table 2.1. Sugar Consumption in the United States, 1830–1930

Year	Estimated Population	Consumption (tons)	Lbs. per Capita
1830	12,866,020	69,711	12.1
1840	17,069,453	107,177	14.1
1850	23,191,876	239,409	23.1
1860	31,443,321	428,785	30.5
1870	38,558,371	606,492	35.3
1880	50,155,000	922,109	43.9
1890	62,979,766	1,522,731	54.0
1900	75,994,575	2,477,423	65.2
1910	91,972,266	3,467,354	75.4
1920	105,710,620	4,519,129	85.5
1930	122,775,046	6,728,073	109.6

Sources: Paul S. Vogt, *The Sugar Refining Industry of the United States: Its Development and Present Condition* (Philadelphia: Publications of the University of Pennsylvania, 1908), 17; Richard Daniel Weigle, "The Sugar Interest and American Diplomacy in Hawaii and Cuba, 1893–1903" (Ph.D. diss., Yale University, 1939), 25; *Historical Statistics of the United States, Colonial Times to 1970* (Washington, D.C.: U.S. Government Printing Office, 1970), 331.

competition and declining profits. The problem was not competition per se but *excessive* competition. The explanation of the refiners has been echoed by some analysts of the sugar refining industry, who have concluded that the formation of the Sugar Trust was a response to hard times characterized by falling prices and increasing competition. Paul Vogt concludes that "the transition that took place leading up to the formation of the Sugar Trust was a natural result of overproduction due to excessive movement of capital into this industrial group at a time when the capacity for production was being greatly increased by remarkable improvements in methods of refining."[19]

The refiners' rationale for the formation of the Sugar Trust may have been sincere, but in any case what the refiners were actually pondering was the future cost of increasing competition versus the future benefits of some form of consolidation, which now seemed feasible and profitable. Domestic consumption of sugar was increasing rapidly concomitantly with falling prices (see Table 2.1), but scanty evidence about the rate of profit in the industry exists. Joe Moller, of the refining firm of Moller and Sierck, complained that "there was not much money in sugar refining," referring to conditions in 1886. When he was pressed by a colleague to answer why he did not withdraw from the refining business, Moller answered, "Well, we are still making 5 or 6 per cent [return on our money] and if I go out I will only get 4."[20] Consolidation would control prices and allocate market shares among the refiners. It had the effect of increasing prices and profits, within certain limits set by the barriers to foreign competition in the form of the tariff on refined sugar and by the barriers to entry created by the large amount of capital needed to establish a new sugar refinery. Within these limits, the new Sugar Trust sought to exercise all the market power it could muster. Henry O. Havemeyer, the preeminent sugar refiner in the United States and the president of the Sugar Trust, expressed his sincere belief that such concentration of power was not incompatible with the functioning of the free market: "I think it is fair to get out of the consumer all you can, consistent with the business proposition."[21]

According to Edwin F. Atkins, a prominent Boston sugar merchant, refiner, and owner of plantations in Cuba, the sugar refining industry of the United States was healthy and showing no signs of distress at the time of the formation of the Sugar Trust. The industry's productive capacity had been rising steadily and rapidly in the period before trust's formation. All the refineries were running full, according to Atkins. It does not seem reasonable to call such an industry "sick."[22] But the particular interest of each refiner cannot be equated with the state of the industry as a whole, which is probably why the formation of the trust appeared to some as a reaction to hard times, while others considered it simply a creative innovation designed to boost profits. The output of the industry as a whole kept rising while the number of enterprises fell, but the actual measure of the state of health of the industry for the refiners was neither total output nor the level of prices but the rate of profit. In the absence of detailed figures for the rate of profit of individual refineries, we can conclude that the formation of the Sugar Trust was both possible and profitable.[23]

The Formation of the Sugar Trust

The trust was formed in 1887. Henry O. Havemeyer and John Searles, a sugar refiner and a banker, undertook the organization of the sugar refining industry along the lines of John D. Rockefeller's reorganization of the petroleum industry. Rockefeller had found a way of turning the trust device from a means of holding property as fiduciary agent into a mechanism for industrial consolidation. What Searles originally had in mind was to form a corporation (not a trust) that would own all the refineries in the United States. This corporation would act as a holding company, the stock would be distributed to the refiners in a proportion equivalent to their output in relation to the total output of the industry, and the corporation would be capitalized at $19.5 million, $3.5 in preferred and $16 million in common shares. The $3.5 million figure probably represented what the various refineries were thought to be worth as independent concerns. The $19.5 million figure probably represented what the same refineries were thought to be worth when consolidated into a single enterprise.[24] The promoters of the trust were actively seeking to capitalize the future profits of the consolidated enterprise. In his famous study on finance capital, the German social democratic economist Rudolf Hilferding noted the importance of promoters' profit in the mergers of the late nineteenth century:

> The American Sugar Trust was formed in 1887 by Havemeyer through the amalgamation of fifteen small companies which reported their total capital as being 6.5 million dollars. The share capital of the Trust was fixed at 50 million dollars. The Trust immediately raised the price of refined sugar and reduced the price of unrefined sugar. An investigation conducted in 1888 revealed that the Trust earned about $14 a ton of refined sugar, which allowed it to pay a dividend of 10 percent on the share capital, equivalent to approximately 70 percent on the actual capital paid when the company was formed. In addition, the Trust was able to pay extra dividends from time to time, and to accumulate enormous reserves. Today [1910] the Trust has 90 million dollars of share capital, of which one half comprises preference shares entitled to a 7 percent cumulative dividend, the other also being ordinary shares which at present also bring in 7 per cent.[25]

The original plans for forming a holding company were changed when Searles's lawyer, John Dos Passos, suggested that the trust device would be more adequate because, unlike a corporation, its affairs would not be open to public scrutiny. Once this form of organization was chosen, there followed a series of negotiations between the promoters of the new trust—a "core" group—and the remaining refiners. The inside group of promoters was composed of Henry O. Havemeyer, John Searles, attorneys John Dos Passos and John Parsons, and a small periphery of the "giants" of the industry composed of Theodore and Hector Havemeyer, F. O. Matthiessen of Matthiessen & Wiechers, "Captain" Joseph B. Thomas of the Standard Sugar Refining Company in Boston, and William Dick of Dick and Meyer.[26] The Havemeyer family was undoubtedly the predominant group among the refiners and within it Henry O. Havemeyer was the outstanding organizer. A committee was set up, composed of Henry and Hector Havemeyer, plus J. O. Donner, to appraise the value of each sugar refining plant according to its capacity and figure out the distribution of trust certificates. In principle, each refiner would receive a proportion of trust certificates equal to the ratio of the output of his refinery to total output. In practice, however, the committee negotiated secretly with each refiner and the actual distribution of trust certificates corresponded to the power each wielded by refusing to enter the combination. Thus the tendency was for the largest ones to receive a higher proportion of certificates because the threat of their withdrawal menaced the existence of the combination more than that of the smaller ones. According to William Havemeyer, the distribution was decided "not scientifically at all. A man simply said, 'I will not come in unless I get so much.' "[27] After several months of negotiations seventeen refineries plus the American Sugar Refinery of California entered the combination.[28]

The Havemeyer family held the primary position in the trust for two interconnected reasons. The Havemeyer and Elder Plant was the largest in the United States and the most efficient in the world. It was, with one exception, the only plant capable of producing high-quality "cut loaf" sugar, it was located at the water's edge, and it could refine low-grade sugars.[29] Without the participation of Havemeyer and Elder any attempt at consolidation was doomed to failure. In addition to this plant, Henry O. Havemeyer represented the branch of the family that controlled the Donner and De Castro refineries. The other branch of the family, represented by John Searles, controlled the two other Havemeyer refineries.[30] The power of the Havemeyer family in sugar overshadowed that of its competitors. The seventeen consolidated refineries controlled 84 percent of the output of the industry east of the Rocky Mountains. The price margin between raw and refined sugar rose from an average of 0.768 cents per pound in 1887 to 1.258 cents in 1888, that is, by approximately 63 percent, as a result of the formation of the trust.

The Price War with Spreckels and the Origins of Vertical Integration

As soon as the original combination developed, a competitive problem arose on the West Coast. The incorporation of the American Sugar Refining Company of California is chronologically proximate to the formation of the trust, but it belongs to a new period in its history, characterized by a struggle against Claus Spreckels of California.

In late 1887 and early 1888 John Searles and Henry O. Havemeyer, having consolidated the industry in the eastern United States, turned their attention to the West. The dominant firm in the West was the California Sugar Refining Company, owned by Claus Spreckels. The trust approached Spreckels about joining the new consolidation. John Searles, who negotiated with Spreckels, explained the advantages of consolidation in no uncertain terms: "He suggested . . . that in the event of one concern being put out of operation . . . by a fire, [its owners] would still have an interest in the other refineries and would not, therefore, be deprived of any revenue."[31] The zealously independent Spreckels refused to join the Sugar Trust on the grounds that the combination was dominated by the Havemeyer interests. Searles then threatened to buy the American Sugar Refinery of California and to dump cheap sugar on the western markets in order to ruin Spreckels. Spreckels vehemently refused to enter. The trust bought the American of California and began to "pound" Spreckels.

The price war with Spreckels had three stages: the initiation of the price war on the West Coast by the trust, the extension of the price war to the East through the building of a Spreckels refinery in Philadelphia, and the resolution of the conflict through the merger of the Havemeyer and Spreckels interests on both coasts, on terms favorable to both. The Havemeyer interests were unable to subdue Spreckels, even though they commanded financial resources approximately ten times greater.[32] Spreckels's capacity to resist the onslaught of the Havemeyer interests was related to the structure of his sugar empire, which was vertically integrated. The Sugar Trust learned from this price war with Spreckels the advantages of vertical integration. The lessons learned in this price war have important consequences for the development of the sugar industry of the Caribbean. The extension of the trust's interests in the Caribbean began in the 1890s, shortly after the price war with Spreckels, and took a great leap forward into the Caribbean and the Philippines after the Spanish-American War of 1898.

Spreckels had built in Hawaii an integrated system of irrigation ditches, sugar plantations, and railroads to carry the sugar to port. The Spreckels interests owned a steamship line that carried the raw sugar to California, refineries in California, and even sections of California railroads. In partnership with William G. Irwin, Spreckels had formed a sugar factors company that dominated the independent Hawaiian planters.[33] Thus when the Havemeyers and the trust bought their plant in California to compete with Spreckels in the spring of 1888, they expected to crush him in a short time. But when they tried to corner the market for Hawaiian raw sugar so as to leave Spreckels without raw material, they found that it was already cornered by Spreckels, who began to play a complicated price game against them.

Spreckels would first reduce the price of sugar and induce an increase in orders for refined sugar for both his refinery and that of the trust. The trust's refinery, having limited access to Hawaiian sugar (that which had been previously contracted with Hawaiian planters), was forced to buy any additional raw sugar from

Spreckels so it could meet the orders. Having created this situation, Spreckels would then force the price of *raw* sugar in California up to the price at which the trust had contracted to sell *refined* sugar by closing the price margin between refined and raw sugar. Through the vertically integrated structure of his western "sugar trust," Spreckels was able to force the Havemeyers' refinery in California to operate at a loss.

The *New York Times* reported on "a curious sugar war" being waged between Spreckels and the trust:

> A curious sugar war is being carried on by Spreckels's California refinery and the American Company. The later being a local member of the trust, prices go up and down in an exceedingly erratic manner. Fluctuations are a part of the battle against the trust. Some time ago the American Refinery changed its rules regarding prices that should be charged to purchasers. It had always been the custom to sell the sugar at figures ruling on the day of delivery and not those of the day that the order was given. When E. L. G. Steele retired from the control of the American Company this rule was changed. It was provided that sugar should be billed at Monday's prices if ordered on Monday and not according to the prices of the day of delivery. This is where the opportunity is given for the fight. Both here and in the East at the time Claus Spreckels cornered the sugar market and gouged the trust, the refineries were loaded up with orders but they had little or no raw sugars. He has them at his mercy and shoved up prices all around while the trust refiners had to fill the orders at prices current when they were given. In many instances they had to buy raw sugar of Spreckels and 6¼ cents a pound and refine, and sell at the same figures.
>
> Taking advantage of the situation, Frazer, Harrison & Co., E. C. Knight, Spreckels, and outsiders generally gathered in all orders they could. As soon as the trust refiners secured some sugar they commenced to receive orders again. Prices, in the meantime, had fallen, and they offered to deliver sugar at low quotations. This was the signal for Spreckels to put up prices once more so as to compel the trust to deliver more sugar at a loss. They are compelled to go to him for their supply of the raw article, he having control of available raw sugar.[34]

The limitations of the economic power of Spreckels's western "trust" in its fight against the eastern trust were threefold. First, raw sugar could be obtained from the Dutch East Indies within six weeks.[35] Second, the eastern trust could make up for the losses caused by the price wars in the West with profits made in the East, whereas Spreckels enjoyed no comparable advantage. Third, the trust was finally able to exploit the hostility of the Hawaiian planters against their monopolistic overlord and pierce through Spreckels's corner on raw sugar.[36] Piercing Spreckels's corner of the market was not coextensive with cornering the market against him because his own plantations in Hawaii accounted for 30 percent of the output of the islands. Thus, at best, the trust could survive against Spreckels in the West but not subdue him. Thus a smaller but vertically integrated structure was capable of resisting an offensive by a much larger horizontal combination.

Once he beat back the offensive of the Havemeyers in the West, Spreckels decided to eliminate the greatest advantage the trust held over him: control of the market of the East. He built a modern refinery in Philadelphia in 1889, capable of refining two million pounds of sugar daily, and announced his intentions to double its capacity to four million pounds daily.[37] The Havemeyer interests then tried, unsuccessfully, to control the market for raw sugar in the East. Their failure was so thorough that Spreckels even sold part of his stock to the trust for a $20,000 profit.[38] Once again, the trust was able to appreciate the advantages of vertical consolidation. Unfortunately for Havemeyer and the Sugar Trust, they were not able to exercise control over the sources of raw sugar on the East Coast in the same way that Spreckels had in the West.[39]

The great eastern Sugar Trust of the Havemeyers had gone to war against the considerably smaller western trust and discovered that it could not defeat it. The secret of Spreckels's endurance was the concentrated force of the structure of his sugar enterprises. Sugar refiners learned that the price war between Havemeyer and Spreckels held an important lesson about the advantages of vertical integration. Judging by what happened in the territories acquired in the war of 1898, it seems that this lesson was not forgotten. Although the refiners were surely aware of the advantages of vertical integration, the war with Spreckels forcefully impressed on their consciousness the resilience of a vertically integrated enterprise in struggle against a much larger, horizontally integrated predator. The vertical relation that developed between the refining interests in the United States and the sugarcane estates in the Caribbean has its origin, at least in part, in this price war. Hawaii, in a sense, could show the future to the Caribbean. The price war between the eastern and western refiners ended in late 1891. In 1892 Henry O. Havemeyer and his cousin Charles Senff became interested in the Trinidad Sugar Company in Cuba and joined Edwin F. Atkins, who presided over the company in Cuba.[40] Although this investment did not yet represent a massive pattern of vertical integration, it was nevertheless an exploratory venture into the possibilities of vertically integrated colonial enterprise.

The price margin between raw and refined sugar in 1888 and 1889 stood at 1.258 and 1.207 cents, respectively. In 1890 the extension of the price war to the eastern United States brought it down to 0.720 cents, it remained low at 0.828 in 1891, and went up again above 1 cent in 1892 as a result of the signing of the Havemeyer-Spreckels peace in late 1891. The terms of the peace were the granting to the Havemeyers of a 45 percent interest in the Spreckels Sugar Refining Company of Philadelphia and the merger of both California refineries into the Western Sugar Refining Company, a corporation formed for that purpose and divided exactly in half between the two contenders.[41] The result of the price war was merger and a lesson for the future. The events of the price war were summarized by the American tariff expert F. W. Taussig: "Claus Spreckels became king refiner on the Pacific slope, the Sugar Trust gradually gathered in the whole industry in the rest of the country; the two great rivals quarrelled and fought, made friends and combined."[42]

The Price War with Spreckels and the Emergence of Oligopoly

One of the side effects of the price war of 1890–91 was the ruin of some smaller refineries, which were forced to sell out to the Sugar Trust. Among them were the E. C. Knight refinery and the Delaware Sugar House of George R. Bunker. Being less concentrated and efficient than the trust, and having smaller financial assets to withstand a prolonged price war, the smaller refiners, who had previously benefited from the price increase brought about by the formation of the trust, were now facing economic difficulties. The competition to which the refiners were subjected was monopolistic—oligopolistic, technically—and they had no means to meet it. After the merger with Spreckels and after buying the smaller refineries during the price war, in 1892 the trust controlled 98 percent of the output of refined sugar in the United States.[43] The one independent refinery in the United States, the Revere Refinery in Boston, worked harmoniously with the trust and was, through the brokerage house of Nash, Spalding and Company, the largest minority holder of American Sugar Refining Company stock. It cannot be called an independent refinery.[44] For all practical purposes, the sugar refining industry was fully monopolized.

Some of these smaller refiners bought out by the trust, particularly the Bunker interests, later became important producers of raw sugar in plantations in the Caribbean. Just as some of the displaced refiners took new positions inside the trust, for example, administering particular refineries, some others were drawn into the process of vertical integration and became involved in sugar estates. That some of the capitalists who appear in the lists of directors of the sugar companies were at one point independent refiners does not mean that competitive capital entered the sphere of sugar production in the Caribbean. Quite the opposite is true. These smaller capitalists were displaced by the formation of the monopolistic Sugar Trust and became cogs in its machinery later on.

In 1891 the American Sugar Refinery Company, a trust, became the American Sugar Refining Company, a New Jersey holding company. The change in legal form came about as a response to litigation brought by the state of New York against one of the refineries that had joined the trust. The decision to bring a suit against the North River Sugar Refining Company, which was owned by Searles and was being dismantled by the trust to reduce refining capacity, was designed in such a way as to establish the principle that trusts were illegal without actually doing economic harm to the Sugar Trust. Once that company was dissolved, all others that had joined the combination would be open to legal prosecution. The desired effect would be achieved without harming the trust economically.

The attorneys of the Sugar Trust argued that the combination did not hold a monopoly and that large size brought economies of scale that were passed on the consumer and, even further, that if combinations of capital were going to be outlawed, the same principle had to be applied to combinations of labor. "The mischief of oversupply and inadequate value in commodities," answered the prosecution, "the producer can and will correct by a reduced supply, thus restoring the equilibrium of prices. But sentient labor cannot withdraw from the market. It must eat or die."[45] The decision to annul the charter of the North River Sugar Refining Company was matched by a California decision dissolving the American Sugar Refinery. The latter decision was part of the struggle of Spreckels against the trust, which was still going on.

In 1890, the Sherman Antitrust Act was passed in Congress, putting an end for the moment to the trust form of industrial consolidation but not to industrial consolidations themselves. As a result, the American Sugar Refining Company reorganized itself as a New Jersey corporation. The legal advantages offered by New Jersey's 1888 corporate statutes account for the decision to reorganize there. According to New Jersey law, a corporation was allowed to own stock in other corporations either inside or outside that state. The holding company was used extensively, particularly after 1898, to link U.S. sugar refineries and centrales in the Caribbean into vertically integrated complexes that were on paper composed of totally independent enterprises.

The effect of the reorganization of the Sugar Trust as a holding company was to strengthen the horizontal consolidation among the refiners. The case of the American Sugar Refining Company helped to determine the form of future industrial combinations, which were predominantly mergers and predominantly New Jersey holding companies.[46] The trust certificates were exchanged for stock in the American Sugar Refining Company, "half in the form of cumulative preferred shares and half in the form of common stock. The preferred shares were intended to represent the value of the new company's assets; the common stock, the capitalized value of its expected profits."[47] A prominent firm of investment bankers, Kidder Peabody & Company, took charge of the financial aspects of the consolidation.[48]

In a posterior case against one of the refineries of the trust in 1898 (*United States v. E. C. Knight et al.*) the Supreme Court declared that Congress had a right to prohibit monopoly in commerce but not in manufacture. The Sherman Antitrust Act was in practice annulled by the decision, at least for a while. Together with the Supreme Court's decision in the Addyson Pipe and Steel case, this ruling on the Sugar Trust laid the legal basis for the merger movement that began in 1895 and ended with the Rich Man's Panic of 1907.[49] Consolidations under a single corporation, generally New Jersey holding companies, became the mark of the movement. After the passage of the New Jersey holding company law and the Sherman Antitrust Act, no new large trusts in the strict sense of the word were erected. Within a few years all the trusts converted to holding companies, with Standard Oil—the first trust—being the last one to convert to a holding company in 1899.[50] Thus the forms adopted by monopolistic combinations in the United States were influenced to a great degree by the cases against the Sugar Trust and by its organizational history.[51] The merger movement radically transformed the economic structure of the United States and created monopolistic industrial consolidations patterned after the early trusts, such as Standard Oil and the American Sugar Refining Company, although on a new legal basis.[52]

In addition to the natural barriers to entry associated with the large investment required to establish a sugar refinery, the Sugar Trust sought to create artificial barriers by granting rebates to the wholesale grocers and to the railroads. The grocers were concerned about the prevalence of widespread price-cutting competition. They established a system with Havemeyer in which they received rebates from the trust according to the amount of sugar they sold at cost. For practical purposes, the wholesalers became mere distributors for the trust on a commission basis. The system guaranteed a constant margin of profit to the wholesalers—a margin that had previously been threatened by competition—and in exchange the trust received a commitment from the wholesalers not to sell any other competing sugars should they appear on the market. The system amounted to cartelization of the wholesalers under the leadership of the trust. As Alfred Eichner described it, "the wholesale grocers were to be protected against competition among themselves in return for the American's being protected against competition from new refiners."[53] Sugar accounted for 40 percent of the business of the wholesale grocers.

With the railroads the system was different. Competition for the business of carrying sugar was severe. The bulk of the material transported by the railroads moved from west to east—grain, timber, and so on—whereas sugar was the main commodity moving east to west. Since the cost of operating the railroads were fixed, the compulsion to cut the prices of the sugar contracts was intense. It was better to carry sugar for a low price than to move empty cars to the West. This difficulty in turn created others: the American Sugar Refining Company constantly switched carriers, creating instability in the railroad business. An accommodation was reached in which each railroad received a fixed percentage of the sugar tonnage in exchange for preferential rates to the American. Any other sugar refiner would have to pay a higher rate. This system allowed the trust to quote prices at distant locations which were low enough to discourage entry into the industry, all without having to reduce its own margin of profit. The rebate system was more of a device to discourage entry than to increase profits.

Despite these barriers, three firms were able to enter the sugar refining business in the early 1890s. The price margin between raw and refined sugar was 1.035 and 1.153 cents per pound in 1892 and 1893, respectively, a margin sufficiently high to encourage new entries. Eventually, Havemeyer became convinced that a one-cent margin was too high and adjusted the trust prices accordingly in the future. After the complicated absorption of rival refineries and the price war with Spreckels, the outcry of public opinion and of the press against the sugar monopoly, and the legal cases brought against the combination, it was best not to attempt a merger with the independents. The three refineries that did enter the business, however—the Mollenhauer Sugar Refining Company built in Brooklyn in 1892, the National Sugar Refining Company formed at Yonkers, and the McCahan Sugar Refining Company of Philadelphia, which began operations in 1893[54]—were all tied in one way or another to the Havemeyer's American Sugar Refining Company. The Mollenhauers were related by marriage to the Dicks, one of whom, William Dick, was a director of the American Sugar Refining Company. Charles Senff, a cousin of Henry O. Havemeyer, owned three thousand shares of stock in the Mollenhauer firm and exchanged them later for stock in the American so that the American came to own a 30 percent interest in the Mollenhauer firm. The

McCahan Refinery in Philadelphia, in turn, harmoniously worked out quotas of production with the trust's subsidiary in that city, the Franklin Sugar Refinery. George Frazier, chief salesman of the Franklin refinery, would notify McCahan of the amount of sugar he was allowed to refine each month in order to keep the prices at the desired level. After 1898 the principals of the Mollenhauer, National, and McCahan refineries became empire builders in the Caribbean, controlling through multiple mechanisms dozens of sugar companies producing hundreds of thousands of tons of sugar each year.

The National Sugar Refining Company was established by interests from B. H. Howell Son and Company, a firm of commission merchants. According to Alfred S. Eichner's study of the Sugar Trust,

> it was through the Mollenhauer Sugar Refining Company that the National was linked to the American, for the Mollenhauer and National refineries relied on the same firm of commission merchants—B. H. Howell, Son & Company—to handle their purchases of raw sugar and their sales of refined. James H[owell] Post, one of the senior partners in B. H. Howell, was, in fact, directly responsible for the establishment of both enterprises. It was at his urging that the principals in the companies decided to undertake the construction of their respective refineries, and in the first few years, when they might have had trouble obtaining credit through normal banking channels, Post saw to it that they were provided, out of B. H. Howell's own funds, with all the working capital they needed.[55]

This original connection between James H. Post, of the firm of B. H. Howell and Son, with the Mollenhauer refineries on the one hand and the trust on the other helps us to understand the composition of the board of directors of many corporations established by these refiners in the Caribbean after 1898. Post became the most influential U.S. investor in sugar plantations after 1898, controlling through holding company mechanisms some of the largest sugar concerns of Cuba, the Dominican Republic, and Puerto Rico. Post became an important linchpin in the machinery of the American sugar empire in Cuba, the Dominican Republic, and Puerto Rico.[56] The Mollenhauers, Bunkers, and McCahans also figured prominently in the sugar centrales of the three countries after 1898.

The links between James H. Post of B. H. Howell & Company and the trust solidified during the great price war in which the trust was forced to engage after 1898. Between 1893 and 1898, that is, after working out an informal agreement with the independent refiners—the National, Mollenhauer, and McCahan refineries—and until the beginning of the price war of 1898, the trust was able to hold sugar prices around seven-eighths cent per pound. The administrators of the sugar monopoly, and Havemeyer in particular, had learned by successive approximations that exceedingly high prices invited entry and that it was possible to keep control of the industry price in coordination with the independents through a system of price leadership. In 1896–98, however, the sweet peace of the trust was broken by a firm of coffee roasters, Arbuckle Brothers.

The price war with Arbuckle Brothers caused a merger between the Mollenhauer, National, and McCahan refineries into a firm that became the second largest in the industry. This merger was promoted by James H. Post but financed by Havemeyer, which meant that the largest competitor of the American Sugar Refining Company was tied to the Sugar Trust, in substance if not in form or appearance. The price war between the American Sugar Refining Company and Arbuckle brothers was the first time that the trust was unable to incorporate an opponent into its structure. Henceforth, the trust abandoned its attempt to establish a total monopoly of sugar refining in the United States and settled instead for an oligopolistic structure based on acknowledged market shares and a system of price leadership. The chronology of this price war, which lasted from 1898 to 1900, is a bit more complicated than the previous ones because it was fought in the sugar and coffee markets simultaneously.

Arbuckle Brothers occupied in coffee roasting a position analogous to that of the American Sugar Refining Company in sugar refining. It owned a patent for a machine capable of measuring a pound of roasted coffee, putting it in a paper bag, and sealing it. Arbuckle Brothers began to pack sugar in two pound bags with this machine. As the firm's volume of packaging increased, a conflict developed with the Havemeyer interests, as described by Eichner:

> James N. Jarvie and H. O. Havemeyer had a consultation about the price the Arbuckles were to pay for sugar in the future. Reports differ. The Havemeyer people assert that Jarvie, representing the Arbuckles, demanded a lower price for sugar, considering the magnitude of their purchase. The Arbuckle people say that Havemeyer wanted this business for himself and refused to furnish the sugar any longer at a price which made the business profitable. Whoever is right, there was a sudden severing of relations, early in 1896, between the Arbuckle interests and the Havemeyer interests, and the Arbuckles started to fight the sugar trust.[57]

The National and Mollenhauer refineries refused to sell to Arbuckle Brothers at a price lower than that of the American Sugar Refining Company, a further indication of the informal monopolistic agreement that existed between these firms and the American.[58]

The war began when Havemeyer purchased the Woolstone Spice Company in Toledo, Ohio, the leading competitor in coffee roasting, in an effort to depress prices. The Arbuckle interests retaliated against the price decrease in coffee by constructing a sugar refinery, which was ready for operations in the fall of 1898. In November of that year the New York Sugar Refining Company of Claus Doscher also started operations, but the price war remained centered on the Havemeyer-Arbuckle dispute. Havemeyer blocked Arbuckle's access to wholesalers, and Arbuckle Brothers started its own retail network. In 1899 the price margin between raw and refined sugar fell to half a cent, the lowest ever in the United States. As a result of this price war, the smaller refiners began to face serious difficulties. The National refinery of James H. Post closed down, and the Mollenhauer refinery had to cut back production.[59]

In June 1900 Havemeyer was able to consolidate the New York, National, and Mollenhauer refineries. According to Jack Mullins, "Working secretly through James H. Post of B. H. Howell, Son, and Company, he organized the National Sugar Refining Company of New Jersey for the purpose of merging and operating in unison these three refineries."[60] The new consolidation, the National Sugar Refining Company of New Jersey, had the appearance of being independent from the trust. In fact, the purchases of the refineries were carried out by Post, of the B. H. Howell firm, with credit granted personally by Havemeyer and his wife. Havemeyer received the lion's share of the stock. Havemeyer placed the stock in the name of James Howell Post but retained the legal right to claim ownership. The president of the American Sugar Refining Company voted one hundred thousand shares through Post and was always in a position to control the National's policy through his ownership of virtually all of the corporation's common stock. In addition, the Sugar Trust owned over 50 percent of the preferred stock of the National Sugar Refining Company.[61] The National Sugar Refining Company in turn purchased a 25 percent interest in the McCahan refinery in Philadelphia, extending to Havemeyer and the trust, if not control, at least a guarantee of harmony.[62] In 1902, at the time the Cuban Reciprocity Treaty was negotiated, the Sugar Trust held more than half the $10 million of preferred stock of the National Sugar Refining Company, while Havemeyer personally held all but a small block of the $10 million of common stock.[63] All the special advantages enjoyed by the American Sugar Refining Company in the form of railroad and wholesaler rebates were extended to the National. As a result of the price war with Arbuckle,

the trust extended its influence through informal means. According to one interpretation of the history of the Sugar Trust, "the formation of the National Sugar
Refining Company was, in a sense, the capstone of the career of Henry Havemeyer
and the zenith of the American Sugar Refining Company's power."[64]

The price war with Arbuckle ended in 1900.[65] Peace on the sugar front came
about in the form of an armed truce rather than a conquest. Havemeyer was not
able to subdue Arbuckle Brothers. Price wars were costly, and his firm stopped
pursuing the goal of achieving a perfect monopoly in sugar refining. When the
dust settled, Arbuckle Brothers began to follow the price leadership structure of
the American firm. The industry as a whole began to approximate oligopoly—
with the important qualification that the two largest firms, the American and
National, were merged through informal means.

Until Henry O. Havemeyer's death in 1907, the daily price of refined sugar in
the United States was determined as follows. At 10 o'clock each morning the price
set by Havemeyer was posted outside the American Sugar Refining Company's
door in Wall Street. The trust's refineries throughout the country—in Boston,
Philadelphia, New Orleans, and San Francisco—were telegraphed. Independent
refiners simply followed the price posted by the American.[66]

But the market being what it is, a place of competition, the Sugar Trust had to
face a challenge from a new source: beet sugar.[67] In addition to its 90 percent
control of the cane sugar market, the trust owned interests in beet factories
representing 70 percent of the beet processing capacity of the United States.[68] The
trust owned significant timber and cooperage interests—related to the fabrication
of sugar barrels—and some glucose interests. At the time of Henry Havemeyer's
death the American Sugar Refining Company had settled into a position of leadership in the oligopolistic cane sugar refining industry and had acquired a substantial
interest in the beet sugar industry. The American Sugar Refining Company was
the sixth largest industrial corporation in the United States. John Moody listed the
American Sugar Refining company as one of the seven "greater industrial trusts"
of the United States.[69]

The death of Henry Havemeyer marked a transition from dynastic family management to a professional or bureaucratic management structure. The sugar empire of the American Sugar Refining Company—including its beet companies—
had become too vast for one-man management. Henry Havemeyer's son Horace
did not succeed his father immediately as head of the corporation. After World
War I Horace Havemeyer surfaced as an important refiner with major interests in
the Cuban sugar industry. The Havemeyer family had divested itself of its share of
American Sugar Refining Company stock and invested its money in New York

City real estate. Washington B. Thomas was the largest stockholder after Henry Havemeyer's death. Thomas and Edwin F. Atkins, the American sugar magnate of Cuba, emerged as the leading forces. Nevertheless, the ologopolistic structures created by Henry O. Havemeyer outlived him and became institutionalized. These oligopolistic structures played an important role in the expansion of American capital into the colonial and semicolonial territories of the United States in the Caribbean, particularly Cuba, the Dominican Republic, and Puerto Rico.

The Oligopolistic Network

In 1910 Congressman Thomas B. Hardwick initiated an investigation of the American Sugar Refining Company. The process was similar to Congressman August O. Stanley's contemporary investigation of the steel trust. The investigation revealed that the weight of stockholding in the American Sugar Refining Company had shifted to New England. Henry Lee Higginson, a prominent Boston banker, intervened with Charles D. Norton, President William Howard Taft's secretary, on behalf of the Sugar Trust.[70]

During the Hardwick Committee investigation, Washington B. Thomas and Edwin F. Atkins sought to impress upon the committee the same argument that Henry Lee Higginson had used with the Taft administration on behalf of the Sugar Trust, namely, that the American Sugar Refining Company was under a new management and thus should not be penalized for the faults of the Henry Havemeyer era. The Hardwick Committee concluded, however, that the power of the Sugar Trust was not based on the personal qualities of its first president but rather on the web of interlocking corporate relationships which Havemeyer had created.[71]

After the death of Havemeyer, several individuals occupied the presidency of the American Sugar Refining Company. Charles H. Allen, who was president of the company between 1912 and 1915, had been the first civil governor of Puerto Rico (1900–1901) and was connected to the House of Morgan through his vice-presidency of both the Guaranty Trust Company of New York and the Morton Trust Company.[72] Much had changed in the sugar world since the Spanish-American War of 1898. United States corporations were making rapid inroads into the production of raw sugar in centrales in Cuba and Puerto Rico. During World War I they expanded their influence into the Dominican Republic. The period of horizontal consolidation and oligopolistic price wars among refiners was giving way to a new phase of vertical integration. Refiners were acquiring sugar plantations and incorporating them as independent enterprises, which were nevertheless constituent parts of larger corporate structures consisting of clusters of enterprises. Vertical integration allowed the corporate groups controlling refineries in the United States and plantations in the Caribbean to sell the sugars of the Caribbean to the refineries in the United States at administered transfer prices. Vertical integration permitted refiners, among other things, to have a stable supply of raw sugar and prices that were more stable than those of the open market. Allen was governor of Puerto Rico during the period when the largest U.S. sugar companies first established themselves there. During his governorship, a tax on landed property known as the Hollander Act forced many poor peasants to sell lands and accelerated the process of proletarianization in the Puerto Rican countryside. The prominent people in the sugar world were henceforth those involved in colonial enterprises in the Caribbean, duplicating a pattern initiated earlier by Claus Spreckels in California and Hawaii.

The investigation and prosecution of the Sugar Trust under the Sherman Antitrust Act became a prolonged affair and was suspended during World War I. During the war, the U.S. government was forced to rely on the largest corporations, including the Sugar Trust, for the organization of the war economy.[73] The populist farmer-based revolt against big business, which sought to break the power of the trusts by returning to nineteenth-century competitive structures, subsided, and public attitudes toward the large corporations became more lenient. The government case against U.S. Steel concluded in 1920 that the corporation was not a monopoly "in restraint of trade." In the case of the American Sugar Refining Company, the decision handed down on May 9, 1922, stated that the Sugar Trust had once violated the Sherman Antitrust Act but was no longer doing so.

Both the steel and sugar refining industries underwent a monopolistic phase, with one firm in control of the industry, and then a phase of oligopolistic stabilization as the powerful monopolies broke down into a limited number of large companies. The transition to oligopoly in these industries was characteristic of the period. In the United States, the share of oil refining output controlled by Standard Oil fell from 90 percent in 1899 to 80 percent in 1911, while the market share of International Harvester fell from 85 percent in 1902 to 64 percent in 1918, and that of AT&T in the telephone industry from 100 percent in 1884 to 50 percent in 1907. The top four copper producers controlled 76 percent of output in 1890 and 39 percent in 1920.[74] In the new oligopolistic structures one firm was the price leader and competition was periodically reactivated. World War I brought the state and the large corporations into increasingly close contact. The state increased its reliance on big capital for the organization of the war economy, while the industrialists came to terms with government regulation of business as a guarantee of profitable stability.[75]

The attacks against the Sugar Trust withered away with the decline of the populist antitrust movement. The emergence of oligopolistic structures with less blatant price-fixing mechanisms, and the increasing symbiosis between the state and business after the experience of the war economy, displaced the Sugar Trust from the limelight of public attention. In the 1922 decision, the American Sugar Refining Company was allowed to retain a 25 percent interest in the National Sugar Refining Company (the second largest cane sugar refining company), a 31 percent interest in the Great Western Beet Sugar Company, and a 34 percent interest in the Michigan Sugar Company (the leading beet producer).[76] Henry O. Havemeyer, had he been alive, would have in all probability repeated his pronouncement on the reorganization of the Sugar Trust from a trust into a holding company in the 1890s: "From being illegal as we were, we are now legal as we are: change enough, isn't it?"

But in the dynamic business world of the early 1920s, the real changes lay elsewhere. By 1922 United States capital had experienced an unprecedented period of expansion in the colonial sugar business. In Cuba the war of 1914–18 brought about fantastic sugar prices and an unprecedented period of prosperity called the Danza de los Millones. Hundreds of millions of dollars were invested in sugar plantations and railroads.[77] Horizontal consolidation was no longer the principal issue in the minds of the sugar refiners.

The Sugar Tariff and Vertical Integration

The price war of 1890 pitted sugar refiners from the East Coast of the United States against those of the West Coast. The process of horizontal consolidation was a struggle for control of the market for refined sugar in the United States. The refiners' attempt to monopolize sugar refining spilled over into a contest for the sources of raw sugar outside the United States. These attempts to control foreign sources, in turn, brought refiners face to face with the tariff, which regulated competition between domestic and foreign sugar producers selling in the U.S. market. The tariff was crucial to the struggle among refiners for control of the sources of unrefined or raw sugar. Capitalist enterprises always compete with each other in a terrain regulated by the state. In the case of the American Sugar Kingdom, what role did the state play in regulating the sugar market? How did the sugar tariff affect the different producing regions within and outside the United States? Since the United States was the main purchaser of colonial sugar from the Caribbean, did the tariff affect the redistribution of income between raw sugar producers and refiners? How did the tariff affect vertically integrated enterprises that sold raw sugar from their colonial plantations to their own metropolitan refineries? Did the regulatory capacity of the state through the powerful mechanism of the tariff have the same impact on producers within the customs area of the United States and producers abroad? What constit-

Table 3.1. Typical Duties on Raw Sugar

Year	On Raw	On Refined	Differential
1789	1 cent	3 cents	2 cents
1802	2½ cents	7 cents	4½ cents
1816	3 cents	10–12 cents	7–9 cents
1842	2½ cents	6 cents	3½ cents
1861	¾ cents	2 cents	1¼ cents

Source: F. W. Taussig, *Some Aspects of the Tariff Question: An Examination of the Development of American Industry under Protection* (Cambridge, Mass.: Harvard University Press, 1934), 100.

uencies shaped state policy in tariff matters? What interests were represented in the decisions of the state? How did state regulation of the sugar market evolve as the United States acquired an empire of sugar-producing colonies? Were metropolitan interests producing in the continental United States at odds with metropolitan producers in the colonies, or at odds with colonial producers? In short, what role did state policy have in the new era of colonialism, in which U.S. enterprises organized sugar production in the colonies for sale in the United States?

In the last decade of the nineteenth century there were three constituencies interested in the sugar tariff and two different tariffs on sugar. The Louisiana cane growers were traditionally opposed to free trade in raw sugar because of their natural disadvantages relative to Caribbean producers. The beet farmers of the Midwest and West of the United States represented an infant but very promising industry which agreed with the Louisiana planters on the need for tariff protection. The Sugar Trust represented the combined interests of the sugar refining industrialists. The tariff on raw sugar was a form of protection to the sugar growing regions of the United States. The tariff on refined sugar was a form of protection to the industrialists who refined sugar. Toward the beginning of the nineteenth century, the tariff on refined sugar served to protect a nascent industry from British competition. Toward the end of the century the tariff dictated the upper limit of prices within which the trust could exercise its monopolistic influence on the market for refined sugar. The tariff shielded the trust from international competition, while placing an upper limit on prices in the country. Throughout the nineteenth century, the two tariffs—on raw and refined sugar—provided ample protection to agricultural producers as well as to the sugar refiners (see Table 3.1).

In the 1890s sugar refiners in continental Europe enjoyed export bounties and tariffs designed to tax local consumers for the cost of dumping sugar cheaply in foreign markets. The sugar tariff of the United States, however, did not function as a dumping tariff, for the United States sold very little refined sugar abroad. Its function was circumscribed to limiting foreign sugar sales in the United States. Sugar refining was in fact protected by tariff walls everywhere. Raw sugar was traded internationally in much greater volumes than refined sugar. The amount of refined sugar of foreign origin sold in the U.S. market was negligible. Refiners defended the tariff on refined sugar on the grounds that European refiners enjoyed the benefits of export bounties. Continental European production of beet sugar, for example, enjoyed government bounties financed through higher prices of sugar in the domestic market, and beet sugar was dumped in the British market at the expense of local refiners. In 1893, an international conference met to discuss international sugar tariffs, with very little success. In 1902, at the time the United States was negotiating a reciprocity treaty with Cuba, the Brussels convention eliminated the export bounties on European sugars.[1]

In addition to protecting the sugar refiners and the producers of raw sugar, the sugar tariffs were also an important source of revenue to the federal government.[2] Both duties were high, but the duty on refined sugar was higher. Before the Civil War the high tariff on refined sugar was associated with the fact that it was considered a luxury item consumed mostly by the rich, while the majority of the population consumed brown sugar. The differential between the two tariffs discouraged the importation of refined sugar and encouraged the development of a domestic refining industry. From 1789 until the 1930s the differential on the duties on unrefined and refined sugar protected the domestic refining industry.[3]

Until approximately 1880, the domestic production of raw sugar in the United States—mostly cane sugar from Louisiana—amounted to 10 percent of national consumption. The remaining 90 percent was imported. After 1880 there was a marked increase in Louisiana production but also an increase in imports, so that despite the absolute increase, the share of total consumption accounted for by that state remained at around 10 percent. Without the tariff on raw sugar, it seems, the industry could not have survived. As Taussig concludes, "The indications are that in fact free sugar would have caused most of the Louisiana planters, perhaps all of them, to give up sugar and turn into something else."[4] Thus the Louisiana industry needed the tariff to survive.

The sugar refiners had different concerns. They were interested in high tariffs on refined sugar and low tariffs for their raw material, raw sugar. The profits of the refiners depended on the difference in price between the refined and raw products. An increase in the price of the raw material meant an increase in costs for the refiners. Passing on this increase potentially reduced demand or else reduced the margin of profit of the refiners. In short, the refiners were interested in cheap raw sugar and expensive refined sugar.

The three organized constituencies that lobbied for the sugar tariff struggled against each other and made alliances with each other, depending on specific circumstances. Of all the sugar interests, the trust was the most influential. In the struggles over tariffs the Sugar Trust usually had to find some accommodation with the Louisiana cane interests and after 1890 with the beet regions also. In practice, therefore, the refining interest was not able to eliminate the tariff on raw sugar but had instead to enter into an "exchange" with the Louisiana cane representatives—and with the beet industry after 1890—by supporting a tariff on raw sugar and requesting their support for a tariff on refined sugar. The domestic sugar producers, on the other hand, had to contend with the trust's influence. In 1901–2, for example, domestic beet producers were unable to persuade the Sugar Trust to give up its campaign for reciprocity with Cuba, which would have eliminated tariffs on Cuban sugar and reduced the profits of the domestic cane and beet producers. In a final assault against the trust's drive for free trade in raw sugar, congressmen from the beet-growing states were able to kill a bill to establish Cuban reciprocity by including it as an amendment to the elimination of duties on refined sugar.[5]

Conflicts over the tariff affected the nature and even the coherence of U.S. expansionist policies abroad. In 1876, a reciprocity treaty allowed Hawaiian sugar to enter the U.S. market duty-free. In 1890, the McKinley Tariff removed Hawaii's special status and helped trigger the Hawaiian revolution of 1893.[6] In 1894 Hawaii returned to duty-free status, and in 1898 annexation guaranteed the permanence of the tariff advantage enjoyed by its producers of sugar. After 1901, sugar from Puerto Rico was admitted free of duty. In 1903, after the beet interests defeated a reciprocity bill that would have granted free access, Cuban sugars were admitted at a 20 percent reduction of the tariff. Philippine sugar entered the United States free of duty in 1909, with a restriction on maximum importation of three hundred thousand tons a year. Beyond this amount, the duty applied to Philippine sugar. These quantitative limitations were lifted in 1913.[7] U.S. tariffs evolved from a purely domestic affair affecting continental producers into an international structure regulating both domestic production of sugar and the production of sugar in the colonial territories. Regulating sugar production in the continent and in the territories was a complicated affair. Louisiana and the beet-growing states had representatives in Congress, but the colonial territories—Hawaii, Puerto Rico, the Philippines, and the semicolonies such as Cuba and the Dominican Republic—did not. In the case of Cuba, for example, these contradictions had a significant impact. J. R. Benjamin underscores the contradictions that the struggles between refiners and planters imprinted on U.S. policy toward Cuba once the latter became a semicolony of the United States. Whereas industrial capital was interested in lower tariffs for raw sugar, the protectionist farming interests wanted a shield from Cuba's potential competition in the sugar and tobacco markets. "The struggle between the two forces caught the Cuban economy in a crossfire which on the one hand tended to make of it a sugar plantation to feed the U.S. east coast refineries, while on the other placed the benefits to be gained from such a role in the hands of U.S. congressmen hostile to the rational functioning of such an arrangement."[8] As the United States acquired overseas possessions, tariff issues became ever more complex, affecting not only the continental producers but also the outlying areas in which U.S. investors initiated operations.

The Tariff in the Outlying Areas: Hawaii, 1876

Hawaiian sugar was granted duty-free status by a treaty of January 30, 1875, which was ratified the following June. The treaty was passed as a commercial and strategic measure, with hardly any input from domestic sugar producers, for Hawaiian sugar did not yet represent a threat to the Louisiana sugar planters. The Hawaiian product could not be shipped east from California except at great expense, just as Louisiana cane sugar was expensive to ship to California.[9] Large blocks of capital were attracted to Hawaii as a result of the treaty, and the sugar industry prospered. Claus Spreckels, the California refiner, originally opposed the treaty, but once it passed he decided to take advantage of it. Spreckels originally opposed the treaty with Hawaii in the belief that it would ruin the refining business.[10] He was joined by some East Coast refiners who also opposed the treaty. Once the treaty was approved, refiners worked to have refined sugar excluded from the free trade agreement. They demanded that no sugars above number thirteen Dutch Standard—the highest grade of unrefined sugar—be allowed to enter duty free.[11] When the reciprocity treaty was passed, Spreckels boarded the ship that carried the news to Honolulu on August 24, 1876. During the next three weeks, Spreckels purchased more than half of the anticipated fourteen-thousand-ton sugar crop before the news of the treaty had time to cause a rise in price.[12] The reciprocity treaty and Spreckels's trip to Hawaii mark the beginning of the speedy growth of Hawaiian sugar output and of Spreckels's Hawaiian sugar empire.

Hawaiian sugar production increased dramatically, supplying 1 percent of the consumption of the United States in 1875 and 10 percent in 1898.[13] So-called free trade with Hawaii did not include refined sugar. Spreckels's original opposition to reciprocity waned as the threat of importation of raw sugar disappeared. The treaty actually gave duty-free status to certain specified Hawaiian products, including "muscovado, brown, and all other *unrefined* sugar . . . syrups of sugar cane, melado, and molasses."[14] Refined sugars from Hawaii were subject to the tariff. But while the threat to the refining industry disappeared in the fine print of the treaty, the challenge posed by Hawaiian production to the domestic producers of sugar increased over time. By 1884 the renewal of reciprocity with Hawaii was facing opposition from the Louisiana planters. Sugar sales from San Francisco were extending into the Mississippi valley and displacing eastern sugars in the areas west of the river. Better railroad communication and the fact that eastward railroad rates were cheaper than westward rates allowed Hawaiian production to penetrate eastward, making the Louisiana planters feel the competition for the first time. The Louisiana cane interests secured opposition to the renewal of Hawaiian reciprocity from the eastern refiners—notably from John Searles of the Havemeyer group.

Duty-free Hawaiian sugar permitted Spreckels to compete with the eastern refiners in the Midwest. The raw material of the eastern sugar refineries came mostly from the Caribbean and paid tariffs. Naturally, the eastern refiners joined with the Louisiana sugar growers against Spreckels, who defended the existing reciprocity treaty after the fact, side by side with the Hawaiian planters. Spreckels and the eastern refiners worked together to exclude refined sugar from the reciprocity agreement with Hawaii. The Louisiana planters and the eastern refiners worked together to defeat the effects of Hawaiian reciprocity on the market for unrefined sugar. To the Louisiana planters, duty-free Hawaiian sugar represented an expanding challenge as decreasing transportation rates allowed California refineries to ship sugar eastward. To the eastern sugar refiners, reciprocity with Hawaii meant a disadvantage relative to the California refiners, who were able to obtain raw sugar below the cost of the duty-paying Cuban sugars refined on the East Coast. The advance of the railroad network and the reduction in transportation costs threatened eventually to break down the relative isolation of the East and West Coast markets.

The opponents of the Hawaiian reciprocity treaty clothed their arguments in the robe of antimonopoly rhetoric, arguing that the benefits of the duty did not accrue to the planters but rather to the monopolistic refining interest represented by Spreckels. A duty on raw sugar could only increase the price to the consumer, however. In 1902, protectionist beet farmers used exactly the same argument to oppose a reciprocity treaty with Cuba, arguing that the real beneficiary was the Sugar Trust and not the sugar planter. In an epoch of widespread populist anti-trust sentiment, these arguments had ample resonance in the circuits of public opinion. The Louisiana sugar growers could not afford to have the duty eliminated, for this would spell ruin to their business. They wanted both a high tariff and the exclusion of Hawaii from the protection it afforded so that Louisiana could occupy an exclusive place inside the tariff wall. The eastern refiners were unwilling to forgo their alliance with the Louisiana lobby in the struggle against Spreckels, so they did not demand duty-free sugar from the Caribbean, at least for the moment. When they merged, formed a monopoly, and set out to conquer Spreckels, they set out to change the tariff. After 1887, the main monopolistic interest in sugar refining was not Spreckels but the American Sugar Refining Company, which gathered together the very refiners who had joined with the Louisiana planters in denouncing Spreckels's monopoly.[15]

In 1890, coinciding with the Havemeyer-Spreckels price war, the McKinley Tariff placed all sugars on the free list and introduced a direct government subsidy to domestic producers (called at the time a bounty). The American tariff expert F. W. Taussig estimated that the difference between the tariff and the bounty, as far as the Louisiana cane growers were concerned, was not real but "psychological": "After 1890 there was a substantial gain, no doubt due in part to the effect on men's imagination of the bounty given by the McKinley tariff act. It is true that the bounty was intended to do no more, and in fact did no more, than make up for the abolition of the duty, but a bounty seems to make a greater impression than a duty—not only on the general public, but also, strange as it may seem, on the producers whose affairs are directly concerned."[16]

In addition to inducing an increase in Louisiana cane production, the McKinley bounties gave the original impulse to the nascent beet sugar industry of the United States. But the effects of the tariff were not simply psychological, as Taussig claims. Under the previous tariff system all the producers from the continental United States were exempt from payment of duties. Hawaii had been exempt from payment of duties since the reciprocity treaty of 1875. Under the McKinley Tariff of 1890, the duty on imported raw sugar was eliminated and a bounty was paid to the producers in the continental United States but not to Hawaii. Before 1890 Hawaii enjoyed the same advantages as Louisiana or any other domestic producer. With the McKinley Tariff the Hawaiian islands found themselves having the same access to the U.S. market as any foreign producer because all foreign sugar was now admitted duty free. But unlike Louisiana, Hawaiian sugar did not receive a bounty. Thus the displacement of Hawaiian sugar from the U.S. market has a lot to do with the prosperity of the Louisiana cane producers, with the growth of beet sugar after 1890, and with the phenomenal expansion of Cuban sugar sales to the United States.

The effects of the McKinley Tariff were not merely psychological. The replacement of the duty by a bounty was not a merely formal change: it involved the displacement of Hawaiian sugar from the U.S. market.[17] The McKinley Tariff rendered ineffectual the Hawaiian reciprocity treaty. Sugar production in Hawaii increased from 242,165,835 pounds in 1889 to 263,656,715 pounds in 1892. The crop of 1889, however, sold at $108.10 per ton, while that of 1892 sold at $55.20 per ton. The total value of Hawaiian sugar exports declined from $13,089,302 in 1889 to $7,276,549 in 1892. So, while the quantity of sugar imported from Hawaii increased slightly between 1889 and 1992, its value decreased sharply (by 44 percent) as a result of the McKinley Tariff.[18]

The sharp drop in the value of Hawaii's sugar exports affected every sector of commerce and industry in the islands. Sugar permeated the economic structure of the Hawaiian archipelago, and inevitably the fortunes of local business houses in all branches of commerce and industry depended on prosperity or depression in the sugar industry.[19] In the Hawaiian revolution of 1893, a faction grouping the majority of the American settlers overthrew Queen Liliuokalani, established a republic, and subsequently demanded annexation to the United States. The influence of the McKinley Tariff and the interests of the sugar planters in these events were contradictory. On the one hand, the advantages Hawaiian planters enjoyed over Cuban producers were wiped out, and sugar prices in Honolulu dropped suddenly. The properties of the planters suffered an estimated $12 million decline in value. It was natural that planters would seek annexation to the United States and enjoyment of the bounty paid on domestic sugar.[20] On the other hand, annexation to the United States entailed the loss of the contract labor system and the consequent rise in labor costs for the planters. Most of the largest planters opposed the revolution, including Spreckels, who was one of the creditors of the Hawaiian monarchy. The majority of the other U.S. settlers in the islands, however, favored it and participated in it. So while the events cannot be characterized strictly as a planters' revolution, the influence of the crisis caused by the removal of reciprocity was nevertheless paramount.

Hawaiian annexation was an extremely popular cause in 1893, and the California legislature adopted a joint resolution to endeavor to bring annexation whenever Hawaii was willing. The influence of the beet sugar interests was not yet strong enough to counteract the influence of trade and commercial groups, who supported reciprocity in the interest of the increased commerce that would follow annexation. The American cane and beet sugar interests were far more concerned with the loss of the bounty in the Wilson Tariff of 1894 and with the heavy competition from bounty-fed European sugars.[21]

The 1890 McKinley Tariff has a different significance when analyzed from the point of view of the sugar refining industry. Havemeyer and the Sugar Trust gained in their contemporary economic struggle against Claus Spreckels. By eliminating Hawaii's advantage in the American market, the tariff also eliminated Spreckels's crucial advantage over the Sugar Trust: duty-free Hawaiian raw sugar for Spreckels's California refineries over duty-paying Cuban sugar for Havemeyer and the Sugar Trust's eastern refineries. All island sugars were now admitted duty free. This change equalized the costs of the raw materials across the United States and eliminated Spreckels's advantage. According to one author, the struggle between the refiners is the only rational explanation for the McKinley Tariff of 1890, which abandoned the duty in favor of a bounty, only to return to the duty system again in the Wilson-Gorman Tariff of 1894. The McKinley Tariff and the return to the duty system in 1894—by which time the trust and Spreckels had merged—also gave a basis to the opinion that the McKinley Tariff had been tailored and passed through Congress by the Sugar Trust. The journalist Judson C. Welliver expressed it in 1912 as follows:

> Long before the war with Spain the sugar tariff had been regularly dictated by the Trust. The people were misled in 1890 to believe they had won a great victory by getting raw sugar placed on the free list, when in fact the necessities of the Trust at that particular period made it especially important that raw sugar be free. The greatest competitor at that time was Spreckels. He was in control of most of the raw sugar from Hawaii, which was given free admission at American ports under a reciprocity treaty. Therefore it became necessary for the Trust to temporarily get all raw sugar admitted free, in order to place itself on an equality with Spreckels. It got just that in the McKinley bill of 1890.[22]

The McKinley Tariff eliminated Spreckels's advantage and helped to bring about the eventual merger of the Havemeyer and Spreckels interests.

Whether or not the Sugar Trust was instrumental in passing the McKinley Tariff, it no doubt benefited from it. Cuban producers benefited also. Free entrance of Cuban sugar into the U.S. market eased the transition from slavery to free labor in the Cuban sugar industry. After emancipation in 1886, the Cuban sugar planters began to reorganize sugar production. The conversion of the old ingenios to new centrales was given an immense impetus by free trade, to the point that sugar production did not decline but rather increased precipitously after abolition, contrary to what one might expect. In 1892 Cuban sugar production crossed the landmark of 1 million tons of sugar.[23] The McKinley Tariff also propelled U.S. direct investment in the Cuban sugar industry. Initially, Spain reacted to the free entrance of Cuban sugar into the United States with a supplementary duty of 25 percent on all imports into Cuba and Puerto Rico. The Foster-Cánovas Treaty between the U.S. and Spanish governments, however, restored free trade and created an unprecedented volume of exchange between Cuba and the United States. Between 1890 and 1894, Cuban sugar production increased by 74 percent. The value of sugar exports increased from $35.4 million in 1890 to $60.6 million in 1893. The McKinley Tariff's exclusion of Cuban finished tobacco products from the free list further strengthened the overwhelming predominance of sugar in Cuba's export basket. In 1890 sugar accounted for three-fourths of the value of Cuban exports, 90 percent of which were purchased by the United States.[24]

United States capitalists began to invest in Cuban sugar production after 1890. Henry Havemeyer visited Atkins in Cuba that year and was impressed with the future prospects of the sugar industry. In 1892 Havemeyer, his cousin Charles Senff, and Atkins purchased the Trinidad estate in Cienfuegos. Havemeyer invested 40 percent of the $600,000 capital, Senff 40 percent, and Atkins 20 percent. Atkins later stated that he had only a minority interest, "but to oblige Havemeyer, I became president."[25] Stephen C. Gallot and Francis H. Ludlow incorporated the Mapos estate in Sancti Spiritus and the Victoria sugar company in Sagua la Grande. Juan M. Ceballos, Manuel Rionda, and I. C. Clark of New York incorporated the Tuinucú estate in 1891, which produced its first crop in 1893. Many Cuban planters became naturalized U.S. citizens and incorporated many smaller companies as American enterprises. The Hormiguero estate of Elías Ponvert, of French extraction, and Los Caños of Paul Brooks, of English origin, became "American" properties. Many other Cuban planters took out citizenship mainly to seek American protection for their property.[26] Still, the share of the Cuban sugar industry owned by Americans remained small and had not reached significant proportions at the time of the Spanish-American War. Americans owned approximately $5 million in plantations in Cuba, while naturalized Spaniards and Cubans owned approximately another $5 million. Adding holdings in mines and other scattered enterprises, total American holdings in Cuba were perhaps $20 million, considerably less than the holdings of Americans in Hawaii at the time of the revolution.[27]

The Wilson-Gorman Tariff of 1894 was a return to the pre-1890 system. Bounties were eliminated, a duty was imposed on foreign sugars, and reciprocity once again put producers in Hawaii on the same footing as domestic producers in the United States. The impact on Cuba, however, was extremely negative, for Cuban sugars lost their free entrance into U.S. markets. Massive deflation affected the Cuban economy and added to the political unrest brewing against the outdated Spanish colonial regime. When Cubans launched their revolution seeking independence a year later in 1895, they targeted the sugar industry for destruction. The Cuban Revolutionary Party's struggle against Spanish colonialism was combined with social struggle against the planter class of Cuba. The revolutionaries set cane field after cane field afire. The preeminent U.S. planter in Cuba, Edwin Atkins, who had lobbied against the passage of the Wilson-Gorman Tariff,[28] presented his argument to the Cleveland administration against recognizing the Cuban insurgents. Atkins continued to seek a solution within the colonial framework, an extension of autonomist reforms to the Cubans. Atkins was concerned that Spanish obligations to protect American properties would cease the minute the U.S. government recognized the insurgents. The Cleveland administration was determined in its policy of non-recognition of the insurgents, on the grounds that the Monroe Doctrine would compel it to intervene to expel Spain from Cuba if it recognized the Cuban insurgents. The American interest in Cuba was not primarily in direct investment but in commerce. Commercial interests had a big stake in the Cuba trade and pressured the McKinley administration in 1898 for relief against the collapse of trade with Cuba, without specifying any course of action. According to prominent New York merchants, commerce with Cuba had been affected in the amount of $100 million yearly over the three years of the conflict.[29]

The United States finally intervened, not only against Spain but against the cause of the independence of Cuba, the Philippines, and Puerto Rico, which were all invaded and occupied in the war of 1898, at a time when the beet sugar industry of the United States was in the midst of a rapid process of expansion and had articulated its opposition to Hawaiian reciprocity. In 1897, when it seemed that Hawaiian annexation was imminent, Spreckels worked with Henry T. Oxnard of the American Beet Sugar Company to prevent the annexation of Hawaii. Oxnard agitated in the beet states against annexation. Spreckels and Oxnard also conducted a campaign in California, primarily at Sacramento, the state capitol. Petitions were circulated to congressmen in the states where beet cultivation was expanding.[30] In California, commercial capital interested in reciprocity with Hawaii wanted annexation and had more influence on the congressmen and state legislature than did the protectionist beet farmers. The strategic importance of Hawaii in the battle of Manila Bay, however, overrode all sectoral considerations, and Hawaii was annexed to the United States. There was no determined opposition to annexation, for Hawaiian sugars were already exempt from the duty and annexation merely fixed the status quo. The struggle over Hawaiian reciprocity, however, prepared the domestic beet sugar interests for the battle against Cuban reciprocity, which lasted until 1903.

The Struggle over Cuban Reciprocity

The sugar beet industry was in the middle of a boom in 1898. The pioneer in the beet industry was Henry T. Oxnard, whose sugar refinery in Brooklyn had been absorbed by the Sugar Trust in 1887. Oxnard had gone to Europe to study beet sugar production methods in 1887–88 and had returned to organize a beet sugar company with New York financial backing. The Oxnard Beet Sugar Refining Company, valued at $350,000, was established in Grand Island, Nebraska. Oxnard persevered in various beet sugar ventures and was instrumental in the expansion of the industry in the United States. When the Dingley Tariff was enacted in 1897, it raised duties to $1.685 per hundredweight of unrefined sugar and $1.95 per hundredweight of refined sugar. Under increased protection from foreign competition, the beet sugar industry thrived. Between 1897 and 1903, forty-nine sugar factories were built in the United States, raising the total number of factories in operation to fifty-two. Beet sugar production increased from 35,536 long tons in 1897 to 195,463 in 1903. Growth was vigorous in Michigan after the state legislature offered a two-cent-per-pound bounty to the sugar producers. In 1897, Henry Oxnard incorporated the American Beet Sugar Refining Company with a capitalization of $20 million.[31] Oxnard was the outstanding spokesman in the battle of the beet sugar interests against the Cuban reciprocity bill.

Powerful interests promoted reciprocity with Cuba. Leonard Wood, military governor of Cuba, was an ardent defender of reciprocity. President Theodore Roosevelt favored reciprocity along the lines suggested by Wood and expressed his sentiments to the general: "I exactly agree with the policy you indicate. A differential rate in favor of Cuba would tie her to us, and we must consistently give as well as get if we expect to make our policies a success."[32] The planters of Cuba were unanimously in favor of reciprocity and the Spanish planters advocated annexation. General Wood circulated literature in favor of reciprocity to eighty thousand "leaders of thought" in the United States—editors, businessmen, ministers, teachers, and others. Wood ordered the circulation of ten thousand pamphlets on "industrial Cuba" to the president, members of the cabinet, all senators and representatives, and 9,550 newspaper editors, at a total cost of $15,627 to the

Cuban Treasury. F. B. Thurber, president of the United States Export Association, distributed General Wood's literature as well as his own in favor of reciprocity. In his statement to the House Ways and Means Committee, Thurber posed as a protectionist Republican who was interested in giving some concessions to relieve economic conditions in Cuba because poor economic concessions merely increased the annexationist sentiment. If annexation were achieved, the beet interests would be ruined. Thurber argued that it was in the interest of reasonable protectionist Republicans to favor a reduction of the Cuban duty so as to forestall annexation. Henry O. Havemeyer personally contributed $2,500 toward the publication of Thurber's propaganda. All of this was merely the icing on top of a much deeper popular sentiment in favor of trade concessions in favor of Cuba. Yet the bill to establish Cuban reciprocity was defeated in Congress.

The protectionist beet farmers of the western states and the Louisiana planters mounted a concerted campaign against Cuban reciprocity. The main theme of the campaign was that given the Sugar Trust's control over the purchases of raw sugar from Cuba, any tariff concession to Cuba would actually accrue to the U.S. monopoly of sugar refining, not to the Cuban producers. In testimony to the Committee of Ways and Means, Edwin F. Atkins stated that he was chairman of the Associated American Interests of Cuba, which was endorsed by almost all the sugar planters of Cuba. His association therefore spoke for 90 percent of the producers in the island. Atkins urged the removal of the duty on Cuban sugars and argued for a 50 percent reduction on all other tariffs between Cuba and the United States. Upon examination, Atkins admitted that he owned American Sugar Refining Company stock and that he was interested jointly with Havemeyer in the Trinidad estate. To the protectionist congressmen who sympathized with the antimonopolistic, populist arguments against the trust, this was confirmation that the reduction in the tariff was merely a ruse to fill the pockets of the Sugar Trust. Atkins further admitted that his Soledad estate had made a profit the preceding year and that there was no unemployment in Cuba, further weakening the sense of urgency of Leonard Wood's propaganda about the tariff as a necessary reconstruction measure. The committee also heard testimony from Hugh Kelly, an American planter who also owned Centrales Ansonia and Porvenir in Santo Domingo, and from Robert B. Hawley, head of the Cuban American Sugar Company.[33] The opponents of reciprocity successfully stressed the importance of protection to the domestic beet industry, undermined the idea of economic distress in the occupied island, and impressed upon the Congress that the Sugar Trust was the real force behind the drive for reciprocity with Cuba. Six of the seven state delegations that voted unanimously for the Cuban reciprocity bill represented sugar constituencies: California, Colorado, Louisiana, Michigan, Utah, and Washington. The Florida delegation voted against it probably for fear of competition from Cuban tobacco. States voting partially against the bill because they had sugar constituencies were Minnesota, Ohio, Wisconsin, Nebraska, and Illinois. New York had beet producers but voted for reciprocity, probably because the sugar refining interests had greater influence. The vote showed "a remarkable adherence to geographical lines of sugar interests."[34]

When the government of Cuba was turned over to President Tomás Estrada Palma, the Roosevelt administration had not achieved its goal of establishing reciprocity through a bill in Congress. It then tried to achieve reciprocity by means of a treaty with Cuba. By the time the treaty came for ratification in Congress, the opposition of the sugar beet interests had dissipated, and congressmen found that their constituents were quiet on the issue of Cuban reciprocity. The Sugar Trust increased its capital stock from $75 million to $90 million in 1901 and purchased a large interest in beet factories in 1901 and 1902. The trust purchased the Lehi Sugar Company of Utah in March 1902 and acquired a substantial interest in the Bay City Sugar Company, Alma Sugar Company, and Peninsular Sugar Refining Company in Michigan. Havemeyer personally acquired a $200,000 interest in the Sanilac Sugar Company in Michigan and sold a fourth of it to the American Sugar Refining Company, which acquired in addition one-half of the $1 million capital of the Great Western Beet Sugar Company at Longmont, Colorado. The Logan Sugar Company and Ogden Sugar Company of Utah were consolidated with the Oregon Sugar Company in a transaction in which the American Sugar Refining Company ended owning $1,151,925, representing half of the stock of the merged enterprise. Additional beet factories were purchased in Fort Collins, Windsor, Longmont, Port Morgan, and Brush, Colorado. In December 1902 Havemeyer purchased for the Sugar Trust seventy-five thousand shares of Oxnard's American Beet Sugar Company, which owned six enterprises with a combined capacity of six thousand tons of sugar daily. In 1901 the Sugar Trust had engaged the American Beet Sugar Company in a price war along the Missouri River markets, which no doubt helped persuade Oxnard to merge with his arch-enemy in 1902. The American Sugar Refining Company then set up a committee made up of three directors—Washington Thomas, Arthur Donner, and Lowell Palmer—to manage the beet sugar companies acquired.[35]

When reciprocity was finally achieved in 1903, Cuban sugars were granted a 20 percent tariff reduction, leaving 80 percent of the tax in effect. This was a historical victory for the beet interests. The American Sugar Refining Company's decision to invest in the beet industry reflects the victory of the beet interests in preserving the tariff. It also represented a change of strategy for the Sugar Trust, which realized that it could now profit from its investment in the protected beet industry, while also reaping the benefits of the moderate reduction in the tariff on Cuban sugars because the net effect would be the displacement from the U.S. market of foreign sugars that paid the full duty. Between 1900 and 1913, foreign, full-duty sugars were gradually displaced from U.S. markets.

In 1900, the United States imported 1,397,214 tons of full-duty sugar, distributed by area of origin as follows: 581,101 tons from the Dutch East Indies (Java); 173,865 from the West Indies (excluding Cuba and Puerto Rico); 350,769 tons of European beet sugar, and 273,477 from all other sources. In 1913, total full-duty imports had decreased to 112,549 tons, distributed by area of origin as follows: 6,380 tons from the Dutch East Indies (Java); 1,965 tons from the West Indies (excluding Cuba and Puerto Rico); 91,324 tons of beet sugar from Europe; and 12,880 sources from all other sources.[36]

The 20 percent reduction of the duty on Cuban sugars became a permanent feature of the U.S. tariff structure and provided relief to domestic producers until the entire system of tariffs was replaced by sugar quotas in 1934. The big winners in addition to the beet interests were United States corporations doing business in the annexed territories, which by virtue of being American possessions were granted duty-free status. Hawaii, the Philippines, and Puerto Rico experienced dramatic productive expansion and eventually cut into Cuba's share of the U.S. market. In the period 1900–1913, the displacement of full-duty sugars for the U.S. market left sufficient space for the beet producers and Cuba to coexist in a rapidly expanding market.

Muscovado Bias: The Tariff on Refined Sugar
and the Colonial Division of Labor

In the market for refined sugar, protectionism was even more severe than in the market for unrefined. The industrial process of refining was reserved for the metropolis while much of the process of production of raw sugar was done in the sugar islands. An essential feature of all plantation economies is a pattern of colonial division of labor in which the subordinate, or peripheral, regions dominated by metropolitan capital specialize in the production of raw materials according to the needs of the core economy that dominates them. The Caribbean social scientist Lloyd Best has termed this pattern of specialization in the production of raw materials "Muscovado Bias," referring to the tendency for metropolitan powers to force upon colonial possessions the role of complementary producer of raw materials for the industries of the core regions of the world economy. According to Best, one of the defining features of a plantation economy is that it is limited to the production of raw materials and terminal activities that concentrate little value added.[37]

Because industrialists from the United States zealously guarded for themselves the role of sugar refiner, they sometimes opposed the full annexation of the colonial territories. Sugar refiners opposed the annexation of Hawaii and the islands of the Caribbean if it meant the possibility of refining sugar in the territories, for free trade in refined sugar could jeopardize the refining industry's control over sugar prices, and indeed its very existence. Free trade threatened the refiners with competition not only from sugars produced in Europe but also with the possibility of a shift of the refining industry to the cane-growing territories. If refined sugar were admitted to the United States free of duty, what could prevent the development of a refining industry by the powerful hacendado bourgeoisie of Cuba or by the wealthy American planters in Hawaii? Given the technologies in operation, it was natural for central mill owners to continue processing the sugar into the refined state. To prevent a shift of the refining industry to the cane-producing regions, the refining industry of the United States needed a tariff on refined sugar, and it also needed to keep these new regions outside the tariff walls of the United States. This explains the seemingly contradictory position of an industry that was interested in reciprocity and free trade in the raw sugar market but was nevertheless highly protectionist when it came to refined sugar. From this point of view, the full annexation of Cuba threatened the refiners as much as it did the domestic cane and beet producers.[38]

In 1897 the California sugar baron Claus Spreckels lobbied intensely against the annexation of Hawaii, in the belief that it would enable Hawaiian planters to export sugar refined in Hawaii, while the island planters, fearing the defeat of annexation, opened their own refinery at Crockett, California, under the name of the California and Hawaiian Sugar Refining Company.[39] This represented a pattern of upward vertical integration for the Hawaiian planters. The refinery lost money and operated inefficiently and was finally destroyed in the San Francisco earthquake of 1906.[40] It reopened as part of the struggle of the Hawaiian planters against Spreckels.[41] Even after annexation in 1898, no refined sugar from Hawaii was allowed into the United States, representing a significant concession to the U.S. sugar refining industry.

The tariff was directed toward the reproduction of an international division of labor that forced the specialization of the islands as producers of cane and raw sugar, while reserving the industrial process of refining for the metropolitan industrial centers. Despite so-called annexations and free trade, in practice the importation of refined sugar remained banned from the U.S. market. In Puerto Rico in the 1920s, for example, the establishment of a sugar refinery by the landowning and rum-distilling Serrallés family caused a complicated litigation in the U.S. courts, the outcome of which was that the family received permission to operate the refinery for sale of refined sugar only in Puerto Rico. It could not export sugar to the United States.[42]

If the interests of the domestic producers of beet and cane were a nuisance to the framers of the large policy of colonial expansion in 1898, the interests of the sugar refiners were at the heart of the colonial division of labor on which imperialism was predicated. The closure of the frontier gave way to a new phenomenon of colonial expansion, characterized by the domination of the annexed territories by big capital from the mainland. The new phenomenon was strange and contradictory, for its essence was not the full incorporation of the territories to the polity under conditions of equality. Contemporary observers were puzzled by the exclusionary character of the new phenomenon, by the extreme domination of big business, and by its refusal to promote full annexation. What was puzzling was not that big business should want to guzzle Cuba but rather its semimercantilist refusal to do so completely. The terms attributed by the press to the barons of the sugar industry reflect this contradiction. Claus Spreckels supposedly said about Hawaiian annexation: "By and by, sometime, they will be annexed, but not now. I'll guarantee to deliver them at any time."[43] Judson C. Welliver, a muckraking journalist who studied the investments of the Sugar Trust in Cuba, believed the trust held a similar position toward that island: "Cuba will be annexed when the Sugar Trust gives the order."[44] The implication was that full annexation was anathema to the refining interests. And indeed, it is not in the nature of big business to expand in order to incorporate the conquered regions on the basis of political and economic equality, but rather the opposite, to develop in the colonies only those industries that are complementary to those it controls. Until 1898, the American experience of expansion was based on the acquisition of territory by settlers who demanded recognition and statehood from the federal government, often after subjugating and disfranchising local populations of Native Americans or Mexicans. The term "annexation" in that context precluded the kind of colonial division of labor that characterized the economic relation between the United States and the possessions acquired after 1898. As in the case of European imperialism in Africa and Asia, the colonial territories were to specialize in the production of raw materials. The Supreme Court of the United States reminded the treasurer of Puerto Rico,

Table 3.2. Tariff Advantage of Territorial Sugars (Hawaii, Philippines, Puerto Rico) over Cuban Sugar in the U.S. Market (cents per pound)

Year	Duty on Foreign Sugars	Duty on Cuban Sugar	Average Price in U.S.: 96 centrifugal	Cuban Price	Cuban Price as % of Customs Area Price
1898	1.685	1.685	4.419	2.734	62
1899[a]	1.685	1.685	4.566	2.881	63
1900[b]	1.685	1.685	4.047	2.362	58
1901	1.685	1.685	3.542	1.857	52
1902	1.685	1.685	3.72	2.035	55
1903[c]	1.685	1.348	3.974	2.626	66
1904	1.685	1.348	4.278	2.93	68
1905	1.685	1.348	3.686	2.338	63
1906	1.685	1.348	3.756	2.408	64
1907	1.685	1.348	4.073	2.725	67
1908	1.685	1.348	4.073	2.725	67
1909[d]	1.685	1.348	4.007	2.659	66
1910	1.685	1.348	4.188	2.84	68
1911	1.685	1.348	4.453	3.105	70
1912	1.685	1.348	4.162	2.814	68
1913[e]	1.256	1.0048	3.506	2.5012	71
1914	1.256	1.0048	3.814	2.8092	74
1915	1.256	1.0048	4.642	3.6372	78
1916	1.256	1.0048	5.786	4.7812	83
1917	1.256	1.0048	6.228	5.2232	84
1918	1.256	1.0048	6.447	5.4422	84
1919	1.256	1.0048	7.724	6.7192	87
1920	1.256	1.0048	12.362	11.3572	92
1921[f]	2.000	1.6000	4.763	3.163	66
1922[g]	2.206	1.7648	4.632	2.8672	62
1923	2.206	1.7648	7.02	5.2552	75
1924	2.206	1.7648	5.964	4.1992	70
1925	2.206	1.7648	4.334	2.5692	59
1926	2.206	1.7648	4.337	2.5722	59
1927	2.206	1.7648	4.73	2.9652	63
1928	2.206	1.7648	4.229	2.4642	58
1929	2.206	1.7648	3.769	2.0042	53
1930[h]	2.500	2.0000	3.387	1.387	41
1931	2.500	2.0000	3.329	1.329	40
1932	2.500	2.0000	2.925	0.925	32
1933	2.500	2.0000	3.208	1.208	38

Sources: Benjamin Allen, *A Story of the Growth of E. Atkins & Co. and the Sugar Industry in Cuba* (Boston: N.p., 1926); U.S. Tariff Commission, *Sugar: Report to the President of the United States* (Washington, D.C.: U.S. Government Printing Office, 1934), 172, 173, 176.

[a] 85% reduction of duty on Puerto Rican sugar.
[b] Free entrance of Puerto Rican sugar.
[c] Cuba reciprocity: 20% reduction on tariff.
[d] Payne Aldrich Act.
[e] Underwood Act.
[f] Emergency Tariff Act, May 28, 1921, to September 22, 1922.
[g] Fordney-McCumber Act.
[h] Hawley-Smoot Act.

Table 3.3. Crop Sources of Sugar Marketed for Consumption in the United States (in thousands of short tons)

| | United States | | United States Insular Areas | | | | |
5-year average	Cane	Beet	Hawaii	V.I.ª	P.R.ᵇ	P.I.ᶜ	Total I.A.ᵈ
1897–1901	267	77	289		50	18	357
1902–6	339	244	385		136	25	546
1907–11	378	508	514		267	82	863
1912–16	237	725	579		355	119	1,053
1917–21	223	803	540	7	394	98	1,039
1922–26	171	959	601	5	418	313	1,337
1927–31	145	1,064	800	6	610	642	2,058
1932	150	1,232	957	4	851	974	2,786

Source: U.S. Tariff Commission, *Sugar: Report to the President of the United States* (Washington, D.C.: U.S. Government Printing Office, 1934), 159.

ªUnited States Virgin Islands included in "other foreign" until 1917.

ᵇPuerto Rico.

Alan H. Richardson, during a lawsuit against the Fajardo Sugar Company, that "the Constitution of the United States does not ipso facto follow the flag," and "upon the whole, Porto Rico is much more in the nature of a dependent State external to the United States, and corresponding to what are called possessions of the British Crown, more than to a technical territory of the United States."[45]

Changes in Sources of Supply to the United States

The triumph of the protectionist beet farmers had long-term effects on Cuba, but the most extreme effect was felt in the colonial territories that were granted free trade with the United States. In the Caribbean the principal beneficiary was the sugar producers of Puerto Rico, a colonial possession that was granted free trade in 1901. Free trade favored the importation of U.S. commodities at the expense of foreign commodities and reoriented the productive structure of the island from the production of coffee, the principal export in 1897, to sugar. Incorporation into the U.S. tariff structure had a powerful effect in reorienting the Puerto Rican economy. Puerto Rico's trade with the United States expanded at the expense of trade with other countries because of its inclusion within the U.S. customs area, almost on the same ground as a state of the Union. Inclusion within the U.S. customs area was probably the main factor in the phenomenal transformation of Puerto Rican trade and industry between 1898 and 1934. Products protected by

U.S. + I.A.[e]	Cuba[f]	Other Foreign	Misc.	Total Supply U.S.
701	401	1,287	18	2,407
1,129	1,139	702	27	2,997
1,749	1,508	339	19	3,615
2,015	2,057	46	19	4,137
2,065	2,116	149	24	4,354
2,467	3,262	72	2	5,803
3,267	2,918	24	1	6,210
4,168	1,647	25		5,840

[c] Philippine Islands.

[d] Total duty-free imports from insular areas (Hawaii, Virgin Islands, Puerto Rico, Philippines).

[e] Continental United States plus insular areas (total duty-free sugar).

[f] After 1903, Cuban sugar paid only 80% of duty on foreign sugar.

the tariff, such as raw sugar and tobacco, received a tremendous boost, while unprotected products that had been protected in the Spanish customs area before 1898, such as coffee, declined.[46] Direct colonial rule in the political sphere was accompanied by free trade in the economic sphere, producing a momentous transformation of the Puerto Rican economy. Sugar could be produced in Puerto Rico under tropical conditions comparable to those of Cuba, while enjoying the added advantage of customs protection equivalent to that enjoyed by Louisiana and the beet states.

In 1900 the United States imported a considerable amount of full-duty sugar. After the acquisition of Cuba, Puerto Rico, and the Philippines, full-duty sugar was displaced from the U.S. market. Before the Spanish-American War, 53 percent of the sugar consumed in the United States was imported from areas that paid the full tariff. By 1913, Cuban sugar, which enjoyed a 20 percent tariff reduction, accounted for 50 percent of U.S. consumption, and sugar produced within the U.S. customs area accounted for 49 percent. Less than 1 percent of the sugar consumed in the United States paid the full duty. "Imperial preference" for the colonies created a sort of U.S. trading block comparable to the European colonial spheres. The drastic decrease of imports from full-duty regions was a consequence of U.S. colonial expansion.

Hawaii, Puerto Rico, and after 1913 the Philippines were within the customs area. In that year domestic cane accounted for 6 percent of U.S. consumption, while domestic beet accounted for 18 percent. Hawaii produced 14 percent of the

Table 3.4. Crop Sources of Sugar Marketed for Consumption in the United States (percentage)

| 5-year average | United States | | United States Insular Areas | | | | |
	Cane	Beet	Hawaii	V.I.[a]	P.R.[b]	P.I.[c]	Total I.A.[d]
1897–1901	11	3	12	0.00	2	1	15
1902–6	11	8	13	0.00	5	1	18
1907–11	10	14	14	0.00	7	2	24
1912–16	6	18	14	0.00	9	3	25
1917–21	5	18	12	0.16	9	2	24
1922–26	3	17	10	0.09	7	5	23
1927–31	2	17	13	0.10	10	10	33
1932	3	21	16	0.07	15	17	48

Source: U.S. Tariff Commission, *Sugar: Report to the President of the United States* (Washington, D.C.: U.S. Government Printing Office, 1934), 159.

[a] United States Virgin Islands included in "other foreign" until 1917.
[b] Puerto Rico.

sugar consumed in the United States, Puerto Rico 9 percent, and the Philippines 3 percent. The 20 percent reduction was significant enough to direct most of Cuba's exports to the United States, and Cuba continued to provide the greatest share of the sugar consumed in the U.S. market. Cuban and Puerto Rican production for the U.S. market soared as a result of reciprocity in the former case and of free trade in the latter. During World War I, U.S. investors flocked to Cuba to take advantage of soaring prices and world shortages of sugar, consolidated their holdings in Puerto Rico, and extended their operations into the Dominican Republic after U.S. Marines occupied the island in 1916.

In the period between the Spanish-American War and 1913, the price of sugar was stable, averaging about 4 cents a pound duty paid in the U.S. market. Extreme price fluctuations were a problem for the future. The years with lowest prices were 1902 and 1913 (3.5 cents) and the years of high prices were 1900 and 1911 (4.5 cents). Under these conditions, the system of imperial preference worked smoothly, balancing the output of the colonial regions and the protected regions in the United States. The tariff on sugar did not change between 1897 and 1914, until the Wilson administration lowered the tariff from 1.685 cents per pound to 1.26 cents per pound on March 1, 1914. John Dalton contends that "the absence of wide fluctuations in sugar prices was a factor conducive to profitable agricultural and industrial operations. The steadiness of the national price resulted from the stable world price for sugar, the prosperity in domestic sugar being a manifestation in the tranquillity in the world market."[47]

U.S. + I.A.[e]	Cuba[f]	Other Foreign	Misc.	Total Supply U.S.
29	17	53	1	100
38	38	23	1	100
48	42	9	1	100
49	50	1	0	100
47	49	3	1	100
43	56	1	0	100
53	47	0	0	100
71	28	0	0	100

[c] Philippine Islands.
[d] Total duty-free imports from insular areas (Hawaii, Virgin Islands, Puerto Rico, Philippines).
[e] Continental United States plus insular areas (total duty-free sugar).
[f] After 1903, Cuban sugar paid only 80% of duty on foreign sugar.

Sugar production in the American Sugar Kingdom increased from approximately 450,000 tons in 1900 to 3 million tons in 1913. U.S. interests linked to the refining industry together with local interests in the islands established and expanded the output of sugar in new or refurbished sugar mills. The early expansion of the U.S. mills in Puerto Rico and Cuba, carried out primarily by refining interests, was exemplified by the formation of the Cuban American Sugar Company and the Aguirre, Fajardo, and South Porto Rico companies. The stability of the world market price meant that, under the U.S. tariff agreement, Cuba could sell its sugar in the U.S. market at a profitable rate. The volume of the Cuban *zafra* determined the price in the United States. Cuban producers received the domestic price in the United States minus the tariff. At 3.5 cents a pound duty paid in the United States, a producer in Cuba received 2.15 cents a pound for raw sugar. All the while a producer of sugar in Puerto Rico or Hawaii received the full 3.5 cents for sugar produced under similar conditions. The U.S. market was able to absorb most of the Cuban output while keeping domestic producers afloat with the protective tariff essentially because both were able to expand their output at the expense of foreign sugars that paid the full duty. A combination of natural conditions and technological advances allowed the Cuban sugar industry to prosper despite its tariff disadvantage in the U.S. market.

In the period between Cuban reciprocity and World War I, the main effect of the tariff was to displace foreign sugar that paid the full duty from the U.S. market. By 1914 the displacement of full-duty foreign sugar was almost total, and the

Table 3.5. Sugar Production in the American Sugar Kingdom, 1898–1934 (thousands of short tons, 2,000 pounds)

Year	Cuba	Dominican Republic	Puerto Rico	American Sugar Kingdom (Cuba + D.R. + P.R.)	World Production (Beet + Cane)	American Sugar Kingdom as % of World Production
1898	350	54	60	464	8,472	5.48
1899	384	57	60	501	8,719	5.75
1900	343	51	39	433	9,287	4.66
1901	728	50	90	868	10,740	8.08
1902	973	51	103	1,127	12,186	9.25
1903	1,143	57	100	1,300	10,497	12.38
1904	1,191	53	138	1,382	11,574	11.94
1905	1,332	53	151	1,536	10,676	14.39
1906	1,350	62	214	1,626	15,625	10.41
1907	1,599	68	235	1,902	16,203	11.74
1908	1,077	70	224	1,371	15,590	8.79
1909	1,695	79	283	2,057	16,311	12.61
1910	2,021	104	345	2,470	16,707	14.78
1911	1,661	101	330	2,092	19,021	11.00
1912	2,124	109	411	2,644	17,992	14.70
1913	2,720	96	398	3,214	20,393	15.76
1914	2,909	119	364	3,392	20,648	16.43
1915	2,904	122	345	3,371	20,703	16.28
1916	3,369	142	483	3,994	18,894	21.14
1917	3,387	147	502	4,036	19,157	21.07
1918	3,860	143	464	4,467	19,469	22.94
1919	4,448	179	406	5,033	17,697	28.44
1920	4,178	199	485	4,862	17,363	28.00
1921	4,408	210	491	5,109	18,658	27.38
1922	4,476	178	405	5,059	19,771	25.59
1923	4,035	208	379	4,622	20,566	22.47
1924	4,555	259	448	5,262	22,510	23.38
1925	5,741	351	661	6,753	26,867	25.13
1926	5,471	400	606	6,477	27,246	23.77
1927	5,045	342	630	6,017	27,034	22.26
1928	4,493	416	751	5,660	29,222	19.37
1929	5,775	400	594	6,769	30,870	21.93
1930	5,232	407	866	6,505	30,673	21.21
1931	3,497	410	788	4,695	31,894	14.72
1932	2,915	483	992	4,390	29,489	14.89
1933	2,234	406	834	3,474	26,951	12.89
1934	2,593	432	981	4,006	27,882	14.37

Sources: Production series for Cuba, Puerto Rico, and total world production for 1906–34 are from U.S. Tariff Commission, *Sugar: Report to the President of the United States* (Washington, D.C.: U.S. Government Printing Office, 1934), 144. Puerto Rico figures for 1898–1906 are from U.S. Tariff Commission, *Sugar: Report of the United States Tariff Commission to the President of the United States* (Washington, D.C.: U.S. Government Printing Office, 1926), 13. Figures for the Dominican Republic for 1898–1934 and for Cuba and total world production for 1898–1906 are from Food and Agriculture Organization of the United Nations, *The World Sugar Economy in Figures, 1880–1959* (Geneva: FAO-UN, 1961), using 1 ton of 2,000 pounds = 0.9 metric tons as the conversion factor.

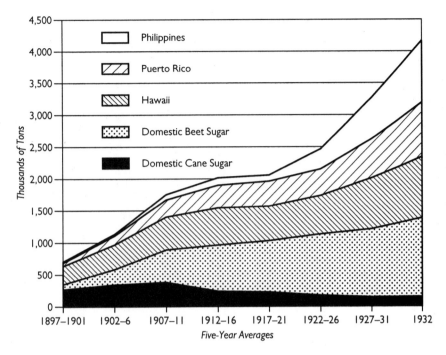

Figure 3.1. Sugar Production in the U.S. Customs Area, 1897–1932

expansion of Cuban sugar production came into direct competition with protected, duty-free sugar. The customs area expanded in 1913 as a result of the
granting of free entrance to Philippine sugar.

But just at the moment when Cuba and the customs area producers came into
competition with each other, World War I opened the prospect of sugar shortages
in Europe and created a boom for everyone in the sugar business. During World
War I, U.S. and native Cuban investors expanded the output of existing mills
and built new ones at an accelerated pace. Cuban sugar production soared from
2,442,000 tons in 1913 to 3,742,000 in 1920, while the value of sugar exports
increased from $115 million to $1,016 million. The sixteen largest mills built by
U.S. corporations alone during World War I were producing 997,000 tons of sugar
in 1925. When the price of sugar began to fall in 1921 as a result of the recovery of
the European beet crops, Cuban producers who had borrowed heavily during the
boom began facing difficulties, while domestic beet and cane farmers began demanding added protection against low prices from their government. Throughout
the 1920s, the sugar industry faced problems of overproduction.

The sugar tariff was raised from 1.256 cents per pound in 1913–20 to 2 cents a

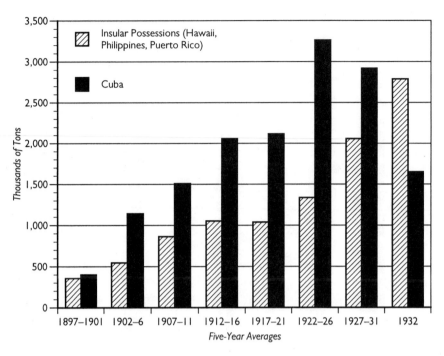

Figure 3.2. Crop Sources of Sugar Marketed for U.S. Consumption, 1897–1932

pound in 1921 and 2.2060 cents in 1922. This was a rude blow to the Cuban economy, for Cuban sugars had to pay 80 percent of the tariff. During the world war, when prices soared and the duty on foreign sugars was 1.25 cents, Cuban sugars paid a 1-cent-per-pound duty, after the 20 percent reduction. With an average price of 7.24 cents per pound in 1919 in the U.S. customs area, a duty of 1 cent per pound represented a burden of 15 percent on Cuban sugar. In 1920 with average prices at 12.362 cents per pound, the tariff represented a mere 9 percent of the Cuban price. In 1922, with the decline in prices and the raise in tariffs, the levy on Cuban sugar represented 77 percent of the price paid to producers in Cuba. By 1929, Cuban producers were receiving less than half of the price paid to producers in the U.S. customs area. In 1932, with average sugar prices in the United States at 2.925 cents a pound and a duty of 2 cents a pound, producers in Cuba received 0.925 cents per pound. Producers in Hawaii, the Philippines, and Puerto Rico received the full 2.925 cents per pound for their sugar. This was an enormous difference, and it progressively displaced Cuban sugars from the U.S. market (see Tables 3.2, 3.3, 3.4, and 3.5 and Figures 3.1 and 3.2).

The protectionist cycle of the 1920s was a vicious circle. Domestic beet and cane producers requested added protection as a shield against falling prices, and the Congress granted it in 1921, 1922, and again in 1930. But almost every pound of Cuban sugar displaced from the U.S. market by the increased tariff was replaced by duty-free sugar from Hawaii, Puerto Rico, and the Philippines, leaving the domestic producers without relief and once again requesting higher tariffs. In 1933, raw sugar prices averaged 3.208 cents within the U.S. customs area. The tariff was 2.5 cents, of which the Cuban producers paid 2 cents, leaving them with 1.208 cents per pound of sugar produced, on average. The tariff represented 166 percent of the Cuban price.

By 1925 Cuban producers were feeling the combined pressure of overproduction in the world market and protectionism in the United States. Horace Havemeyer, the son of Henry O. Havemeyer and an important investor in the South Porto Rico Sugar Company, communicated to Manuel Rionda, the principal organizer of the gigantic Cuba Cane Sugar Corporation, his concern about the effect of the tariff on the profitability of enterprises in Cuba. Havemeyer boasted that tariff protection allowed the South Porto Rico Sugar Company to earn $3.79 per sack of sugar whereas the Cuba Cane Sugar Corporation was making $1.07 per sack. The U.S. corporation with operations in Puerto Rico was making 254 percent more per sack than its counterpart in Cuba. Rhetorically, he asked whether "we are in the business to produce quantity or to produce profits."[48] The historic victory of the beet sugar interests against Cuban reciprocity in 1902 became, in the course of the 1920s, a victory for U.S. corporations in the annexed territories.

Vertical Integration
in the Colonies

It is commonly recognized that the sugar economies of Cuba, the Dominican Republic, and Puerto Rico in the period 1898–1934 were dominated by large foreign corporations. The corporations were absentee owned. The structure of ownership of these corporations, however, has not been studied. How was United States capital organized in these semicolonial and colonial territories? Were the firms small and independent, or were they interlocked with each other and linked to oligopolistic structures in the United States? Were they controlled by managers, as managerial theory would have us believe? Or were they under proprietary control, and if so, how was this proprietary control organized? Were they linked to one another, related to banking capital, or vertically integrated? Were North American interests organized separately in each island, or were they organized regionally into corporations and groups of companies encompassing the three islands?

This chapter seeks to answer these questions by looking at the history and interlocking directorate structure of the large concerns that controlled sugar production in the Spanish Caribbean before the Great Depression of the 1930s.[1] The exact extent and precise form of organization of absentee capital in the islands of the Spanish Caribbean had a direct bearing on the process of development. Direct foreign investment in plantations contributed to the overspecialization of the islands in the production of sugar and blocked an alternative path of development based on national ownership and a diversified economy. Whereas the precise forms of political rule of the territories occupied by the United States varied considerably, from direct colonial rule in Puerto Rico to indirect rule in Cuba under the provisions of the Platt Amendment, the pattern of industrial organization in the sugar industry was similar across the islands. Vertically integrated enterprises, controlled by the same groups of U.S. refiners, owned a considerable share of sugar production in each island. The empirical evidence examined here shows, furthermore, that U.S. capital was organized into structures that encompassed the three islands. Some groups of U.S. refiners owned plantations in all three islands. This opens the possibility of studying the sugar industry and the process of underdevelopment comparatively across the islands and gives rise to an important methodological question in the study of development and underdevelopment in the region. Given the fact of common absentee ownership, does it not make more sense to study the region as a whole and comparatively instead of each "national" economy separately? Most scholars who have studied U.S. investments in the Spanish Caribbean have focused on one island and have thus lost sight of the regional framework within which U.S. capital operated.

The evidence also suggests that the so-called managerialist thesis is inadequate for explaining overseas corporate expansion. The managerialist paradigm holds that the emergence of the modern corporation signified the emergence of manager control over the assets of capitalist enterprises. Its main weakness when applied to a colonial context is that it is incapable of explaining the expansion of metropolitan capital because such control was based on ties organized essentially around property rights, not around managerial prerogatives. A wide structure of proprietary control existed, and it encompassed the sugar refining industry of the United States, large New York banks, and colonial plantations in Puerto Rico, Cuba, and the Dominican Republic. The findings confirm the analysis of Maurice Zeitlin and support the notion that the theory of managerial control is based on paucity of information about real centers of proprietary control.[2] The process of vertical integration of U.S. corporations was not an unproblematic or "efficient" market response to increased demand for raw materials. Instead, power struggles among refiners gave initial impetus to the process of vertical integration, and the final emergence of vertically integrated groups of plantations and refineries depended on the power of the metropolitan state, which created the conditions for the expansion of U.S. big business through colonial military intervention and through the enforcement of a colonial division of labor imposed by the metropolitan tariff system.

United States military interventions paved the way for the expansion of U.S. capital and the development of a monocultural sugar plantation economy encompassing Cuba, Puerto Rico, and the Dominican Republic. In contrast to the United States South after the Civil War, there were no major movements of settlers or carpetbaggers to the islands. Instead, highly organized capital came to reap the profits of colonial enterprise. Many of the sugar companies operating in the Spanish Caribbean were vertically integrated concerns controlled by the sugar refining industry of the United States. The sugar corporations operating in Cuba, Puerto Rico, and the Dominican Republic had similar structures of ownership and management and formed part of a larger sphere of investment of U.S. corporations—the sphere of investments to which Eric Williams intuitively pointed when he called the region "the American Sugar Kingdom in the Caribbean."[3]

The expansion of the United States as an imperialist power in the Caribbean took place in a period in which economic concentration had advanced precipitously, producing qualitative changes in the structure of capitalist property. The modern corporation replaced family-owned enterprises as the basic unit of production in metropolitan capitalist societies in the last three decades of the nineteenth century. The transition from family to corporate ownership facilitated a process of centralization of capital to put in motion the technologies of the second industrial revolution, which transformed one industrial branch after another, featuring steel production, electricity, internal combustion engines, refrigeration, electric lighting, and much else. Standard Oil became a model of organization for the new enterprises. After Standard Oil, horizontal consolidation advanced in one industry after another, leading to the formation of industrial trusts.[4]

Because the sugar refining industry was a pioneer in the process of horizontal consolidation, the prosecution of the American Sugar Refining Company (ASRC) under antitrust legislation helped to forge corporate law and forced sugar refiners to reorganize their enterprises. Holding companies that owned the stock of other companies were used to bring the industry into formal compliance with antitrust legislation. The underlying reality of economic concentration, however, proved to be more enduring. Analyzing the power structure of the U.S. sugar companies in the Caribbean requires breaking down and reassembling the structure of interlocking directorates which link together multiple, formally independent enterprises. In the analysis that follows, I have focused on the directors with the greatest number of interlocks.

Vertical Integration: Cuba

United States investors acquired a predominant position in the production of sugar in Cuba in the first decade after the Spanish-American War. The investment of United States concerns in agribusiness was the largest of such investments by United States companies anywhere in the world.[5] Their magnitude can be appreciated in the following figures: in 1924 U.S. sugar investments in Cuba represented 63 percent of total U.S. agricultural investments worldwide, and the largest eight U.S. sugar companies in Cuba had an average investment of $45 million.[6] The importance of Cuba and the Caribbean as a whole is further revealed in the figures for U.S. investments abroad by geographic area. U.S. investments in 1924 were concentrated in the Western Hemisphere: in Canada ($2,631 million), in South America ($1,411 million), in Cuba and the Caribbean ($1,103 million), and in Mexico ($1,005 million). U.S. investments in the Caribbean were almost as large as its investments in all of South America, larger than its investments in Mexico, almost twice as large as its investments in all of Asia, and about thirty times larger than its investments in all of Africa.[7] Whereas in 1897 U.S. investments in Mexico were almost four times larger than those in the Caribbean, by 1924 the Caribbean had a larger share. If one takes into account the size of the territories in this comparison, their populations, and the fact that U.S. investments in Puerto Rico are not accounted as "foreign," one can see that the Caribbean, especially Cuba, had the largest concentration of U.S. investments in the world.

United States intervention in Cuba in 1898 altered dramatically the existing property relations in the island. The extremely destructive war between Cubans and Spaniards of 1895–98 left the sugar economy in a disastrous condition. During the war, the sugar fields became part of the economic battlefield. The insurrection against the Spanish became an economic war waged against the planters in an effort to paralyze the economy and reduce the revenue of the Spanish colonial state. A decree by Máximo Gómez, the commander in chief of the Cuban insurrection, warned in 1895: "All sugar plantations will be destroyed, the standing cane set fire and the factory buildings and railroads destroyed." Cane field after cane field was set afire and la tea (the torch) became "the most devastating weapon in the insurrectionary arsenal."[8]

In 1898 Cuba was a destroyed country. United States direct control of the government, and indirect control after 1902 under the Platt Amendment, contributed to the displacement of the Cuban planters from the dominant position they had enjoyed in the Cuban economy before 1895. The output of sugar reflects the levels of destruction during the war. The one-million-ton crop of 1894 fell to 225,000 tons in 1896 and 212,000 tons in 1897. The North American occupation dealt the planter class a second blow by depriving the Cubans of the opportunity to reorder their economy according to national priorities. The United States seized control of the government, controlled the collection of revenues, and determined the disbursement of public funds. With the state at the service of foreign interests, the creole bourgeoisie was displaced from its position of economic primacy. As might be expected, "the beneficiaries of North American rule were North Americans."[9]

Lands and agricultural establishments were transferred to United States owners in a great feast of division of the colonial bounty. In a matter of a few years there were thirteen thousand North American landowners in Cuba, in agricultural pursuits ranging from tobacco to pineapples. The strategic heights of the Cuban economy—the sugar economy—came under the control of a few gigantic concerns interlocked among themselves, with the sugar refining industry of the United States, and with the biggest banks. In railways, mining, shipping, and public utilities, North American capital was preeminent. But among all the sectors, sugar production was the most important. Many of the other important branches of investment (e.g., railroads) may be considered ancillary to the sugar economy. The Cuban rail network was built to serve the sugar industry.[10]

There were two waves of investment in the Cuban sugar economy: in the years immediately following the U.S. occupation and during the boom of 1914–19. In the first wave of investments, U.S. corporations purchased existing sugar mills and built new ones. By 1913, North Americans owned thirty-nine mills representing 23 percent of the grinding units of the island and 37 percent of the sugar produced (1,033,275 tons).[11] Following the arrival of North American capital, Cubans owned sixty-seven mills producing 917,342 tons of sugar. Although Cubans owned a larger number of mills than North Americans, their total output was smaller than that of the U.S. mills. The Spanish owned forty-one mills with a total output of 510,357 tons, or 18 percent of Cuba's output. The U.S. mills were on average larger and had a higher output of sugar. Mills belonging to U.S. owners had the highest agricultural productivity, which is probably an indication that many of them were of recent construction and were therefore located in new regions of sugar cultivation.[12] In the second wave of investments (1914–19), U.S. investors deepened their control of the Cuban sugar economy.

The effects of the U.S. occupation on transfers of property can be estimated from a sample of eighty-two mills built before 1898, still in operation in 1913, with identifiable owners at the date of foundation and in 1913 (see Table 4.1). While British, Cuban, and U.S. owners benefited, French and particularly Spanish own-

Table 4.1. Transfer of Mill Ownerhip in Cuba before 1913

Owner in 1913	British	Cuban	French	Spanish	U.S.	Total
British founder	1					1
Cuban founder	2	19	1	2	2	26
French founder	1	2	1	1	3	8
Spanish founder		13	1	14	5	33
U.S. founder		1			13	14
Total	4	35	3	17	23	82

Source: Secretaría de Agricultura, Comercio y Trabajo de Cuba, *Portfolio azucarero: Industria azucarera de Cuba, 1912–1914* (Havana: La Moderna Poesía, 1914).

ership declined in the Cuban republic. It is likely that many of the mills counted as Cuban in 1913 were owned by naturalized Spanish citizens.

The achievement of reciprocity with the United States offered producers in Cuba a 20 percent reduction on the tariff on raw sugar. Commercial exchange with the United States increased, and the new prosperity benefited the Cuban planter class. But under the United States neocolonial system, the dominant owners in the sugar industry were American citizens. The Cuban planters were displaced from a position of preeminence into a secondary position although their total output of sugar expanded. The new colonial overlords were, in contrast to the period of Spanish colonialism, the principal purchasers of Cuban sugar. For the Cuban planter class, the U.S. occupation of 1898 and the neorepublican government implanted under the Platt Amendment signified the realization of a long-sought access to the U.S. market.

The National Sugar Refining Company Group in Cuba

In the aftermath of the U.S. occupation American corporations began to make inroads in the sugar industry. The U.S. corporation with the most obvious links to the oligopolistic sugar refining network was the Cuban American Sugar Company, established in 1899 and reorganized in 1906 by a group of refiners from the U.S. firms of B. H. Howell Son & Company and the National Sugar Refining Company (NSRC). Prominent figures from this group include James Howell Post, the president of the NSRC, Thomas A. Howell, the vice-president of the same firm, the Bunker and Mollenhauer sugar refining interests, Lorenzo D. Armstrong, and John Farr. When the Cuban American Sugar Company was reorganized in 1906 into a holding company controlling a multiplicity of centrales, the reorganization received the financial support of Henry O. Havemeyer. The Cuban American was a holding company incorporated in New Jersey, which owned the entire capital stock of the Chaparra Sugar Company, the Tinguaro Sugar Company, the Cuban Sugar Refining Company, the Unidad Sugar Company, and the Mercedita Sugar Company. In 1908, the Cuban American acquired the Colonial Sugars Company, which owned a sugar refinery in Granmercy, Louisiana, and in 1910 it purchased the San Manuel Sugar Company in Cuba, "the latter comprising an estate adjoining the property of the Chaparra Sugar Co.; these two properties, operated as a single unit, forming the largest sugar estate in the world."[13]

Judson C. Welliver, an investigative journalist, estimated that the Sugar Trust controlled fourteen centrales spanning 116,000 acres producing 297,000 tons of raw sugar in 1910.[14] The total surface covered by the companies controlled by the Cuban American exceeded five hundred thousand acres of land in 1910, according to one source,[15] but the holdings of the oligopolistic network of sugar refiners in Cuba were in fact much larger. The B. H. Howell–NSRC group achieved by 1924 control of seventeen sugar mills in Cuba with a total production of 452,550 tons of sugar. Tracking the ownership of the group requires assembling information about holding companies that owned the capital stock of other companies and identifying the most important officers and directors in the enterprises. The seventeen mills under the control of the NSRC group in Cuba produced more sugar than all the mills of Puerto Rico in 1924 (447,972 tons) and more than double the combined production of all the mills of the Dominican Republic in the same year (256,898 tons). In addition to the mills owned by the Cuban American Sugar Company, the NSRC group controlled the Sugar Estates of Oriente and the Guantánamo, New Niquero, and Cuban Dominican companies.

The documents of incorporation of the largest concern controlled by the NSRC, the Cuban American Sugar Company, include a list of the principal stock owners.[16] The corporation issued a total of 13,750 shares. The largest stockholder was Robert B. Hawley with 2,524 shares, followed by James Howell Post with 2,299.5 shares. A careful look at the list, however, indicates that a large block of shares were controlled by the B. H. Howell–NSRC group.[17] The group constitutes in my view a clear example of what Maurice Zeitlin and Richard Ratcliff have termed a "kinecon group," an economic entity in which blocks of stock are held by groups organized through ties of kinship.[18]

In addition to the sugar mills owned through the Cuban American holding company, the B. H. Howell & Son–NSRC group controlled additional holding companies, which in turn owned other mills. The Guantánamo Sugar Company established in 1905 owned three sugar mills—Isabel, Los Caños, and Soledad—located in the vicinity of the city of Guantánamo in eastern Cuba. The sugar company owned over one hundred thousand acres of land in eastern Cuba and controlled, through leases and mortgages, another seventeen thousand. The Guantánamo Railway was owned by the company and provided transportation essential to link the cane farms to the mill and the mill to the port of Deseo. The lines of the Guantánamo Railway extended over one hundred kilometers in addition to the narrow rails used in the farms.

In addition to the Cuban American and Guantánamo companies, the NSRC group controlled the New Niquero Sugar Company, a holding company that owned Central Niquero, established in 1905. It controlled sixty-seven thousand acres of land in eastern Cuba in the vicinity of Manzanillo and had access to another eighty-five hundred acres of colono cane. New Niquero had an internal railroad system, and its location on the seaboard gave it an advantage in reduced freight costs. James Howell Post, president of the NSRC, was president of the New Niquero Sugar Company.

The Sugar Estates of Oriente was a product of several reorganizations. At the end of World War I, Thomas Howell of the NSRC was president of Central Cupey and vice-president and director of Central Alto Cedro and of Central Palma. The Sugar Estates of Oriente was established in 1922 under a Maryland charter "to acquire the assets of the Alto Cedro, Cupey, and Palma estates."[19] In May 1923, Sugar Estates of Oriente acquired the entire capital stock of the Compañía Central América. Thomas A. Howell was vice-president and director of the new company. Eleven of the directors of the Sugar Estates of Oriente were also directors of the Cuban Dominican Sugar Corporation, which owned centrales in the Dominican Republic and Cuba.

The Cuban Dominican Sugar Corporation was also a product of several reorganizations carried out by the NSRC refiners. The reorganizations first converted the properties of the West India Sugar Finance Corporation into the Cuban Dominican Sugar Development Syndicate in 1920, which in turn was succeeded by the Cuban Dominican Development Company. In 1924, the Cuban Dominican Development Company became the Cuban Dominican Development Corporation, a holding company that controlled 100 percent of the stock of the Santa Ana Sugar Company, Central Altagracia, and the Sugar Estates of Oriente, which in turned owned Compañía Central América. Gordon S. Rentschler, an executive in charge of reorganizing the properties of City Bank after the sugar crash of 1921, and William A. Rockefeller were directors of the Cuban Dominican.[20]

A total of fifty individuals occupied positions as officers and directors of the

Table 4.2. Interlocking Officers and Directors of the National Sugar Refining Company and Related Enterprises in Cuba (numbers)

	CASC	CDSC	GSC	NSRC	NNSC	SEO
CASC	—					
CDSC	1	—				
GSC	4	2	—			
NSRC	2	2	3	—		
NNSC	3	2	3	2	—	
SEO	0	11	1	2	1	—

Sources: Farr & Co., *Manual of Sugar Companies* (New York: Farr & Company, 1926); Directory of Directors Company, *Directory of Directors in the City of New York* (New York: Directory of Directors Company, 1921); Oscar Pino Santos, *El asalto a Cuba por la oligarquía financiera yanqui* (Havana: Casa de las Américas, 1973). Muriel McAvoy Weissman, "Officers and Directors of United States Companies Investing in Cuban Sugar: A Listing with brief Biographical Data," manuscript, 1990, made available by the author. The model for this matrix is taken from the methodological appendix in John Scott, *Capitalist Property and Financial Power: A Comparative Study of Britain, the United States, and Japan* (New York: New York University Press, 1986), 210–20.

Note: CASC = Cuban American Sugar Company; CDSC = Cuban Dominican Sugar Corporation; GSC = Guantánamo Sugar Company; NSRC = National Sugar Refining Company; NNSC = New Niquero Sugar Company; SEO = Sugar Estates of Oriente, Inc.

five companies owning centrales in Cuba linked to the NSRC. Of these, sixteen held multiple positions in the complex of companies.[21] Table 4.2 shows the interlocks among the companies, represented in the matrix as lines of multiplicity *n*. In graph theory language, we say that the Cuban Dominican Sugar Corporation and the Sugar Estates of Oriente are adjacent points joined by a line of multiplicity 11. Table 4.3 shows the individuals interlocking the corporations.

According to the Cuban economic historian Oscar Pino Santos, finance-capital groups penetrated the Cuban economy during World War I to take over sugar properties at the time of a boom in sugar prices. Before 1914, the Cuban sugar industry had recovered largely at the initiative of the Cubans themselves.[22] After the crash of sugar prices in 1921, U.S. capital acquired new properties through foreclosure.[23] Finance capital groups first made their presence felt shortly after 1898. Michael Soref has operationalized the concept of "finance capitalist" by selecting individuals who sit on boards of industrial corporations and on the board of a bank or other financial institution.[24] Such individuals typically hold central positions in interlocking networks and represent a greater number of corporations than do nonfinancial capitalists. Both James Howell Post and Thomas Howell are represented in five of the six corporations of the NSRC group. Post had been a member of the board of directors of City Bank since 1898, and Howell was a director of the board of the First National Bank in the city of New York. Thus

Table 4.3. Interlocking Officers and Directors of the National Sugar Refining Company and Related Enterprises in Cuba (names)

Directors	Companies					
	CASC	CDSC	GSC	NSRC	NNSC	SEO
Frederick B. Adams		1				1
Lorenzo D. Armstrong		1				1
George R. Bunker	1		1	1		
Guy Cary		1				1
George H. Houston		1				1
Thomas A. Howell		1	1	1	1	1
George C. Keiser	1		1			
George E. Keiser	1				1	
Arthur Kirstein		1				1
Charles G. Meyer		1				1
George S. Minde		1				1
James Howell Post	1	1	1	1	1	
E. N. Potter		1				1
Gordon Rentschler		1				1
William A. Rockefeller		1				1
Walter J. Vreeland	1				1	

Note: CASC = Cuban American Sugar Company; CDSC = Cuban Dominican Sugar Company; GSC = Guantánamo Sugar Company; NSRC = National Sugar Refining Company; NNSC = New Niquero Sugar Company; SEO = Sugar Estates of Oriente.

finance capitalists, representing the fusion of banking and industrial capital (but not necessarily bank control of industry) were present in Cuba from the beginning of the period of U.S. neocolonialism.

Several important facts about the Cuban American Sugar Company and its directors help us to understand the significance of the distinction between these notions of finance capital. Among the top stockholders in the corporation not listed above was James Stillman, who held 670 shares.[25] Stillman had helped to subscribe a loan of $200 million to finance the Spanish-American War.[26] James Howell Post, president of the NSRC, had served on the board of directors of City Bank since 1898.[27] The link with City Bank is additionally revealing because of the bank's historical role in financing the Cuba-U.S. sugar trade since the days of slavery. Moses Taylor, an important nineteenth-century New York merchant, made a fortune trading in Cuban sugars and joined the board of National City Bank in 1837.[28] Under Taylor, City Bank expanded into a banking institution of prime importance in the United States.[29] In addition to the historical ties of City Bank to the Cuban sugar trade through Moses Taylor, Stillman and City Bank were already involved with the sugar refining interests in the 1890s: by 1904 the

Table 4.4. Cuban Centrales Controlled by the National Sugar Refining Company, 1924

Company	Mill	Province of Cuba	Sugar Production (tons)
Cuban American Sugar Co.[a]	Tinguaro	Matanzas	36,538
Cuban American Sugar Co.[a]	Delicias	Oriente	[b]
Cuban American Sugar Co.[a]	Chaparra	Oriente	80,971
Cuban American Sugar Co.[a]	Mercedita	Pinar del Río	19,936
Cuban American Sugar Co.[a]	Constancia	Santa Clara	20,670
Cuban American Sugar Co.[a]	Unidad	Santa Clara	14,043
Cuban Dominican Sugar Corporation[c]	Hatillo	Oriente	17,284
Cuban Dominican Sugar Corporation[c]	Santa Ana	Santa Clara	14,884
Cuban Dominican Sugar Corporation[c]	Altagracia	Oriente	26,271
Guantánamo Sugar Co[d]	Isabel	Oriente	16,671
Guantánamo Sugar Co.[d]	Los Caños	Oriente	15,925
Guantánamo Sugar Co.[d]	Soledad	Oriente	15,145
New Niquero Sugar Co.[e]	Niquero	Oriente	33,880
Sugar Estates of Oriente, Inc.[f]	Alto Cedro	Oriente	36,190
Sugar Estates of Oriente, Inc.[f]	Cupey	Oriente	23,471
Sugar Estates of Oriente, Inc.[f]	Palma	Oriente	49,534
Sugar Estates of Orinte, Inc.[f]	América	Oriente	31,137
Total of NSRC in Cuba			452,550

Sources: Directory of Directors Company, *Directory of Directors in the City of New York* (New York: Directory of Directors Company, 1921); Farr & Co., *Manual of Sugar Companies* (New York: Farr & Co., 1924 and 1926); Muriel McAvoy Weissman, "Officers and Directors of United States Companies Investing in Cuban Sugar: A Listing with Brief Biographical Data," manuscript, 1990, made available by the author.

[a] James Howell Post, president of the NSRC, was vice-president, treasurer, and director of the Cuban American Sugar Company; Thomas Howell, vice-president of the NSRC, was a vice-president of the Cuban American Sugar Company.

[b] The production of Delicias is reported jointly with that of Chaparra.

[c] Thomas Howell, vice-president of the NSRC, was chairman of the board of the Cuban Dominican Sugar Corporation.

[d] James Howell Post, president of the NSRC, was president of the Guantánamo Sugar Company.

[e] James Howell Post, president of the NSRC, was president of the New Niquero Sugar Company.

[f] Sugar Estates of Oriente was a subsidiary of the Cuban Dominican Sugar Corporation.

board of City Bank included men such as Henry O. Havemeyer (American Sugar Refining), Cyrus H. McCormick (International Harvester), James H. Post (National Sugar), P. A. Valentine (Armour Company), William Rockefeller (Standard Oil), and the Union Pacific's E. H. Harriman.[30]

Thus the formation of the Cuban American Sugar Company in 1906 represents an incursion into Cuban terrain of North American finance capital, understood in the broader sense of a fusion of banking and industrial capital.[31] The group of refiners it represented were heavily interlocked and historically tied to City Bank.

The sugar trade remained central to City Bank from the time of Moses Taylor until at least the 1930s. Sugar played a crucial role in the rise of Taylor's fortune and therefore that of City Bank. Under the direction of Stillman, the top U.S. sugar refiners were members of its board. The sugar crash of 1921 resulted in Stillman's resignation in 1921 and his succession by Charles Edwin Mitchell. City Bank nearly collapsed as a result of its overextension of Cuban sugar loans at a time of plummeting sugar prices in the world market, and the bank had to be rescued.[32] The linkages of City Bank to the Cuban sugar industry, however, overflow the limits of the B. H. Howell–NSRC group. After the sugar crash of 1921, the bank organized the General Sugars Company to take over foreclosed or bankrupt mills. Table 4.4 shows the sugar mills owned in Cuba by the NSRC group in 1924.

World War I and the Sugar Boom in Cuba

The war of 1914–18 destroyed the beet crops of Europe and prompted a marked rise in sugar prices, which in turn produced a sugar boom in Cuba. The pace of U.S. investment in Cuba accelerated during the war to a level never reached in any previous or succeeding period in the history of the island. Some observers even concluded that during the war "Wall Street" acquired definitive control over the Cuban economy.[33] A National City Bank pamphlet referred to Cuba during the war as "the most valuable piece of agricultural real estate on the globe." "The actual production," according to this euphoric pamphlet, "has increased over 50 percent during the war period, and Cuba now produces about 25 percent of the world's sugar as against an average of about 11 percent in the decade preceding the war." Predicting that the European sugar industry would be slow to recover because of the Bolshevik Revolution and the breakdown of Austria-Hungary, the pamphlet concluded that "the enlarged demands upon Cuba will continue indefinitely." In 1919, National City Bank opened local branches in Artemisa, Caibarién, Cárdenas, Camagüey, Ciego de Avila, Cienfuegos, Guantánamo, Havana, Manzanillo, Matanzas, Pinar del Río, Sagua la Grande, Santa Clara, Santiago, and Unión de Reyes. Americans owned, according to the National City Bank, "between 40 percent and 50 percent of the approximately $600,000,000 worth of sugar mills, plantations and other appurtenances of sugar production in Cuba," the remaining share belonging to Europeans and Cubans.[34] During the war years, the sugar-producing provinces of Cuba experienced a frenzied increase in their production, with the exception of Pinar del Río, a tobacco-growing province (see Table 4.5).

Table 4.5. Production and Value of Cuban Sugar, 1913–1920

Year	Production (tons)	Value ($ millions)	% of total Export Value
1913	2,442,000	$115.8	72
1914	2,615,000	163.4	77
1915	2,609,000	202.4	84
1916	3,034,000	308.5	85
1917	3,063,000	332.2	86
1918	3,473,000	347.1	85
1919	4,012,000	472.1	89
1920	3,742,000	1,016.8	92

Sources: Susan Schroeder, *Cuba: A Handbook of Historical Statistics* (Boston: G. K. Hall, 1982), 43; Louis A. Pérez, *Cuba: Between Reform and Revolution* (New York: Oxford University Press, 1988), 225.

Some of the foreign capitalists who invested in Cuban sugar plantations purchased existing mills in the expectation of rising sugar prices during the world war. The Cuba Cane Sugar Corporation's massive investments exemplify this pattern. Other foreign capitalists came to the island to build new, more efficient mills in the eastern provinces and to take advantage of the foreseen price increases. This second group of investors included the promoters of the Punta Alegre Sugar Company, the American Sugar Refining Company, Manuel Rionda and a group of associated investors, the Hershey Corporation, and the Hires Root Beer Company. All built or refurbished sugar mills in the island during 1914–19. The share of the Cuban sugar crop owned by U.S. nationals increased during the wartime boom. When the war ended, the beet crops in Europe recovered and the price of sugar fell again. Cuban producers who had incurred massive debt during the period of the fabulous prices found it increasingly difficult to meet the payments on loans acquired under expectations of much higher sugar prices, and foreign banks began to foreclose on their properties. Thus the sugar boom increased foreign ownership in the Cuban sugar industry, and the crash augmented it even further. City Bank acquired a group of mills in the early 1920s.

Shortages of sugar in Europe increased the demand for Cuban sugar and promoted the inflation of sugar prices. In July 1914, raw Cuban sugar sold in New York at 1.93 cents a pound. The next month it sold at 3.66. In 1915–16, the three-million-ton crop sold at an average of 4.37 cents, and a year later a crop of roughly the same size sold at 4.62 cents.[35] Nine new mills were erected in 1916, and in 1917, the year the United States entered the war, another seven mills were built. Six more mills were built in 1918, two in 1919, two in 1920, and five in 1921.[36]

Several important corporations emerged during this period. The Cuba Cane Sugar Corporation, the Punta Alegre Sugar Company, the Rionda interests, and the ASRC, all linked to the House of Morgan, experienced the most dramatic expansion during the war.[37] Some groups continued to expand after the conclusion of hostilities, such as the General Sugars Company, a concern owned by City Bank, which foreclosed a number of mills after the price of sugar collapsed in 1921.

The Cuba Cane Sugar Corporation

In January 1916, Manuel Rionda went to Cuba with financial resources drawn from J. W. Seligman Brothers and purchased in one month seventeen plantations at a cost of $48,120,000.[38] The Cuba Cane Sugar Corporation was established to take advantage of imminent increases in the world market price of sugar as a result of World War I. Incorporated in New York in late 1915, the corporation drew on capital resources from the House of Morgan. Prominent in the corporation were Manuel Rionda, of the firm of Czarnikow-Rionda, Alfred Jaretzky of Sullivan & Cromwell,[39] Alfred Strauss of J. & W. Seligman Brothers,[40] and Charles Sabin of Guaranty Trust Company.[41] The sheer size of the enterprise and the fact that it was created by bankers who purchased already existing mills, instead of industrialists who built them, is one of the reasons why the boom of the world war has been considered a period of takeover of the Cuban economy by Wall Street. In the expectation of increasing prices for sugar as a result of the European war, the House of Morgan decided to establish its own production of raw sugar in Cuba.[42] The expectation of shortages of sugar in Europe as a result of the destruction of the beet crops exerted a strong influence on the financiers who conceived the idea of the Cuba Cane Sugar Corporation. Raw sugar prices had hovered around 3 cents a pound in the period 1898–1914.[43] By March 1916, raw sugar was selling in New York at 5.75 cents per pound. In 1920, raw sugar prices reached the unprecedented level of 20 cents a pound and Cuba experienced the famous Danza de los Millones. Considering trends in sugar prices, the motives for the establishment of the Cuba Cane Sugar Corporation in late 1915 were well founded. The sugar refining establishment was represented on the board of directors of the corporation through Horace Havemeyer of the ASRC and James N. Jarvie of Arbuckle Brothers. Banking capital brought together competing industrialists in a single enterprise, according to the long tradition of the House of Morgan of developing "communities of interests," which dated back to the reorganization of the railroads in the 1870s and 1880s.

By 1918 the Cuba Cane Sugar Corporation was the largest sugar enterprise in the world.[44] Like the refiner-controlled Cuban American Sugar Company, the board of the Cuba Cane Sugar Corporation included directors from the sugar refining business (Havemeyer and Arbuckle), sugar brokers and owners of centrales (Rionda interests, sugar brokers who operated the Tuinucú, Francisco, and Manatí mills), and American banking interests from the House of Morgan and J. W. Seligman. The bankers were the dominant interest in the Cuba Cane, however, not the refiners. The corporation achieved control of 15 percent of the Cuban crop. The case of Cuba Cane reveals a trend in the process of vertical consolidation that also existed in Puerto Rico and the Dominican Republic: the fusion of industrial and refining interests with banking interests in the process of vertical integration and colonial expansion.

Manuel Rionda, of the New York branch of the firm of Czarnikow-Rionda (London-based sugar brokers),[45] presided over the formation of Cuba Cane. Rionda had entered the Cuban sugar business in 1897 as a representative of the London-based Czarnikow MacDougall & Company, which, according to Rionda's own account, was "the first foreign house to enter the Cuban field immediately after the War of Independence, advancing money to the many needy Cuban planters."[46] The Rionda-owned Tuinucú estate had been devastated during the War of Independence and had to be abandoned. Beginning in 1900, the Riondas resumed operations, making 3,400 bags of sugar on their first crop, 153,767 by 1913, and 277,000 by 1919. Although the Rionda interests were connected with the refining establishment,[47] the capital for the formation of Cuba Cane originated in the House of Morgan. The linkages of the Rionda interests to the House of Morgan dated back to 1906, when Manuel Rionda came into contact with Sullivan & Cromwell in connection with the reorganization of the Stewart Sugar Mill.[48] In 1912 Rionda launched the Manatí Sugar Company, a new venture in Oriente. Important figures in its formation were the president of the Bankers Trust (Edmund C. Converse), Captain Joseph R. DeLamar of the International Nickel Company, and the firm of Sullivan & Cromwell.[49] In 1915, when sugar prices soared, the House of Morgan financed the creation of Cuba Cane. Manuel Rionda's ties with the House of Morgan, developed in the operation of the Manatí Sugar Company since 1912, led to his appointment as president of the gigantic new corporation. The bankers wished to purchase sugar mills immediately to take advantage of the practically certain increases in the price of raw sugar. In the formation of Cuba Cane, according to Manuel Rionda, the chief banker "was J. P. Morgan & Co., although their name does not appear in the syndicate for reasons of their own."[50]

Among the important banking figures involved in the formation of Cuba Cane was Charles H. Sabin, of the Guaranty Trust Company of New York, another institution of the House of Morgan. On November 24, 1915, at a meeting with the bankers, Rionda was assured that the corporation would be in full swing within two weeks. On December 31, Cuba Cane was incorporated. On January 1, 1916, Rionda left for Cuba. Within a month, Rionda had purchased for Cuba Cane seventeen centrales in Cuba.[51] The prospect of rising sugar prices impelled the bankers to invest large sums in the sugar business of Cuba. The bankers supported the formation of the corporation on the assumption of a price of 3.5 cents per pound of raw sugar. By March 1916, Cuban centrifugals were selling in New York at 5.75 cents,[52] and they would climb to over 20 cents by 1920. Cuba Cane was presided by Rionda, but the Riondas as a group held less than 2 percent of the voting stock as of September 15, 1916.[53]

The Czarnikow-Rionda group, however, managed the sales of sugar and the purchases of equipment and sugar bags for the Cuba Cane Sugar Corporation. The volume of the transactions was sufficient to interest the Riondas in management of the Cuba Cane. Between 1916 and 1918, the charges by Czarnikow-Rionda to Cuba Cane for handling sales and purchases amounted to $8,147,230.12, or an average of $2,715,743 per season.[54] In 1919, an audit report of Cuba Cane criticized the Rionda interests severely for these charges. In addition, the audit noticed that most of the sugar mills owned by Cuba Cane were older properties located in the western part of Cuba. Out of the seventeen mills purchased by Cuba Cane, thirteen were in the west and four in the east. The eastern mills, auditors found, were much more profitable than those of the west.

The Punta Alegre Sugar Company

Not all investors in Cuban sugar followed the pattern of Cuba Cane. The Punta Alegre Sugar Company built new mills in eastern Cuba instead of buying older ones in the west. The corporation was presided over by Edwin F. Atkins, the foremost U.S. sugar baron in Cuba. The Atkins family had been involved in the Cuban sugar trade since 1838. Elisha Atkins, a Boston merchant, started a business with William Freeman in 1838 importing molasses and sugar from Cuba. The firm of Atkins and Freeman, located at 26 India Wharf, imported sugar for sales to U.S. grocers before the sugar refining business was fully developed. Atkins and Freeman served as merchants and bankers, advancing funds to Cuban merchants and planters. On the Boston-Havana route, the ships carried cooperage stocks for the manufacture of hogsheads, fish, dried goods, boots, and shoes. In 1843, the Atkins and Freeman firm began trading with the city of Cienfuegos, which became the main sugar market on the southern coast of Cuba. Elisha Atkins built commercial relations with Fowler and Prosper, Monzón, Abrieu & Company, the Torriente Brothers, and Hernández & Terry. The introduction of steam-driven mills on the Cuban plantations increased the extraction of cane juice to 60 to 65 percent on the weight of the cane and recovered 6 percent of the sugar. The Cuban crop and the slave population of Cuba continually increased.

In 1849, William F. Freeman decided to concentrate on the manufacture of logwood and dyestuffs, and Elisha Atkins continued the trade with Cuban planters by himself. Atkins traded with Cuba, the Windward Islands, St. Thomas, Jamaica, and St. Croix. His vessels went to Guatemala for coffee, cochineal, and granadilla wood, and sometimes to Río de Janeiro to import coffee to the port of New Orleans. In the 1850s the Atkins firm built stable relations with the Torriente Brothers, Thomas Terry, and the Montalvos of Cienfuegos. By 1868, Cuban sugar production had increased to 749,000 tons, and the business of Atkins firm increased in proportion. According to Benjamin Allen, "The homeward cargoes often numbered fifty in a single season, with bills of lading covering a total of twenty-five thousand hogsheads of sugar and thirty-five hundred hogsheads of molasses, which all found a market under his care, the amount of business running into the millions every year."[55]

In 1874 Edwin F. Atkins, son of Elisha, was admitted into the firm at the age of twenty-four. Edwin joined the firm during the Ten Years' War in Cuba (1868–78), which destroyed many plantations in the eastern part of the island. The process of abolition of slavery in Cuba (1880–86), the increasing competition of beet sugar in the world market, and the transition to the system of centrales and to the colono system left many planters bankrupt. After the Ten Years' War, the Sarria family's Soledad estate was in no position to pay its indebtedness to the Torriente Brothers, and the Torriente Brothers were in turn unable to pay their debt to E. Atkins and Company. A long and complicated series of negotiations resulted in the acquisition by the Atkins firm of the Soledad estate in 1883. Under the initiative of Edwin Atkins, then resident in Cuba, the forty-five-hundred-acre estate was modernized, railroad track was installed, and plantings were extended. By 1887 the Soledad produced four thousand tons of sugar.[56]

The merchant firm of E. Atkins & Company acquired a sugar refinery in Boston in 1878, also through foreclosure. In 1888, a year after the foundation of the Sugar Refineries Company, predecessor of the ASRC, Elisha Atkins agreed to join the consolidation of the sugar refiners. In exchange for his stock in the Bay State refinery, Atkins received trust certificates in the new horizontally consolidated firm. A year after the Bay State was acquired by the Sugar Trust, it was dismantled and its machinery transferred to other plants.[57] From its original role of intermediary between planter and sugar refiner, the Atkins firm extended, though unwillingly, into the production of raw sugar in Cuba through ownership of the Soledad estate and into the refining of sugar in the United States through the acquisition of the Bay State refinery.

In 1892, shortly after the conclusion of the price war between the ASRC and Spreckels, Henry O. Havemeyer and his cousin Charles Senff became interested in the Trinidad Sugar Company in Cuba. Edwin F. Atkins joined them, presided over the newly acquired company, and managed its affairs in Cuba.[58] The Trinidad estate was a private Havemeyer-Senff-Atkins venture rather than a corporate extension of the ASRC. This was perhaps typical to the extent that the process of formation of trusts was presided over by "captains of industry" who retained extraordinary independence even after they created immense corporations. The emergence of the modern corporation was a long process. In its initial stages in the nineteenth century the capitalists still retained many aspects of the rugged individualism of an earlier competitive era of firms led by private entrepreneurs. In another sense, the venture into Trinidad expressed the desire of prominent refiners from the eastern seaboard of the United States to establish vertically integrated structures after the Havemeyer-Spreckels price war of 1890–91. Vertical integration had allowed Spreckels, the "Sugar King" of Hawaii, to resist a predatory price war against a much larger rival.

The trajectory of the Atkins firm represents the structural forces propelling the rise of vertical integration in the sugar industry. The acquisition of the Soledad estate occurred as a result of a foreclosure in which E. Atkins attempted to recover funds loaned to planters, not through a voluntary purchase. The acquisition of the Bay State refinery likewise propelled the merchant firm, almost involuntarily, into sugar refining, through its having taken over the Bay State refinery in Boston, upon its insolvency in 1878.[59] Through this double process of foreclosure in Cuba of a plantation during the difficult period of the abolition of slavery and foreclosure of a refinery in the United States in the period of intensified competition among refiners leading to the formation of the Sugar Trust, the merchant firm of E. Atkins & Company ended up in possession of a small, vertically integrated complex consisting of a plantation in Cuba and a refinery in the United States, both involuntarily.

After the death of Henry O. Havemeyer in 1907, Atkins took charge, with Washington B. Thomas, of the ASRC. Allen notes that "it was only natural that the New England interests who had for many years been large stockholders in the American Sugar Refining Company, should elect Edwin F. Atkins to represent them on the Board."[60] Atkins served as first vice-president and then as chairman of the board, a position from which he resigned on July 13, 1915. On August 3, 1915, the Punta Alegre Sugar Company was incorporated in Delaware.[61] The Punta Alegre wanted to take part in the development of new centrales on virgin territory in expectation of increased demand for Cuba's sugar. According to Allen, "Realizing the possibilities of development of this virgin territory, the Atkins family decided to participate in it, and land was acquired in the north western section of the province on which the erection of the Punta Alegre central was started and the land cleared and cane planted."[62]

The Punta Alegre Sugar Company owned the new Punta Alegre mill and the older Trinidad mill. The Florida mill in the province of Camagüey, constructed in 1914–15, was acquired in 1916 by the Punta Alegre. The Caracas estate near Cienfuegos changed hands from the Terrys of Cuba to the United Railways of Cuba and then to E. Atkins and Company. Robert W. Atkins, son of Edwin, was in charge of the operations of the Punta Alegre mill. In 1920, E. Atkins & Company acquired an interest in the management of the San Agustín mill in Santa Clara province, assisted John Randolph in securing control of the Ermita mill in Oriente province, and became a minority stockholder in the Ermita company, which owned a mill built in 1914–15. The Baraguá sugar mill was built in Camagüey in 1915 by a group of investors from Pittsburgh and acquired by the Punta Alegre in 1922. Centrales Tacajó and Báguanos, constructed in 1918 and 1920 respectively, were acquired by the Antilla Sugar Company in 1924 "under the leadership of the members of the firm of E. Atkins & Company and the Punta Alegre Sugar Company." The Antilla Sugar Company purchased in 1925 the San Germán and Presidente mills. The Presidente was dismantled and the capacity of the San German was increased. The Antilla was a subsidiary controlled by the Punta Alegre. In addition, the Punta Alegre "represented" Bernabé Sánchez Adán's Senado mill and the Hormiguero mill of the Ponvert family in Santa Clara.[63]

The Atkins firm and the Punta Alegre interests produced a pattern of upward vertical integration to safeguard their sugar estates in Cuba against the wide fluctuations in raw sugar prices at the conclusion of World War I. When sugar prices were at a height in 1920, and expecting a sudden slump, according to Benjamin Allen, E. Atkins & Company proposed to the Pennsylvania Sugar Company a contract "whereby the Pennsylvania would manufacture their sugars for them on a toll basis, that they might be able to ship their raw sugars to the United States without being sold and dispose of them to willing buyers in the form of refined sugar."[64] Once again, the Atkins interests were bridging the gap between the production of raw sugar in Cuba and refining in the United States through vertical integration. Allen concludes that "the signing of this contract brought Mr. Edwin F. Atkins, who had twice headed a refinery, back into the refined sugar business again for the third time, but this time his raw and refined sugar interests were consolidated."[65] The Atkins–Punta Alegre–Pennsylvania Sugar Company arrangement replicated a pattern already begun by the United Fruit Company, which sold its sugars through the Revere Refinery in Boston, and the Hawaiian Planters Association, which marketed its sugar through the California & Hawaiian Sugar Refining Corporation of San Francisco. Frank C. Lowry of the Federal Sugar Refining Company joined the Atkins firm to assist in the process of vertical integration. In September 1921, Eugene V. Thayer joined the Atkins group to manage the finances of the business. Thayer had been president of the Merchant's National Bank of Boston and of the Chase National Bank of New York (1917–21).[66] In 1924, an alcohol distillery was built next to the Pennsylvania refinery in Philadelphia to distill Cuban blackstrap molasses for the production of industrial alcohols because of the increased demand for alcohol in the winter as an automobile antifreeze medium.[67]

Of the directors of the Punta Alegre Sugar Company, Edwin F. Atkins had been president of the Bay State Sugar Refining Company of Boston from 1878 to 1888 and a director of the Boston Sugar Refining Company. In addition to his multiple positions in the Cuban sugar industry, Atkins was a director of the Union Pacific Railroad between 1888 and 1895 and was president of the Aetna Mills and the Boston Wharf Company and chairman of the board of the ASRC until 1915. His positions in the field of banking included directorships in the American Trust Company, National Shawmut Bank, and Second National Bank of Boston. Atkins was also a director of Westinghouse Electric. The Punta Alegre Sugar Company and the First National Bank of Boston shared four directors. Clifton H. Dwinnell, first vice-president, and Charles E. Spencer, vice-president of the same bank, were directors of the Punta Alegre. Henry Hornblower and Galen L. Stone were directors of the Punta Alegre and of the First National Bank of Boston. Robert W. Atkins and Ernest B. Dane were directors of both the Punta Alegre and the Merchant's National Bank of Boston. Robert W. Atkins, Clifton H. Dwinnell, and Ralph Hornblower of the Punta Alegre Sugar Company were directors of Aetna Mills, of which Edwin F. Atkins was president. Two of the directors of the Punta Alegre and the First National Bank of Boston, Henry Hornblower and Galen L. Stone, were directors in the Atlantic, Gulf & West Indies Steamship Lines, together with Punta Alegre director Richard F. Hoyt. Louis K. Liggett and Ernst B.

Table 4.6. Mills Controlled by E. Atkins & Company and the Punta Alegre Sugar Company

Mill	Province	Owner in 1925	Tons of Sugar Produced, 1924–25
Baguanos	Oriente	Antilla Sugar Co.[a]	41,493
Tacajó	Oriente	Antilla Sugar Co.[a]	41,945
Presidente	Oriente	Antilla Sugar Co.[a]	16,966
San Germán	Oriente	Antilla Sugar Co.[a]	28,458
Caracas	Santa Clara	E. Atkins and Company[b]	48,770
Ermita	Oriente	E. Atkins & Co./John Randolph	26,015
Baraguá	Camagüey	Punta Alegre Sugar Co.	98,406
Florida	Camagüey	Punta Alegre Sugar Co.	61,463
Punta Alegre	Camagüey	Punta Alegre Sugar Co.	87,862
Soledad	Cienfuegos	Punta Alegre Sugar Co.	19,653
Trinidad	Santa Clara	Punta Alegre Sugar Co.	16,391
San Agustín	Santa Clara	Robert W. Atkins/Mr. Caldwell (Compañía Azucarera Mercantil Central Agustín)[c]	29,165
Total production of sugar			516,587

Sources: Benjamin Allen, *A Story of the Growth of E. Atkins & Co. and the Sugar Industry in Cuba* (N.p., ca. 1926); Farr & Co., *Manual of Sugar Companies* (New York, Farr & Co., 1926); Directory of Directors Company, *Directory of Directors in the City of Boston* (Boston: Directory of Directors Company, 1914 and 1921); Directory of Directors Company, *Directory of Directors in the City of Philadelphia* (Philadelphia: Directory of Directors Company, 1917); Directory of Directors Company, *Directory of Directors in the City of New York* (New York: Directory of Directors Company, 1921).

[a] The Punta Alegre Sugar Company owned all the preferred stock and a majority of the common stock of the Antilla Sugar Company.

[b] E. Atkins and Company also had a special relation with Bernabé Sánchez Adán's Senado mill in Camagüey and the Ponvert family's Hormiguero estate in Santa Clara. No ownership relation has been shown, however. The two mills are therefore excluded from the calculation of the mills controlled by the E. Atkins–Punta Alegre group.

[c] Robert W. Atkins, son of Edwin, was admitted to the firm of E. Atkins and Company in 1910 and administered the Soledad estate in Cuba during the time his father headed the American Sugar Refining Company.

Dane of the Punta Alegre were directors of John Hancock Mutual Life Insurance Company (see Table 4.6).

Finance Capital

The sugar refining industry expanded into the colonial world of sugar plantations within the framework of a wide network of interconnected interests. The business of sugar refining experienced a transformation characterized by the emergence of holding companies and by increasing fusion over time with banking capitalists through interlocking directorates. The original Sugar Trust was formed in 1887 with little help from banking capital. When it was reorganized in 1891, the investment banking house of Kidder Peabody and Company floated the issue of securities. By the time the monopolized refining interests expanded into the Caribbean massively, they established holding companies which facilitated collaboration with finance capitalists. Finance capitalists occupied central positions in interlocking networks, and the refineries and plantations of the American Sugar Kingdom were no exception.[68] The Punta Alegre Company, for instance, had eighteen interlocks with banking institutions. Not all interlocks are equally meaningful, and the financial institutions in question are of varying importance. The interlocks with the First National Bank of Boston and Merchant's National Bank of Boston are more significant than those with small savings institutions in which the members of the board of Punta Alegre were also directors.[69]

According to the Cuban economist Oscar Pino Santos, the expansion of American interests in Cuba in the period between the Spanish-Cuban-American War and World War I was accomplished primarily by industrial capital, that is, by the refiners. After 1913, a combination of industrial and banking capital took over. This transition took place simultaneously with an increase of the share of the Cuban crop controlled by American capital. Whereas in 1913 American interests owned thirty-nine centrales in Cuba representing 37 percent of the sugar production, in 1924 they owned seventy-four centrales that produced 60 percent of the 4.2-million-ton crop.[70] U.S. refiners continued to hold important positions on the boards of directors of sugar companies that owned centrales in Cuba. The most prominent refiners joined boards of directors of important banks as sugar refining prospered and colonial expansion of the businesses of the refiners advanced in the Caribbean.

Bankers entered the world of industry, and industrialists entered the world of high finance. The banker-controlled Cuba Cane Sugar Corporation had important links with the refining establishment. Horace Havemeyer of the ASRC and James N. Jarvie of Arbuckle Brothers were members of its board of directors.[71] The fusion between industrial and banking capital, however, did not only take the form of representation of the banks on the board of directors of sugar companies. The refiners were also represented on the boards of directors of the great banks. Horace Havemeyer was a director of the Bankers Trust (House of Morgan).[72] James H. Post, president of the NSRC, and Earl D. Babst, President of the ASRC, were both directors of City Bank.[73] The Banker's Trust was heavily represented on the board of directors of the South Porto Rico Sugar Company (a concern I will discuss in detail below), which places this company in relation to the Cuba Cane Sugar Corporation and in the sphere of influence of the House of Morgan.

The Puerto Rican sociologist Rafael Bernabe has argued that Cuba Cane was among a group of companies linked together in the sugar world. The complex includes the Cuba Cane, the Manatí, and the Punta Alegre companies in Cuba, the South Porto Rico Sugar Company, and its subsidiary in the Dominican Republic, the Central Romana. Horace Havemeyer, of the refining establishment, was a director of the Cuba Cane, the Manatí, and the South Porto Rico. Manatí and Cuba Cane were linked through the presence in both of them of Manuel Rionda, a prominent partner in Czarnikow-Rionda, one of the largest merchants of both beet and cane sugar in New York and London. Frank Dillingham and Frank C. Lowry were directors of the South Porto Rico. Both were, like Havemeyer, directors of the Punta Alegre Sugar Company. Richard F. Hoyt was a director of the Punta Alegre, like Dillingham and Lowry, and of the Cuba Cane, where he sat with Havemeyer and Rionda.[74] Rionda was president of Cuba Cane, which was controlled by the House of Morgan, a finding consistent with the South Porto Rico's orientation toward the House of Morgan through the presence of important members of the Bankers Trust on its board (Seward Prosser, Albert A. Tilney, and Horace Havemeyer).

When the exceedingly high price of sugar in the world market returned to a level only slightly above prewar prices in 1921, several native-owned Cuban sugar estates began to face financial difficulties. The National City Bank found itself with $30 million to $35 million in loans that could not be collected. The bank appointed an Ohio manufacturer of sugar mill machinery, Gordon S. Rentschler, to "look over the mortgaged sugar properties." In 1922 the bank approved Rentschler's plan and organized the "really sound properties" into the General Sugars Company, which by 1923 was producing 5.1 percent of the Cuban crop in eleven mills.[75] Gordon Rentschler became a director of the National City Bank in 1923, vice-president in 1925, and president in 1929, which reflects the importance of sugar to the bank.[76] The National City Bank floated fifteen bond issues for American companies in Cuba between 1921 and 1931, of which six were for sugar—including the Cuban American and Cuban Dominican companies—and the rest were for railroads.[77]

The sugar crash of 1920–21 caused a massive takeover of nationally owned Cuban estates by American capital, but this was by no means the only source of the increased role of the banks in the island. Cuba's Banco Nacional, the largest in the island, closed in April 1921. The second largest bank, the Banco Internacional, folded in May. By the end of the year eighteen other banks had closed. The only major banks to survive the crisis without much harm were the National City Bank and the Royal Bank of Canada. The Spanish and Cuban banks disappeared. Whereas Cuban banks dispensed 70 percent of all loan money and had 80 percent of all deposits in 1920, after the banking crisis of 1921 they dispensed 18 percent of all loans and had 31 percent of all deposits.[78]

The abnormally high prices during the war were a product of scarcities caused by the destruction of beet crops in central Europe. The postwar recovery of the beet crops brought prices down as total output in the Continent approached prewar levels. In 1920–21 prices came tumbling down, and both sugar mill owners and colonos began to face difficulties meeting payments on debts acquired during the period of fabulous prices. Banks were unable to collect debts and began to withhold payments. The government declared a moratorium on all bank payments. City Bank in New York approached bankruptcy as a result of an excess of uncollectible sugar loans. James Stillman resigned, and the bank was practically rescued from bankruptcy by a consortium of bankers.[79]

The fall in the price of sugar triggered a Cuban banking crisis. In October 1920, there were still one million tons of unsold sugar from the previous zafra in the Cuban warehouses. Prices fell to 5.25 cents in October and to 4.5 cents in November. By prewar standards, these were good prices, but the massive indebtedness of the sugar producers in Cuba was acquired under expectations of much higher prices. Sugar producers who had not yet recovered all their expenses from the previous crop were faced with an approaching zafra without the necessary working capital to pay the wages and to set the entire mechanism of the plantation economy in motion. On Sunday, October 10, 1920, an extraordinary edition of Cuba's *Gaceta Oficial* announced Presidential Decree no. 1583, a moratorium on all bank payments until December 1, 1920.[80]

Cuban businesses were facing imminent bankruptcy, and normal business activity practically came to a halt. Goods stopped flowing through the port of Havana. Frightened by the prospect of generalized insolvency, the public ran to the banks to withdraw their deposits. The shortage of funds caused by the panic of the depositors forced the banks to import hard currency. During the month of October the Bank of Nova Scotia received from abroad $4,215,186. Between November 14 and November 30, the Havana branch of the National City Bank received from abroad $16,100,000; the Royal Bank of Canada in Havana received $17,668,000; the Banco Español de la Isla de Cuba received $2,100,000; the Canadian Bank of Commerce $350,000; N. Gelats y Compañía $800,000; Pedro Gómez Mena $2,000,000; Banco de Comercio $50,000; Banco Mercantil Americano de

Cuba $2,915,000. Other smaller companies received $210,543. As of November 3, 1920, banks in Cuba had called on their main branches or on other banks abroad for hard currency to the amount of $49,573,728.[81]

In the countryside the situation was bleak. Mills lacked the resources to prepare for the new grinding season. Mill owners and colonos owed beyond their capacity to pay. The banks, trapped under the mass of debt of sugar mills and colonos, began to withhold payments. Short-term credit to lubricate the wheels of commerce became scarce. The workers were idle and the shopkeepers in the countryside were bankrupt. The prominent planter José Gómez Mena wrote to the president of the Cuban republic, General Mario García Menocal, to express his concern about the possibility of a social crisis: "The storekeepers in the countryside cannot buy but with cash, which is running out, but the agricultural worker cannot pay and is not paid, and the continuation of this lack of obligations will bring misery principally in the countryside, and it also prevents a decrease in the cost of living so necessary to reduce wages and cheapen production costs."[82]

President Menocal was in direct communication with the president of the Cuban American Sugar Company in New York, Robert Hawley. Through Hawley, Menocal requested funds to set the coming harvest in motion. On November 22 Hawley cabled Menocal that National City Bank had agreed to assist in overcoming the crisis. The bank was willing to advance $10 million to assist "bona fide mill owners" to prepare them for the coming zafra. The gigantic North American concerns negotiated directly with the president of the republic, who turned to them for the public financial needs of the island. After securing the loan for Cuba, Hawley requested from Menocal "some word of expression" to the bank. President Menocal's answer can be understood only in the context of the economic dependence on foreign capital that had developed in neocolonial Cuba's plantation economy: "I shall appreciate it if you will be good enough to convey to the Board of Directors of the National City Bank my personal appreciation of their attitude and to assure them that such disinterested and friendly action will not soon be forgotten."[83] Menocal had an interest in the Cuban American Sugar Company and the Chaparra mill kept a mansion—euphemistically called a "presidential chalet"—for Menocal on company grounds.[84]

The failure of the Banco Nacional and the Banco Español and the high degree of indebtedness of the Cuban producers generated widespread failure to meet payments, bankruptcies, and transfers of ownership. In some cases the transfers were overt, as in the case of City Bank's acquisition of several mills through foreclosure and their reorganization as the General Sugars Company. In other instances, the transfers of properties, particularly to U.S. owners, were less obvious although no less real.

The case of Central Confluente offers an interesting example. The Confluente Sugar Company could not meet its payments to Cuba's Banco Nacional after the harvest of 1921–22. The Banco Nacional was in turn bankrupt, and a liquidating commission was in charge of collecting its loans. The management of Ingenio Confluente wrote to the bank arguing that "the economic situation of Ingenio Confluente becomes more difficult each day, to such an extreme that in the past zafra of 1921 to 1922 despite the good intentions of the Company, it has been materially impossible to make payments to the creditors."[85] The Confluente Sugar Company postponed payment of its loans for three years, attempting to survive as an independent entity. By 1925 the mill was totally ruined.[86]

The Guaranty Trust Company of New York intervened and seized control of Confluente in an interesting transaction in which it also collected its debt from Cuba's Banco Nacional. After the crash of 1921, Cuba's Banco Nacional defaulted on a loan of $416,571 made by the Guaranty Trust Company of New York. By 1925, Guaranty Trust had not been able to collect this debt from the liquidating commission of the Banco Nacional. That year, after admitting bankruptcy, the management of the Confluente Sugar Company negotiated with the liquidating commission of the Banco Nacional the cancellation of all its debt through payment of $60,000 in cash and delivery of the note which the Guaranty Trust Company had been unable to collect from Cuba's Banco Nacional. Evidently, the Guaranty Trust Company took over the Confluente Sugar Company and paid its debts with the notes for the loan which it had been thus far unable to collect from the Banco Nacional. Confluente was no longer in debt to the liquidating commission of the Banco Nacional, the liquidating commission of the Banco Nacional was no longer in debt to Guaranty Trust, and Guaranty Trust was in control of Confluente. These transactions were carried out by the management of Confluente, which remained in place, so that no formal transfer of ownership can be observed. Evidently, the price for such debt cancellation was control of the sugar producing enterprise by the Guaranty Trust Company. The president of the Confluente Sugar Company reminded its creditors, in attempting to persuade them to accept the note from Guaranty Trust as payment, of "the sacrifice which the acquisition of the credit note of the Guaranty Trust Company represents to this Company."[87] This debt-for-equity swap was made through the management of the bankrupt Confluente Sugar Company, which continued to appear as legal Cuban proprietor of the sugar mill, even though in reality the Confluente had been acquired by U.S. interests.

In the aftermath of the crash a substantial increase occurred in the share of Cuban sugar produced by American-owned or controlled companies. In the zafra of 1919–20, American enterprises produced 12,689,816 sacks of sugar, representing 48.37 percent of Cuba's total production. The figure increased to 14,747,219 sacks in 1920–21 (53.59 percent), and 16,352,475 sacks in 1921–22 (58.46 percent). The 16,020,731 sacks of sugar produced by American companies in 1924 represented 63.53 percent of Cuba's total production. In the four years after the sugar crash, U.S. companies acquired another 15 percent of Cuba's foremost export industry, increasing the American share from 48 to 63 percent.[88]

North American banks played a central role in the expansion of the share of the Cuban crop produced in mills owned by U.S. entrepreneurs. It is difficult to overemphasize the fusion between the banks and the U.S. sugar refining interests in Cuba. But this fusion should not be equated with total harmony. In practice, there were differences between these two sectors, especially after the onset of chronic overproduction of sugar which plagued the world market, and Cuba especially, after 1921. The crisis elicited divergent reactions to the problem of overproduction among different sectors of the sugar industry. Native Cuban producers, who generally owned the smallest, least productive mills, were hit the hardest by the fall in price. The U.S. refiners who owned sugar estates were sheltered to a degree from the fall in price because a large part of their profit came from refining. Refiners were able to compensate for the decrease in the price of raw sugar and sometimes were even able to profit from it, provided the price margin between raw and refined remained stable or increased. Vertical integration cushioned the refiners from the fall in the price of raw sugar.

Vertical integration allowed the mills controlled by the refiners to sell their raw cane sugar to themselves, rather than in the open market. The output of the centrales was an input to the sugar refineries. A decrease in the price of raw sugar lowered the cost to the refinery. The profit of the refining industry depended on the spread between the prices of raw and refined sugar and not, as in the case of cane operations, which sold on the open market, on that between the cost of milling and the raw price.[89]

The banks can be considered a third sector of the sugar industry. They loaned money and were generally involved with both the Cuban-owned and the refiner-controlled estates. As a result, the banks tended to take the larger view of the problems posed by the sugar depression. Their interests were not always identical with those of the sugar refiners. Thus the banks could claim a position as arbiters between the factions. The banks had a comprehensive vision of the economy and how to attempt to reorganize it.

The oligopolistic network that developed in the process of horizontal consolidation of the sugar refining industry (see Chapter 2) is crucial in understanding the interlocking structure of the U.S. concerns in Cuba. Yet the period of colonial expansion of the refining interests differed somewhat from the previous stage of horizontal consolidation in that the latter was characterized by a more developed fusion between industrial and banking capital. The expansion of the refining interests proceeded in strict collaboration with high finance. The City Bank and the House of Morgan were the main institutions connected to the expansion of the oligopolistic network in Cuba. This structure becomes more visible once one examines the interests of the U.S. refiners and banks in the neighboring colonies of the Dominican Republic and Puerto Rico.

Vertical Integration: The Dominican Republic

The development of the sugar industry of the Dominican Republic, unlike that of Cuba, does not date back to the early nineteenth century. Sugar was of relatively minor importance in the Dominican Republic, beginning its ascent in the second half of the century as a result of two external factors. First, the Spanish reoccupation of the Dominican Republic in 1861–65 brought Spanish and Italian immigrants interested in the development of the industry. Second, the immigration of Cuban planters during the Ten Years' War of 1868–78 in Cuba introduced to the Dominican Republic the technology of the Cuban mills and steam power for refining and transport.[90] Sugar production began to expand in the 1870s, but production figures were even smaller than those of Puerto Rico. The primacy of sugar in the export basket of the Dominican Republic was consolidated by the North American occupation of 1916–24. The Dominican sociologist Wilfredo Lozano argues that "its most immediate and direct outcome was the strengthening and definitive entrenchment of the most important productive pole of the structure: the sugar pole, generally controlled by North American investors."[91]

Under the combined influence of a favorable military government and high international sugar prices during World War I, the North American interests in the Dominican Republic propelled the expansion of Dominican sugar production from its prewar level of 86,734 tons in 1913 to 371,419 in 1926.[92] In 1920 sugar exports amounted to $45 million, or 413 percent greater than that of the other three largest crops combined. In 1926 sugar represented 88 percent of the export tonnage and about 60 percent of export value. The sugar companies claimed that the Dominican government received 65 percent of its income of $7.4 million from sugar-related taxes.[93]

The sugar estates and the power of the corporations were consolidated during the military occupation, but the expansion of North American sugar interests predates the military intervention of 1916. Central Romana, for example, began to grow cane in 1911 with the purpose of shipping it over the Mona Passage to grind in the Guánica mill of the South Porto Rico Sugar Company in Puerto Rico. Nevertheless, the real growth of the sugar-producing latifundia occurred mostly in the period 1917–20 under the American occupation.[94]

At the beginning of the century, the Dominican sugar industry was in disarray for several reasons. First, the beet sugar industry had achieved tremendous progress and was displacing cane sugar in the world market. Beet sugar accounted for 69 percent and cane sugar for the remaining 31 percent of total world sugar production in 1899–1900, estimated at 8,043,000 tons.[95] A 20 percent reduction on the tariff for Cuban sugar associated with reciprocity and the Platt Amendment, free entrance of Hawaiian sugar since 1876 and of Puerto Rican sugar after 1901, and free entrance of sugar from the Philippines up to a limit of three hundred thousand tons put Dominican sugar at a disadvantage in the United States market.[96]

At the turn of the century William L. Bass, the North American owner of the Consuelo estate in the Dominican Republic, expressed the distress of the Dominican situation arguing that fourteen ingenios had disappeared as a result of the crisis of the sugar industry and that the remaining twelve ingenios were in danger of bankruptcy.[97] The solution Bass proposed for the "crisis" was to be expected from a sugar producer: reciprocity, that is, free entrance for Dominican sugar into the U.S. market. The Dominican industry never received the tariff relief that Bass proposed, and the increased difficulties translated into further economic concentration at the milling stage.

In 1907, of the fourteen ingenios in operation, four belonged to the General Industrial Company (Vicini Group), three to Bartram Brothers and associates, and two to Hugh Kelly. Together, these nine ingenios accounted for 67 percent of the land planted in cane in the republic, taking into account the lands of colonos associated with the mills. Foreign capital was represented by seven ingenios belonging to North Americans and one to Cubans established in the republic, which together accounted for 62 percent of cane lands. The General Industrial Company of the Vicinis was incorporated in New Jersey. The ingenio Puerto Rico belonged to Sucesores de Juan Serallés, a Puerto Rican family, and the ingenio Mercedes of Puerto Plata to J. Bartle & Company. Geographically, sugar production was concentrated in San Pedro de Macorís, with its seven ingenios accounting for 67 percent of cane lands; in Santo Domingo, with three ingenios representing 16 percent of the cane lands, and in Puerto Plata with one ingenio representing 2 percent of the cane lands. It must be underscored, however, that all these enterprises were individually owned and the corporate phenomenon was still unknown.[98]

Sugar still did not have the overwhelming predominance in the Dominican export basket that it acquired after 1916. In fact, in 1907 and 1908, the value of cocoa exports, a peasant-produced crop, surpassed that of sugar.[99] Regionally, El Cibao continued to be a land of tobacco, cocoa, and petty commodity producers. Coffee, the fourth export by value, was spread throughout the republic, while sugar was concentrated in the east, particularly in San Pedro de Macorís.

The uncertain state of land titles in the Dominican Republic opened opportunities for U.S. capital to acquire vast estates. The process of conversion of *haciendas comuneras* into private property under the laws of the Dominican Republic allowed foreign corporations to acquire vast expanses of relatively unpopulated land for the development of sugar production.[100] Through the acquisition of haciendas comuneras the Barahona Company, organized in New York in 1916, soon became the owner of the second largest sugar estate in the Dominican Republic, with an extension of 49,400 acres of land. The expansion of this estate occurred through the extensive "purchase" of *pesos comuneros* and through the acquisition of extensive water rights. By 1917 the Barahona Company owned 10 percent of the land in Barahona Province. Although the titles to many of the lands were false, Barahona could afford to hire the best lawyers in the country. The land speculators in effect deprived many peasant households of land, as Bruce Calder argues, by "taking advantage of the ignorance and poverty of the inhabitants of the Neyba Valley who, for lack of unity and financial resources, cannot hire a good lawyer to defend their legal rights."[101] The Barahona Company also acquired rights under the Ley Sobre Franquicias Agrarias to the waters of the Yaque del Sur River, against the protestations of the peasant communities along the riverbanks. The protesters claimed that ten thousand people would be left destitute and would be forced to become tenants of the Barahona Company if the government granted its demands for water rights. As in Cuba, however, the beneficiaries of North American rule were North Americans. The actions of the company were legal and favored by the local elite, who believed that the Barahona Company's multimillion-dollar investment would improve the economy of the region.[102]

In some instances foreign sugar companies obtained titles to whole villages. In 1921, the Central Romana estate, a subsidiary of the South Porto Rico Sugar Company, burned to the ground two hamlets, El Caimonal and Higueral, which stood in the path of its expanding fields. One hundred fifty families were left homeless, the company having made no provision for them.[103] The degree of land concentration which the United States military occupation of 1916–24 brought about can be appreciated in the fact that out of the 438,182 acres of land owned by the sugar estates in 1924, 326,416 were owned by the five largest mills. The Central Romana alone owned 144,418 acres of land; the Barahona company 49,400; the Consuelo estate some 49,354 acres; the Santa Fe 61,069; the Cristóbal Colón 22,175. A sixth estate, San Isidro, spanned 20,727 acres of land.[104]

This concentration of land is misleading. Actual concentration in the sugar industry was much higher. In the Dominican Republic, three groups of investors were in almost complete control of the industry: out of nineteen large centrales the Cuban Dominican Sugar Company owned ten, the Central Romana (South Porto Rico Sugar Company) owned two, including a truly gigantic one, and an Italian-Dominican group (Vicini) owned three estates. The Cuban Dominican Sugar Company was controlled by the B. H. Howell & Son group. Central Romana was a subsidiary of the South Porto Rico Sugar Company, so that its linkages to the Havemeyer interests through Horace Havemeyer, and to the Bankers Trust, a Morgan institution, replicate those of its parent company. Thus the links with the oligopolistic sugar refining network were organized through institutional connections which implied close ties with banking capital (City Bank, House of Morgan) as in Cuba.

Central Romana alone owned 30 percent of the cane lands of the Dominican Republic. Individually, the Barahona estate was smaller than Central Romana, but it belonged to the Cuban Dominican Sugar Company, whose mills, taken as a group, produced most of the sugar of the republic. The investments of North Americans in the cane sugar industry of the Dominican Republic were totally controlled by two groups: the Cuban Dominican company and the South Porto Rico group. These two "baronies in Sugardom" represented North American interests. A smaller Italian group, plus five independent ingenios, represented the remainder of the Dominican industry.[105]

The Barahona mill was launched in 1916, the year the United States invaded, and became a voracious land grabber. The wider structure to which Barahona belonged, the Cuban Dominican Sugar Company, was typical among sugar companies and serves to illustrate, according to Melvin Knight, "the structure of such concerns, which interlock in a way suggesting nothing else so much as a feudal system."[106] The Cuban Dominican Sugar succeeded the West India Sugar Finance Corporation after a reorganization in 1924. Both the West India and the Cuban Dominican were controlled by the NSRC and the firm of B. H. Howell Son &

Table 4.7. Important Interlocks among the Cuban Dominican, Fajardo, and Cuban American Companies

Directors or Officers	West India Sugar/ Cuban Dominican Company	Fajardo Sugar Company	Cuban American Sugar Company
Lorenzo D. Armstrong	Director	Director	Director
James B. Coombs	Treasurer	President	
Loring D. Farnum	Director	Director	
Thomas Howell[a]	President	Director	Vice-president
James H. Post[b]	Director	Director	President

Source: Directory of Directors Company, *Directory of Directors in the City of New York, 1921* (New York: Directory of Directors Company, 1921).

  [a]Vice-president of the NSRC.
  [b]President of the NSRC.

Company.[107] Because the NSRC controlled the Cuban American and both were interlocked with City Bank, the Cuban Dominican Sugar Company has been considered a National City concern.[108] Thus, for example, when the Barahona Company ran into difficulties and required loan money in 1920, it obtained it from the International Banking Corporation, a National City subsidiary. For all these interlocking directorates, see Table 4.7.

When the West India ran into difficulties as a result of the crisis of the 1920s, it reorganized itself as a holding company with centrales in both Cuba and the Dominican Republic and changed its name to Cuban Dominican Sugar Company. As of 1919, the West India controlled in Cuba the Cupey Sugar Company (Cupey Mill), the Central Alto Cedro Sugar Company (Alto Cedro Mill), and the Palma Soriano Sugar Company (Palma Mill). After the fall in sugar prices, the Cuban mills were reorganized as the Sugar Estates of Oriente. City Bank supported the reorganization and acted as trustee of all the operations. A posterior reorganization created the Cuban Dominican Development Company, which acquired the Sugar Estates of Oriente, which in the meantime had acquired three more mills in Cuba: the Santa Ana, Hatillo, and Altagracia. With new emissions of stock ($11.5 million preferred, 1,630,000 common without par value) the entire complex was renamed Cuban Dominican Sugar Company. National City Bank underwrote a bond emission of another $15 million, and in 1925 William A. Rockefeller and Gordon Rentschler from National City Bank joined the board of directors of the Cuban Dominican.[109] Thus, as the process of vertical integration advanced, the ties between the banking groups and the refining oligopoly also advanced. The emergence of the Cuban Dominican represents further expansion of the NSRC

Table 4.8. Ownership Groups in the Sugar Industry of the Dominican Republic, 1930

Mill	Owner in 1929–30	Tons of Sugar Produced
Monte Llano (1928)	Chase National Bank	5,905
Barahona	Cuban Dominican Interests	56,708
Consuelo	Cuban Dominican Interests	51,965
Quisqueya	Cuban Dominican Interests	27,705
San Isidro	Cuban Dominican Interests	15,900
Las Pajas	Cuban Dominican Interests	15,476
Boca Chica	Cuban Dominican Interests	14,335
Porvenir	Kelly Interests	16,655
Ansonia	Kelly Interests	727
San Luis	S. Michelena, Jr. & Oscar Michelena	13,570
Romana	South Porto Rico Sugar Company	99,084
Santa Fe	South Porto Rico Sugar Company	47,805
Angelina	Vicini Interests	13,480
Italia	Vicini Interests	12,237
Cristobal Colón	Vicini Interests	8,798
Total		400,350

Source: A. B. Gilmore, *The Porto Rico Sugar Manual, Including Data on Santo Domingo Mills* (New Orleans: A. B. Gilmore, 1930), 249–80.

and B. H. Howell Son & Company group in Cuba and the Dominican Republic in collaboration with City Bank.

The Central Romana represents a second group of North American investors in the Dominican Republic. A subsidiary of the South Porto Rico Sugar Company, the Central Romana established itself in the Dominican Republic in 1911. In 1910, according to a company report, the officers of the South Porto Rico Sugar Company were confronted with a decision to expand and purchased twenty thousand acres in La Romana in 1911 because of the natural limits on sugar lands and the increasing cost of lands and leases in Puerto Rico.[110] A Dominican law of 1911 granted duty exemption for the importation of agricultural machinery and tax exemption for eight years to firms established under the new law. Central Romana, which was in the process of development and was linked to the oligopolistic network of refiners, was the principal beneficiary of this regulation because for many years it exported its canes to Puerto Rico, where another associated enterprise—Central Guánica—ground them. In so doing, the sugar produced evaded the strong tariff restrictions of the North American market because Puerto Rican raw sugars, even if produced from Dominican cane, enjoyed 100 percent tariff exemption in the U.S. market.[111] Seventy-three hundred acres were under cultivation in 1917 when the officers authorized the construction of a factory at La

Romana, but some Dominican cane was still ground in Puerto Rico. By 1921, twenty-four thousand acres of Dominican land were under cultivation, producing 500,000 tons of cane. La Romana and Guánica produced an aggregate of 110,000 tons of sugar in 1921.[112] The composition of the officers and directorate of the South Porto Rico Sugar Company suggests important links not so much with City Bank and the NSRC as with the oligopolistic network—the "vague central organization of Sugardom," in the words of Melvin Knight—through Horace Havemeyer, on the one hand, and through the House of Morgan on the other (see Table 4.8).[113]

In 1930, the Cuban Dominican Sugar Company owned six mills and produced 45 percent of the Dominican crop. The South Porto Rico Sugar Company owned two mills and produced 37 percent of the island's sugar. In combination, these two foreign concerns produced 82 percent of the sugar of the island. Sugar was the main export of the Dominican Republic in 1930. The Vicini interests owned three mills and produced 9 percent of the island's sugar. Santiago Michelena owned one mill, and the Chase Bank owned another through a receivership.[114]

Vertical Integration: Puerto Rico

Puerto Rico's special status as a formal colony of the United States gave metropolitan capital advantages and guarantees of stability which it did not enjoy elsewhere. Its special status as a United States territory granted its sugars free entrance into the U.S. market. Free trade gave sugar enterprises an advantage over Cuban mills, whose products had to pay 80 percent of the duty to enter the U.S. market, and over the production of the Dominican Republic, which paid the full tariff.[115] Puerto Rico's status as a formal colony of the United States ruled by a presidentially appointed U.S. governor created an investment climate that gave U.S. investors guarantees of political stability they could not dream of in Cuba or the Dominican Republic.[116] The *Fiftieth Anniversary Report* of the South Porto Rico Sugar Company acknowledged the special advantages of colonial rule and free trade: "Before the Spanish American War . . . there had been too much risk involved to interest American investors. The conditions changed when the American Army landed on July 25, 1898, at Guánica Bay, near where the company's Guánica factory now stands. With Puerto Rico (then spelled Porto Rico) under the wing of the American government, and in a preferred position under its tariff system, opportunities in the island appeared more attractive."[117] The expansion of U.S. corporate capital was not an automatic, unmediated response to increasing demand for raw sugar in the United States. The presence of the U.S. Army in the colony created the conditions that enabled the establishment of U.S. enterprise.

Vertical integration allowed U.S.-owned centrales to sell raw sugar to continental refineries at administered transfer prices, allowing the corporations to shift profits out of Puerto Rico to escape taxation. Four large sugar corporations dominated the economic life of the island by the early 1930s. The Aguirre, Fajardo, South Porto Rico, and United Porto Rico companies produced approximately 60 percent of the sugar on the island by the late 1920s.

The principal interlocking directors in the U.S. corporations with centrales in Puerto Rico were finance capitalists including James Howell Post, Horace Havemeyer, and Thomas Howell, who were both leaders in the sugar refining industry and directors of important banks. Also among the pioneers in some of the sugar companies were independent capitalists who were later displaced by the refiners. Central Aguirre Sugar Company was established by a group of adventurous capitalists from Boston who were unrelated to the sugar refining industry. Within five years of its foundation, sugar refiners purchased the majority interest in the Aguirre Sugar Company. The former were colonial frontiersmen who embarked on colonial expansion in search of windfall profits. The latter represented the organized power of the oligopolistic sugar refining establishment, who had spent a decade integrating horizontally and who turned to vertical integration with plantations in the Caribbean as a means of increasing control over the supply of raw sugar, the essential raw material of the refining industry.

The founders of Aguirre (Henry De Ford, Francis Dumaresq, William Sturgis Hooper Lothrop, and John Dandridge Henley Luce) established a banking firm, De Ford and Company, in 1898. Each man held a quarter share. Luce and Lothrop had received training in the foreign banking department of the banking business in Kidder, Peabody and Company.[118] De Ford and Dumaresq had been sugar brokers in Boston since 1886. Henry Cabot Lodge, the senator from Massachusetts who was Luce's brother-in-law, intervened with President William McKinley to allow De Ford and Company to secure the position of fiscal agent of the U.S. military government in Puerto Rico. This special concession from the colonial state was the starting point of the Aguirre.[119]

In February 1899 De Ford and Company entered the sugar business through the purchase of the two-thousand-acre Aguirre estate in the south of the island and the leasing of the Carmen (937 acres), Josefa (1,300 acres), and Amadeo (231 acres) estates, with option to buy. The emerging corporation contracted with the Esperanza, Margarita, and Caños estates for the grinding of their sugarcane and purchased the franchise for a railroad line between Ponce and Guayama from the French Railroad Company. In July 1899 a partnership, known as the Central Aguirre Syndicate, was formed, with initial capital of $525,000, which was increased to $2 million in 1903.[120] Of the original partners in De Ford and Company, Dumaresq returned to Boston in 1901 and died there a year later, De Ford moved on for unknown reasons, and Lothrop died in Ponce in 1905 during an appendectomy. Only Luce survived the initial years. After the death of Lothrop, Luce entered into a partnership with Charles Lemuel Crehore, his classmate from Harvard University, to manage Aguirre through the firm of Luce, Crehore and Company. Within a few years, however, the pioneering capitalists from New England were replaced by much more organized capitalists linked to sugar refining in the United States.

In 1905 the company was organized as a trust incorporated in Massachusetts. Seven of the directors of the new corporation were from Boston, but three, including the vice-president, John Farr, were from New York. The other two were James Howell Post and Frederick D. Mollenhauer, the president and vice-president of the NSRC, respectively. When Mollenhauer retired from the NSRC in 1911, his replacement, Thomas Howell, took his post on the board of Aguirre. The replacement of broken ties in an interlocking structure generally indicates formal relations between enterprises. [121] When Thomas Howell replaced Frederick Mollenhauer as vice-president of the NSRC, he also took over his seat on the board of directors of the Aguirre Sugar Company.

Seven years after the founding of Aguirre by Boston interests, the company was taken over by the New York refining interests associated with the NSRC.[122] The Boston interests had the numerical advantage on the board because of the origins of the corporation, but the New York capitalists linked to the sugar refining business had strategic leverage over them. The board of Aguirre was composed of three central men from the NSRC, plus a periphery of Boston capitalists who were there because the company had originally been founded by Boston interests. After the 1905 reorganization, the interests from Boston came to occupy a position of secondary importance, even though J. D. H. Luce, one of the founders, was retained as president.[123]

When a refiner retired from the board of Aguirre he was replaced by another from the same sugar refining company. When the pioneering president of the Aguirre corporation, who did not represent the larger interests of the Sugar Trust, died in 1921, he was not replaced by a capitalist representing the continuity of a corporate lineage. Luce had remained in Aguirre as president even after the company was taken over by the New York refiners of the NSRC. Luce's only son,

Stephen Bleeker Luce, wrote to his uncle Henry Cabot Lodge that he felt he should occupy his father's position in the Aguirre company. His uncle advised him against it and explained that Aguirre was no longer controlled in Boston.

> Your father built up [Aguirre] and made it successful for himself and for everyone connected with it. He was, of course, retained as president because his knowledge and experience were invaluable, but you must bear in mind that the company was not controlled by your father or the interests he represented. The company is owned and controlled in New York and has been for some time. . . . You and the people you care about are minority stockholders—just how large a minority I do not know, but a very decided minority.[124]

The positions of Luce and his son were not analogous to the position of the sugar refiners on the board of Aguirre. There were, to be sure, capitalists from Boston on the board of Aguirre with linkages to the sugar refining establishment of the United States.[125] Charles Francis Adams of the Aguirre Sugar Company was one of the eleven directors of the ASRC, the largest sugar refining corporation in the United States. A descendant of an old Boston family, Adams had access to the highest circles of power in the country. In 1921, he was director of a multitude of corporations. From 1929 to 1931, he was secretary of the navy.[126] Although linked to the sugar business, however, Adams made a career as a politician instead of as a businessman. What makes the directorships of the sugar refiners from New York in the Aguirre company especially meaningful is the larger structure of corporate affiliations within which they functioned. The most important linkages of Aguirre with the sugar refining establishment were James Howell Post and Thomas H. Howell of B. H. Howell Son & Company and the NSRC. An analysis of their positions in 1921 clarifies their situation in the Aguirre company by showing the extent of their involvement in the sugar industry of the Dominican Republic and Cuba as well as in Puerto Rico. Their influence derived from their centrality in the network of interlocks between banks, sugar refining companies, and colonial sugar plantations.

In 1921, the structure of the complex system of refineries in the United States and the vertically integrated plantations in the Caribbean had taken definitive form. James H. Post was president and Thomas Howell vice-president of the NSRC. Both had been originally members of the firm of B. H. Howell Son & Company, which, together with the McCahan, Bunker, and Mollenhauer refineries, consolidated and formed the NSRC in 1900. The merger of the previously independent refining interests into the NSRC was caused by low prices in the refined sugar market at a time when two giant corporations in the industry, the ASRC and Arbuckle Brothers, were engaging in a price war. In 1921, the ASRC still held important interests in the NSRC. In 1922, the court decision that ended prolonged antitrust litigation against the sugar refining "monopoly" (the Sugar Trust) allowed the ASRC to retain a 25 percent interest in the NSRC. After the formation of the NSRC in 1900, the process of horizontal consolidation in the sugar industry gave way to a process of vertical expansion of the refiners into the newly acquired colonial regions of the United States—Cuba, Puerto Rico, the Philippines, and, a bit later, the Dominican Republic. Changes in the structure of the sugar market led the sugar refining oligopolists, who had spent a decade fighting each other and then merging, to initiate a process of vertical integration through the acquisition of colonial plantations.

The directors from the sugar refineries on the board of Aguirre held many other positions in sugar companies in the Caribbean (see Table 4.9). Corporations created innovative organizational forms through which capital sought to avoid government prosecution through the Sherman Antitrust Act. The New Jersey holding company allowed an inner group of refiners to control a multiplicity of vertically integrated refineries and colonial sugar plantations through a series of corporations that were formally independent of one another.

The process of horizontal consolidation in sugar refining entailed organizational transformations of the merged firms and new roles for the capitalists involved. The transition from the family-owned enterprise to the corporation signified new roles and imposed new limitations on previously independent entrepreneurs. When the ASRC was formed, sugar refiners merged their properties and received trust certificates roughly in proportion to their share of the refined sugar market. The loss of independence and their subordination to the "captain of industry" in sugar refining, Henry O. Havemeyer, were compensated by the increased profits generated by restriction of output and increased prices. Corespective behavior in larger institutions replaced the competitive dynamics of an earlier era. The process of socialization of capital[127] replaced individual enterprise and created a highly organized industry among previously independent sugar refiners. Vertical expansion into the Caribbean opened new fields for the refiners, who used holding companies and expanded in groups rather than individually in the establishment of colonial plantations.

Albert and George R. Bunker were directors of the Fajardo Sugar Company. Like the Mollenhauers, they had been independent sugar refiners who had integrated into the oligopolistic network. The Bunkers had sold their Delaware Sugar House to the Sugar Trust in 1892. They participated in the organization of the

Table 4.9. Directorships of National Sugar Refining Company Officers in the Caribbean Sugar Industry, 1921

Company	Thomas A. Howell	James Howell Post	John Farr
National Sugar Refining Company	Vice-president + Director	President + Director	
Cuban American Sugar Company[a]	Vice-president + Director	Vice-president + Treasurer + Director	Director
Tinguaro Sugar Company			Director
Chaparra Sugar Company	Director	First Vice-president + Treasurer + Director	Director
Unidad Sugar Company			Director
Cuban Sugar Refining Company			Director
Colonial Sugars Company	Vice-president + Treasurer + Director	First Vice-president + Treasurer + Director	President + Director
Chaparra Railroad Company			Director
West India Sugar Finance Corporation[b]	President + Director	Director	
Barahona Sugar Company	Vice-president + Director		
Aguirre Sugar Company[c]	Director	Director	Vice-president + Director
Ponce and Guayama Railroad Company			Director
Atlantic Fruit Company	Director		
Central Alto Cedro	President + Director		
Central Cupey Sugar Company	President + Director		
Compania Azucarera Dominica C. por A.	President + Director		
Fajardo Sugar Company[d]	Director	Director	
Guantanamo Sugar Company		President + Director	
Holly Sugar Corporation	Vice-president + Director	Director	
New Niquero Sugar Company	Director	President + Director	
Palma Soriano Sugar Company	Vice-president + Director		
Santa Ana Sugar Company	President + Director		
Santos Company	Director	President + Director	
Sugar Planters Corp.	Director		
U.S. Casualty Company		Director	Vice-president + Director
U.S. Industrial Alcohol Company	Director		

Source: Directory of Directors Company, *Directory of Directors in the City of New York* (New York: Directory of Directors Company, 1921).

[a] CASC was a holding company that controlled the Mercedita, Tinguaro, Chaparra, Unidad, San Manuel, Cuban Sugar Refining, Colonial Sugars, and Chaparra Railroad companies in Cuba.

[b] WISFC was a holding company that controlled the Consuelo, Barahona, Quisqueya, San Isidro, Las Pajas, San Marcos, San Carlos, Santa Fe, Porvenir, and Ansonia sugar mills in the Dominican Republic.

[c] Aguirre Sugar Company owned the Aguirre, Cortada, and Machete mills in Puerto Rico.

[d] Fajardo Sugar Company owned the Fajardo and Canóvanas mills in Puerto Rico.

NSRC of Yonkers, which, together with the Mollenhauer Refinery and the New York Sugar Refining Company merged in 1900 to form the NSRC of New Jersey. Both the Mollenhauer and the National of Yonkers had been set up with capital from the firm of B. H. Howell and Son (James Howell Post–Thomas Howell). Their merger in 1900 was promoted by Post but financed by Havemeyer. George R. and Albert Bunker eventually came to occupy positions in the B. H. Howell–National Sugar–Cuban American–West India Sugar–Aguirre Fajardo complex of refineries and plantations. Table 4.10 illustrates the positions these refiners held in the Caribbean sugar industry in 1921.

The Fajardo Sugar Company was incorporated in New York in 1905 by Charles P. Armstrong of New York and Jorge Bird Arias of Fajardo, Puerto Rico.[128] The company emerged in a context of mergers of larger interests in the sugar world. In 1905 Aguirre was taken over by New York sugar refiners. A year later the Cuban American Sugar Company was reorganized with the participation of the central capitalists of the sugar refining duopoly, Henry Havemeyer of the ASRC and James Howell Post of the NSRC. The community of interest between the National and American refining companies was confirmed in the process of colonial expansion. Havemeyer emerged as the owner of 12 percent of the value of all the shares issued by the new Cuban American company.[129]

James Bliss Coombs, the president of Fajardo Sugar, was an attorney with the firm of L. W. and P. Armstrong of 106 Wall Street. Coombs's directorships were limited to the Fajardo Sugar Company (president), the Fajardo Development Company (president), and the West India Sugar Finance Corporation (treasurer). All of these enterprises were linked to the NSRC through interlocking directors. Lorenzo D. and Frederick S. Armstrong, of the same firm as Coombs, were directors in the Fajardo Sugar Company. Lorenzo was a director of the Cuban American Sugar Company. Frederick was vice-president of the West India Sugar Finance Corporation, which owned multiple plantations in Cuba and the Dominican Republic, a director of the Atlantic Sugar Refineries Company (Montreal), and treasurer of the Fajardo Sugar Company. The Armstrongs and Coombs were part of a larger system encompassing the NSRC in the United States, the Cuban American Sugar Company, the West India Sugar Finance Corporation (Cuba and Dominican Republic), and the Fajardo and Aguirre companies in Puerto Rico.

Of the original group that formed the NSRC of New Jersey, Post and Howell were on the boards of both Aguirre and Fajardo sugar companies. These two outstanding investors fit Zeitlin and Soref's definition of a "finance capitalist" and confirm their findings. Capitalists who sit on the boards of directors of industrial enterprises and on the boards of banks typically occupy central positions in the

Table 4.10. Interlocking Directors and Officers of the Aguirre, Cuban American, and Fajardo Sugar Companies, 1921

Directors	B. H. Howell Son and Company	National Sugar Refining Company
James H. Post	President and Director	President and Director
Thomas A. Howell	Director	Vice-president and Director
B. Huntting Howell	Director	
John Farr		
Frederick D. Mollenhauer		
J. Adolph Mollenhauer		
Lorenzo D. Armstrong		
Frederick S. Armstrong		
George R. Bunker		Secretary and Director
Albert Bunker		

Source: Directory of Directors Company, *Directory of Directors in the City of New York, 1921* (New York: Directory of Directors Company, 1921).

There were thirteen directors of the Cuban American Sugar Company. Seven directors were represented in Puerto Rico.

business networks and have a greater number of interlocks.[130] James Howell Post was the most densely interlocked director in the entire structure and was strategically placed as a director of City Bank (Figure 4.1). In 1926, a new U.S. corporation, the United Porto Rico Sugar Company, entered the sugar business. In 1934 National City Bank purchased it and subsequently reorganized it as the Eastern Sugar Associates (see Figure 4.1).

The South Porto Rico Sugar Company is an interesting example of vertical integration of a central in Puerto Rico with cane farms in the Dominican Republic. The company owned the largest sugar mill in Puerto Rico and eventually built the largest sugar mill in the Dominican Republic. The complexities of the structure of corporate control of this corporation require knowledge not only of the formal aspects of interlocking directorates but also of the relationships on which interlocking directorates are based.[131] The presence of the president and vice-president of the Bankers Trust on its board of directors indicates the influence of the House of Morgan, which had a particular pattern of bank control over industry, unique in the investment banking world. Paul Sweezy concluded that "the directorship of a Morgan partner is a fact of first importance in determining the orientation of a corporation."[132] This fusion of banking and industrial capital, in which banking capital dominates, has been the object of studies in the United States because it is so important as an organizational form. Sweezy, for example, concluded that this pattern of bank control over industry was weakened during

Aguirre Sugar Company	Cuban American Sugar Company	Fajardo Sugar Company
Director	Vice-president and Treasurer	Director
Director	Vice-president and Director	Director
	Director	
Vice-president and Director	Director	
Director (1905–11)		
		Director
	Director	Second Vice-president
		Director
Secretary and Director	Director	Director
		Vice-president

the Great Depression of the 1930s.[133] There has been a long debate about the theory of "bank control"[134] and its evolution, but there is no question that in the 1920s House of Morgan institutions controlled the industrial operations they financed. The prominent presence of the president and the vice-president of the largest commercial bank of the United States on the board of the South Porto Rico Sugar Company is indeed "a fact of first importance." Seward Prosser, president of the Bankers Trust, entered the board of the South Porto Rico Company in 1918. When he left the board in 1922, he was replaced by the vice-president of the Bankers Trust, Albert A. Tilney, who remained on the board of the company until 1937.[135]

The South Porto Rico Sugar Company was established by capitalists from the firm of Muller, Schall & Company, a group of bankers in New York who knew about the opportunity for development in the island from two sources. Edmund Pavenstedt, one of its partners, had managed his father's sugar plantation there from 1885 to 1890. Muller and Schall did business with Puerto Rican firms, including Fritz, Lundt, and Company, the largest sugar exporting firm in Puerto Rico at the turn of the century.[136] Karl H. Lundt was the German consul in San Juan and Henry C. Fritze was the German vice-consul in Ponce. Muller and Schall had linkages in Puerto Rico, therefore, through Pavenstedt the planter and Fritz and Lundt the merchant-bankers. In 1899 Muller and Schall in conjunction with Porto Ricans established the American Colonial Bank of Porto Rico, with an

Director of the National City Bank of New York and the National City Safe Deposit Company		Director of the American Colonial Bank of Porto Rico

Other	**James Howell Post**	**Cuba**
Director of Holly S. C. and American Hawaiian Steamship Co.	President and director of the National Sugar Refining Company of New Jersey	(other than Cuban-American) President of New Niquero Sugar Company President of Santos Company President of Guantanamo Sugar Company

Cuba	**Puerto Rico**	**Dominican Republic**
Vice President, treasurer, and director of the Cuban American Sugar Company, which controlled the following: Chaparra S. C. San Manuel S. C. Delicias S. C. Tinguaro S. C. Nueva Luisa S. C. Unidad S. C. Cuban Sugar Refinery at Cárdenas Constancia S. C. Granmercy Refinery, Louisiana	Director of Aguirre S. C. Director of Fajardo S. C. United Porto Rico S. C.– Eastern Sugar Associates, owned by City Bank after 1934	Director of West India Sugar Finance Corporation, which owned the following mills in the Dominican Republic: Consuelo Barahona Quisqueya San Isidro Las Pajas San Marcos San Carlos Santa Fe Porvenir Ansonia

Source: Directory of Directors Company, *Directory of Directors in the City of New York, 1921* (New York: Directory of Directors Company, 1921).

Figure 4.1. Directorates of James Howell Post, 1921

authorized capital of $1 million and William Schall as its president.[137] The U.S. secretary of war promptly appointed the firm to share U.S. government deposits with De Ford and Company, the predecessor of the Aguirre company.[138]

Like DeFord and Company, therefore, Muller and Schall first established itself on the island by doing the banking business of the occupation army. When Puerto Rican sugar was granted tariff-free entrance to the United States, Muller and Schall moved toward investment in sugar. The South Porto Rico Sugar Company's *Fiftieth Anniversary Report* explicitly acknowledges the importance of direct U.S.

colonial rule over Puerto Rico to the investors who established the company. The incorporation of the company in New Jersey in 1900 raised rumors in Puerto Rico that the Sugar Trust would take over the best coastal lands.[139]

Whether or not the Sugar Trust was involved, the founders of the South Porto Rico were organized around a number of German-American capitalists, with the firm of Muller and Schall at the center.[140] The German-American capitalists occupied six of the ten seats on the board of directors of the South Porto Rico when it was founded. But by 1921 the company had experienced a transformation similar to that of the Aguirre Sugar Company.

Two factors combined to produce a drastic change in the ownership and management of the South Porto Rico company: anti-German chauvinism during World War I and the expansion of the House of Morgan into sugar production in Cuba, the Dominican Republic, and Puerto Rico. Gustav Kulenkampff, a director of the South Porto Rico company, was arrested in May 1918 as an "enemy alien." Kulenkampff, Edmund Pavenstedt, and Frederick Muller-Schall resigned from the SPRSC.[141] Upon their departure, prominent bankers from the House of Morgan entered the board of the South Porto Rico. Horace Havemeyer, son of the founder of the Sugar Trust and a member of the "vague central organization of Sugardom," joined the board of the SPRSC in 1916 representing the Bankers Trust.[142] The Cuba Cane Sugar Company and the Punta Alegre Company, both underwritten by the House of Morgan, were rapidly expanding simultaneously, and the SPRSC itself built Central Romana in the Dominican Republic during World War I.

The relation between the Bankers Trust and the South Porto Rico is similar to that between the Aguirre and Fajardo sugar companies and National City Bank. Horace Havemeyer points to a community of interest between banking and industrial capital on the board of the SPRSC. Prosser, the president of the Bankers Trust, was a director of Central Romana, SPRSC's subsidiary in the Dominican Republic.

The organization of sugar corporations in clusters which included plantations, refineries, and important banks permitted the transfer of profits from colonial plantations to metropolitan refineries. Sales of raw sugar from the centrales to the refineries were really transactions by refiners selling raw sugar to themselves at administered prices not ruled by the market. In a series of litigations against the sugar companies, the treasurer of Puerto Rico attempted to establish the fact of vertical integration and the existence of transfer price mechanisms. The sugars of Puerto Rico were not sold at the price of the open market in New York but were delivered to U.S. corporations at lower prices established by contract before the harvest season. Consequently, the profits registered by the sugar centrales in Puerto Rico were inferior to the actual profits calculated on the basis of the market price of sugar in New York. This implied a diminution of the taxes the corporations had to pay locally. The conflict between the treasury of Puerto Rico and the sugar companies became acute during the period of high sugar prices occasioned by World War I and led to discoveries about the patterns of vertical integration.

A lawsuit initiated by Manuel Domenech, treasurer of Puerto Rico, against Horace Havemeyer and the South Porto Rico Sugar Company forced the company to uncover its organizational structure. The court determined that the South Porto Rico Sugar Company of Porto Rico was controlled by the South Porto Rico Sugar Company of New Jersey, which owned 29,990 shares out of the 30,000 issued by the Puerto Rican corporation. The total property of Russell and Company, which owned the lands surrounding the company's mill in Puerto Rico, was mortgaged to the New Jersey corporation. The Puerto Rican company sold its sugars to the New Jersey company below market prices.[143]

In the litigations the treasurer of Puerto Rico established the existence of a community of interest between refineries and centrales. Domenech initiated three simultaneous court suits against the local company, against the parent company in New Jersey, and against Horace Havemeyer. The opinion of the Boston Circuit Court of Appeals, where the case finally arrived, did not find legal cause against the holding companies because they were formally "independent" of one another. The court, however, did admit that

> the partnership (Russell & Company) owns the sugar land, grows the cane, and sells it to the Porto Rican corporation (the mill); which in turn sells the raw sugar to the New Jersey Company which puts it on the market. The New Jersey corporation owns all the stock of the Porto Rican corporation except qualifying shares of directors. The majority of the shares of the New Jersey corporation belong to Russell & Company. *It is obvious and conceded that there is identity of interest between the two corporations.*[144]

The connections between Horace Havemeyer and the refining establishment were not the object of the lawsuit. But Havemeyer represented the heights of the sugar refining establishment and it is only in connection to the refining industry that vertical transfer prices acquired importance. When the SPRSC sold in New York the sugar produced in Guánica, the sale represented a transfer of raw materials between plants owned by the same group of investors. Instead of a market price, the transactions took place under administered transfer prices. The legal fiction of independence between the enterprises allowed the corporations to declare reduced profits and to pay reduced taxes in Puerto Rico.

The pattern of industrial organization of sugar centrales in the Caribbean in the early twentieth century raises important questions about the structure of capitalist enterprise in general. It reveals the limitations of studying colonial economies simply in relation to the metropolitan economy to which they are linked. Lateral relations with other colonial economies may hold the key to understanding the full scope of metropolitan capitalist organization. Very often, the distorted view derives from the assumption that the legal entity of the corporation represents the actual unit of capitalist enterprise. Once these corporations are accepted as the basic units of capital, the appearance of management control is reinforced. When these smaller manager-controlled units become established as the real economic actors, the organization of the colonial economies becomes unintelligible. It would be impossible, for instance, to understand the place of the South Porto Rico Sugar Company, taking French T. Maxwell, general manager of the corporation in Puerto Rico, as one's point of departure. One would inevitably discover an independent enterprise competing in a market. It would be difficult to explain why this profit-maximizing enterprise sold its sugar below market prices.

In reality, the proper unit of capital may be much larger than a corporation. This larger entity can be a cluster of enterprises functioning as a complex, in which the assets are legally broken down into smaller units to hide the actual economic concentration, vertical integration, and monopoly power. Managerial theory cannot provide an adequate analysis of these wider structures of power because only property can provide the cohesion necessary to the functioning of a larger complex of legally "independent" enterprises. The phenomenon of vertical integration in the Caribbean sugar industry is an excellent example of this problem. Property links the economic behavior of abstract enterprises in a market to capitalist class domination. Property also helps us to analyze the true scope of the empire of the sugar companies, which encompassed the entire Spanish Caribbean. The sugar economy of the islands was dominated by a specific segment of the capitalist class: the oligopolistic sugar refiners in alliance with the largest metropolitan banks.

The process of vertical integration was not an automatic, unmediated response to increased demand for raw sugar in the United States. It emerged from a power struggle among sugar refiners for control of the market for refined sugar in the 1890s. But it was not until massive state intervention in the form of colonial conquest created the proper conditions in the Caribbean that metropolitan capital was able to integrate backward into the production of raw sugar on a massive scale. The power exercised by the state through armed intervention and colonial occupation enabled U.S. ownership of the majority of sugar production in the colonies and the specific pattern of vertical organization and control by metropolitan sugar refiners described in this chapter. In the debate on the rise of the large corporation in America, the functionalist belief that the large modern corporations rose and spread in the U.S. economy because they were efficient has been challenged by explanations that emphasize power relations, and not efficiency, as an important determinant.[145] The process of vertical integration analyzed here is unthinkable without the armed power exercised by the metropolitan state in the process of colonial conquest and occupation. Conversely, very little in the pattern of industrial organization of the American Sugar Kingdom has to do with efficiency, which in the abstract would have been better served by forward vertical integration of Caribbean-owned enterprises expanding into sugar refining located in the Caribbean. There was no reason, other than the metropolitan tariff system, why the processing of raw sugar into refined sugar had to stop when sugar reached 96 degrees on the polariscope test. Vertical integration in a colonial context depended more than elsewhere on the power of the metropolitan state, whether in the form of armed intervention, tariff regulation, or directly through the imperial court system, as in the case of transfer prices in Puerto Rico. Put differently, colonialism is not at all about efficiency, it is about power. International industrial organization reflects the basic reality of metropolitan state power, not abstract arguments about corporate efficiency.

The Colonos

The penetration of U.S. capital into the economies of Cuba, the Dominican Republic, and Puerto Rico transformed the technological base of sugar production. The new mills featured increased grinding capacities, internal railroad networks, the introduction of internal combustion engines, and electrification in the plantation zones. But in contrast to the technological revolution of cane grinding, the planting and harvesting of cane continued to use the same immemorial technologies and displayed resistance both to transformation and to the penetration of metropolitan capital. Cane farmers known as colonos produced most of the cane ground in the mills of Cuba, the Dominican Republic, and Puerto Rico. In contrast to the industrial end of producing sugar, which was uniformly dominated by big capital, mostly metropolitan but also local, the production of cane was carried out by a great diversity of rural producers, ranging from large corporations employing workers in the thousands to small farmers who produced cane with family labor. The term "colonos" refers to a multiplicity of social layers, all of which specialized in the production of cane for delivery to the mills. A large farmer operating thousands of acres of land with wage labor and a small farmer working his cane lands only with family labor were both called colonos. The use of the term "colonos" to refer to such a diverse set of rural producers may create a certain homogenizing illusion, hiding to some degree the highly stratified land tenure structure that characterized cane farming.

The degree of industrial concentration at the milling stage led many of the critics of the sugar industry in the early twentieth century's Spanish Caribbean to focus on the immense wealth at the upper pole of the sugar economy, represented by U.S. agribusiness and local *centralistas*, and the lower pole, represented by the resident and migrant agricultural proletariat. Between these two poles, however, stood a complex and highly differentiated group of cane farmers. Were these mainly working farmers tilling the land with their families or capitalist farmers who employed wage labor? Did they own the land they worked, or was the land under the control of the sugar mills? Were they in a position to activate competition between mills for the cane, or were they subject to the monopsony power of the mills? If the sugar mills did not harvest all of the cane they ground, why not? Were previously settled farmers affected by the transition from ingenio to *central* after the abolition of slavery? How? Did most rural workers work directly for U.S. corporations or for local farmers?

The relation between metropolitan capital and native labor was mediated by the role of these farmers, who produced, under a variety of circumstances, the majority of the sugarcane of the American Sugar Kingdom. Most agricultural workers were employed by native colonos rather than by foreign corporations. In the literature of the 1930s, the role of the cane farmers is downplayed while metropolitan capital and local labor occupy center stage.[1] This homogenizing illusion was not purely a creation of U.S. social scientists. In fact, local anti-imperialist social scientists emphasized the role of metropolitan capital while contributing to an image of the colonos as a group with uniform social interests. The great Cuban scholar Ramiro Guerra y Sánchez is perhaps the foremost exponent of this vision. Guerra y Sánchez was acutely aware of the stratification of the colonos. He distinguished between colonos who worked the land, whom he called *labradores*, and colonos with sufficient land and employing enough workers to be classified as agricultural entrepreneurs. The former *colonias* were called also *sitios* or *sitios de labor*, and they combined the production of cane with local food crops. The condition of working colonos who owned their land resembles what John E. Davis has called the "propertied laborer," which describes family farmers controlled by the corporations and credit institutions that supply inputs and market their crops.[2] In Cuba as in the Dominican Republic and Puerto Rico, their income was higher than that of the rural proletariat, but they did not exploit wage labor. Guerra y Sánchez's term "labrador" includes also working colonos who rented lands from the corporations or who were sub-colonos of landowners who did not own mills. Of the 30,020 colonos in Cuba's sugar industry in 1934, 18,639 (62 percent) were classified as labradores. These colonos combined subsistence agriculture with cane agriculture. Guerra y Sánchez saw them as the embodiment of the Cuban nation and idealized their permanence on the soil: "The power of resistance of the large colonos is that of capital and credit, both of them power-ful economic forces which nevertheless end up annulled or destroyed when there are continuous losses. The power of resistance of the small colonos is that of life, struggling to maintain itself under the most adverse circumstances, and he does not abandon the countryside except through annihilation or death."[3] The small working colonos were for Guerra y Sánchez the "salt of the earth" of the Cuban nation.

Ramiro Guerra y Sánchez classified all colonos producing over thirty thousand arrobas[4] of cane above the group classified as labradores. This group was not composed of labradores but rather of owners and administrators of sugar colo-nias. Colonos producing between fifty thousand and one hundred thousand arro-bas were residents of their colonias but were no longer classified as labradores. This stratum marks "the point of transition between the sitio or subsistence farm, and the large colonia, an industrial agricultural enterprise dedicated to the busi-ness of producing cane."[5] All colonias producing more than one hundred thou-sand tons of cane were unambiguously cane producing enterprises, without any subsistence component on the part of the owners or operators. While describing in fascinating detail the stratification of the colonos and the distinction between those who worked the land and those who merely administered the colonias, however, Guerra y Sánchez also argued that the large colonos were the *líderes naturales* of the smaller cane growers.[6] The large colonos had the leisure and time to become the political representative of the smaller farmer, strengthening his personal influence "with the support of thousands of small colonos spread out throughout the national territory; these, in turn, support their spokespersons, to whom they delegate the *representation of the class*. In this way, the union and coopera-tion of small and large colonos is guaranteed to the benefit of all."[7] Guerra y Sánchez's defense of the small colonos as the foundation of the Cuban nation was coupled with a conservative agrarian ideology linking small farmers to large land-owners in a common interest.

Guerra y Sánchez pointed out that the land tenure structure of the *colonato* was characterized by uneven regional development. In the 1930s, the majority of small colonos were concentrated in the western provinces of Havana, Matanzas, and Santa Clara. The majority of colonos producing over five hundred thousand arrobas of cane were located in Camagüey and Oriente. As one moved from west to east in Cuba, the average size of colonias increased.[8] As in the case of the size of the Cuban sugar mills, this fact reflects the difference between the older and newer regions of sugar culture, the conversion from ingenio to centrales in the west, and the introduction of the colossal U.S.-owned plantations in the east after the Spanish-American War.

The colonato as an institution emerged in full force in the aftermath of the abolition of slavery. Instead of a simple transition to wage labor in agriculture, the expansion of sugar production after abolition took place under hybrid conditions. The new central mills hired wage labor but also ground cane from independent and tenant cane farmers. These colonos often subleased lands to smaller sub-colonos who worked the land with the labor of their families, while some of them also employed wage workers during the harvest. The problem of scarcity of capital seems to have been paramount in the transition to the colono system after abolition. Originally, the colono system served as a cushion against the scarcity of capital. The division of labor between cane farmer and mill owner allowed the mills to expand their grinding capacity and to modernize their technologies without having to increase the areas of land planted in cane in the same proportion as their milling capacity. It also allowed unsuccessful mill owners to continue growing cane by hiring wage labor or subleasing to smaller colonos. It served as an expedient to the uneasy process of land consolidation, which would have otherwise been needed to expand sugar production. Because land is a natural monopoly—both limited in quantity and a relatively immovable form of capital—capital accumulation takes place in a different form than in industry. In industrial production, increases of scale and concentration of production do not necessarily entail the suppression of smaller capital. But in agriculture, where the land is fragmented, accumulation generally requires the centralization of smaller properties.[9]

The origins of the colonato are associated with the uneven development of the agrarian aspect of sugar production relative to the industrial phase. An impressive process of concentration eliminated most ingenios and replaced them with more efficient centrales. In agriculture, however, the pace of concentration was not as fast. Because land cannot be socially multiplied or transported to more suitable locations,[10] the process of capital accumulation in agriculture is slower than in industry. The increase in scale of the cultivation of sugarcane could be achieved only through the centralization of smaller farms. In this sense, the process of accumulation encountered obstacles based on the property divisions of land which were in place at the time of the abolition of slavery. The emergence of the colono system is in some measure a reflection of this obstacle. On the one hand, owners of modernized mills could grind more cane than they could plant. On the other hand, planters who were unable to modernize their mills continued to plant cane and took it to grind to the ingenios centrales. In contrast to the transition in the cotton belt of the U.S. South after abolition, the freed slaves were excluded from ownership and even from tenancy of cane farms.[11] The large colonos of western Cuba were overwhelmingly a class of white landowners who had once been planters. Relying on petty commodity producers or even on farmers who employed wage labor allowed the mill owners to specialize in the industrial operations. The colono system was also a form of insurance in which the risks of a bad crop were borne by the farmer, not by the mill.

The colono system spread during the process of transition from ingenio to central, but the term "colonos" is of much older origin. One meaning referred to communities of immigrants recruited to populate frontier zones by settling on divided Crown lands of haciendas comuneras. An example is the "colonia blanca" recruited to settle Xagua Bay in Cienfuegos, Cuba, early in the nineteenth century. Another meaning refers to renters recruited to work the lands of former ingenios that had difficulties meeting their labor requirements after abolition. A third meaning refers to a class of owners of land who grew cane on their mills and who could be substantial landowners.[12] Yet a fourth meaning refers to farmers imported by the planters after abolition to work the land mainly with family labor, employing a few wage workers during the zafra. This was the case of the Canary Islanders imported into Julián Zulueta's central Zaza in Cuba in the 1890s.[13] In the twentieth century colonos were classified principally as owners (*colonos independientes*) and as tenants (*colonos controlados*).

In the aftermath of abolition in Cuba, the expansion of the railroads permitted the developing central mills to draw cane from a much larger area than was possible under the previous ingenio system, and this led to a significant expansion of sugar cultivation by the colonos. In addition to the incorporation of more distant farms into the radius of operation of the enlarged centrales, many planters who dismantled their ingenios subdivided their cane lands and leased them to sub-colonos. In Cienfuegos in the mid-1890s, the lands of centrales Hormigueros that had previously belonged to ingenio Santa Isabel were divided into thirty-seven farms, twenty-one of them under one *caballería*, ten of them between 1 and 2 caballerías, and six of over 2 caballerías. Mean farm size was 1.1. caballería. Central Constancia in Cienfuegos ground cane from thirty-five colonias, of which thirty-three were over 2 caballerías (63 acres) in extension.[14]

A sample of 1,257 colonos in the province of Matanzas in 1895 indicates that a small number of colonos at the top of the social scale (7.9 percent) occupied 52.9 percent of the farmland. At the opposite end of the spectrum, the bottom 60 percent of colonos controlled 8.9 percent of the land. In this sample, even the smallest colonos hired wage labor. Cuban land measures make it difficult to distinguish between the smallest colonos because the unit of land, the caballería, is equivalent to 33.6 acres of land, and statistics are not very specific for farms under 1 caballería. Even a colono with 1 caballería of land, however, may have employed wage labor during the harvest. In 1899, the manager of colonia Guabairo in Matanzas reported to U.S. military authorities that 350 workers were needed to harvest 33 caballerías of cane, or slightly more than 10 workers per caballería. In the Matanzas sample, 81 percent owned more than 1 caballería (33.6 acres) of land.[15] Although it was perhaps possible for a colono to harvest one caballería of cane with family labor with extreme exertion, above that amount the colono had to hire wage labor. Thus a conservative estimate is that more than 80 percent of these colonos employed wage labor. The colonos of Cuba would appear from the beginning to have been principally a class of capitalist farmers who hired wage labor during the harvest. But the statistics offer a limited picture because many of these farmers may have leased lands to sub-colonos instead of hiring wage labor, but subleasing agreements generally are not well represented in the official sources.

A census of Cuba's 174 sugar mills taken in 1913–14 reveals some aspects of the evolution of the colonato on the eve of World War I but leaves some essential aspects in the dark. The *Portfolio azucarero* of 1914 classified cane lands into two basic types: those owned by the sugar mills and those owned by independent colonos. It revealed that the strength of the independent colonato lay in the west of the island. The *Portfolio*, however, did not offer a breakdown of the lands owned by the mills but planted by tenant colonos. Thus the *tierras de administración* owned and planted under the management of the mill and the lands of colonos who were tenants of the mill were aggregated into a single category, obscuring the expansion of tenant farms in the newest regions of cane cultivation in eastern Cuba. The *Portfolio* indicates the total amount of land owned by independent colonos and by the mills, but it does not offer a farm-by-farm breakdown that would permit an analysis of the stratification of cane farms.

In the western provinces, in which plantation slavery had a greater impact and lasted longer, the mills controlled a smaller share of the cane lands than in the eastern provinces, which constituted the frontier of plantation agriculture in the twentieth century. The established class of planters who had become colonos retained the ownership of cane lands in the west. In Matanzas, the center of plantation agriculture in the nineteenth century, 58 percent of the cane lands were controlled by colonos independientes, the mills controlling the remaining 42 percent. In Pinar del Río and in Santa Clara independent colonos controlled 55 percent of the cane land, while in the province of Havana they controlled 38 percent. The two eastern provinces displayed a different structure of landownership. In the eastern province of Camagüey, where sugar production hardly existed in the nine-

Table 5.1. Lands in Cuba Planted by Mills and Independent Colonos, 1913

Province	Area Planted in Cane by Mills and Dependent Colonos[a]	Area Planted in Cane by Independent Colonos[a]	Percent of Land Planted by Independent Colonos
Pinar del Río	433	536	55
Havana	2,670	1,662	38
Matanzas	4,253	5,769	58
Santa Clara	6,510	8,084	55
Camagüey	2,266	209	8
Oriente	5,994	1,766	23
Cuba	22,126	18,026	45

Source: Secretaría de Agricultura, Comercio y Trabajo de Cuba, Portfolio azucarero (Havana: La Moderna Poesía, 1914).

[a]All areas are expressed in caballerías. A caballería is equal to 33.6 acres.

teenth century, independent colonos owned only 8 percent of the cane land, while in Oriente, which had a mix of older and newer mills, independent colonos controlled only 23 percent. Reflecting the division between east and west, new and old sugar mills, the vitality of the independent colonato varied according to the antiquity of the cane regions. In 1913–14 54 percent of the cane crushed in the mills founded before the abolition of slavery in 1880 was grown by independent colonos. In the mills established between 1880 and 1898, independent colonos produced 35 percent of the cane. In the mills established after 1900, the independent colonos produced only 14 percent of the cane (see Table 5.1).[16] Clearly, the independent colonato was principally a product of the pre-1898 sugar economy.

The phenomenal expansion of sugar production during World War I opened opportunities for Cuban agricultural entrepreneurs. Some of the them acquired extensive holdings through leases or purchases and planted more cane than some of the smaller sugar mills could process. The region of Ciego de Avila in the Cuban province of Camagüey underwent a process of plantation growth in the twentieth century. In a frontier of sugar cultivation with high yields per acre of land, the modern mills of Camagüey exemplified the new type of central. Large sugar mills owned vast tracts of land. Instead of undertaking the management of cane agriculture, the sugar mills leased most of these lands to colonos who took over the agricultural phase. The pattern of subcontracting reveals the difficulties experienced by the sugar mills administering the agricultural phase of sugar production. In sugarcane agriculture, the difference between production time and labor time could be considerable. Cane was harvested from December–January to June–July. During the rest of the year, the labor requirements of cane agriculture shrank to

one-third of the labor requirements during the harvest. After planting, the maintenance task of weeding was the only other important activity. As a result, for a
period of six to seven months of the year, most cane workers were unemployed.
The labor requirements in cane agriculture were highest in the months of January
to July. During August, September, and October, payrolls shrank to one-half of
the level of January to July. In November, the labor used in cane agriculture was
only a third of that during the harvest, which means that two-thirds of the agricultural laborers and small working colonos were idle.[17]

In Ciego de Avila in central Cuba, the Baraguá mill hired 1,500 men during the
harvest for operations in the mill yard (*batey*). During the *tiempo muerto*, the number
of employees was reduced to 500. Of the 6,000 laborers who worked in its cane
farms (colonias), the overwhelming majority were unemployed half of the year.
The Santo Tomás mill, a Cuban-owned enterprise, hired 125 men in the industrial
operations during the harvest and 75 during the tiempo muerto. Central Stewart
hired 1,800 workers during the harvest in 1918, but only 300 remained during the
dead season. Central Jagüeyal of the Cuba Cane Sugar Corporation hired 500 men
during the harvest, 250 during the tiempo muerto. Central Pilar hired 1,000 men in
its batey and retained only 110 during the off-season.[18] The fluctuations in the
industrial sector are indicative, on a reduced scale, of the fluctuations in the
agricultural sector. The agricultural phase displayed more drastic reductions in
employment than the industrial sector, although these reductions are harder to
quantify in these mills farm by farm.

The seasonal nature of cane agriculture and lack of diversification presented
some obstacles to capital accumulation. In industry, specialization and the development of capitalism go hand in hand, but in the agrarian sector the penetration of capital is generally accompanied by diversification, which permits the
investments to be used continuously throughout the year. Interruptions to the
labor process present obstacles to investment because tools, animals, and machinery must remain idle for a prolonged period. Ramiro Guerra y Sánchez argued that
one of the virtues of the colono labrador was that he could use his farm imple-
ments in producing food crops during the tiempo muerto. Mills attempted to
overcome these obstacles by leasing lands to colonos instead of taking on the
entire burden of agricultural investments that would remain idle part of the year.
The management of vast amounts of land under a single ownership required
freezing assets during the tiempo muerto. In addition, the centralization of all
wage labor under a single employer increased the possibilities of unionization.
Even though many of the large mills owned enormous amounts of land, they
opted to lease them to large colonos rather taking on their operation. In Ciego de

Table 5.2. Farm Sizes of 305 Colonias of Centrales Algodones, Baragua, Ciego de Avila, Jagüeyal, Jatibonico, Pilar, Santo Tomás, and Stewart in Cuba, 1919

Size of Farm (in acres)	Number of Farms	Percentage of Farms	Area in acres	Percentage of total area
Less than 10	6	1.97	46	0.03
10–19	6	1.97	101	0.07
20–39	17	5.57	556	0.39
40–59	7	2.30	344	0.24
60–79	16	5.25	1,075	0.75
80–99	2	0.66	176	0.12
100–399	114	37.38	26,214	18.31
Over 400	137	44.92	114,667	80.09
All farms	305	100.00	143,179	100.00

Source: José Ramón Cabrera Pérez, *Memoria explicativa e ilustrada de varios centrales del término municipal de Ciego de Avila, Provincia de Camagüey* (Havana: Montalvo, Cárdenas & Co., 1919).

Avila farms over 400 acres in area predominated, followed by farms of 100 to 399 acres (see Table 5.2).

The size of the holdings indicates that these colonos were not exactly a class of small farmers but a class of agricultural entrepreneurs. Thus the great concentration of land under the ownership of the newest and largest mills actually fostered the expansion of the colonato. Unlike the independent colonos of western Cuba, the eastern colonos were generally tenants bound by contract to deliver the cane to a specific mill. This arrangement made it harder to activate competition for cane among the mills. Nevertheless, the prosperity of the sugar industry benefited Cuban capitalist farmers, who produced most of the cane and therefore hired most of the workers. Class conflict in the Cuban countryside pitted Cuban and immigrant workers principally against Cuban capitalist farmers.

The majority of the cane was produced on farms of far greater acreage than could be properly called a sitio de labor. The dynamic expansion of the sugar industry also allowed some colonos in the eastern zone to become large landowners, a process that is sometimes obscured in accounts that emphasize the expansion of U.S. enterprises "at the expense" of Cuban producers.[19] Domingo Dones, for example, took advantage of rising prices during World War I to build a small empire of cane-growing farms. This agricultural entrepreneur owned twelve large colonias with a total area of 15,523 acres in the region of Ciego de Avila. Each colonia was run by a hired manager. Dones did not own sugar mills. Miguel Robaina, another agricultural entrepreneur, owned the Unión, América, and Vencedora farms, which together occupied 3,461 acres of land in the Ciego de Avila region.[20] If the figures provided for Central Baraguá are accurate, 6,000 field workers were required during the harvest of 1918 for the tasks of cutting and loading 21,790 acres of cane, which amounts to one worker for each 3.63 acres. A farmer with 400 acres of land would require, under these conditions, 110 workers during the harvest. At this rate, the farms of Domingo Dones required over 4,000 workers during the harvest. The division between industry and agriculture in this case was not a division between industrial capital and working farmer but between industrial and agrarian capital. Under the specific circumstances of plantation agriculture in Cuba, U.S. capital penetrated into the industrial side of sugar production, while Cuban colonos hired Cuban and immigrant workers from other islands of the Caribbean on large cane farms in which the colonos were in charge of organizing the cane cutting. Despite the persistence of the small colonos, the great expansion in the area cultivated in cane after 1898 took place on large farms employing wage labor. Capitalist relations of production emerged in the absence of fundamental changes in the technology of cane harvesting. Except for advances in the lifting and transporting of cane through railroads and later on trucks, cane continued to be harvested with the machete.

If the mills in the east were able to acquire sufficient lands to guarantee their entire supply of cane for the grinding season, why did they sublease to colonos instead of managing the production of cane? The colossal sugar mill introduced a new division of labor into Cuban agriculture in which the principal actors were corporate mills and tenant capitalist farmers. The decision to sublease to colonos instead of planting administration cane reflected problems associated with placing vast numbers of agricultural workers under the same management. Subcontracting to colonos provided a flexible production strategy, shielding foreign mills from the vicissitudes of managing native labor. The organization of production based on subcontracting transferred to Cuban capitalist farmers the problems associated with control of the labor process in Cuban agriculture.

The case of Central Francisco in southern Camagüey is illustrative of the issues confronting a foreign enterprise in the virgin soil of eastern Cuba shortly after the U.S. occupation of the island. Francisco was located in a region of the island which experienced a dramatic social transformation in the early years of the twentieth century.[21] When the Francisco company purchased land in eastern Cuba in 1899, it obtained a title to 45,527 acres in southern Camagüey which included the lands of the town of Guayabal. The town was made up of sixty common Cuban country houses and four hundred inhabitants.[22] Having literally purchased the town and the land surrounding it, the company proceeded to build a sawmill and a wharf. The clearing of the forests was subcontracted to entrepreneurs who hired work crews. Francisco did not hire the workers directly. With the wood from the cleared forests, the company built houses for the administration and small cottages and *barracones* for the workers. In a matter of two years, a sparsely populated wilderness of southern Camagüey was transformed into the nucleus of what would become an immense sugar mill yielding high profits to foreign entrepreneurs. In 1901, Central Francisco processed its first sugarcane crop. Francisco was connected to markets and sources of labor power through the weekly trips of steamboats to its pier. Overland travel was not yet feasible. U.S. sugar refiners (the McCahan family of Philadelphia) and Manuel Rionda, an important sugar merchant in New York, were among the principal owners of the new corporation.

Francisco grew at an impressive rate. During its first harvest in 1902, the mill produced 1,651 tons of sugar. By 1910 production had increased to 19,814 tons. In 1918, at the height of the sugar fever produced by the great demand caused by World War I, Francisco produced 51,774 tons of sugar. The area planted in cane increased from 1,233 acres in 1901 to 26,578 acres in 1918. An internal railroad linked the central yard of the sugar mill (batey) to the cane farms (colonias). After 1906 Francisco established rail connection to main lines in Cuba. The production of sugar required coordination between the cane farms, the internal railroad, and the mill. Because sugarcane must be processed within twenty-four hours of being cut, the term "vertical integration" has been used to refer to the linkages between cane farm and mill. Strictly speaking, the term is inaccurate because many of the cane colonias in twentieth-century sugar mills were independently owned. In Francisco, however, the colonos were overwhelmingly tenants of the mill. The emergence of the pattern of subleasing to colonos reveals some of the difficulties associated with labor which the mills encountered.

Because Central Francisco owned all the land surrounding the sugar mill, it initiated its first grinding season with cane planted under the management of the mill itself. Canes planted in 1901 were harvested when the mill started grinding on April 2, 1902. By April 25 the manager of Francisco reported "great difficulty in continuing to grind, owing to strikes of the field hands, preventing sufficient supply of cane and causing the work in the factory to be only partial and more expensive."[23] Before the end of the first month of operations, the management of Francisco decided to contract with colonos for the planting of additional cane on its lands, a thousand acres to be planted in the spring of 1902 and an additional nine hundred in the spring of 1903, "which it is believed will give us all the cane that our present machinery can handle. The cane is planted by colonos . . . to whom in some cases, advances of money was made from $15 to $30 per acre."[24] James McCahan, a U.S. sugar refiner who was one of the principal investors in the Francisco Sugar Company, immediately established a fund of $10,000 for loans to colonos. Thereafter Francisco did not hire wage labor to plant and harvest sugarcane directly under the administration of the company. Instead, it leased lands to tenant farmers who raised cane for the mills under terms specified in the leases, with credit provided by the mill. The subcontracting of cane agriculture freed the sugar mill from the problems of labor unrest, but the mill still had to face the problem of colono unrest. In 1912, the corporation was faced with the decision of either taking over the management of a farm from an unsatisfied tenant complaining of low cane prices or contracting with another colono. It decided to contract with a new farmer, "it not being advisable under the present labor conditions in Cuba for the company to increase its own plantings."[25] The colono was simply replaced. A similar action against the workers of a colonia would have surely resulted in a strike.

It would appear from the evidence that the principal obstacle to the expansion of the plantings of the mill was labor control. The creation of a subcontracting system buffered the clash between foreign capital and Cuban labor, leaving the process of planting and harvesting cane, and the confrontation with Cuban workers, in the hands of Cuban agricultural entrepreneurs. Cane agriculture in Central Francisco displayed a classical tripartite division into landowner, capitalist farmer, and wage worker. But the landowner was industrial capital itself, the corporation owning the sugar mill or some subsidiary corporation set up for that purpose. Unlike traditional landowners, the mill was principally interested in industrial profit as opposed to land rent. The colono was a tenant of the mill and a capitalist farmer, while both resident and migrant laborers constituted a seasonal agricultural proletariat. During World War I, faced with increasing production demands and shortages of labor, Central Francisco resorted to the importation of Haitian workers for the duration of the harvest. The company brought in "from eight to nine hundred of these laborers at an average cost of up to $10.00 per man. Many of these laborers were distributed among the Colonias at the same expense to them as had been incurred by the Company in bringing them."[26] The company was responsible for the importation of the immigrant laborers, but the colonos hired them during the sugar harvest. Thus, even though the corporation took on the expense of importing foreign workers, it preferred to continue using the subcontracting system instead of increasing its own plantings.

The sugar mill controlled the principal inputs in the production of sugarcane and inspected closely the condition of the colonias. It gave incentives to plant new cane or to allow a new crop of ratoon cane to grow, depending on the circumstances. It granted allowances to colonos for cleaning and weeding and lent them money to clear forests and plant new cane lands. After the harvest, inspectors decided to grant the colonos allowances for old cane, depending on the condition of the fields. The colono was paid a certain percentage of the sugar contents of the cane. Typically, one hundred tons of cane yielded thirteen tons of sugar. The colonos received five tons of sugar for every one hundred tons of cane delivered. At the end of the season, the mill and the colono closed accounts at this rate, after discounting credits advanced to the colono, land rent, transportation charges on the railroad of the mill, and other miscellaneous charges. Payments to colonos were based on the average price of sugar in the port of Havana during the two-week period in which specific deliveries of cane were made to the mill. The contracts between sugar mill and cane farmer were complicated documents which stipulated in great detail how much cane the colono had to plant and how much rent he had to pay. Payment for the cane was based on its sucrose content as measured by a chemist employed by the mill. The mill kept exact account of charges for planting and weeding, the costs of cutting, and so on. The mill owned the lands and inspected the fields, making determinations about the use of fertilizers and even importing wage laborers for the colonos. The degree of control by the sugar mill over the enterprise of the colonos was in conflict with the entrepreneurial prerogatives of this emerging agrarian middle class. Nevertheless, the fact that most colonos planted great extensions of cane and hired wage labor prevents their identification with any precapitalist or noncapitalist class. The term "propertied laborer" is not applicable to these colonos, who employed far too many workers to fit the concept.

The development of cane subcontracting controlled by Cuban capitalist farmers is inconsistent with some of the characterizations of the development theorists of the so-called plantation school.[27] The idea that the persistence of precapitalist relations of production and extraeconomic coercion are defining features of plantation economies does not always fit the case of U.S. agribusiness corporations in the Caribbean.[28] If anything, the dynamic expansion of the Cuban capitalist entrepreneurs suggests that the flexible strategies of subcontracting which are in such vogue at present may have a longer lineage in the history of capitalism than is currently apparent.[29] Subcontracting to Cuban capitalist farmers guaranteed a supply of cane to the mills at prices not subject to competition between mills while at the same time freeing the corporations from the burdens of managing a vast agricultural labor force. The expansion of the new mills offered Cuban capitalists opportunities for production of a cash crop which would have otherwise been unavailable. The hierarchical control of industrial capital over agrarian capital should not obscure the fact that the expansion of sugar monoculture dominated by foreign capital nevertheless provided Cuban agrarian entrepreneurs with a dynamic field of expansion. Over a period of years, some prosperous colonos were able to purchase land. In the Francisco Sugar Company, by 1918 colonos owned 18 percent of the lands planted in cane. The supply of cane to the sugar mill derived from three sources: lands planted by the administration of the sugar mill (15 percent), lands planted by tenants, known as *colonos de administración* (67 percent), and lands planted by farmers who owned their lands, known as colonos independientes. Eighty-two percent of the cane for the Francisco mill derived from lands owned by the company. Both the tenants of the mill and the independent colonos were a stratified group. But in Central Francisco, all farms were very large by any Caribbean standards of the time, averaging 531 acres.

The price paid for cane to the colonos of Central Francisco differed greatly from the terms of colonos independientes in other regions of Cuba. The terms of delivery of cane at the mill varied according to whether the colono was an owner or a tenant and whether the railroad lines and the location of the mills allowed the farmer to take advantage of competition for cane between mills. The contracts with the colonos of the Francisco Sugar Company were strict and specified in advance the terms of delivery of cane to the mills. The lease agreements left no room for negotiation at the time of delivery. The inputs to the farming of cane were controlled by the mill, including the transportation of the immigrant labor for distribution to colonos, which was organized by the corporation. The corporation made credit advances to the colonos based on a fixed amount per unit of area planted in cane. At the end of the season, an inspector determined whether another ratoon crop would be grown or whether new canes would be planted. Special "bonuses" were given after inspection for fields clean of weeds (see Table 5.3). Elsewhere in the American Sugar Kingdom conditions were similar. In Puerto Rico, contracts of dependent colonos generally stipulated that the mill was "an interested party" in the business of the colono with a right to stipulate the timing of irrigation and cutting.[30]

Colono contracts stipulated that the mill would determine when the cane had to be cut. Because cane must be crushed within twenty-four hours of being cut, the mill had to organize the schedule for cutting and crushing cane, colonia by colonia, in a system of "just-in-time" delivery. The obstacles which big capital encountered in Cuban agriculture were not solved through the establishment of noncapitalist relations of production but through the development of a production system based on subleasing of lands to capitalist farmers and through the importation of immigrant labor.

Subleasing offered corporate capital advantages relative to the mills located in regions with an entrenched colonato. The price of cane was higher in districts in

Table 5.3. Land Use by the Francisco Sugar Company, by Type of Farm, 1917

Type of Farm	No. of Farms	% Farms	Area in Acres	Area Average Farm	% of Farm Area
Administration cane	5	10	4,033	807	15
Colonos (tenants)	32	63	18,205	569	67
Colonos (owners)	14	27	4,865	348	18
All farms	51	100	27,103	531	100

Source: Francisco Sugar Company, "Manager's Report, Francisco Sugar Company, 1917," Record Group IV, series 96, Braga Brothers Collection, University of Florida, Gainesville.

which cane farmers owned the land, and especially in places where the railroad structure allowed them to activate competition between mills. The records of the Cuba Cane Sugar Corporation offer an interesting example of the importance of the independent agrarian middle class in western Cuba. The Cuba Cane was established in 1915 through the purchase of seventeen sugar mills by Manuel Rionda, an established Spanish merchant in the sugar business of New York and Havana. The funds for the purchase of the mills were provided by bankers from the House of Morgan. Unlike other enterprises established by U.S. corporate capital, the Cuba Cane purchased existing sugar mills instead of building new ones. The banker-financed corporation bought mills mostly in the western part of the island in 1916, expecting sugar shortages and increasing prices during World War I. By 1919 the management of the Cuba Cane discovered the difference in cost of production between mills that owned all of their cane lands and those in which independent colonos supplied the cane.[31]

The mills of the corporation were unable to control the price of cane in the western part of the island, where an entrenched class of colonos was in firm possession of the land. An audit report of 1919 complained that "nearly all the cane used by the Cuba Cane Corporation *is Colono cane.*" Thirteen of the corporation's seventeen mills were located in the western part of the island and only four in the eastern part.[32] The strength of the independent colonos in the west was formidable.

According to the audit report, "Many colonos grow cane on land not under the control of the centrales, and, where favorably located with respect to a number of centrales, they are able, through competition, to receive higher prices than the general average in the locality. The control by centrals of sufficient cane to work the mills to full capacity is, therefore, an important factor."[33]

The mills located in western Cuba had to purchase cane from independent colonos. The centrales of the Cuba Cane Sugar Corporation in the eastern provinces of Camagüey and Oriente owned most of the lands that supplied cane in patterns similar to that of Central Francisco. The difference in the price of cane in the corporation's eastern and western mills was noticeable. A report stated: "The cane situation for the Corporation's western centrals is not so favorable. The number of independent colonos is greater and there is a larger number of mills, so that in some localities the competition is very keen."[34] High prices of sugar during the war attenuated the impact of the independent colonato on the sugar mills of the Cuba Cane. But the corporation's auditors questioned whether the western mills could resume production at profitable rates once world competition was restored at the end of the war: "Considerable doubt has been expressed by those familiar with the Cuba situation whether the mills in the west will be able to make any profit after the resumption of world competition, unless the price of cane is materially reduced. It may compel centrals to consider seriously the growing of more administration cane by the most scientific and efficient methods."[35] This concern reflected the meticulous calculations of the management and the conclusion that the corporation was earning $2.092 per bag of sugar (325 pounds) in its eastern centrals but only $1.166 per bag of sugar in the western mills. Where the corporation owned the land, it earned 79 percent more per bag of sugar. The case of the Cuba Cane Sugar Corporation confirms Alan Dye's finding that the existence of independent colonos was negatively correlated to the expansion of grinding capacity of the sugar mills. Mills expanded where they controlled the land and avoided expansion where colonos controlled the land. Sugar mills preferred to expand their supply of cane through subcontracting to dependent tenants. Mill-grinding capacity was positively associated with the increase of cane area planted by dependent colonos. Where the independent colonato was strong, the increase in mill capacities was not as vigorous as in the zones of dependent colonos.[36]

Cuban agriculture evolved toward the system of independent colonos in the older zone of sugar cultivation where the planter class was differentiated into centralistas or independent colonos after abolition. In the newer regions of sugar cultivation, agribusiness corporations acquired sufficient land to guarantee the entire supply of cane to vastly superior mills and chose to sublease land to dependent colonos. In both cases, the result was the expansion of the Cuban colonato. By the mid-1920s, 85 percent of the cane of Cuba was planted and harvested by dependent and independent colonos.[37] The corollary to this figure is that the overwhelming majority of agricultural workers in the fields of Cuba were employed by Cuban capitalist farmers, not by foreign corporations. The colonos classified by Ramiro Guerra y Sánchez as labradores represented 62 percent of all cane farmers but grew less than 3 percent of the cane. By contrast, colonos who hired wage labor harvested 97 percent of the cane. The upper stratum of colonos producing above five hundred thousand arrobas occupied less than 4 percent of the farms but produced over 40 percent of the cane. Thus, while it is true that the overwhelming majority of colonos were working farmers, the immense majority of the cane was harvested in the farms of colonos who employed wage labor. In Cuba and the rest of the Spanish Caribbean metropolitan investment in the age of classical imperialism propelled a rapid transition to capitalist agriculture dominated by native farmers.

This successful transition to capitalist agriculture seems to have taken place in the absence of substantial increase in agricultural productivity. The facets of production amenable to technological improvement and changes in the organization of labor were taken over by industrial capital. The technologies of cane grinding were altered dramatically, and industrial yields doubled between the abolition of slavery and World War I. Similarly, transportation was revolutionized by the introduction of new railroad lines and later trucks. Still, the cutting of cane proceeded in essentially the same fashion as in the nineteenth century, and the organization of labor remained unchanged between abolition and the 1930s. Between 1878 and 1913 the extraction of sugar from cane increased from 5.5 tons sugar per one hundred tons of cane, to 13 tons sugar per one hundred tons of cane. Agricultural yields, however, probably declined from around eighty thousand arrobas per caballería to approximately fifty thousand arrobas per caballería.[38] A comparison of the 1913 data with nineteenth-century Cuban ingenio figures shows that industrial yields increased but agricultural yields declined. The improvement of industrial yields, however, was so significant that it compensated for the decline in agricultural yields. The increase in industrial yields was caused by three fundamental changes: improvements in the technology of crushing cane and extracting juice, improvements in the technologies of making sugar out of cane juice, and new varieties of cane that produced more sugar per unit of cane weight.

At the agricultural end, yields of cane in arrobas per caballería were not higher than during the days of slavery, and often they were lower. Laird Bergad has noted in his examination of agricultural yields in the 1830s and at the turn of the twentieth century that the transformation of the social organization of cane agriculture was not matched by changes in productivity.[39] The data presented here suggest that agricultural yields actually declined between 1878 and 1913.[40] In 1913, agricultural yields ranged from 83,000 arrobas per caballería on the first-rate lands of Central Manatí in the province of Oriente, to a low of 26,600 arrobas per caballería on Central Nuestra Señora de Regla in Santa Clara. The mills of Camagüey, the frontier of sugar cultivation, reported high yields: Central Jatibonico reported

75,000 arrobas per caballería; Central Francisco 74,106; Central Jagüeyal, 74,884; Central Senado, 70,000; and Central Morón, 69,741.[41]

The contrast with the preemancipation period of Cuban cane agriculture is striking. It is not possible to draw exact comparisons between yields of cane per unit of land between the mills of 1913 and those of preemancipation Cuba at the aggregate level because the range of yields in the nineteenth century was broader than in the twentieth. The larger, highly capitalized plantations of the nineteenth century are better represented in the studies than the small marginal *trapiches*. The ingenios of the nineteenth century were unitary enterprises in which the mill owners operated the cane lands and the grinding units, with the consequence that the cane was not weighed. The centrales, by contrast, had to keep exact accounts of the weight of the cane of each colono so as to determine the amount to be paid for the cane delivered. As a result, the figures of cane production per unit of land are much more reliable in the twentieth century than in the nineteenth. Despite the uncertainties about agricultural yields in the nineteenth century, the existing information indicates that the most developed plantations recorded higher yields per unit of land that the most developed plantations of the twentieth century. In the 1850s, the most productive mills in Banagüises produced over 100,000 arrobas per caballería, and in the mid-1880s agricultural yields ranged between 75,000 and 80,000 arrobas per caballería.[42] Ingenios Narciso, Urumea, and Santa Elena produced over 100,000, and the Alava mill in Banagüises produced 97,500 arrobas per caballería. In ingenio Las Cañas of Juan Poey, some of the sugar fields recorded yields of over 120,000 arrobas per caballería in the 1877–78 season.[43] By comparison, the highest yield recorded in 1913 (Central Manatí) stood considerably below nineteenth-century standards at 83,800 arrobas per caballería. If these figures are accurate, the decline in agricultural yields after the abolition of slavery was not an isolated phenomenon but occurred across the breadth of Cuban cane agriculture. A possible explanation is the spread of extensive agriculture because of abundance of land and increased ease of transportation. In the 1930s, cane farms in Cuba had much lower yields per unit of land than those of Puerto Rico, where land was relatively scarce and the development of irrigation systems in the south of the island contributed to the rise of intensive cane agriculture.[44]

Within the overall trend of decline in agricultural productivity, there are differences between small and large mills. The mills with larger grinding capacity had higher agricultural yields. Yields also exhibited regional differences. Mills located in the eastern provinces of Camagüey and Oriente had higher average yields than the mills of the west. The lower yields of the western provinces suggest possible soil exhaustion of the older lands of sugar cultivation. The virgin lands of the east simply had higher yields than those of the west. In the case of the mills with ascertainable dates of foundation, the pattern is similar. In arrobas per caballería, the mills founded before 1880 had an average yield of 48,575 arrobas per caballería; mills established between 1880 and 1898 had an average yield of 50,676; mills founded after 1898 had an average yield of 63,022.

The decline of agricultural yields, however, must be considered in combination with the increase of industrial yields. While the former declined, the latter more than doubled in the period 1860–1913. In the 1860s the most mechanized and capital-intensive mills of Cuba reported sugarcane yields of between 4.5 and 5.5 percent.[45] In the 1880s and 1890s industrial yields reached 8 percent in some mills.[46] In 1913, by contrast, mills reported yields of 11, 12, and even 13 percent of the weight of the cane. The increase in industrial yields (weight of sugar per weight of cane) more than compensated for the decline in agricultural yields (weight of cane per area of land).

The combination of increasing industrial yields and decreasing agricultural yields produced a net increase in the amount of sugar per unit of land. A caballería of land that produces 80,000 arrobas of cane (1,000 tons) will yield 55 tons of sugar in a mill with an industrial yield of 5.5 percent, whereas a caballería of land that yields 50,000 arrobas of cane (625 tons) will yield 75 tons of sugar in a mill with an industrial yield of 12 percent, the actual yield in Cuba in 1913. Under the very generous assumption of agricultural yields of 80,000 arrobas per caballería and industrial yields of 5.5 percent for Cuban sugar agriculture as a whole under the regime of slavery, the combination of declining agricultural yields and increasing industrial yields resulted in a net increase of 36 percent in the sugar obtained per caballería of land. The combined agricultural-industrial yield increased significantly after abolition because of increased industrial yields and despite the drop in agrarian yields. Extensive capitalist agriculture with relatively low yields per unit of land characterized the transition to twentieth-century sugar monoculture in Cuba.

In Puerto Rico, the transition took a slightly different form. United States capital did not encounter contiguous extensions of sparsely populated frontier land comparable to those of the eastern Cuban plantations. The South Porto Rico Sugar Company owned the largest mill in the island, Central Guánica. In contrast to the Francisco Sugar Company in Cuba, 56 percent of the cane of the Guánica mill was grown and harvested by independent colonos.[47] In 1932–33, 46 percent of the cane lands were planted by the administration of the centrales, 54 percent by colonos.[48] This fact reflects the obstacles to the centralization of landownership in a densely populated island. The establishment of a large central required purchasing lands from a multiplicity of owners and entering into contracts with surrounding farmers. The island did not resemble the sparsely populated eastern provinces of Cuba. Because of the decline of the sugar industry after abolition, the island did not resemble the western province of Matanzas either. In contrast to Cuba and the Dominican Republic, Puerto Rico did not import migrant laborers from the neighboring Antilles. The process of proletarianization which had taken place in the coffee-producing highlands in the last three decades of the nineteenth century[49] combined with the decline of coffee cultivation in the twentieth century accelerated a process of proletarianization and migration of landless laborers from the highlands to the coastal lands after 1898.

The problem of land scarcity led U.S. corporations to attempt to grow as much cane as possible on irrigated lands with high yields per unit of land under the direct management of the central. This was the case of the Aguirre Sugar Company in the south coast, which derived 90 percent of the supply of cane for its Aguirre, Cortada, and Machete mills from tierras de administración. The South Porto Rico Sugar Company sought to bypass the problem of shortages of land and cane entirely by importing cane from the neighboring Dominican Republic, but it was unable to consolidate its local landholdings to supply all the cane needed by its gigantic mill. Fifty-six percent of the cane from Puerto Rico ground by Guánica was grown by colonos.[50] Instead of the Cuban pattern of owning more land than the mills were willing to manage and subleasing to colonos, in Puerto Rico sugar mills leased lands from landowners to place them under the direct management of the mills as tierras de administración. The United Porto Rico Sugar Company owned 30,967 acres, the Fajardo Sugar Company 29,240, the Central Aguirre Sugar Company 24,234, and the South Porto Rico 21,275. In addition to these holdings, the sugar companies leased an additional 56,000 acres, controlling a total of approximately 160,000 acres. The four U.S. corporations controlled approximately 24 percent of the cropland in cane farms.[51] Under conditions of land scarcity and plentiful labor, the U.S. corporations developed intensive, irrigated cane agriculture, assigning as much land as possible to direct management by the centrales. Under the management of the corporate mills, lands benefiting from the government-built irrigation works produced high yields in land-scarce Puerto Rico. Colono farms produced 28 tons of cane per acre in 1931–32, while company farms averaged 37 tons per acre, which is more than double the Cuban average of 18.26 tons of cane per acre in that same year.[52] Land scarcity and plentiful labor propelled the corporations to manage as much cane land as possible, to increase yields per unit of land without concern for labor supply, which was plentiful. Nevertheless, 76 percent of the cane lands were owned either by local colonos or local centralistas, which means that approximately three-quarters of all wage laborers were employed by local capitalist farmers or mills, imparting a high Creole inflection to the local struggle between capital and labor. In Puerto Rico as in Cuba, most agricultural workers in the cane fields were employed by native capitalists.

In Puerto Rico, there were far more small colonos who worked solely with family labor than large colonos who employed laborers. Instead of a broad intermediate layer of medium capitalist farmers, tenure was polarized into a small group of large farms and a large group of small farms. The expansion of sugar production led to a process of land concentration, on the one hand, and to a process of formation of a micro-colonato that supplied cane to the mill on the other.[53] Puerto Rican social scientist Esteban Bird described the plight of these small colonos in terms reminiscent of Guerra y Sánchez's portrayal of the small Cuban colonos. Bird, however, avoided grouping the small colonos into a single "class" with large landowners:

> The *colonos* are very important producers from a social point of view. Although probably they are not the most efficient sugarcane producers, and they do not own most of the productive land, most of them are small farmers, bound emotionally to the soil they cultivate, actual toilers of the land. Most of them are the only actual farmers remaining in the cane areas. They and their families live and have their being in the midst of the waving cane fields. They have endured economic pressure from stronger elements in the sugar industry; they have weathered the fury of the tropical hurricanes; they have survived economic depressions, credit stringency, and a downward price trend for over a decade. The small *colono* is the romantic figure of individualism in an industry controlled by a handful of corporations or powerful partnerships.
>
> While farming to the sugarcane corporation is merely a manufacturing business, it is a way of living for most *colonos*.[54]

The expansion of the sugar mills in an island with high population density and numerous smallholders led to the incorporation of the small farmer into the sugar economy as a supplier of cane to the sugar mills. The number of these petty farmers was large but their production very small. The majority of colonos in Puerto Rico worked their lands with their families.[55] After three decades of expansion of sugar production, by the 1930s a clear landowning structure had emerged. On the one hand, a large number of small farmers produced cane in farms sufficiently small to cultivate only with family labor. At the other pole, large farms produced the bulk of the cane using wage labor in the planting and harvesting of the cane (see Table 5.4).

Table 5.4. Area and Production of Farms Growing Sugarcane, by Size of Farm, Puerto Rico, 1934–1935

Size of farm (cuerdas in sugarcane)	No. of Farms		Area in Farms		Area Planted to Sugarcane		Estimated Production	
	Farms	Percent	Cuerdas	Percent	Cuerdas	Percent	Tons	Percent
0.01–3.00	3,486	45.2	27,253	3.5	5,566	1.9	100,882	1.1
3.01–6.00	1,329	17.2	25,847	3.4	6,277	2.1	115,441	1.3
6.01–10.00	839	10.9	26,271	3.4	6,904	2.3	131,997	1.5
10.01–25.00	989	12.8	49,031	6.4	16,090	5.4	330,454	3.7
25.01–50.00	472	6.1	54,487	7.1	16,932	5.7	376,251	4.1
50.01–75.00	175	2.3	28,094	3.7	10,855	3.6	250,815	2.8
75.01–100.00	104	1.4	25,649	3.3	9,136	3.1	220,926	2.4
100.01–200.00	144	1.9	43,680	5.7	20,365	6.9	514,480	5.7
200.01–499.99	111	1.4	66,090	8.6	33,457	11.3	928,976	10.3
500.00 and over	59	0.8	421,409	54.9	171,337	57.7	6,070,190	67.1
Total	7,708	100	767,811	100	296,919	100	9,040,412	100

Source: Sol L. Descartes, *Organization and Earnings on 130 Sugar Cane Farms in Puerto Rico, 1934–35* (San Juan: Bureau of Supplies, Printing and Transportation, 1938), 11.

The expansion of sugar mills in densely populated areas with preexisting land fragmentation opened possibilities for cash crop production to a large number of farmers who would have otherwise dedicated their land to food crops or cattle. When the Fajardo Sugar Company built a mill in eastern Puerto Rico in 1900, it encountered local conditions that were very different from those of the newly exploited sugar lands of eastern Cuba. Land was occupied and fragmented. The sugar mill bought some lands, obtained leases from the larger landowners, and built railroad lines throughout the district which enabled the small landowners to turn to the farming of cane. The majority of the lands purchased belonged to preexisting *haciendas azucareras* with outdated milling equipment.[56]

> The practice is to buy some of the larger estates lying in the immediate vicinity, to secure long term leases, usually from five to fifteen years, from the owners of the other large estates adjoining, and to make cane grinding contracts with the owners of small outlying farms. The centrale then constructs railroads at its own expense through this territory—a main line, with spurs running off to the more remote estates and up the valleys and mountains. Each day cane cars are placed on sidings conveniently near the various cane fields, and each day, hauled away, loaded, to be ground. Thus the owners of large plantations find as convenient an outlet as if they had mills of their own, while owners of small farms find a ready and equally convenient market for as much cane as they are able to raise.[57]

The construction of a central sugar mill required a large investment of capital in machinery, railroads, and sometimes wharves. Before financing a large mill, investors searched for a guaranteed stable supply of cane. In the case of Central Francisco in eastern Cuba, this was achieved through land concentration in the hands of the sugar mill and the development of a class of tenant farmers whose contracts specified the terms of delivery of cane. But under the conditions of scarcity and fragmentation of land in Puerto Rico, the sugar mills did not enjoy such latitude. Sugar mills had to control at least some of the lands to assure themselves a minimum supply of cane and to negotiate the terms of delivery of the cane to the mill by the colonos. Lack of ownership of a minimum amount of cane lands could potentially expose sugar mills to cartelization by the colonos and an increase in the price of cane. Sufficient amounts of cane lands under the control of the central enabled the mills to begin and to continue grinding cane while negotiating the price with the independent farmer. If a farmer asked for prices which the central considered too high, his cane was left standing, waiting to be ground at a later date. To organize competition among suppliers of cane, the central needed to assure itself of a minimum of cane under its direct control. A sugar mill, therefore, did not need to own all the cane lands in its vicinity, but it needed to own some. The management of the Fajardo Sugar Company expressed the need to own some land as follows:

It is not necessary for a centrale to own all the land required for its supply of cane, nor is such a method practised, but it should own a certain percent, to insure against failure in case the planters of the lands accessible to that centrale should divert them to the production of cattle, or fruit, or tobacco, or some other product, which they would be very apt to do, should the low price of sugar, or a change in tariff rates, or any one of many other causes make the production of something else more profitable. Previous to 1900, a great deal of land now planted in sugar-cane was used for grazing, because, owing to the tariff rates, it was very profitable to raise cattle for export to Cuba and the French and English West Indies; and this might well happen again. We can very well imagine circumstances where, although there might be a fair profit in the raising of sugarcane, there would be much more in the production of something else, so that the colono, with no capital invested in expensive machinery and with absolutely nothing to lose by the change, might stop supplying cane to the factory at any time, leaving it stranded with a great amount of capital invested in machinery, building and railroads, and with no cane to grind, bankrupt.[58]

Most cane farms were small micro-enterprises, but most cane was not grown on small farms. Large landowners were integrated into sugar production as colonos, while a process of differentiation polarized landownership. Small farms of peasant households were subdivided to heirs and became even smaller. The number and total area occupied by farms of 0–19 acres increased between 1900 and 1930. At the other pole, large farms of over 500 acres became larger through the absorption of middle-sized farms of 100 to 499 acres. A double dynamic of land concentration at the upper pole and land fragmentation at the lower pole reduced the number of middle-sized farms.[59] As in Cuba, the majority of the rural proletariat was hired by local employers, not by the U.S. corporations. The substantial colonos of Puerto Rico employed large numbers of wage workers. The locally owned sugar mills, which produced more than half of the sugar in Puerto Rico in the 1930s, ground cane from tierras de administración or from colonos.

Central Guamaní of the Cautiño family in Guayama owned 8,400 acres. Only 2 percent of its cane was grown by colonos. Central Caribe in Salinas, owned by the Godreau family, owned 4,000 acres and ground cane from a handful of farms, most of them controlled by the Goudreau family itself. Central Mercedita of Ponce, owned by the Serrallés family, owned 12,700 acres of land in Juana Díaz and Ponce. Twenty-two percent of its cane was grown by colonos. Central Lafayette, located in Arroyo, owned 10,300 acres. Although only 19 percent of its cane was grown by colonos, the mill purchased cane from approximately two hundred farmers. In Central Victoria in Carolina, about 60 percent of the cane was grown by colonos. Twenty-five percent of the cane of the small Central Vannina in Río Piedras was grown by colonos, in addition to cane grown on the mill's 3,900 acres of land. The Roig family of Humacao owned 12,500 acres of land which produced most of the cane processed in the family mills. In Central Eureka, a locally owned enterprise, a fourth of the land was planted by colonos. In Central Igualdad of the Ramírez de Arellano and García Méndez families, most of the cane was produced on farms owned by large colonos who were close relations of the mill owners. In the north-central coast of the island, between Bayamón and Arecibo, colonos played a major role and all mills were locally owned.[60] Agricultural laborers in all of these cases worked either for native colonos or native centralistas. But in either case, the employer was not a foreign corporation. In the north coast west of Canóvanas and in the west coast of Puerto Rico, all sugar mills were owned by native centralistas or native corporations. Agricultural workers were employed by native capitalists, whether native centralistas or colonos of these locally owned mills. Thus, despite land concentration in the hands of the big four (Aguirre,

Fajardo, United Porto Rico, South Porto Rico), approximately three-quarters of the agricultural proletariat in the cane industry was hired by native employers.

The existence of a class of very small colonos in Puerto Rico is in part owing to the high profitability of the sugar industry through the tariff advantage of Puerto Rico relative to Cuba. In the early 1930s, Puerto Rican sugar producers were paid more than twice the price received by Cuban producers because they received increasing protection in the United States.[61] These relatively high prices were an incentive for the mills to purchase cane from producers who would have been considered uneconomical in the Cuban sugar economy. Intensive development of cane agriculture in Puerto Rico through increase of cane yields per acre of land and the development of sugar mills in areas that would otherwise be considered unsuitable for large-scale investment are also attributable to the special tariff advantage enjoyed by producers in the island. Sugar mills developed intensive cane agriculture, extended plantings to less productive lands, and incorporated small farmers into the sugar economy as micro-colonos.

In the Dominican Republic the colonato was much weaker than in Cuba or Puerto Rico. The late development of the sugar industry and the extreme concentration of production in the hands of U.S. corporations translated into almost universal control of the cane lands by the mills. The Central Barahona of the Cuban Dominican Sugar Company produced 100 percent of its supply of cane in tierras de administración. The Cuban Dominican company owned another five mills which grew most of their own cane in tierras de administración. Excluding the Barahona mill, in 1930 approximately 878,000 tons of cane were produced by the administration of the Cuban Dominican, 100,000 by dependent colonos on administration land, and 23,000, or about 2 percent, by independent colonos. The cane grown was crushed in four centrales owned by the company. The Consuelo mill processed 466,108 tons, the Quisqueya 147,450, Las Pajas ground 140,292, and the San Isidro mill the remaining 147,450. The fields of Central Consuelo alone produced 600,000 tons of cane in administration lands, of which a considerable supply was sent to the Quisqueya mill for grinding. In Central Boca Chica, the smallest mill of the Cuban Dominican Sugar Company, colonos grew about half of cane on company lands, while the other half was managed by the mill.[62]

Central Romana was the largest producer of cane in the Dominican Republic, supplying more cane than the Romana mill could process. Every year several hundred thousand tons of cane were sent by barge to the Guánica mill in Puerto Rico, which was owned by the same parent company as the Romana mill. The Cuban Dominican mills and the Romana mill of the South Porto Rico Sugar

Company together produced 82 percent of the sugar of the Dominican Republic and grew most of their cane on administration lands. This alone guaranteed that the share of colonos in the production of cane in the Dominican Republic was minimal. But even some of the smaller, locally owned mills grew their cane on tierras de administración. In Central Angelina of the Vicini interests there were only two independent colonos and 90 percent of the cane was grown on administration land. In the Ansonia Mill of Hugh Kelly, 80 percent of the cane was *caña de administración*. Some of the smaller mills, however, had contracts with dependent colonos. In the San Luis mill of the Michelena family, 95 percent of the cane was grown on company land subcontracted to colonos, and in Central Porvenir of Hugh Kelly, the company advanced funds to growers who produced 90 percent of the cane on company lands and were paid for the cane on the basis of its weight. The San Luis and Porvernir mills, however, were relatively small enterprises producing 3.4 and 4.2 percent of the output of the Dominican Republic, respectively. The sugar economy of the Dominican Republic was similar to that of eastern Cuba in terms of the predominance of large mills owned by U.S. capital but differed in that the mills took on most of the cane plantings.

The Spanish Caribbean as a whole made a surprisingly quick transition to capitalist agriculture with large farms employing wage labor predominating. In contrast to the transition to sharecropping in the South of the United States, in the Caribbean cane agriculture experienced a transition to wage labor after abolition. After 1898, the spread of U.S. colonial power in the region fostered even faster development of capitalist agriculture. Sugar production soared as U.S. corporations moved in, purchased existing mills, renewed them, and built new ones in regions previously untouched by cane agriculture. The process of expansion was highly uneven. The industrial processes of crushing cane and extracting sugar from cane juice were revolutionized. Cane agriculture, however, achieved only marginal improvements, and evidence suggests that agricultural yields actually declined in some regions.

The consolidation of land in the areas where it was fragmented by an anterior plantation system was especially problematic. In western Cuba the planters became colonos and retained ownership of land. Because land is not movable and cannot be created by social labor, the concentration of production requires the centralization of smaller capitals. Technological change was slow, and the machete remained the essential hand tool during the harvest. In regions where independent producers of cane survived, the mills had to own at least a minimum amount of land to organize competition among the farmers. Surprisingly, in the newer regions of cane agriculture, where the corporations owned all the land, there emerged a pattern of subcontracting in which cane agriculture was assigned to local producers under strict supervision and contractual obligations to the sugar mill. In specific areas of the American Sugar Kingdom privileged by special tariff concessions, even very small farmers were incorporated into the sugar complex as suppliers of cane. In all areas, however, the bulk of the cane was produced on large farms that hired wage labor, resident and migrant. There were, to be sure, important obstacles to the penetration of capitalism into cane agriculture in the American Sugar Kingdom in the Caribbean. But these obstacles were overcome, not through the generation of noncapitalist relations of production, as in the South of the United States, but rather through a system of subcontracting, flexible production, and just-in-time delivery.

Labor and Migration

The expansion of the sugar industry in the Spanish Caribbean in the twentieth century was so dramatic that it changed the economic balance between regions in each island, established new demographic patterns of settlement, and resulted in the settlement of lands that had hitherto remained largely depopulated. As new regions were opened up to the cultivation of sugar, the demand for labor, particularly in the agricultural phase of the process, which was labor intensive and required dedicated labor during the zafra, propelled workers into the new plantation zones. While the sugar industry experienced expansion everywhere, the supply of labor power for the plantations varied considerably from region to region. Why were workers scarce in some regions and abundant in others? What are the historical differences between the regions? Why was the process of proletarianization more advanced in some regions than others? What is the connection between the availability of labor power in each region and the history of the abolition of slavery? What happened to the slaves after abolition in Cuba and Puerto Rico? Did they become peasants or rural proletarians? How did the presence or absence of an agricultural proletariat influence the patterns of immigration of workers in the different sugar-producing zones? In other words, how was the history of immigration to the plantations of the Caribbean conditioned by the previous history of rural settlement, structure of landownership, and proletarianization in each zone? How did corporate enterprises owned by essentially the same groups of investors react to local preexisting social conditions, availability of labor power, and extent of local ownership of the land? Answering these questions requires looking at the interaction between the powerful corporate interests that irrupted into the Caribbean in 1898 on the one hand, and preexisting social conditions on the other, and will yield some answers to the question of how much the pattern of development was determined by preexisting class structures and not simply by external economic forces or absentee capital.

In Cuba, the expansion of the plantation economy into the eastern provinces of Camagüey and Oriente produced new settlements and advanced concomitantly with the expansion of the railroad network of the island. By the mid-1920s, the eastern provinces caught up and surpassed the traditional western regions of sugar cultivation in total sugar output, so that the center of gravity of the sugar industry shifted to the east, away from the traditional locus of sugar cultivation inherited from the period of slavery. The population of the eastern provinces increased at a faster pace than that of the western provinces. After 1912, the labor needs of the Cuban sugar industry, particularly in the eastern provinces, were met with immigrant labor from Jamaica, Haiti, and the British West Indies. In the Dominican Republic, the same process of expansion of the plantation economy occurred, although on a smaller scale. The existence of an entrenched peasantry with possession of land in the context of abundance of land and relatively low population densities blocked the emergence of an agricultural proletariat sufficiently large to meet the demands of the expanding sugar economy. As in eastern Cuba, the completion of the zafra required the yearly importation of foreign labor, which in the Dominican case was composed initially of workers from the eastern Caribbean and after World War I mostly of Haitian workers. The island of Puerto Rico, by contrast, was more densely populated and had a surplus of landless laborers available for work in the plantations. Even during the periods of accelerated expansion of sugar production labor needs were met locally. The expanding sugar mills were unable to employ all the landless workers in the island, and laborers continued to emigrate throughout the period despite the expansion of the sugar industry.

Historically produced differences in social structure between as well as within the islands explain the variability in the supply of labor power. In eastern Cuba and the Dominican Republic labor power was scarce. Puerto Rico, by contrast, was at the opposite end of the spectrum, with an overabundance of local labor for work in the plantations. Everywhere the demand for labor was conditioned by the unchanging nature of the labor process in the harvest and the increased mechanization in the transportation sector with the introduction of portable track, tractors, and trucks. Still, the relatively uniform increased demand for labor power produced by corporate capital across the islands encountered, as in the case of the colonos, local variations in social structure that determined the development of specific class relations in each region. In some areas, peasants had already been dispossessed of the land and landless workers were available for hire. In other regions, independent household production survived, peasants retained access to the land if not outright ownership, and the plantations found it difficult to recruit labor locally. Planters resorted to the importation of migrant laborers to fulfill their needs for labor power. Thus the specific class structures that emerged were a product of the interaction of foreign investment with local social conditions. The plantation proletariat in the islands has a specific history that was constructed in the course of struggle against previous colonial powers. The process of class formation was influenced by the history of the abolition of slavery, which took place at different times and under different conditions in each island, and by the history of the struggles between landlords and peasants in each region of each island, which varied considerably. Slavery and Spanish colonialism disappeared simultaneously in Santo Domingo but not in Cuba or Puerto Rico. The struggles between landlords and peasants took place in a colonial context in Cuba and Puerto Rico throughout the nineteenth century, but in the Dominican Republic it took place in the context of a weak national state that needed peasant support for its intermittent wars with the neighboring Haitian state. The rich histories and local struggles of masters and slaves, landowners and peasants, colonial authorities and revolutionary separatists in each island, and not simply the external relations of insertion into the capitalist world economy, determined the formation of agrarian social classes in the American Sugar Kingdom.[1]

Slavery was abolished in Puerto Rico in 1873 and in Cuba in 1886. In the Dominican Republic, by contrast, slavery had been abolished much earlier, in 1822, as a result of the occupation of the island by Haitian forces under General Jean Pierre Boyer.[2] By the time sugar plantations reemerged in the Dominican Republic in the 1870s, the former slaves and their descendants had become an entrenched peasant class, with possession if not titles to the land. In Cuba and Puerto Rico, however, abolition took place much later and did not result in the elimination of plantations, but rather in their transformation from ingenios to centrales. Emancipation was not accompanied by agrarian reform or land distribution to the former slaves, and slaves did not always become peasants as in other regions of the Caribbean. The fate of the former slaves after abolition poses both theoretical and empirical problems. Theoretical problems revolve around the meaning of abolition to the *libertos*, as many of them continued to labor after emancipation on the plantations where they had once been slaves. Some social scientists who argue for the continuity of plantation life in the Caribbean consider that abolition without indemnification in the form of land grants meant in essence the continuation of extraeconomic coercion.[3] In reality, it signified a transition to free wage labor similar to the process of original accumulation and expulsion of the peasantries from the land described by Karl Marx. After abolition, libertos migrated to the cities, where they became urban workers or joined the service economy, and also to less populated regions, where they could squat on land and obtain guarantees of a subsistence life. How many of the former slaves moved to the cities or to regions where they could become subsistence farmers is still an empirically open question, particularly in Cuba, where a significant movement to the east of the island seems to have taken place. Because the period of slavery has been subject to more studies than the period after emancipation, we still lack a clear representation of the evolution of class relations in the islands after emancipation.

The social structure of the peasantry and the processes of proletarianization in each region of the American Sugar Kingdom developed as a function of a multiplicity of factors: the density of population in the region, the existence or lack of existence of a state capable of guaranteeing a system of land titles and enforcing landowners' rights against squatting peasants, the previous level of integration of a region to the market economy, and the course of the process of emancipation. At the turn of the century Puerto Rico and the western provinces of Cuba had abundant supplies of labor power for the plantations. In eastern Cuba the expansion of the sugar industry outpaced the flow of population from the western provinces, and in the Dominican Republic labor shortages were perennial. In labor-scarce regions, plantations relied increasingly on the importation of *braceros* from other islands of the Caribbean for the sugar harvest. The contrasts between labor conditions in the different regions were a product both of the evolution of class relations in each region in the period 1868–98 and of new conditions created by U.S. intervention and capital investment after 1898.

The availability of land for subsistence cultivation affected the ability of planters to recruit labor. Historically, peasants in the Caribbean have withdrawn from the labor market whenever they have had enough land to guarantee subsistence. Depending on the amount of land at their disposal and on the level of wages, they have combined independent household production with wage labor. Even when the peasants were formally landless, they continued to interact with local ecologies, drawing subsistence as peasants for generations after they began to work as proletarians in the plantations. Because many of the workers on the plantations continued to draw subsistence from lush tropical ecologies where landowners' rights were difficult to enforce—such as the food-rich coastal mangroves—it is difficult to locate in the Caribbean a pure "plantation proletariat."

Even in Puerto Rico, where the process of proletarianization was most advanced, the plantation proletariat retained throughout the twentieth century some access to independent household production even in the absence of land titles. In a study of the Loíza region in Puerto Rico, Juan Giusti found that the boundary between "peasants" and "proletarians" was not fixed:

> Universal rural proletarianization and wholesale destruction of peasant subsistence—assuming it were possible—was not necessarily in the interest of large scale sugar plantation production, for the following reasons: (a) the reproduction costs of the laborer would fall fully upon the wage or (b) the laborer would be able to reproduce his labor only partially, and his productivity would plummet amidst disease, in the end imperiling the existence of the laborer population itself (c) wholesale destruction of peasant subsistence was difficult or impossible to accomplish anyway.[4]

Measuring the depth of the process of proletarianization is thus complicated by the fact that many peasants with land nevertheless worked in the plantation sector, while many landless peasants were able to engage in subsistence and market production despite the absence of land titles. In the region of Piñones in Puerto Rico, a formally landless peasantry continued to engage in subsistence and independent production for the market well into the twentieth century, even though title to the land was owned by various landlords and corporations since the late eighteenth century. Fishing, crabbing, cutting mangrove woods, and charcoal making persisted, in addition to the cultivation of garden crops, so that what appears on the surface as a completely proletarianized labor force drew a considerable share of its sustenance from household production. Plantations came and went, but the peasant community persisted on the land. Since the late eighteenth century, when Piñones and the Loíza region were the *casabe*-producing center of Puerto Rico and the road to Piñones was known as the casabe road, the slaves of the plantations engaged in subsistence activities. In the late nineteenth century a British firm with plantations in Guyana developed the first modern sugar central in Puerto Rico in the area of Piñones. In the early twentieth century, a Spanish/Creole group of investors established the Loíza sugar company. In the 1920s the U.S.-owned Fajardo Sugar Company operated Central Canóvanas, where many of the Piñoneros labored. Throughout the entire period, Piñoneros never worked more than half of the year or derived all of their subsistence from work on the

plantations. The Piñoneros were capable of subsisting in the periods when plantations were in decline and employment as wage laborers was not available.[5]

Conversely, peasants who did have some land also worked on the plantations.
Ownership of land in some cases may act to conceal an underlying process of
proletarianization, and there have been arguments in favor of so-called concealed
proletarianization.[6] It is not easy to determine the amount of land necessary to
shield a peasant family from proletarianization because, as an observer of labor
conditions in Puerto Rico stated in 1905, "it is still possible for a small acreage to
maintain life in the same manner as life was maintained in the island two hundred
years ago."[7] Thus many peasant households had members who worked as proletarians in plantations, and many fundamentally proletarian households retained
some household production well into the twentieth century. Yet despite these
overlaps, it is possible to obtain a sense of the advance of the process of proletarianization from the structure of landholding and the history of migrations in
the region. For though the peasant communities and household production may
have persisted everywhere, labor power for the plantations was not equally available everywhere. In some regions of peasant entrenchment, or of low population
densities, the plantations relied on immigrant workers. The history of this variability in the twentieth century is connected to labor conditions in the last three
decades of the nineteenth century.

Agrarian Transformations, 1868–1898

The epoch of slavery came to a close in two stages and through two distinct
processes in the island of Cuba. In the eastern provinces, most slaves acquired
their freedom in the course of the Ten Years' War of Independence (1868–78).
Slavery and plantation agriculture declined rapidly in Camagüey and Oriente, the
centers of the insurgency. Camagüey, a cattle-raising area then known as Puerto
Príncipe, and the province of Oriente, an area of smaller sugar mills and much
small-scale farming then known as Santiago, lost slaves rapidly during the war.
These two provinces were the center of the anticolonial struggle, which caused
the destruction of many plantations and the liberation and migration of many
slaves.[8] By 1877, the slave population of Camagüey was only 15 percent of what it
had been in 1862, and that of Oriente declined by 74 percent in the same period.[9]
In the western provinces, however, where the plantation system was more developed, slavery persisted and sugar production prospered. Matanzas, Santa Clara,

and Pinar del Río retained a higher percentage of slaves than Santiago de Cuba or Puerto Príncipe. The uneven impact of the Ten Years' War by region had the effect of intensifying the geographical concentration of slavery in those regions with a more developed plantation economy. Whereas Matanzas and Santa Clara had 46 percent of Cuba's slave population in 1862, by 1877 they had 57 percent.[10] Slavery was decimated in the two eastern provinces in the course of a colonial revolution demanding national sovereignty. The reconcentration of slavery in the western provinces left the task of emancipation in the hands of the Spanish colonial state, which assumed it in the interest of the preservation of Spanish sovereignty over Cuba.

The abolition of Cuban slavery in its western bastions took place administratively between 1880 and 1886. Unlike Haiti, where slavery was abolished in the course of a revolution, or the United States, where it was abolished in the course of a civil war, the moderate process of abolition in Cuba never threatened the social or political power of the planter class. An apprenticeship system known as the *patronato* attempted to eliminate slavery gradually and to bring about a transition to free labor while retaining the plantation as an institution and avoiding the radical process of emancipation which ended slavery in the eastern provinces during the Ten Years' War of 1868–78. Emancipation may have been conceived in one fashion in the minds of the colonial administrators and planters, but in practice it unfolded in the context of a struggle between planters and slaves over the conditions of abolition. Both attempted to use the process to advance or defend their positions, and this early struggle established many of the parameters of the future social life of the libertos. On the one hand, slaves accelerated their path to freedom through self-purchase, flights, lawsuits, and negotiations. Within the first year of the patronato 6,000 slaves obtained their freedom, followed by another 10,000 in the second, 17,000 in the third, and 26,000 in the fourth. Of the almost 200,000 slaves in Cuba in 1877, by 1883 there were but 99,566 *patrocinados* in the registers and by 1885 just 53,381.[11] More than 100,000 slaves gained their freedom before final abolition in 1886. Their determined struggle to accelerate abolition sealed the pipeline to freedom and rendered emancipation irrevocable.[12] On the other hand, Cuban slaves never heard even the promise of forty acres and a mule. Ownership of land by Afro-Cubans remained very limited, and those slaves who remained on the plantations did so principally as wage workers. The census of 1899 enumerated 26,000 "colored" men and women who worked in agriculture in the province of Matanzas, but only 537 farms were owned or rented by people of color, occupying less than 4 percent of the agricultural land. In Cuba as a whole, by

1900 only 1 percent of the land planted in cane had colored owners, while colored renters occupied a mere 4 percent.[13] The initiation and administration of the process of abolition by the colonial state from above meant that it lacked the mobilization that accompanied the Civil War in the United States after the Emancipation Proclamation, which W. E. B. Du Bois characterized as "the general strike."[14] In the province of Matanzas, only 6.6 percent of all landowners were black or mulatto, and only 20 percent of all renters were people of color.[15] Slavery disappeared in the absence of a social revolution, and the plantation remained a central institution of the Cuban economy as the social system of the ingenio evolved toward the system of central sugar mills after abolition. Despite the movement of slaves to the eastern provinces to escape proletarianization, most slaves became wage workers.[16]

Slavery departed from the Cuban landscape, but the plantation did not. For the former slaves, freedom did not signify access to land but dispossession in a sudden transition to wage labor. Libertos attempted to escape proletarianization by moving to areas that offered the possibility of engaging in independent household production. Santiago received a large influx of former slaves who settled there as subsistence farmers. In the plantation heartland of western Cuba, however, the colono system began to develop. In the aftermath of a process of abolition which had conquered only very precarious rights for Afro-Cubans, former planters continued to own their plantations, white farmers became owners or renters of the subdivided sugar lands of the planters, and blacks became workers on the lands of the farmers as well as those of the ubiquitous planters. The developing central system entailed a separation of the industrial process of sugar milling from the agricultural task of sugar growing, in contrast to the earlier ingenio system, in which the planter controlled harvesting and grinding operations. A process of differentiation of the planter class ensued, in which success meant the acquisition of a central mill, and decline meant closing the old mill and becoming a colono who took cane to the neighboring centrales. Through this process, many former owners of ingenios became colonos, sometimes dividing their plantations and leasing land to farmers who produced cane for the mills. To retain laborers, landowners allocated small areas of land for food crops to former slaves. Afro-Cubans were not successful in this process because most lands remained the property of whites, particularly in the western province of Matanzas, but this was also true in Havana, Puerto Príncipe, and Pinar del Río. In Santa Clara, most people of color labored for wages, but there were 2,737 farms with colored owners or renters in 1899, or about 11 percent of the number of workers in agriculture. In

Santiago 30 percent of the people of color working in agriculture were small owners or renters. Both Santiago and Santa Clara had a history of smallholding by free people of color before abolition.[17]

Thus the end of Cuban slavery brought about some economic changes but also lack of change and continuity in other respects. The central aspect of emancipation in Cuba was the lack of compensation to the slaves, or even the promise of compensation or agrarian reform. This produced enormous pressures toward rural proletarianization, from which many libertos tried to escape by moving to areas where they could become peasants engaging in independent household production, or by moving to urban areas where they could work in the service sector as urban rather than rural proletarians. The labor force that remained on the plantations was semipeasant in appearance because of the allocation of small amounts of land in usufruct for small-scale production but actually proletarian in the sense that the usufruct and residential rights were conditional upon wage labor in the new centrales and colonias. The end of Cuban slavery granted a new mobility to the former slaves, who began to move away from the core regions of the ingenio economy into the areas with the best possibilities of landownership or squatting, such as Oriente. The geography of Oriente made squatting difficult to control and large-scale plantations did not yet have a monopoly of the land. In Oriente many slaves and their descendants had the greatest opportunity to obtain access to small plots of land with or without titles to engage in independent household production.[18]

The displacement of the black population away from the province of Matanzas into Oriente is associated with the attempts of the libertos to reconstitute themselves as a peasantry and thereby escape proletarianization.[19] The province provided extensive lands for squatting and a tradition of smallholding by colored people. This movement of population to Oriente to obtain lands for subsistence production was accompanied by an expansion of sugar production in the province, from 6 to 17 percent of Cuban output from 1864 to 1899. By 1899, 34 percent of the planted land in Oriente was allocated to sugar. Yet the combined acreage devoted to corn, bananas, potatoes, yams, and manioc surpassed that of sugar and made Oriente the most agriculturally diversified of all the Cuban provinces.[20] The lands of Oriente were contested terrain, offering an internal frontier for the development of a reconstituted peasantry made up of former slaves, on the one hand, and fabulous opportunities for plantation development, on the other.[21] The contest between peasants and plantations continued throughout the twentieth century, right down to the revolution of 1959, whose initial social base were the *precaristas* of Oriente, semipeasant squatters who worked part of the year as proletarians on the plantations.[22] Cuba's immense eastern province functioned as a haven to libertos seeking to move away from the plantations. In the twentieth century it also served as a frontier to the newest, most technologically advanced, and best capitalized plantations of the island. The acquisition of immense amounts of land by U.S. corporations in the early twentieth century altered the balance between small farmers and the large estates in eastern Cuba. The area of Oriente under cultivation in 1899 (205,761 acres), for example, was smaller than the land owned by the Cuban American Sugar Company's Chaparra-Delicias plantation complex in 1919 (331,600 acres).[23]

Abolition ended the strict association between slavery and plantation labor. In 1877 72 percent of the workers in the ingenios of Cuba were slaves, 11 percent were Asian contract workers, mostly Chinese coolies, and another 16 percent were free workers. As abolition approached, planters sought a variety of solutions to the problem of labor, including the use of prisoners assigned by the state to the plantations. Mills contracted groups of 50, 100, and even 150 prisoners, who were paid twelve gold pesos a month, of which nine went to the treasury, two to a special fund, and one to the contracted laborer. Workers toiled from dawn to dusk, except Sundays, Good Thursday and Friday, Corpus Day, and Immaculate Conception Day, with an hour for the morning meal and two hours at midday for rest. As a result of the failure of planters to pay even these wages to their laborers, a Royal Order of July 30, 1887, abolished the contracting of prisoners to the plantations.[24]

In 1886, a report of the Círculo de Hacendados to Madrid estimated that there were 45,000 whites, 30,000 Asians, 100,000 free blacks, and 25,000 patrocinados (slave "apprentices" in the process of transition to freedom) working in the sugar plantations of Cuba. During the tiempo muerto those employed earned between fifteen and twenty-five pesos a month without meals, and during the zafra wages ranged between twenty-five and forty pesos a month. Plantations began using tokens redeemable only at the ingenio store for payment to both black and white workers, and the rigors of the contract labor system were applied to peninsular Spaniards and Canary Islanders as well as Asian laborers. Peninsular workers had greater means of resistance because of their legal status as nationals under the Spanish colonial system. Galician workers who toiled under extreme duress, for example, revolted and were able to avoid being sent to the plantations, in violation of their contracts. Peninsular Spaniards, who came to Cuba in increasing numbers after 1880, were treated by the colonial authorities as a superior stratum of colonial society, despite their generally low level of literacy and skills.[25] As slavery disappeared, Cuban planters attempted to extend coercive measures to other workers through the system of contract labor and through payment in scrip. But the shortages of labor also generated movements of seasonal migration of Spanish workers. Between 1882 and 1890 145,912 passengers entered Cuba while only 91,768 left, leaving a balance of 54,144. The records of entries to and exits from the Cuban ports indicate seasonal fluctuations that coincide with the beginning and end of the harvests.[26] The complex scenario of the late 1880s and early 1890s thus includes the development of new responses to the labor scarcities generated by abolition: experiments with penal labor, extension of the contract labor system, introduction of payment in scrip in the plantations, and seasonal peninsular migration. At the lower end of the spectrum of the colonato, workers toiled with their families essentially as agregados and were paid by the amount of cane they delivered. Agregados received plots of land for food production under agreements that required their employment in cane agriculture for wages during the zafra. The statistics on the number of farms rented and owned by people of color in Cuba in 1899 indicate, however, that a sharecropping class equivalent to that of the cotton South of the United States never developed. Afro-Cubans owned few cane farms, and they rented far too few to constitute a sharecropping class. The general tendency in the Cuban countryside after abolition was toward Afro-Cuban proletarianization. In 1899, 77.9 percent of all black and mulatto males and 36.6 of the black and mulatto women in the province of Matanzas were classified as laborers.[27]

By the early 1890s Cuban agriculture had made a successful transition from the ingenio to the central system, the division of labor between industry and agriculture had advanced considerably, the planter class had experienced a process of differentiation and was polarizing into centralistas and colonos under the system of division of labor, while the class of slaves suffered a sudden transformation into an agricultural proletariat, with some peasant adaptations. The process of proletarianization was already advanced at the time of the U.S. occupation of the island. In 1892 and 1894 the Cuban sugar harvest surpassed one million tons. Despite complaints by centralistas and colonos about lack of liquid capital and credit, which undoubtedly sent many ingenio owners under, the system of sugar plantations as a whole made a successful transition to wage labor. And despite the flight to other provinces and to Havana, the bulk of the rural proletariat was composed of former slaves. Patrocinados received wages of three to four pesos a month during the period of transition to freedom, while free workers received fifteen to twenty pesos. After final abolition planters had to pay more to attract workers to the plantations. For many planters accustomed to the privileges of extraeconomic coercion, the transition was difficult, particularly because of the lack of operating capital and the primitive state of the credit system in Cuba. For the libertos, the reality was even harsher, as the euphoria of emancipation gave way to the stark reality of proletarianization. This resident proletariat, however, was not sufficient to fill the needs of the expanding plantation economy. More than nineteen thousand seasonal workers from Spain and the Canary Islands came to Cuba every year. Arrivals increased in the months of September to November, just before the commencement of the zafra, and ceased in March. Emigration peaked in May at the end of the harvest.[28] Between 1882 and 1894, approximately seven thousand of these workers settled in Cuba every year.[29] The increase in the volume of the harvests was accompanied by supplementing the existing supply of labor power, composed of former slaves who now labored for wages, with immigrant labor from Spain. This influx of workers helped planters avoid the rise in Cuban wages which labor scarcity would have otherwise provoked.

The brief but substantial prosperity of the sugar industry from 1890 to 1894 was driven by the liberalization of tariffs and increased trade with the United States. The destruction caused by the war of 1895–98 interrupted the expansion of the sugar industry and caused a catastrophic population decline in some plantations zones. The labor force was able to lend much greater logistical support to the insurgents during the Second War of Independence than the slaves had been able to provide during the Ten Years' War. As Rebecca Scott has noted, "Once they had moved into the sugar zones, the insurgents could count upon estate populations for various kinds of informal support—a crucial change since the Ten Years' War."[30] Workers in the sugar mills were able to join the insurgency, and in some instances members of the insurgent forces were hired during harvest time.[31] The Spanish policy of *reconcentración* forced the rural population to move to concentration camps in the cities in an attempt to eliminate the base of support for the anticolonial insurrection in the Cuban countryside. The Cuban revolutionaries targeted many plantations for destruction. The Spanish retaliated and targeted the peasantry with their policy of reconcentración. These two processes devastated the Cuban countryside. At the time of the U.S. occupation of Cuba in 1898, the island had already made a successful transition to a new plantation system based on centrales, colonos, and wage laborers. The destruction caused by the war devastated many Cuban planters and opened the field for U.S. investors to take their place. The reconstruction of the Cuban plantation economy after 1898 began through the restoration of the productive system that was already in place before the devastation of 1895–98 and through the establishment of new U.S.-owned mills.

The Dominican Republic had a totally different class structure at the end of the nineteenth century. The central characteristic of the Dominican rural class structure was the widespread availability of land for household production. The strength of the Dominican peasantry was a product of three historical processes whose impact extended well into the twentieth century. Since the late eighteenth century, low population densities and the development of extensive cattle ranching, which functioned as a food-producing complement to the Haitian slave economy, guaranteed a low level of social differentiation in the countryside. The Haitian occupation of 1822 abolished slavery and carried out a policy of land redistribution, further strengthening the peasantry. Intermittent border wars with the neighboring republic of Haiti throughout the nineteenth century forced the Dominican state repeatedly to raise peasant armies, which had to be compensated with land grants. The combination of these three processes enabled the small peasant farm anchored in subsistence production to survive into the twentieth century as the main unit of economic activity in the Dominican Republic.

The collapse of the sugar plantation economy of Saint Domingue as a result of the Haitian Revolution meant the collapse of the market for the cattle of Santo Domingo. During the first half of the nineteenth century, mahogany became the main export of the Spanish portion of Hispaniola. The Haitian occupation of 1822–44 ended slavery and occasioned an emigration of the European ruling classes, which were concentrated around the capital city of Santo Domingo. Under the Haitians and subsequently after independence in 1844, Santo Domingo became a society of subsistence farmers and petty commodity producers. The Haitian policy of land redistribution stimulated commodity production in the Spanish-speaking part of the island, and the integration of the island under a Haitian government introduced absolute private property in land along the pattern existing in the French-speaking portion of the island.[32] There was relatively little socioeconomic differentiation among the peasantry and no clearly demarcated class relations in agriculture. Control over these petty producers was exercised commercially, principally by the foreign import-export houses based in Santo Domingo and Puerto Plata. A chain of credit and imported goods extending from the foreign merchant houses to the wholesalers and from these to the retailers, and a chain of commodities originating in the peasant farms and moving to the small towns and from these to the ports, passing through the hands of the middlemen, organized the linkages of this society of petty commodity producers to the outside world.[33] In the south of Santo Domingo, mahogany cutting was controlled by large landowners. In El Cibao, mahogany, as well as the tobacco farms, were controlled by peasants. El Cibao became the demographic as well as economic center of Spanish-speaking Haiti (1822–44) and of the Dominican Republic (1844–).[34]

There were no large-scale sugar plantations comparable to those of Cuba or Puerto Rico in Spanish-speaking Haiti or in the Dominican Republic until the last third of the century.[35] The strength of the Dominican peasantry and the correlative weakness of the landlord class blocked the development of large-scale, commercial agriculture. Small-scale tobacco cultivation for export took place on farms in combination with subsistence production. The peasant units were able to retrench into subsistence production when foreign trade was interrupted. The resilience of household production in peasant units and the widespread availability of land were formidable obstacles to proletarianization. The abolition of slavery by the Haitian state and the ever-present border conflict with it made it difficult to introduce extraeconomic coercion in agriculture. After independence from Haiti in 1844 the Dominican state was forced, time after time, to acknowledge and protect the peasant farm as the main form of economic organization, against the best interest of real or potential landlord classes. The repeated invasions by the Haitians required for their repulsion the creation of peasant armies and the distribution of lands to the soldiers. The ubiquitous small peasant plot created an internal political balance that did not permit a transformation of existing social relations.[36] The state had to rely on the support of the peasantry to repel the repeated Haitian invasions, which in turn forced it to protect and expand the peasant farm as a form of economic organization. The independent peasantry expanded, blocking an alternative path of development based on extraeconomic exploitation of the peasants by a landowning class. This situation blocked the development of a coherent Dominican ruling class and eventually led the richest interests of the republic, led by General Pedro Santana, to seek a solution by handing over the sovereignty of the state to Spain in 1861. Spanish colonialism in the Dominican Republic was quickly repelled during the War of Republican Restoration. El Cibao, the region where the independent peasantry was most deeply entrenched, served as the center of the anticolonial war. During the war, the Haitian state provided material support to the Dominicans, served as the outlet for tobacco exports from El Cibao, and provided a channel for the importation of weapons. The war ended in the expulsion of the Spanish in 1865, served as a measure of strength between the peasantry and their would-be landowners/rulers, and consolidated the historical association between the cause of Dominican sovereignty and the independence of the small peasant farm.

If the Haitian revolution strengthened the free peasantry of the Spanish-speaking part of Hispaniola, the weak ruling classes during the first and second republics (1844–61, 1865–1916) failed to dispossess it. Sugar plantations developed as minute islets in a vast peasant sea. The sugar industry emerged during the last third of the nineteenth century as a result of the first Cuban War of Independence (1868–78), which caused the emigration of planters from Cuba to the Dominican Republic. The effects of the United States Civil War on the plantations of Louisiana and of the Franco-Prussian war of 1870, which involved the major beet producers, provided a favorable international context for the development of plantation agriculture.[37] The mills established by the Cuban planters were concentrated in the south and the east of the republic. They were not based on slave labor but rather on the labor of semiproletarian peasants and on sharecroppers and independent farmers who sold cane to the mills.

Plantation development caused a slow shift of the economic center of gravity of the republic from the tobacco- and cocoa-producing region of El Cibao and its corresponding main city and coastal port, Santiago de los Caballeros and Puerto Plata, back to the capital city of Santo Domingo.[38] The recurrent struggle between plantations and peasants unfolded under conditions unfavorable to the plantations, which faced problems of labor shortages and lack of labor discipline. In the British Caribbean, the establishment of a peasantry had tended to follow the abolition of slavery in 1838 when former slaves began operating as independent farmers on unused Crown lands. In the Dominican Republic, in contrast, a fairly substantial *campesinado* existed before the establishment of the sugar plantations of the late nineteenth century.[39] In a precocious interpretation of the struggle between plantations and peasants, the Puerto Rican social scientist Eugenio María de Hostos conceptualized the crisis caused by low sugar prices in 1884 in the Dominican Republic as an expression of a deeper problem involving the struggle between two opposed forms of agriculture, one based on large estates and the concentration of wealth and the other based on small farms and the widespread distribution of land.[40]

Within the economy of the Dominican Republic the sugar sector remained comparatively small relative to Cuba or Puerto Rico. In 1884, there were thirty-five sugar mills in the republic, occupying 175 caballerías of land under cultivation and including space for factories and machines. There were fifty-five hundred national workers, some five hundred foreign workers, and two hundred machinists and skilled sugar workers.[41] Scarcity of labor was the paramount problem facing the plantations in the late nineteenth century. In the early phase of the sugar economy, planters sought to remedy labor shortages with immigrant labor.

The scarcity of labor was related to the availability of land in a country with low population density and a basically nonexistent system of land titles. In the 1870s the Dominican Republic had a population of between 150,000 and 200,000 inhabitants and the lowest population density of any island of the Caribbean. In the 1880s, the Dominican mills attracted mostly local peasants who sometimes worked for daily wages but preferred piece wages. The clearing of forests for cane cultivation was carried out by peasants under a system of piece wages. Once established in the tasks of clearing forests, the cane farms continued to use piece rates. Monetary inflation in the 1880s and the decline of local food production resulting from the abandonment of the peasant *conucos*, in response to the relatively high wages the planters had to pay to attract workers, caused an increase of food prices. Fresh meat was replaced by imported salted beef and salted codfish in the diet of the workers. Increasing food prices and indebtedness to storekeepers who insisted on being present on pay day and collecting the debt of the workers caused a decline in real wages for these workers and a retrenchment of the peasants to their small farms.[42] These semiproletarianized peasants had the alternative of returning to household production and did so increasingly in the 1890s. Only high wages could attract them away from household production into the ingenios. According to an analysis by Michiel Baud, "the problem with the Dominican sugar plantations was that they made labor a commodity but could not effectively separate workers from the means of agricultural production. The unforeseen effects of the situation did not suit the planters at all. Scarce population and open land resources forced the planters to pay high wages, higher than ever because of fierce competition among the *ingenios*."[43]

Although native laborers worked in the mills and fields, planters began to find the cost of labor power prohibitive. Planters were forced to compete with each other for a limited supply of labor power, which was neither abundant nor cheap, raising wages and reducing the profitability of the mills. This violated one of the principles of plantation development, which is that labor must be both abundant and cheap.[44] After 1890 the Dominican crop began to rely increasingly on immigrant labor.[45] Workers who migrated to the sugar zones of the Dominican Republic soon became integrated into the local peasantry and abandoned wage labor.[46] Initially, planters attempted to solve the problem of labor scarcity by importing Canary Islanders and a few hundred Puerto Rican peasants as temporary workers. Juan Serrallés, who owned Ingenio Puerto Rico in the Dominican Republic, imported Puerto Rican workers in the 1890s.[47] Increasingly, the mills of the eastern Dominican Republic began to rely on migrant workers from the eastern Caribbean, principally from St. Thomas, St. John, St. Kitts, Nevis, Anguila, St. Martin, and Antigua. At the beginning of the twentieth century, these workers were the principal labor force in the mills of the Dominican Republic. Approximately forty-five hundred workers arrived in San Pedro de Macorís every year for the zafra[48] and continued to work in the cane fields through the 1930s. During World War I, the Dominican industry began to recruit increasing numbers of Haitian workers for the harvest, a pattern that increased with time until Haitians became the principal labor force in the industry.[49] By 1910, sugar was the primary export of the Dominican Republic.[50]

Puerto Rico was characterized by an overabundance of labor in the early twentieth century. Its peasantry experienced a dramatic process of proletarian-ization relative to the Dominican Republic in the last decades of the century. The percentage of cultivated land devoted to export crops increased steadily all through the nineteenth century at the expense of local food production, from 29 percent in 1830 to 68 percent in 1899.[51] In the first half of the nineteenth century, sugar produced by slaves was the principal export of Puerto Rico. Sugar growth peaked around 1840 but continued to be the main export until mid-century. The plantations were already in deep decline when slavery was abolished in 1873. The expanding plantations from 1800 to 1850 devoured the choice lands of the coast and displaced the *hateros* and the *estancieros* of the coastal valleys toward the interior highlands of the island. The exodus from the lowlands to the highlands propelled the colonization of the internal mountainous frontier of Puerto Rico, where the peasants sought to reproduce the small-scale subsistence agriculture that had previously supported them in the coastal lands. Although the emergence of plan-tations on the coast of Puerto Rico opened a market for foodstuffs sold by the peasants to the plantations, peasant agriculture remained anchored in subsistence production. The highlands acquired population, but land resources remained essentially open, producing a scarcity of workers for hire in Puerto Rico. The countryside had "*mucha gente, pocos trabajadores.*"[52] In the coastal valleys, sugar plantations could not rely on the labor of *jornaleros*, who, as Francisco Scerano wrote, were characterized by their "high cost and notorious absenteeism. The cost factor reflected the scarcity of supply, as only the prospect of very high wages could lure peasants away from their subsistence plots, even temporarily, for the demanding work of cane harvesting."[53] The Jornalero Law introduced by the colonial government in 1849, which remained in effect until 1873, was in effect a passbook system designed to block customary access of peasants to land and forcing them to register for salaried work. The very fact that such a regulation was established indicates that socioeconomic conditions were characterized by the absence of a viable labor-market. So long as peasants had available land for subsistence, the sugar estates could not obtain a reliable supply of wage workers. The internal frontier provided peasants an escape route from the constrictive expansion of the plantations. The late development of plantation slavery in Puerto Rico (1800–1850) reflected the inability of plantations to constrain the life of the surrounding peasantries when land resources were open. Peasant colonization of the interior highlands set the foundations for the coffee export economy of the second half of the nineteenth century, which was centered in the central and western mountainous regions.

Coffee was the ascendant crop in the second half of the nineteenth century.[54] Though it was originally a small farm crop, the commercialization of the product eventually led to land concentration, differentiation among the peasants, and the development of a class of *hacendados*. From 1870 to 1898, coffee production expanded steadily and proletarianization advanced in the highlands. In the 1850s, there were few jornaleros in the highlands of Puerto Rico. In the municipality of Lares, for example, only 52 jornaleros were registered in 1852, but by 1870 there were 2,210. Coffee planting expanded, the population of the highland *municipios* increased, the usufruct rights of agregados deteriorated, and the number of jornaleros increased. The emergence of a market for land signaled the closure of the epoch of open land resources. By 1885, a clearly demarcated class structure had emerged in the coffee-producing municipalities and coffee plantations began to hire immigrant labor from the coastal municipalities. Rising coffee prices caused an increasing demand for labor. Despite an increasing landless population, wages rose and proletarianization continued to advance from 1885 to 1898. This was the golden age of the Puerto Rican coffee hacendados.[55] In the coastal zone, abolition without land grants for the slaves produced proletarianization. Andrés Ramos Mattei describes the situation of the workers in the coastal cane fields as one of "sharp divorce from the means of production." The North American invasion only completed the transition to the massive incorporation of a pauperized labor force in need of work.[56] In the 1890s, this proletarianized labor force was already seeking employment outside the island. In 1894, for example, 888 Puerto Ricans were reported to have migrated to San Pedro de Macorís for work in the sugar mills.[57] Located at the opposite end of the spectrum from the Dominican Republic, the agrarian class structure of Puerto Rico featured an advanced degree of proletarianization at the moment of the U.S. occupation. When tariff changes affected the coffee region negatively soon after the U.S. invasion, thousands of workers migrated from the coffee highlands to the expanding cane fields of the coast, and the sugar industry was able to expand without having to rely on immigrant labor from elsewhere in the Caribbean. Barely months after the U.S. occupation of the island, workers from the coffee zone began to move to urban slums surrounding the coastal towns of Puerto Rico.[58]

Agrarian Transformations, 1898–1934

The differences in agrarian social structure inherited from the nineteenth century persisted and became accentuated during the U.S. colonial period. The extension of the plantation economy in Cuba and the Dominican Republic accentuated the need for immigrant labor. In Puerto Rico, by contrast, the same process of expansion of the centrales did not produce significant importation of immigrant workers. Instead, the surplus of labor power in Puerto Rico was so significant that it permitted the expansion of sugar cultivation even as the island exported labor to other regions of the Caribbean and the United States. The shortage of laborers in Cuba, by contrast, was acute, and U.S. sugar corporations considered it the main obstacle to the expansion of sugar production. A representative of the Atkins sugar interest stated, for example, that the essential problem of the Cuban sugar economy was the scarcity of workers: "Cuba's great problem is that of Labor supply."[59] In the Dominican Republic, the expanding sugar mills of San Pedro de Macorís, La Romana, and Barahona became dependent on the importation of braceros for the zafra, which was carried out with immigrant labor from the eastern Caribbean and Haiti. Higher population densities, an inherited land tenure structure characterized by an advanced process of differentiation of the peasantry at the time of the U.S. occupation, and direct control of the insular government by U.S. colonial administrators accelerated an already advanced process of rural proletarianization in Puerto Rico, which resulted in the emergence of a large landless population. This population was sufficiently large to cover all the labor needs of an expanding sugar industry while reserves of unemployed and underemployed rural proletarians kept the wages of those lucky enough to find employment in check. This particularity of the Puerto Rican plantation economy is all the more significant in that the island's sugar producers, who were protected by U.S. tariffs and received a much better price for their sugar than those of Cuba or the Dominican Republic, nevertheless paid the lowest wages to local laborers in the industry. At the heights of the sugar economy, the profitability of sugar mills depended to a great degree on the sugar tariff. The price of labor power, however, was primarily a function of the local supply of workers.

Labor Immigration into Cuba

The island of Cuba was characterized by great regional uneven development and immense variations in the availability of labor power for the sugar harvests. In the western provinces and especially in Matanzas, there was a resident labor force in the plantations. The scale of the mills in the sugar industry, the pattern of land-holding, and the persistence of the independent colonato were all conditioned by the preexisting ingenio system. The transformation that took place at the level of industrial capital from ingenio to central was mirrored in agriculture as a transition to the colono system and at the level of the direct producers as a progression from slavery to wage labor. The scarcity of labor power in the eastern provinces was a product of a different history marked by de facto abolition during the Ten Years' War, open land resources, and low population densities. As the railroad made entire sections of the east accessible in the twentieth century, U.S. sugar corporations acquired vast tracts of land, cleared the forests, and initiated sugar cultivation where none had previously existed. Small hamlets were absorbed by newly emerging company towns, and the new centers of population began to increase in size as a result of immigration from nearby towns, from other regions of Cuba, and from abroad. Internal Cuban migration continued, the west continued to lose laborers, but the east never had enough. Between 1900 and 1925 the province of Matanzas lost approximately eighty thousand inhabitants, principally to Havana. The Cuban historian Juan Pérez de la Riva argues that this population could have supplied the deficit of labor power in the eastern provinces if it had chosen to migrate to the eastern plantations.[60] Instead, the movement to the neighboring cities of Matanzas and Havana was stronger than the movement to the more distant east. The internal movement of population from the older plantation heartland to the east did not suffice to fill the void of laborers in the booming eastern plantations.

The vast extension of land newly planted in cane in the eastern provinces required more cane cutters than were available locally in Cuba. Immigration from the eastern Caribbean, Haiti, and Jamaica took off around 1912. Centrales Morón in Camagüey and Delicias and Chaparra in Oriente alone required ten thousand cane cutters.[61] The sugar plantations of the United Fruit Company in eastern Cuba imported laborers from Jamaica, where the same company had extensive holdings in banana production.[62] The flow of seasonal immigrants increased during World War I, slowed down and was even banned for a while after the sugar crash of 1920, picked up again in the mid-1920s, and slowed down again during the Great Depression of the 1930s. In 1919 at the height of the Cuban sugar boom twenty-four thousand Jamaicans arrived along with ten thousand Haitians. In April 1920 the Jamaican press, which circulated among the Jamaicans employed or unemployed in the Panama Canal Zone, reported that mills in Cuba were paying a minimum of $2.70 per day and larger amounts for skilled labor.[63] After the sugar crash of October 1920 some of these laborers became redundant. By November 1920, there were over 10,000 Jamaicans in Cuba wishing to return to their island because of the fall in wages that resulted from the drop in sugar prices. Many of these workers stayed at various mills, which gave them plots of land for subsistence farming during the off-season. In the early 1930s the number of Jamaicans still living in Cuba was estimated at between 60,000 and 63,800.[64]

Estimates of the numbers of immigrant workers who went to work yearly in Cuba vary considerably, for several reasons. The figures for arrivals and departures from the different Cuban ports are not always reliable and show some discrepancies. For example, the demographic calculations of Juan Pérez de la Riva suggest that many Haitians arriving in Cuban ports were listed as North Americans because of Haiti's status as an occupied U.S. colony from 1915 to 1934. The records show that between 1919 and 1931 803,177 "North American" passengers arrived and 684,417 departed from Cuba, leaving a migratory balance of 118,760, but the census of 1931 reported only 7,195 U.S. residents in Cuba. Since the difference of 111,565 persons cannot be exclusively explained as a result of mortality, de la Riva argues that it is a result of the migration sponsored by the U.S. authorities in occupied Haiti.[65] Mills were supposed to be responsible for repatriating the workers at the end of the zafra and had to post a bond with the Cuban government when importing foreign workers. But many of the workers stayed in the mills or went to work in the coffee and tobacco harvests after the termination of the zafra. Some of the largest mills were able to obtain special presidential permits to import workers. Cuban president Mario García Menocal was a large absentee colono of the Chaparra Sugar Company. García Menocal had a presidential "chalet"—a mansion, in fact—in the lands of Central Chaparra near Puerto Padre,[66] which no doubt facilitated the processing of permits to import immigrant workers for all the mills of the Cuban American Sugar Company.

The records of the Cuban American Sugar Company for 1924 suggest that the migrant population was composed mostly of young adult males. The company's records of arrivals and departures indicate the presence not only of Jamaican and Haitian workers but also of workers from the eastern Caribbean. On August 15, 1924, the steamship *Vedette* took 112 Grenadians, 233 Barbadians, and 162 St. Vincentians on a return voyage from Puerto Padre after the conclusion of the zafra. On September 2, in a trip to the eastern Caribbean the Dutch ship *Nueva*

Altagracia took 11 workers to Anguila, 36 to Antigua, 97 to Dominica, 37 to Montserrat, 18 to St. Kitts, 10 to St. Thomas, and 34 to St. Martin. The *Nueva Altagracia* took group of 30 *antillanos* to the eastern Caribbean on October 24: 4 to St. Vincent, 11 to Grenada, 2 each to Montserrat and Antigua, 3 to Barbados, and 4 to Curaçao. The records of the company show the shipments and destinations of the workers after the zafra, their gender, and their ages. With few exceptions, the workers were male, although a few female workers appear in the records: "Christophina Hinds and her daughter Anita" are listed in the records of a ship returning to St. Thomas. "Frances Quailey and 2 children" returned to St. Kitts in the same voyage. A voyage of the ship *Angelita* to the eastern Caribbean featured an all-male cargo with 42 workers ages sixteen to twenty, 105 workers ages twenty-one to twenty-five, 64 workers ages twenty-six to thirty, 10 workers age thirty-one to thirty-five, and 11 workers ages thirty-six or older.[67]

Acute shortages of labor sometimes propelled sugar companies to produce fantastic schemes that did not always materialize to supply themselves with a labor force. The management of the Cuba Cane Sugar Corporation considered the importation of Chinese contract workers during World War I. Plans were laid for importing two thousand Chinese from Hong Kong under a five-year contract. The workers were to be paid $50 a month for a seven-day workweek made up of ten-hour workdays, and the importing company, Guy M. Walker of 61 Broadway, would receive $100 for each Chinese worker delivered at the port of Havana. They were to be housed in "barracks as good as the best now furnished to native Cuban labor of like kind." The contract stipulated that "said laborers shall receive no wages while sick or for holidays or for any other days in which they voluntarily abstain from working and that except when sick and unable to work the said laborers shall have charged against their allowance for rations the sum of thirty cents (30 c.) gold for each day that they so abstain from working." Provisions were made to handle "any Chinese laborer imported under this agreement [who] shall prove to be a troublemaker or otherwise undesirable." A committee made up of a representative of the Cuba Cane Sugar Corporation, one from the importing firm, and, in case of disagreement, a third member appointed by the American consul would decide on the case of troublemakers. "If the cause of complaint shall not be found to be well founded the laborer shall continue in his contract, but if the complaint against said laborer shall be found to be supported by fact he shall be deported and the Sugar Company shall be no longer liable for or on account of said laborer." The plans included provision for Chinese national holidays and stipulated that the workers "may worship their own gods in their own manner."[68] Difficulties of coordination between the U.S. Food Administration, which regulated sugar importing and refining firms during the war, the Cuban government, the importing firm, the Cuba Cane Sugar Corporation, and the Chinese exporters caused the suspension of the project.

In Central Francisco in southern Camagüey, labor shortages were perennial. Francisco was established in 1899 and began production in 1901. The corporation was established by sugar refiners of the McCahan refinery in Philadelphia in conjunction with Manuel Rionda through the purchase of approximately forty-five thousand acres of land in southern Camagüey, about midway between Santa Cruz and Manzanillo. The title to the property included the lands of the town of Guayabal, which at the time of foundation of Central Francisco included sixty "common Cuban Country houses and 400 inhabitants."[69] Access to Francisco, which was located in a remote region along the southern coast of Camagüey with sparse population density, was restricted to the weekly visits of small steamships to the pier of the mill. The central owned all lands surrounding the sugar mill. Colonos were enticed to settle as tenants of the mill. Labor was accommodated in barracks around the mill yard or batey and was always scarce. The company's minute book recorded that

> to secure the necessary labor in former years, permission was given to parties to erect Huts or Houses in our lands at Batey. This has proven troublesome and its correction was decided on. Thirty-six of the structures have been bought and rented to the laborers by the Company. Nineteen new and better houses have been built; a new and combined stable and dwellings; New Barracks for Rural Guards; and four (4) large buildings (know as Baracons) each capable of accommodating sixty (60) laborers were built one at our Wharf and one at each of our three cane divisions.[70]

In 1906, a revolt in Cuba led to complaints by the management of labor shortages. The U.S. intervention of 1906–9 brought both fears and great improvements to Central Francisco. As the minute book stated, "The United States being again in control of the Island, it is hoped that disorder and marauding will be at an end, but we fear, that a greater scarcity of labor to harvest the coming crop, will result from the recent outbreak."[71] As it turned out, the U.S. intervention of 1906 was extremely beneficial to the Francisco Sugar Company because it resulted in the construction of a rail line from Francisco to Martí at government expense, connecting Francisco to the railroad network of Cuba. The minute book concluded:

> The Cuban revolt during the summer of 1906, made clear to the American Provisional Government our rather isolated situation in case of needed pro-

tection and the visiting members of our Executive Committee, together with
the President and our Manager, called on Governor Magoon at Havana last
Spring and submitted to him very full our situation and desires for suitable
action. Governor Magoon has since placed officially on the program of roads
to be built by the State, a road from our Wharf to Martí, a station of the
Cuban railroad, a length of about 30 miles and includes culverts and bridges
(over the Sevilla river to be a steel bridge), the expense of the entire work, to
be paid by the Cuban Government which it is estimated will cost $400,000 to
$650,000.[72]

The Francisco mill was an isolated outpost in sparsely populated countryside,
relying on colonos who were tenants of the mill and on seasonal labor that lived in
the barracks built by the corporation. The problem of labor shortages was related
to the availability of land for subsistence farming in the sparsely populated east,
the existence of haciendas comuneras, and the low population densities. In the
eastern part of the island frontier conditions and open land resources made
subsistence farming an alternative and blocked the formation of a permanent
rural proletariat. The subdivision of the administration lands to dependent colonos prevented the centralization of all labor under one management and the
consequent danger of unionization. During World War I, Francisco began to
import West Indian workers at the expense of the company. The wage workers
were allotted by the central management to the dependent colonos who hired
them. In their drive to avoid the independent colonato the eastern mills encountered the new problem of the shortages of labor typical of regions with low
population densities and available lands for subsistence. This situation in turn
generated an organized drive to recruit immigrant labor for the harvest from
regions of the Caribbean where land was less abundant or less available and where
there existed, therefore, a landless rural proletariat. Central Francisco paid for the
importation of foreign workers, but it allotted them to its dependent colonos.

Demographic calculations of the migratory balance are complicated by the lack
of exact knowledge of the ages of the workers who stayed in Cuba, which hampers
the approximation of mortality rates. Many of the seasonal workers who stayed in
Cuba and never returned to their home countries of Haiti, Jamaica, or the eastern
Caribbean did so clandestinely and after a while integrated into Afro-Cuban
country life, which presents a further obstacle to calculating their exact numbers.
Official figures for Haitian migration to Cuba from 1912 to 1931 are 184,598
(Haitian figures) and 190,255 (Cuban figures). Other estimates are that from 1915
to 1929 Haitian migration to Cuba numbered 200,468. Between 1912 and 1927 the

Table 6.1. Haitian Emigration to Cuba, 1915–1929

Year	Migrants	Year	Migrants
1915	23,300	1922	10,250
1916	4,900	1923	20,100
1917	10,200	1924	21,500
1918	11,300	1925	23,000
1919	7,300	1926	21,600
1920	30,700	1927	14,000
1921	17,600	1928–29	5,500

Sources: Suzy Castor, *La ocupación norteamericana de Haiti y sus consecuencias* (Mexico: Siglo XXI, 1971), 83; Franc Báez Evertsz, *Braceros Haitianos en la República Dominicana* (Santo Domingo: Instituto Dominicano de Investigaciones Sociales, 1986), 44.

province of Camagüey alone received 200,000 braceros from other islands of the Caribbean, but the number who returned to their home countries is unknown. Between 1920 and 1931, 186,393 Haitians and 114, 806 Jamaicans entered Cuba, but the number who returned to their home countries is uncertain.[73] Between 1916 and 1920, 10,685 Chinese migrated to Cuba, despite a decree of June 13, 1917, that banned Chinese immigration.[74] Although Haitians, Jamaicans, West Indians from the eastern Caribbean, and Chinese workers migrated to Cuba to work on the plantations, the largest immigrant group in Cuba was Spanish. Most Spanish immigrants, however, moved into the urban trades and the retail sector. In the west of Cuba, where there was a resident labor force, sugar mills complemented their local supply with some Spanish workers.[75] Although the largest immigrant group into Cuba was Spanish, among immigrant plantation workers the Haitians were the most numerous, representing approximately 40 percent of all immigration to Cuba from 1912 to 1930 (see Table 6.1).

By the late 1920s, Cuba had a population of slightly over three and a half million and a labor force of nearly a million workers. Approximately half of the labor force worked in agriculture and fisheries and of these the largest number, or 396,294 persons, worked in the sugar industry. Of these workers, 380,746 worked in the sugar plantations and 15,548 in the factories and yards. In 1927–28, the provinces of Camagüey and Oriente absorbed approximately 225,000 workers, or approximately two-thirds of the labor force in the sugar industry, and produced 56 percent of the sugar. "A quarter of a century ago," according to the director of the Department of Immigration, Colonization and Labor of the Cuban Ministry of Agriculture, the eastern provinces "hardly produced any sugar at all, and were among the more thinly populated parts of the country: Nor did they receive large influxes of slave population in earlier days. They are now therefore unable to supply the numbers of workers required. Recourse is had to immigration."[76] In good years between 40,000 and 50,000 immigrants arrived for the sugar season. In a bad season the number of immigrants was lower and the number of sending countries was reduced. Approximately 17,500 workers from Jamaica and Haiti, but mostly from Haiti, arrived for these seasons. Computing these numbers was complicated because in practice it was difficult to distinguish between the more permanent immigrants into Cuba and the circular migration or *migración golondrina*. At the termination of each sugar harvest, there was always an unemployment crisis, which was alleviated through employment in the sowing and sorting of tobacco and employment in public works, which the government endeavored to carry out at the end of the zafra.

Wages varied by region. In 1913, when the influx of immigrant workers was barely beginning, labor was both more abundant and more expensive in the west, reflecting the competition for labor between centrales and colonos in a conjuncture of fabulous sugar prices. Wages varied considerably according to the region and the sizes of the mills. In 1913, field wages were lowest in Pinar del Río at 92 cents per day and highest in Camagüey at $1.17 per day. In Havana and Matanzas, field wages averaged $1.01 a day. In Santa Clara and in the province or Oriente field wages averaged $1.07 a day. Wages were higher for mill workers, and the regional variation differed from agricultural wages. Mill wages were highest in Havana at $1.27 per day and lowest in Matanzas at $1.15. In Pinar del Río wages for mill workers were $1.20, in Santa Clara $1.17, in Camagüey $1.22, and in Oriente $1.17. Wages also varied according to the sizes of the sugar mills. In the smallest mills, ranging in production from zero to five thousand tons of sugar yearly, field wages averaged 89 cents a day. In mills ranging in production from five to ten thousand tons, field wages averaged $1.08 daily. In the mills with sugar production ranging from ten to twenty thousand tons yearly, daily wages averaged $1.04, in mills with output of between twenty and forty thousand tons wages in the field averaged 1.05, and in the mills with output of over forty thousand tons, field wages stood considerably higher than in other mills at $1.23. At the top, the largest, most productive mills paid the highest field wages; at the bottom, the smallest mills paid the lowest wages.[77] During World War I, wages increased. A colonial officer observing Puerto Rican labor conditions in 1919, where excess supply of laborers prevented the rise of wages, noted that "a Cuban worker in the sugar industry gets $2 for a 9 hour day and the Porto Rican worker only $1 or 75 cents for a 10 or 12 hour day."[78]

After the collapse of sugar prices following the Danza de los Millones and the continuation of sharp competition in the international sugar market in the 1920s, wages declined and remained depressed throughout the decade. The reduction in wages was attributed to the decline in sugar prices and justified as "apparently the easiest means of meeting the competition of other sugar-producing countries."[79] The reality was that the importation of workers into the eastern regions had generated some permanent settlement of a rural proletariat in the estates and that increased labor availability was beginning to drive wages downward in the eastern mills. In 1926, the Cuban government ordered a restriction of output in the mills in an attempt to restore sugar prices, and after that date employers used the restriction to explain the continuation of depressed wages. In 1928–29 the immense majority of the workers in the sugar industry (96 percent) worked in the fields at piece rates and were paid for every one hundred arrobas of cane cut or loaded. Wages varied regionally, depending on the supply of labor in each province, and individually, depending on the physical capacity of the workers under the system of piece wages. The importation of field workers into Camagüey and Oriente depressed wages in the eastern provinces and tipped the regional wage scale toward the west. In 1913, average field wages in Camagüey and Oriente were the highest in the Cuban sugar industry. In 1928, they were the lowest. In Santa Clara and Matanzas the average field wage was $1.00, and in Havana and Pinar del Río wages for agricultural laborers averaged $1.20 per day. Thus the large importation of immigrant workers to the eastern provinces did produce a shift in the wages, depressing them below the level of the western provinces, even though the gigantic mills of the east were of more recent construction and the lands more productive. The system of piece wages extended the wage disparities depending on the physical ability of the worker. Field workers earned between 65 or 70 cents a day (Oriente) and 1.60 pesos a day, according to their skill and industry.[80]

The settlement of immigrant workers in the eastern province solved some of the most acute labor shortages. Haitian laborers, for example, were atypical in that they created cohesive, stable communities that were geographically stable.[81] Immigrant communities also displayed varying patterns of skill and employment. The least literate of all the workers were the Haitians. Spanish workers were in an intermediate position in literacy but were able to move from plantation labor to urban trades and retail through an extensive kinship network which Cubans referred to as *sobrinismo*, that is, the employment of Spanish "nephews" in businesses owned by their relatives. Jamaicans were the most literate and skilled group. Knowledge of the English language opened possibilities of employment as foremen and supervisors capable of mediating between the rural laborers and management in the U.S.-owned mills. Many Jamaican women were also employed as urban domestics in middle-class residences.[82]

Labor Immigration into the Dominican Republic

The incorporation of Puerto Rico into the U.S. customs area and the preferential tariff rate granted Cuba in 1903 put the Dominican sugar industry at a disadvantage. Not satisfied with the wages offered by the sugar farms, many workers who labored in the plantations returned to their conucos to pursue subsistence farming. These workers had never been fully proletarianized and remained anchored in peasant subsistence production, which offered them the possibility of rejecting the low wages offered for agricultural labor and pursuing instead an independent livelihood based on household production. The semiproletarian character of the native Dominican labor force pressed sugar mills to seek alternative sources of workers for the industry through the importation of foreign field hands.[83]

The Dominican sugar industry relied primarily on immigrant labor. The abundance of land and the lowest population density in the Greater Antilles blocked the creation of a stable labor market.[84] Sugar plantations discovered a basic fact known to entrepreneurs in all previous Caribbean plantation systems: "Free men will not work as employed agricultural laborers if they have access to land which they can cultivate for themselves."[85]

The largest plantations in the Dominican Republic obtained land through the conversion of the customary system of pesos comuneros into private property in land. The uncertainty of land titles and the predominance of customary rights in the Dominican system of land tenure led the United States military government to carry out the first thorough cadastral survey in the history of the country during the military occupation of 1916–24. Corporations were able to manipulate the uncertainty of land titles to obtain land at the expense of the peasantry. As Calder put it, "Peasants faced with sacrificing their land to pay a lawyer, the courts, and other expenses, were probably well advised to sell immediately."[86] The land-grabbing feast was by no means a peaceful process. It created a peasant guerrilla war in the eastern region of the country, which lasted from 1917 to 1922. This guerrilla war stands, along with the campaign against Augusto César Sandino in Nicaragua, as the major military involvement of the United States in Latin America in the twentieth century. Sometimes the corporations used private as opposed to state violence to expel peasants from the lands. The South Porto Rico Sugar Company's subsidiary in the Dominican Republic, the Central Romana estate, burned to the ground two peasant hamlets, El Caimonal and Higueral, which stood in the path of its expanding fields. The company made no provisions for the 150 families left homeless.[87]

The displacement of the peasants pressured them to turn wage labor. The acquisition of large latifundia had the double purpose of guaranteeing land for the sugar mills and expelling the peasantry, altering the social balance in specific regions and intensifying the pressure toward proletarianization. According to the Dominican sociologist Wilfredo Lozano, the discrepancy between the amount of land owned by the South Porto Rico corporation (144,000 acres) and the amount planted in cane (24,000 acres) reflects the attempt to increase the tension impelling peasants toward wage labor. Underuse of land by the corporation affected the peasantry and was aimed at provisioning the mills with an adequate reserve of labor. What was true of Central Romana applied to the entire industry. Barely 28 percent of all lands were actually under cultivation, another 18 percent was used for cattle grazing. Overall, 52 percent of the land under the ownership of the mills was left idle. Land underuse, according to Lozano, was an indicator of "the social nature of the latifundia, in so far as it assigns over half of its land to unproductive use; evidently, what this achieved was a social effect, to the degree that it fragmented and constrained the life of the surrounding peasant settlements."[88]

Despite the pressures toward proletarianization generated by the expansion of the cane-growing latifundia, Dominican mills were unable to secure a stable local supply of labor power. Access to *terrenos comuneros*, state lands, and municipal lands, as well as the lack of regulation of landed property, continued to provide the Dominican peasantry with land for subsistence.[89] The North American mill owner William Bass argued in 1902 that local conditions in the Dominican Republic hampered the development of the sugar industry. The natural fertility of the country, the lack of sufficient population, and the availability of unclaimed virgin lands allowed the "inferior classes" to live without having to search for employment in the principal "modern" enterprises.[90] Since the 1890s, immigrants from the eastern Caribbean had provided the main labor force in the eastern sugar mills of the Dominican Republic. Mills sent agents to the eastern Caribbean to recruit workers, and workers also arrived of their own volition seeking employment on the plantations. Until the U.S. occupation of 1916, these workers, known derisively as *cocolos* in the Dominican Republic, constituted the main labor force in the industry. The Dominican social scientist José del Castillo estimates that approximately 4,400 cocolos entered San Pedro de Macorís for the harvest of 1902–3. As a result of legislation established in 1912, the government began to keep records of immigrant workers, who had to register with the authorities upon arrival. From 1912 to 1920, an average of 4,885 immigrant workers came to labor in the annual harvest, for a total of 39,090 workers. During the period 1921–28, a yearly average of 6,778 braceros arrived to perform labor in the plantations, for a

Table 6.2. "Colored" Braceros in the Dominican Republic, 1921

Origin of "Colored" Braceros in the Dominican Republic	Number	Percent of Total
Haiti	10,124	46
British Caribbean	7,865	36
French Caribbean	1,621	7
Dutch Caribbean	1,279	6
Danish	355	2
Americans (U.S. Virgin Islands)	646	3
Americans (Puerto Rico)	218	1
Other	13	0
Total	22,121	100

Sources: José del Castillo, *La inmigración de braceros azucareros en la República Dominicana, 1900–1930* (Santo Domingo: Centro Dominicano de Investigaciones Antropológicas, 1978), 52–53.

total of 40,668 persons. These numbers reflect the registered braceros. The total number of workers who arrived outside the official channels is unknown. The migratory balance is not clear because the figures for returns at the end of the harvest are not specified. In 1921, residence permits were granted to foreign "colored" workers in the Dominican Republic. The results indicate that Haitian immigration had replaced the immigration of cocolos as the principal source of workers for the industry (see Table 6.2).

Under the U.S. military occupation, the importation of Haitian braceros increased. Of the 22,121 braceros who were granted permits in 1921, 36 percent did not specify the mill or colonia at which they worked, although 43 percent reported working in the mills of San Pedro de Macorís, 10 percent in La Romana, 5 percent in Santo Domingo, 2 percent in Puerto Plata, and 1 percent in Azua, Bajabonico, or Yaguate.[91] The U.S. military governor, Thomas Snowden, banned the emigration of laborers from the Dominican Republic through executive order 278 in 1919. In theory, mills were required to pay for the return voyage of migrant workers at the end of the zafra, but executive order 259 of 1919 banned immigrant workers from requesting those funds before the termination of the harvest. These measures were aimed at guaranteeing a stable supply of workers for the mills. Other measures stigmatized colored workers and contributed to their degradation, making it increasingly difficult for these workers to overcome the superexploitation to which they were subjected in the Dominican mills. Executive order 372 of December 1919 banned the immigration into the Dominican Republic of braceros of any race other than the "Caucasian" and required that nonwhite immigrants obtain a permit within four months of arrival to remain in the country.[92] The majority of the workers in the industry were "colored" foreigners who, under these rules, had to register with the colonial authorities to remain in the country, providing the state with a regulatory power it had not had before.

Immigration from the eastern Caribbean continued until the late 1920s. After that date, the Dominican sugar industry used principally workers from Haiti in the sugar harvest. In 1937, the Trujillo government carried out a massacre of Haitian workers. Estimates of the number of victims range between twelve thousand and thirty thousand. Although the workers in the sugar mills were not the principal victims of the massacre, the killings and the stigmatization of Haitians contributed to the progressive degradation of the condition of mill workers in the Dominican Republic.[93]

Puerto Rico's Labor Surplus

The hurricane of 1899 and the loss of the protected Spanish and Cuban markets devastated the coffee producers of Puerto Rico. The devaluation of the Spanish currency, shortage of credit in the initial years of the U.S. occupation, and the introduction of colonial taxation further aggravated the plight of the smaller coffee farmers. The crisis of the coffee industry generated a movement of laborers from the highlands to the coast in search of employment in the expanding sugar farms. The depth of the nineteenth-century process of proletarianization in the coffee industry became apparent after 1898. A colonial report of 1901 described labor conditions in Puerto Rico: "The dense population, the small area, the inadequacy of employment for all under present conditions, and the comparative scarcity of food effectively combine to prevent immigration of working people, any particular reports to the contrary notwithstanding."[94] The sugar industry expanded continuously until the 1930s, but it was always able to find enough workers, and even during periods of accelerated expansion labor needs were met locally. Puerto Rico is an exceptional case in the Spanish Caribbean in that it never had to import immigrant labor to complete the sugar harvest. On the contrary, from early on the island exported workers even when demand for labor power in the sugar industry was on the increase. In 1900, Puerto Rican workers were recruited to work in the Hawaiian plantations. More than five thousand workers left for Hawaii in 1900–1901. In 1903 the commissioner of labor of Hawaii described the Puerto Rican workers who arrived to work on plantations as "mostly people from the coffee country of their own island, who had been starved out of the mountains when that region was devastated by the hurricane of 1899. This was

Table 6.3. Population Densities in the Spanish Caribbean

Country	Area in Square Miles	Population in 1900	Population Density in 1900 (persons per square mile)	Population in 1930	Population Density in 1930 (persons per square mile)
Cuba	42,804	1,573,000	37	3,838,000	90
Dominican Republic	18,704	700,000	37	1,400,000	75
Puerto Rico	3,515	953,000	271	1,552,000	442

Sources: Country areas are from *Rand McNally Cosmopolitan World Atlas* (Chicago: Rand McNally, 1987), 225, 227; population figures are from Nicolás Sánchez-Albornoz, *The Population of Latin America: A History* (Berkeley: University of California Press, 1974), 169.

followed by a year of idleness, semidependence, and mendicancy in the coast country before they left for Hawaii. They were half starved, anaemic, and, in some cases, diseased."[95] The island also exported laborers to Cuba, the Dominican Republic, Yucatán, and Panama. In 1913 the Arizona Cotton Growers Association recruited workers in Puerto Rico for the cotton harvest.[96] For population densities in the Spanish Caribbean, see Table 6.3.

The already advanced process of proletarianization was accentuated by the policies of the colonial government, which deepened the process of proletarianization through a controversial tax on land. The Hollander Bill introduced in 1901 functioned in effect as an expropriating mechanism for the farmers of Puerto Rico. Tax levies denominated in U.S. currency in a context of currency devaluation and loss of the protected coffee markets forced many owners to sell land. The Hollander Bill stipulated that all landed property had to pay a 1 percent tax on the assessed value of each farm. The process of appraisal of land prices was controlled by the U.S. colonial governor, who appointed all tax assessors. Contemporaries observed that in colonial Puerto Rico, the U.S. democratic tradition of assigning land appraisal functions to elected municipal authorities was violated.[97] Complaints of high appraisals for taxing purposes were matched by lower prices at the time of actual sale. A typical farmer, therefore, was taxed on the basis of a land appraisal that represented the capitalized value of the expected rent once land was turned into capitalist farming. In a society in which subsistence farming was an important component of all agricultural sectors, the effects of the Hollander Bill were understandably devastating for Puerto Rican proprietors.[98] The introduction of colonial taxation and of property assessment under the control of the colonial governor produced widespread public opposition on the part of the largest landowners of the island. Assembled in a *"magna asamblea de propietarios"* in San Juan on February 2, 1901, the large landowners deliberated on possible courses of action against the colonial imposition. The prospect of inclusion in the customs area of the United States, which guaranteed the prosperity of the sugar industry, dissuaded the landowners from pursuing any further opposition. Soon, their protests dissipated, canceled by the desire to gain free access to the U.S. market. Professor Félix Córdova Iturregui of the University of Puerto Rico characterized the conflict around the tax bill as follows: "The law created an immense dust cloud which seemed to be the product of the movement of a large army. But once the dust settled, the combatants had disappeared."[99]

Colonial taxation had a double effect. On the one hand, it increased supply in the market for land and accelerated the process of land concentration. On the other hand, it ruined many small farmers, forcing them to seek employment as proletarians in the expanding coastal sugar lands. The coffee zone was devastated by the new tariff structure and production declined in the first years of the U.S. occupation, forcing many already proletarianized highlanders to seek alternative employment on the coast. Proletarianization advanced concomitantly with land concentration, creating both the necessary land concentration and the labor force necessary for the new centrales. The North American anthropologist Sidney Mintz described conditions in the early years of the twentieth century:

> Although the conditions of life on the south coast haciendas were exceedingly rough at the turn of the century, they were apparently much less so than those which prevailed in the highlands. It is not surprising, therefore, that highland workers came to the coast to fill the need for cheap labor engendered by the expansion of the cane lands.
>
> The migrants from the highlands were mainly farmers and sharecroppers of Spanish ancestry. They had lost their lands because of the hurricanes, the exorbitant rates of interest, and the loss of the European coffee markets.[100]

The descent of thousands of farmers from the highlands produced an inexhaustible supply of laborers,[101] guaranteeing a multiplying labor force to the expanding sugar estates.[102] In 1901, a report of the U.S. Department of Labor stated that "a fact which impresses the observer of labor conditions in Porto Rico is the great excess of labor of the lowest grade."[103]

World War I accentuated the shortage of labor in Cuba and the Dominican Republic because of the conjuncture of high prices and increasing demand. In 1913, agricultural workers in the cane farms of Puerto Rico were paid at the rate of $0.47 per day, whereas in Cuba wages ranged from $0.92 in Pinar del Río to $1.17 in Camagüey.[104] Workers believed that Puerto Rico's special status as a protected territory under the customs area allowed employers to pay wages at least equal to those of Cuba. Although wages rose everywhere, toward the end of the war wages in Cuba were still approximately twice as high as in Puerto Rico. Cuban agricultural wages that year were reported to be $2.00 for a nine-hour day, but in Puerto Rico they ranged between $0.71 and $1.00 for a ten-to-twelve-hour day.[105]

Even at the height of the good prices and high demand for agricultural labor in 1919, labor conditions in Puerto Rico, as described by Joseph Marcus, were characterized by an excess of labor power for the plantations:

> The general complaint of laborers interviewed was that many people were coming down from the hills and cutting the wages down.
>
> Many coffee laborers, when the season is over in December, move to the coastal districts, which brings them just in time to participate in the cutting and grinding of sugar cane. Not all, of course, are able to do so for a good many reasons; and if large numbers of them were to come down they could not expect to find work as there are sufficient workers in the cane regions.[106]

Marketplace bargaining power favored employers and was extremely adverse to workers. Workers attempting to organize against low wages were easily replaced, and labor agents knew specific regions of the island where labor power was abundant. According to Marcus, "The presence of thousands of unemployed in the island at all times provides a ready supply of labor wherever a strike is declared, for if labor is not available immediately at hand an agent is usually sent to another district and men are brought in by the trainload." Workers interviewed by Marcus, a researcher for the U.S. Department of Labor, stated that "in order to keep the price of labor down, the company imports laborers from the hills, who are willing to work for 50 cents a day."[107] Organizers for the Federación Libre del Trabajo had to face severe obstacles because of the surplus of laborers available for work in the plantations.

> Some of the men directing the work of the federation in various parts of the island, and who were interviewed, appear to be well posted on labor conditions and wages paid in the neighboring islands where products similar to those of Porto Rico are produced. That the price of sugar, for instance, is now higher than it ever was before is a matter of common knowledge, and it is their belief that the employers in Porto Rico could well afford to pay better wages than those of Cuba, for instance. The Cuban sugar or tobacco producer has to pay duty on shipments to the United States, while the Porto Rican ships his products free.[108]

The tariff advantage enjoyed by sugar producers in Puerto Rico did not translate into better wages for agricultural labor. While the price of sugar was determined by international competition and conditioned by the tariff, wage rates answered to local supply. The surplus of labor power in Puerto Rico continued into the 1930s, even though the granting of U.S. citizenship to Puerto Ricans in 1917 opened the possibility for free emigration of workers to the United States.[109] In the east of the island, semiproletarian tobacco farmers alternated between work in their tobacco *vegas* and work in the sugar harvest. In the west of the island, migrant laborers alternated between the sugar and coffee harvests.[110] Everywhere in the island, women, men and children produced garments in the domestic needle industry, which was the only source of income for many working families during the tiempo muerto.[111]

The misery of the rural proletariat resident on the plantations became the object of special attention during the New Deal reforms of the 1930s.[112] The reports of the 1930s emphasized the dependence of the island on food imports and high food costs relative to the wages of workers, in addition to the widespread incidence of anemia and particularly the spread of malaria resulting from the extension of irrigation canals in the southern coast, which provided a perfect habitat for the mosquitoes that transfer the disease. The most graphic representation of the misery of the cane cutters, however, is that of Esteban Bird in his classic work *The Sugar Industry in Relation to the Social and Economic System of Puerto Rico*, published in 1937. Bird calculated the yearly wages of cane cutters and their average family size and spread the income to cover the tiempo muerto. He concluded that the average cane cutter spent 94 percent of wages on food, and that at this rate the daily budget for food per family member was twelve cents. "Twelve cents per person per day is only four cents more than the food expense required for feeding a hog in the United States!"[113] During the years of the Great Depression, Central Aguirre Sugar Company paid 40 percent dividends on its common stock, with the exception of the terrible year 1929, when it paid a 27.5 percent dividend to its North American stockholders. The extremes of wealth and poverty generated by the plantation economy were most visible in Puerto Rico. Corporate profits soared in an economy protected by an imperial tariff advantage, while the surplus of labor power available to work on the plantations drove wages below the levels of those received by workers elsewhere in the American Sugar Kingdom.

The Twentieth-Century
Plantation

The occupation of Cuba and Puerto
Rico by the United States in 1898 and the gradual expansion of imperial influence
over the Dominican Republic culminating in the occupation of that island by U.S.
Marines in 1916–24 led to an impressive expansion of sugar production across the
Spanish Caribbean. Sugar production for export was not new to the islands. Was
the extension of monocultural sugar production across the Spanish Caribbean an
entirely new phenomenon attributable to U.S. colonialism, or was it a continuation
of trends already in place before 1898? How did the internal class structure of the
U.S.-owned plantations that developed after 1898, and particularly the relations
between the mills and the cane farmers, differ from that of the plantations that had
already developed across the islands after the abolition of slavery but before 1898?
How did the plantations of the American Sugar Kingdom compare with the
postemancipation plantations of Cuba and Puerto Rico or with the plantations
that developed in the Dominican Republic after 1870? Did United States colonialism and the presence of the imperial state contribute merely to the continuation of
secular economic trends, or did it drastically alter the conditions for capital accumulation in the sugar industry? Had the transition to a plantation system based
on wage labor been completed in the islands in 1898? How was this transition

affected by the entrance of the United States into the region in the Spanish-American War of 1898?

These questions have direct relevance to the study of underdevelopment by outlining how local conditions, local differences in class structure, and preexisting divergent patterns of ownership of land affect the degree of control which absentee capital can acquire. The economic forces emanating from the empire were uniform across the different regions of the American Sugar Kingdom, but the local class structures varied considerably from one region to another. The history of the American Sugar Kingdom is a product of the interaction of the two, which means that much of the raw material that went into the making of the plantations of the Caribbean was of local origin. The study of European and U.S. imperialism in the colonial world too often emphasizes the metropolitan side of the process of underdevelopment at the expense of local social actors. Underdevelopment then appears as an inevitable, unchangeable course determined exclusively by the will and social agency of metropolitan forces. Social transformation promoted by colonial actors appears impossible because only the wider forces of the world market seem to have any bearing on the course of development. Preexisting classes and social structures appear as irrelevant, and even the classes created by the process of capital accumulation—tenant farmers, the agricultural proletariat—appear merely as pawns in a game created entirely by metropolitan capitalists. If, on the contrary, the making of underdevelopment is regarded as a complex process of interaction between metropolitan and colonial social classes, social change promoted by local social forces emerges as a possibility. The imperial construction appears as something that was created jointly with local allies and can therefore be undone or at least refashioned in favor of colonial peoples by local social actors. Development and underdevelopment acquire historical specificity. In the Spanish Caribbean in 1898, the social classes—local mill owners, colonos, and the agricultural proletariat—were the product of the transformation of the plantations after abolition.

The abolition of slavery produced dramatic changes in tropical agriculture and tilted the balance in favor of the production of beet sugar in temperate climates. From 1870 to 1900 European sugar beet production developed swiftly and outpaced the tropical cane sugar regions in total output, so that by the year 1900 beet sugar made up 60 percent of total world output while cane sugar accounted for 40 percent. The crisis of tropical plantation agriculture, however, did not mean the end of the plantation but rather its transformation. This chapter examines the transformation of tropical sugar production in the three islands of the Spanish Caribbean by looking at the transition from the system of ingenios, which prevailed during the slave regime, to the system of central sugar mills, which replaced these ingenios. The transformation from one type of plantation system to another encompassed changes in the relations between classes, changes in the relation between industry and agriculture, and changes within the planter class itself. The transformation of the slaves into an agricultural proletariat, the exceptions to the process of proletarianization, and the increase of the agricultural proletariat through immigration are examined comparatively across the islands. The changes in the structure of enterprise from the ingenio, an integrated agrarian/industrial production unit, to the central sugar mill, characterized by the separation of ownership of the agrarian and industrial components, are also examined comparatively. The separation of industry from agriculture entailed the differentiation of the planter class into centralistas/industrialists on the one hand and cane farmers on the other. At the turn of the century, the transition to capitalist agriculture and the differentiation of the planter class had been completed successfully in Cuba but not in the Dominican Republic or Puerto Rico, where the sugar industry languished and the future of sugarcane monoculture seemed uncertain. In Cuba and Puerto Rico the Creole central had many features inherited from the period of slavery. The transformation of many ingenio owners into colonos or cane farmers created a complex landowning structure in which central sugar mills most often did not own sufficient cane lands to guarantee their entire supply of cane. In the geographical areas that experienced the transition from ingenio to central, sugar mills had to compete with each other for the cane produced by capitalist cane farmers (colonos) who employed wage laborers. In short, after abolition, the richest ingenio owners became centralistas, the majority of ingenio owners became colonos, while most slaves became agricultural wage workers.

This transition led by Creole landowners and centralistas ended in 1898 with the U.S. invasion of Cuba and Puerto Rico. Under the U.S. colonial regime, a second distinct system of central sugar mills began to emerge. This type of central sugar mill not only functioned on a much larger scale, but it was, like the old ingenio, a unitary enterprise in which the cane lands and the sugar mill were under the same ownership. Independent cane farmers did not control the majority of the cane lands, which were instead owned by the mills. The mills planted the cane themselves (administration cane) or subleased lands to dependent colonos who could not activate price competition between mills for the cane. This second type of central sugar mill required enormous capital investment, generated colossal sugar complexes with their own ports and railroad stations, and became veritable company towns in the Caribbean countryside. Because the new mills were established mostly in virgin regions with sparse population, they relied more than the older Creole centrales on immigrant labor for the completion of the sugar harvest. The Creole central whose origin dates to the abolition of slavery and the colossal U.S.-owned sugar mills which developed after 1898 coexisted in all the islands but were often in geographically distinct regions. Thus uneven regional development reflected the different histories of the sugar industry in each area. The structure of landownership and the availability of labor in a sugar mill and its surrounding area depended on the date the mill was founded. Mills built before the abolition of slavery, between abolition and the Spanish-American War of 1898, and during the period of U.S. colonialism had different social structures, particularly concerning the relations between the mills and surrounding independent cane farmers and of the availability or absence of a settled rural proletariat. The Creole central was the product of the transition that took place after abolition but before the consolidation of U.S. colonial power in the Spanish Caribbean. The colossal sugar mills developed only after the Spanish-American War of 1898 and the consolidation of U.S. imperial power in the Spanish Caribbean.

This second system of colossal U.S. centrales, which developed after 1898, contributed to a dramatic expansion of tropical production in which cane sugar overtook beet output in the period 1900–1930. By 1929 tropical cane production accounted for 60 percent or world sugar, beet sugar for the remaining 40 percent. The scales tipped again in favor of tropical agriculture, through analogous processes of modernization in the three principal centers of tropical production: the Spanish Caribbean, the Dutch East Indies (Java), and British India. While the Spanish Caribbean can be seen as a relatively homogeneous center of expansion of the new sugar industry, particularly in comparison with the Javanese or Indian plantation systems, the process of development of the new plantations based on wage labor was different in each island. In the Dominican Republic, shortages of wage laborers had impeded the realization of the island's potential for export agriculture in the nineteenth century. Scarcity of labor continued in the early decades of the twentieth century, propelling many mills to recruit immigrant laborers. In Puerto Rico, difficulties in separating the ownership of the industrial and agricultural components of the sugar industry retarded the development of central sugar mills in the nineteenth century. In the twentieth century, the protection afforded by the inclusion of Puerto Rico in the U.S. tariff system served to attract U.S. capital, eliminating the constraints imposed by the scarcity of capital that had prevailed during the Spanish colonial period. In Cuba the phenomenal growth of a new type of plantation agriculture after abolition suffered a serious setback during the War of Independence (1895–98). Four-fifths of the mills ceased to function or were destroyed by the insurgents. After 1898 the influx of

U.S. capital contributed to the recovery and eventually to the phenomenal expansion of sugar production in the eastern provinces.

Despite the advances in the development of central sugar mills, particularly in Cuba, the period 1870–1900 can be characterized as transitional. In 1898, the transition was most advanced in Cuba and least advanced in the Dominican Republic. The period 1900–1930, by contrast, was characterized by a phenomenal leap forward in sugar production in all three islands. U.S. capitalists and some native entrepreneurs developed new corporate sugar mills that operated on a scale vastly superior to that of the mills of the epoch of slavery or the centrales that developed after abolition. The invasions of Cuba and Puerto Rico in 1898, the U.S. customs receivership of the Dominican Republic in 1905, and the eventual occupation of the country in 1916–24 turned the Spanish-speaking islands of the Caribbean into a colonial zone dominated by the United States. In the war of 1898, Spain's colonial power in the region ended, the Cuban revolution was frustrated, and the long rivalry between Britain and the United States for domination of the Caribbean was settled in favor of the latter.[1] The intervention of U.S. Marines in the Dominican Republic in 1905 resulted in the transfer of the Dominican foreign debt from European to American bankers.[2] Everywhere North American rule benefited North American investors. And everywhere the principal sphere of investment was the sugar industry.

In 1920–21, sugar production in the American Sugar Kingdom reached a peak in the world economy. The European beet sugar industry had suffered severe decreases in output because of the world war, and Cuba, the Dominican Republic, and Puerto Rico produced 38 percent of the cane sugar and 27 percent of all the sugar produced in the world that year. The 240 sugar mills of the American Sugar Kingdom produced 5,108,323 tons of sugar, or an average of 21,285 tons per mill. Across the three islands, at least 500,000 workers participated in the production of a landmark zafra. Of these, at least 450,000 were field workers.[3] The price of sugar was high, and Cuba was experiencing an unprecedented period of prosperity known in the national history as la Danza de los Millones. In that year, the value of Cuban exports reached the record mark of $1 billion.[4]

This phenomenal expansion represented a second, distinct process of transformation of the sugar industry, different in magnitude and in quality from the creole transition that had taken place between abolition and the transfer of the Spanish colonies and the Dominican Republic to the United States. Through a process of vertical integration that was greatly facilitated by U.S. colonial expansion in the Caribbean, U.S. sugar refiners achieved control of about one-half of the output of Cuba and Puerto Rico and of practically all the output of the Dominican Republic.

Throughout the Cuban War of Independence the principal U.S. planter in Cuba, E. F. Atkins, advocated against U.S. recognition of the Cuban insurgents, arguing that such recognition would free Spain from the responsibility of protecting U.S. properties. When the United States declared the war in 1898, U.S. capital seized the opportunity and began to invest. The Chaparra, Cuban American, Francisco, and Mercedita sugar companies initiated their Cuban investments in 1899, Cuban Land and Sugar did so in 1900, and United Fruit, Havemeyer & Welch and Damuji Sugar began to invest in 1901.[5] The conditions for the expansion of capital were much more favorable after state intervention, as investors readily acknowledged. The fiftieth anniversary report of the South Porto Rico Sugar Company grants a central role to U.S. political rule in the history of the corporation: "Conditions changed when the American Army landed on July 25, 1898. With Puerto Rico (then spelled Porto Rico) under the wing of the American government, and in a preferred position under its tariff system, opportunities in the island appeared more attractive."[6] Although some analysts have argued that the transition to the system of centrales that began during the Spanish colonial period continued without interruption in the U.S. colonial period,[7] I will argue in this chapter that United States imperial intervention in 1898 radically altered the terrain for capital accumulation and produced a distinctly new type of sugar mill.

1870–1900: The Transition from Ingenio to Central

In Cuba and Puerto Rico, the emergence of the central sugar mill was both a product of and a reaction to abolition. Slavery was abolished in Puerto Rico in 1873 and in Cuba in 1886. At the time of abolition the sugar industry of Puerto Rico was already in deep decline. In Cuba, sugar production not only survived abolition but actually prospered in the decade following emancipation. The Cuban transformation after abolition restored production to preemancipation levels, and in less than a decade a new plantation system was in place. Under the new system of centrales based on a division of labor between mill and farm, within a decade after emancipation Cuba surpassed all previous records of sugar output.[8] If Cuban emancipation represented a crisis, it nevertheless ushered in a period of further growth of plantations, instead of the decline in sugar production that took place after emancipation in most regions of the Americas. After the emancipation of the slaves between 1883 and 1886, the planter class of Cuba underwent a process of differentiation. Successful mill owners modernized their facilities, increased their cane-processing capabilities, and became planter-industrialists. Unsuccessful mill owners who did not have sufficient capital to modernize dismantled their outdated mills and became simply cane farmers. The social structure of the sugar mills was transformed. Slave labor was replaced by wage labor and by tenancy arrangements, and the industrial process of cane milling was separated from the agricultural processes of planting and harvesting sugarcane. As the industrial units became fewer but larger, they were able to grind more sugarcane than was available from the lands directly under their ownership. The larger mills entered into arrangements with surrounding mill owners who were not able to make the transition to the new technological phase of sugar milling. Because the new mills centralized the grinding of cane previously carried out by many smaller units, they became known as ingenios centrales and eventually simply as centrales. The planters who gave up their obsolete milling operations and turned exclusively to cane farming became colonos.[9]

Under the plantation system in Cuba after slave emancipation, the centrales ground cane from their own lands and from the lands of colonos. The Cuban sugar industry expanded rapidly. In 1892, barely six years after the emancipation of the last slaves from the plantations, the industry produced an unprecedented one million tons of sugar. The expansion was propelled by rising demand for sugar in the United States and by favorable tariff reductions between 1891 and 1894.[10] The industry was restructured in the established regions of sugar culture, where the planter class became differentiated into mill owners and colonos. Central mill owners and colonos moved into unexploited regions and extended the zone of sugar cultivation under the innovative system of division of labor between industry and agriculture. The process of centralization changed the configuration of the sugar industry. The slave ingenio was a unitary enterprise which had little incentives to replace labor with machines. Expansion of milling capacity required a great expansion of the area planted in sugarcane and a proportional expansion in the number of slaves. Mechanization of the milling phase required a proportional increase in fixed capital in the form of slaves. Centralization allowed expansion of the milling operations without the burden of an equivalent expansion in the agricultural facet of the business. Mills were able to modernize without a proportional expansion of the area cultivated in cane by entering into contracts with surrounding colonos. On the other side of the process of differentiation, planters who became colonos were able to specialize in cane agriculture, unhampered by the cost of additional investment in mills and machinery. The increase in the flexibility of each of the facets of sugar production, milling and farming, allowed both centralistas and colonos to increase their output and to advance the productivity of the industry as a whole. New centrales were established in frontier regions and the area planted in cane increased as immigrant labor poured into the island. The sugar frontier moved from its hub in Matanzas toward the east. By the turn of the century the province of Santa Clara had surpassed Matanzas, the traditional locus of slave agriculture, in sugar output.[11]

Freed slaves from the core area of the ingenio economy moved to frontier regions in eastern Cuba, drifted into the cities, or remained on the plantations as wage workers.[12] Although the numbers of former slaves who moved to the east or to the cities is not known, under the emerging central system they did not become owners of land and only rarely became tenants of the mills. In 1900, only 1 percent of the lands planted in cane in the island of Cuba had "colored owners," while "colored renters" occupied only 4 percent of the cane area.[13] Most likely, the former slaves in the plantation zones became agricultural workers in the centrales and in the cane farms (colonias). For most Afro-Cubans in the western provinces emancipation did not signify a transition into smallholding but rather proletarianization. The difference in postemancipation Cuba was that, alongside the former slaves, white Cubans and white immigrants and some Chinese also worked as wage laborers. Labor in the cane fields was no longer exclusively associated with African slavery, but Afro-Cubans who remained on the plantations did so as wage laborers. A pamphlet published in 1893 by "a colono from Las Villas" points to the racial composition of the colonato. Calling on colonos to organize to get better prices for their cane from the sugar mills, the pamphlet is suggestively titled *La esclavitud blanca* (White slavery).[14] The transition to capitalist agriculture and the central system in Cuba occurred before the U.S. occupation of 1898.

There are no complete statistical sources for the Cuban sugar industry between 1878 and 1900. The devastation caused by the war of 1895–98 makes it difficult to use the statistical sources of 1899 and 1900 in reconstructing an accurate image of the sugar industry in the period 1880–1900. In many ways, the figures for agricultural production of the turn of the century reflect more accurately the destruction of the war than the development that took place between abolition and 1895.[15] The U.S. occupation of 1898 brought about a renewed expansion of sugar production in Cuba and transformed the social structure of cane agriculture. Internal factors such as the destruction caused by the War of Independence and external factors such as increased foreign investment and preferential tariffs in the United States reshaped class relations and the patterns of uneven regional development of Cuba's sugar industry. The new mills established by United States corporations in the virgin lands of eastern Cuba were characterized by a more polarized social structure than those of the traditional region of cane agriculture in the western part of the island, where the class of independent cane farmers survived. Labor was both more abundant and more expensive in the western regions. The eastern mills relied more on immigrant labor than those of the west and organized vast movements of workers from other islands of the Caribbean to meet their needs during the zafra. To understand the transition after 1898, it is necessary first to understand the transformation that took place between abolition and 1898.

Planters in Cuba and Puerto Rico were searching for ways to continue sugar production at productivity rates that would allow them to compete in the world market. They were aware of the great advances of the European beet industry and of the relative stagnation of the cane industry. They noticed the advanced milling capacities. They also noticed the separation of the milling from the harvesting and the consequent introduction of the system of division of labor in the beet sugar industry. But of equal importance was that the system of centrales appeared as an alternative to the collapse of the cane industry that many foresaw as a result of the imminent abolition of slavery. Faced with the imminent collapse of slavery, the planters idealized the advantages of Adam Smith's division of labor as a panacea for the sugar industry: "The skill which the worker acquires, the economy of time that is achieved and the spirit of invention that develops and produces machines and procedures which ease work and cheapen articles, are due principally to the fulfillment of the economic law of the division of labor."[16]

The imminent collapse of slavery on the one hand and the advances of the beet industry on the other posed challenges to the planters of the Hispanic Caribbean. From the ranks of the slave owners there arose capitalist entrepreneurs willing to introduce the system of division of labor. The big landowners who wished to convert their ingenios into centrales needed the cooperation of small farmers. The new technologies of cane grinding made possible the construction of mills with an enlarged grinding capacity. But the increase in industrial output required a parallel increase in the area planted in cane. The stagnation of cane agriculture and the lack of significant increases in the productivity of human labor in the growing and harvesting of cane meant that the bottlenecks to the expansion of sugar production were related not to the industrial but rather to the agrarian aspect of the business. The colono system served to solve this bottleneck by freeing the mills from the agrarian aspect of sugar production.

In Puerto Príncipe (Camagüey) the Ten Years' War of 1868–78 had de facto done away with slavery, whereas in the western parts of Cuba slavery continued until final abolition in 1886. In the regions of eastern Cuba where some ingenios had existed, the war of 1868–78 destroyed many sugar mills, and after the war there was no significant recovery.[17] The western mills suffered war devastation later, in 1895–98, at a time when slavery had already been abolished and the central mill had taken the place of the ingenio. In the western regions of Cuba where the ingenios survived the Ten Years' War, the abolition of slavery raised the problem of adapting to the new labor regime while competing internationally against beet sugar. A study by Reed, Ruiz y Compañía concludes:

> The Napoleonic Wars gave birth to the cultivation of beet in Europe, creating thereby a rival to sugar cane which at first elicited contemptuous smiles but later achieved such degree of strength that it was able to achieve primacy over cane sugar and today threatens the existence of that industry. The sugar cane cultivators will not free themselves from the imminent danger in which they find themselves unless they appeal, and very soon, to the same procedures which have transmitted so much vigor to an enemy inferior by nature, but which has been able to take advantage of the last word in science.
>
> The inferiority of beet disappeared when, obeying the economic principle of the division of labor, cultivation was separated from milling.[18]

After explaining the advances of the beet industry over the cane industry and the advantages of the principles of Adam Smith, a promotional pamphlet issued by prospective centralistas explained that "the establishment of ingenios centrales, after the abolition of slavery in 1848 in Martinique and Guadeloupe, saved those islands from the misery into which the reduction of the sugar crops was precipitating them."[19] In the British dominions, planters had solved the problem of scarcity after abolition by importing indentured servants from Asia. In Cuba, according to Rebecca Scott, no such expedient was available. The British planters of Guyana and Trinidad had adapted to the transition to free labor by importing indentured Asians, but Spain could provide no such expedient from its diminished empire.[20]

The separation of milling from growing, argued the prospective centralistas, allowed the farmers with modest means to continue growing cane without necessarily having to invest in an ingenio. The promotional pamphlet issued by the prospective centralistas thus sought to convince the lesser landowners, faced with a coming crisis and the forthcoming split of the landowning class into centralistas and colonos, that it was to their advantage to subscribe to the project of building a central by committing themselves to planting cane to be ground by the prospective mill. The centralistas wanted to ensure an adequate supply of cane before investing in the innovative project. The principal newspapers of Cuba endorsed the project and editorialized about the advantages of the division of labor and how it had helped save the sugar industry in Martinique and Guadeloupe after abolition.[21]

The Transition to Plantation Agriculture
in the Dominican Republic

In the Dominican Republic, there was no ingenio economy as such during the nineteenth century. Slavery had been abolished as a result of the Haitian occupation of 1822–44, and throughout most of the nineteenth century Santo Domingo remained a society of petty commodity producers and subsistence farmers. Consequently, there was no transition to the central system, but rather the creation of central mills on areas not previously occupied by ingenios. In the Dominican Republic the centrales reintroduced sugar cultivation but did not build on any previous ingenio system. Since the sixteenth century, Dominican sugar production had contributed very little to total world sugar output. Perhaps for this reason, Dominicans refer to the twentieth-century sugar mill as "el ingenio," whereas Cubans and Puerto Ricans call it "el central" and "la central," respectively, to distinguish it from the nineteenth-century plantation based on slave labor.

The transition to plantation agriculture in the Dominican Republic began in the 1870s. At the beginning of the decade the Dominican Republic imported beet sugar from France and cane sugar from neighboring Puerto Rico, although there existed small trapiches where the peasants produced small quantities of sugar.[22] In El Cibao, tobacco was produced in peasant farms (vegas) and sold to local middlemen, who in turn sold it to the import-export houses of Puerto Plata. German commercial houses from Hamburg and Bremen purchased 90 percent of all tobacco exported in the nineteenth century, and the port of Saint Thomas provided another important outlet for Dominican exports.[23] The increasing supply of tobacco in the world market as a result of increased Brazilian and Dutch East Indian production in the 1870s affected the output of El Cibao, where production for export began to shift toward cocoa. By 1888 an estimated five million trees had been planted. In that year also, the French firm of Montandon, Descombes, and Company established a large cocoa plantation in Sabaná de la Mar, which contained one hundred thousand trees and used German immigrant labor. By and large, however, cocoa production was a Dominican-owned sector.[24] Cocoa production supplanted tobacco as the principal export, a trend accompanied by increasing integration with the world market.

The expansion of cane cultivation is contemporary with the expansion of cocoa, although very different in the unit of production that predominated. Tobacco and cocoa were produced mostly on peasant farms, but sugar was produced on larger estates. Cuban planters played a prominent role in the initiation of the industry in the Dominican Republic at the time of the Ten Years' War in Cuba. In

1872 a Cuban immigrant named Carlos Loynaz founded two ingenios near Puerto Plata. In 1874 the Cuban entrepreneurs Joaquín Delgado and Rafael Martín introduced steam power in ingenio La Esperanza. This event is a landmark in the development of the Dominican sugar industry, according to one account.[25] According to another source, La Esperanza was established in 1875; in 1876 another ingenio (La Caridad) was founded; four ingenios were established in 1877, six in 1878, five in 1879, another six in 1880, four in 1881, and two in 1882.[26]

By 1882, thirty ingenios had been established. But beginning in 1884, a drop in the price of sugar began to pose difficulties for these ingenios. Units that were not able to increase productivity began to disappear. The more advanced ingenios were able to survive and acquired the lesser ones, producing a centralization of property in the sugar industry. Increasingly, a handful of owners, mostly foreign (Alexander and William Bass, the Cambiaso Brothers, the Cuban Fernández de Castro, the North Americans Hardy and Kelly, and the English-Cuban Hatton) became the main producers. In addition to concentration in foreign hands, the new ingenios became geographically concentrated in San Pedro de Macorís, which became the main economic center of the republic, insofar as "economic" means "belonging to the export economy." The foreign capitalists were not yet absentee owners. They behaved as Dominican capitalists because their only investments were located in the republic and they reinvested their profits locally.[27]

The colono system hardly existed in the Dominican Republic before 1884. After 1884, the mills began to rely more on colonos so as to share the investment risk and administrative responsibilities in the rapidly expanding business."[28] By 1900, a process of concentration in the sugar industry had placed most of the smaller sugar mills out of competition while the larger mills flourished in the hands of foreign owners. Mills that ground colono cane were called centrales, while mills that ground their own cane were called ingenios. Dominicans participated in the industry mainly as colonos in operations that were moderately large ventures in commercial agriculture using seasonal laborers.[29] Despite these developments in the nineteenth century, the sugar industry achieved its modern morphology essentially in the twentieth century as a result of U.S. investments.

Dominican production figures in the late nineteenth century are smaller than those of Puerto Rico, even though the Dominican Republic has a much larger area. In 1880, the Dominican Republic exported 7,000 tons of sugar whereas nearby Puerto Rico exported 78,508 tons.[30] The figure is all the more significant because Puerto Rico was not at that time primarily a sugar exporter, sugar exports representing only 29 percent of export value, in contrast to coffee, which accounted for 55 percent.[31] Nevertheless, the embryo of a posterior plantation economy may be said to have emerged in the Dominican Republic in the period 1870–1900, even though the figures seem low by comparison with those of Puerto Rico, let alone Cuba.

The Transition to the Central in Puerto Rico

The Puerto Rican transition to the system of centrales differed from that of the Dominican Republic in that the centrales were a product of abolition, an attempt to preserve the plantation in the absence of slave labor. The centrales of Puerto Rico differed from the Cuban mills in that the division of labor between agriculture and industry did not spread throughout the industry. The mills and the cane fields continued to operate as unitary enterprises under the same ownership. The centrales were descendants of the ingenios, but they did not transform cane agriculture or sugar production successfully. At the time of abolition, the Puerto Rican ingenio system was already in deep decline.[32] After emancipation in 1873, sugar production survived but did not prosper. When the United States occupied the island in 1898, as Ramos Mattei notes, "the sugar industry offered a devastating panorama. The system of haciendas was on the verge of disappearing; the central had not been able to impose itself as a productive regime."[33]

The case of Central San Vicente in Vega Baja is indicative of the state of the sugar industry in Puerto Rico after abolition. The mill was established in 1873, the year slavery was abolished. Its owner attempted simultaneously to expand the grinding capacity of the mill and the area of land under cane cultivation, contrary to the recommendations of a group of economic thinkers who formulated proposals for restructuring the sugar industry. These economic reformers proposed the concept of centralization and the introduction of the division of labor. They recommended that sugar mill owners devote themselves exclusively to the industrial process of sugar fabrication and that landowners devote themselves exclusively to the cultivation of cane.[34] This would allow mill owners to concentrate on improving their milling equipment by releasing them from the burden of the agricultural phase. Likewise, farmers would dedicate themselves exclusively to cane agriculture without having to meet the capital requirements of operating a sugar mill. When advocates of change referred to the division of labor in agriculture, they meant the division between mill and farm, not the technical division of labor within the mills. Instead of relying on farmers for its supply of cane, San Vicente took on the expenses of planting the canes and delivering them to the mill.[35] The cost of planting vastly superior amounts of land, the combination of increased investments in both machinery and cane lands to feed the more voracious mills, ownership of land in excess of the mill's requirements, and the necessity to hire labor throughout the year for the weeding and maintenance of the sugar lands all weighed against San Vicente's success.[36] The enterprise failed, and within a few years of its foundation its owner landed in jail, unable to pay the debts of the inefficient central. Its failure is a negative confirmation of the importance of the separation of industry from agriculture at a critical time in the development of sugar production. Between abolition and 1898, the sugar industry of Puerto Rico lingered but did not prosper, basically because capital did not flow into the industry. The thriving coffee crop drew most of the investment. Under the Spanish regime, Puerto Rico's coffee enjoyed tariff protection and found a good market in Cuba, which was the outstanding sugar producer. The Puerto Rican sugar economy was in a state of decay in 1898.[37] Unlike Cuba, Puerto Rico did not experience a successful transition to the central system before 1898.

There were, however, some successful examples of centralization. Central Canóvanas in the Loíza region is a case in point. Central Canóvanas was established in 1880 and in 1881 was acquired by a British firm, the Colonial Company. At the time of its establishment, Central Canóvanas was, according to the colonial governor, "the first to be established on the basis of the complete separation between the growing of the cane and the elaboration of the sugar, which principle is unanimously recognized as the only one capable of restoring to this Antillean island its lost preponderance, considered as a center of sugar production, principal source of its wealth." The whole island "paid attention, following step by step with the greatest interest, its rapid development."[38] Central Canóvanas remained the largest mill in Puerto Rico until the establishment of the South Porto Rico Sugar Company's Guánica mill early in the twentieth century.

Thus the sugar industry survived but did not prosper. Depending on the vantage point of the author, scholars have considered the sugar industry before 1898 as either the embryo of the post-1898 plantation economy or as a declining industry that was essentially replaced by corporate agribusiness after 1898. At issue is whether the sugar economy of the twentieth century is an accretion of that of the nineteenth century or an entirely new phenomenon. In his seminal studies, Andrés Ramos Mattei argued that there were elements of continuity in the sugar economy: "Instead of a radical transformation, the Puerto Rican sugar industry went through a period of intense acceleration of processes already in development."[39] Elsewhere he acknowledged, however, the "devastating panorama" of the sugar industry in 1898.[40] In her study of Central San Vicente in Vega Baja, Teresita Martínez Vergne similarly argued for continuity in the development of the sugar industry: "I tend to deemphasize 1898, the year that marks the beginning of U.S. control of the island, as a watershed in the social, economic, and even political life of Puerto Rico."[41] Noting the persistence and prosperity of the local class of centralistas after 1898, Juan Giusti-Cordero also leans toward the notion of continuity in the development of the sugar industry around 1898.[42]

Considering the weight of sugar in Puerto Rico's export economy, the scale of operations of the sugar mills, and the social transformations leading to massive proletarianization, a strong case can be made in favor of discontinuity. Governor George W. Davis wrote in 1900 about the sugar industry, noticed the sugar industry's decline since mid-century, and described its state as one of "industrial prostration":

> Twenty years ago the area under sugar was much greater than now. One can see, all over the island lowlands, the ruins of old mills, properties that have been abandoned to pasturage because the cultivation of cane and the manufacture of sugar with the primitive "Jamaica train" was no longer remunerative, and capital for the installation of modern plants was not available. This condition, which prevails all over the West Indies, has brought about in many of the islands a state of industrial prostration.
>
> In 1878 the number of sugar estates that had been abandoned because no longer remunerative amounted to 138, and 505 remained yet under cultivation. About this time the establishment of "central" factories commenced, and in 1880 there were five such establishments where cane was ground for several estates. In October of last year the number of planters had dwindled to 2,497. There were 22 factories where cane was ground for more than one farmer.
>
> The maximum value of sugar produced in Puerto Rico was in 1878, when the reported export (83,000 tons) was valued at 7,487,211 pesos. The maximum volume of this island's sugar export was in 1879, amounting to 170,000 tons, upon which there was paid an export tax of 313,000 pesos. . . . Sugar production, however, still continued to decline after 1879 until, in 1893, it reached a minimum, the export of that year being only 47,000 tons. It is interesting to note that there were only three years between 1850 and 1880 when the quantity exported fell below this minimum. Since 1893 there has been an increase, the average for the last four years being about 55,000 tons.[43]

The incorporation of Puerto Rico into the U.S. customs area propelled a shift in economic activity, replacing coffee with sugar as the main export of the island. In 1896, coffee accounted for 76.9 percent of the value of exports. By 1920, coffee

Table 7.1. Value of Coffee and Sugar Exports from Puerto Rico as Percentage of Total Value of Exports, 1876–1925

Year	Coffee	Sugar
1876	17.6	62.5
1881	54.5	28.9
1886	49.4	43.6
1896	76.9	20.7
1910	15.5	64.3
1920	6.6	71.8
1925	7.5	60.6

James L. Dietz, *Economic History of Puerto Rico: Institutional Change and Capitalist Development* (Princeton: Princeton University Press, 1986), 27, 117.

accounted for only 6.6 percent of exports. In the same period the value of sugar exports rose from 20.7 percent to 71.8 percent of the island's export trade. The coffee industry's protected markets in Spain and Cuba were lost. In the U.S. customs area, Puerto Rican coffee had to compete without protection with that of Brazil. In contrast to sugar, coffee was not protected in the U.S. market because there were no producers in the United States. The dramatic decline in the value of coffee exports was accompanied by an equally sensational increase in the value of sugar exports (see Table 7.1). Inclusion in the customs area also accounts for the revival of the perishing class of native mill owners.

In addition to the transition from coffee to sugar monoculture in Puerto Rico, mill sizes are an indication of the discontinuities around 1898. The largest centrales before 1898 produced 5,000 tons of sugar, whereas in 1933 the average mill produced 27,000 tons. Total production of sugar in Puerto Rico averaged 81,770 tons a year in the decade 1881–90 and 60,775 tons a year in the decade 1891–1900, when the industry was composed of ten centrales and a periphery of smaller mills. The Guánica mill of the South Porto Rico Sugar Company alone produced 111,867 tons of sugar in 1928 and 151,403 tons in 1933–34.[44] Thirty years after the U.S. occupation, a single mill produced more sugar than all the mills of the island combined before 1898. In the late nineteenth century, a large central typically controlled one thousand acres of land. By the 1930s, the figure was up to fifty thousand acres (in Cuba and the Dominican Republic, eighty to one hundred thousand acres).[45]

The process of rural proletarianization is a third indicator of discontinuity. This process, which was already advancing in the highland coffee region, took a great leap forward after 1898 as a result of the introduction of a colonial tax on landed property. The colonial taxation policy exacerbated the problems of land concentration at one extreme and proletarianization at the other extreme. The increase in the landless population fed the ranks of the emergent agricultural proletariat, while land concentration benefited U.S. corporations and local cane growers. In 1919, there were 79,261 agricultural workers in the sugar industry alone.[46] In 1934, when Puerto Rican sugar workers went on a general strike, the stoppage affected 100,000 workers, counting those employed in the sugar mills.[47] The impressive expansion of sugar production in Puerto Rico was made possible by measures taken by the colonial state, ranging from the free entrance of Puerto Rican sugar into the U.S. market to the expropriating land taxes that helped to create an agricultural proletariat. Direct colonial rule, which allowed U.S. colonial authorities to introduce and enforce taxation on land, along with incorporation to the U.S. customs area, propelled the shift from coffee to sugar monoculture.

Tropical production of sugarcane in the period 1870–1900 was characterized by a transition from the ingenio to the central with different paths and mixed results in the Spanish Caribbean. Across the islands, the emergence of the central signified a shift away from the unitary enterprises of the nineteenth century and introduced the division of labor. Milling was separated from the agricultural process, more successfully in Cuba, less thoroughly in Puerto Rico. The transition to the system of centrales encountered difficulties in each island, which retarded the development of the sugar industry. In the Dominican Republic, the persistence of farmers who owned land or had access to it prevented the creation of a viable labor market for the sugar mills. In Puerto Rico, similarly, the experience of San Vicente indicates shortages of labor and access for agricultural laborers to subsistence plots. The separation of the workers from the means of production advanced in Puerto Rico from 1870 to 1900, as shown by Laird Bergad's study of the highland coffee zone.[48] Nevertheless, lack of capital held back the sugar industry, the separation of milling from cane agriculture did not occur, and the so-called division of labor in the sugar industry remained undeveloped. Cuba's successful transition to capitalist agriculture and to the central system is therefore the exception. In the 1890s, Cuban sugar production reached one million tons as a result of the establishment of new centrales in the province of Santa Clara (Las Villas). But the War of Independence initiated in 1895 destroyed the sugar economy of Cuba and put 80 percent of the industry out of service by 1898. After 1898, Cubans faced the challenge of reconstructing a destroyed sugar economy. In many ways, even in Cuba there was a certain discontinuity, the sugar economy of the twentieth century representing a new phenomenon based on the reconstruction of the destroyed mills of the west and on the erection of radically new, gigantic corporate mills in the east.

The Colossal Mills of the American Sugar Kingdom, 1898–1934

The U.S. invasion of 1898 frustrated Cuban attempts to reorganize colonial society to fit national needs. The Cuban revolution of 1895 became, to use the words of Maurice Zeitlin, "a bourgeois revolution that never was."[49] In the wake of this failed opportunity to free the island from Spanish colonialism on the basis of a Cuban initiative and to restructure society to fulfill local needs, sugar monoculture survived and the plantation economy prospered. The revolutionaries of 1895 considered the sugar industry a bulwark of the Spanish colonial regime and the planter class an obstacle to the achievement of the social goals of Cuba Libre, which included national independence, land for the peasants, and social equality for Afro-Cubans.[50] The Cuban Revolutionary Party had a significant base of working-class supporters among exiled Cubans, principally among cigar makers in New York, New Orleans, Key West, and Tampa. The presence of workers' clubs in the structure of the party gave the cause of Cuba Libre a radical edge beyond the limits of previous independence movements in Latin America.[51] The defeated Cuban revolution is a landmark event seldom considered in U.S. historical accounts. But its impact on the political culture of the Spanish Caribbean is, by contrast, immense. As Zeitlin suggests for the failed bourgeois revolutions of Chile, "the paradox, then, is that to understand the significance of what actually happened, of the actual social world that emerged, we have to assume that something we think was decisive never happened in order to discover what else was *possible*."[52] The failed bourgeois revolution of 1895 is the prism through which the critics of sugar monoculture looked at the social world that actually emerged. Instead of an egalitarian distribution of land, the American Sugar Kingdom featured excessive land concentration. Instead of racial equality for all Antilleans, racial stratification continued in the twentieth century. The emergence of a diversified agriculture, the progressive differentiation of town and country, and industrialization never materialized. Instead, the central sugar mills represented outposts of partial industrialization in the countryside without any corresponding urban development, the ruralization of industry which blocked the progressive differentiation of town and country, as opposed to urban industrialization and rural diversification. The failure of the revolution represents the closure of an alternative path of capitalist development free from colonial domination and the plantation economy. The American Sugar Kingdom was the utopia of Cuba Libre turned upside down.

The period 1900–1930 marks the definite establishment of sugar monoculture in the Dominican Republic and Puerto Rico and the recovery of Cuba's position as premier exporter of sugar in the world. The expansion of the U.S-owned mills occurred in several stages. Before 1914, the Cuban planter class rebuilt many destroyed mills and U.S. interests centered on the refining industry built a group of centrales of very large capacity. During World War I, the increase in the world price of sugar resulting from the destruction of the European beet crops induced a wave of investment by monopolistic interests centered in banking-capital groups. Among these were the banker-controlled Cuba Cane Sugar Corporation, the Atkins interests, the expansion of the South Porto Rico Sugar Company into La Romana in the Dominican Republic, and the reorganization of the National Sugar Refining Company (West India Sugar Finance–Cuban Dominican Sugar Company) interests in the Dominican Republic. The investments of the war period brought very large profits in an industry heavily affected by the shortages in Europe and rising prices globally. In 1919, following the war, the American Sugar Kingdom produced 29 percent of the world's sugar. With the postwar recovery, the share began to drop steadily through the 1920s to 15 percent of world production in 1934, not only because Cuba produced less but because the beet regions of Europe recovered from the devastation caused by the war. The most intense expansion of the centrales in the Caribbean occurred from 1914 to 1919, and a few mills whose construction had been initiated in the war years began operations in the early 1920s.

The state of the Cuban sugar industry after the devastation of the war of 1895–98 was described in detail in the reports issued by U.S. colonial officers shortly after the occupation of the island. In 1900 the situation of the Cuban sugar industry was precarious. The second Cuban War of Independence (1895–98) destroyed the plantation economy of western Cuba.[53] When the United States occupied the island in 1898, only 20 percent of the sugar mills were functioning. Sugar output declined from 1,035,000 tons in 1894–95, to 232,000 in 1896, and to 218,000 tons in 1897. In 1898 the industry experienced a mild recovery when production increased to 315,000 tons.[54] General Leonard Wood's report of 1900 lists the sugar mills of Cuba by province and indicates the levels of destruction during the war.[55] Of 570 sugar mills only 102, or less than one-fifth, were in operation, with a total production of 283,319 tons of sugar. Of these 570 mills, 205 were reported as destroyed during the war. Another 157 mills were reported as

Table 7.2. State of the Sugar Mills of Cuba, 1900

Province	Dismantled	Destroyed	In Production	In Reconstruction
Pinar del Río	3	23	7	8
Havana	24	45	0	0
Matanzas	121	68	0	3
Santa Clara	6	70	0	0
Puerto Príncipe	3	1	0	0
Santiago[a]	n.a.	n.a.	n.a.	n.a.
Cuba (%)	28	36	1	2
Cuba total	157	207	7	11

Source: Leonard Wood, *Civil Report of Brigadier General Leonard Wood, Military Governor of Cuba, for the Period from December 20, 1899 to December 21, 1900* (Washington, D.C.: U.S. Government Printing Office, 1900), vol. 7.

demolidos, a term that refers to the process by which a mill ceased grinding cane and was dismantled during the process of differentiation of the planter class following abolition. Many mills ceased operations after the abolition of slavery, became unprofitable, or were unable to modernize and keep up with technological advances. When the lands of these mills became sugar colonias producing cane for neighboring centrales, the mills were classified as "demolished." Obsolete sugar mills that had ceased grinding cane as well as sugar mills destroyed in the second Cuban War of Independence became colonias. The destruction caused by the war of 1895 accelerated a process of differentiation that had started after abolition, in which successful ingenios became centrales, and unsuccessful ingenios became cane farms without grinding equipment.

Even when the sugar industry was in a state of destruction, the figures for 1900 reveal something about the changes in Cuban agriculture after the abolition of slavery. The transformation of the sugar industry entailed shifts in the distribution of the productive enterprises throughout Cuba. The sugar frontier continued to move toward the east. In 1878 Matanzas had the highest output of sugar of the six Cuban provinces, Santa Clara second. In 1900 under the central system, Santa Clara was the premier producing province. After abolition the system of centrales expanded not only in the old areas of sugar culture, where it was forced to overcome the established fragmentation of land, but also in virgin areas where new centrales were built without the obstacles related to the overhaul of an anterior plantation system. In 1900, forty-nine sugar mills in Santa Clara produced 153,251 tons of sugar, compared to the 108,038 tons produced by the thirty-seven mills in operation in Matanzas.[56] The mills that survived the war or resumed

Not Destroyed	Other Crops	Reconstructed	Total
0	5	0	46
10	0	6	85
20	0	59	271
48	0	34	158
6	0	0	10
n.a.	n.a.	n.a.	n.a.
15	1	17	100
84	5	99	570

[a]Statistics for the province of Santiago (Oriente) were unavailable at the time of publication of Wood's report.

operations soon after it were on average larger than the norm in all of the Cuban provinces. In 1900 the average Cuban mill spanned a land area of 2,150 acres, but the mills that had continued to function during the war had a greater average land area of 3,192 acres (see Tables 7.2 and 7.3). This may reflect the ability of larger mills to buy protection during the war or readier access to sources of capital to restore production soon after the conclusion of the hostilities.

The Centrales of Neocolonial Cuba

In 1903, the United States granted a 20 percent reduction on the import duties on Cuban sugar. After the destruction of 1895–98, the incorporation of Cuba into the U.S. tariff system under preferential terms favored the rapid expansion of the sugar industry that took place between the turn of the century and World War I. To achieve the end of the military occupation, Cubans had to accede to many conditions, ranging from grants of land for military bases to the right of the United States to call troops into the island. Under the Platt Amendment, the Cuban Republic born in 1902 became what Cubans derisively called a "neo-Republic." The free flow of U.S. capital into the island and increasing economic integration to the United States fostered economic expansion in the sugar sector.[57] On the eve of World War I Cuban production stood at 2,765,477 tons of sugar. The number of functioning sugar mills had increased to 172. Average output per mill increased sevenfold from 2,400 tons in 1900 to 16,078 tons in 1913. The average figures conceal the degree of economic concentration. The Cuban

Table 7.3. Land Areas (acres) and Sugar Production of the Centrales of Cuba, 1900

Province	Number of Mills	Land Area	Area of Average Mill	Mills in Production	% of Mills in Production
Pinar del Río	46	101,391	2,204	7	15
Havana	85	159,466	1,876	10	12
Matanzas	271	482,016	1,778	37	14
Santa Clara	158	466,536	2,952	49	31
Puerto Príncipe	10	19,098	1,909	2	20
Santiago[a]	n.a.	n.a.	n.a.	n.a.	n.a.
Cuba total	570	1,228,517	64	105	18

Source: Leonard Wood, *Civil Report of Brigadier General Leonard Wood, Military Governor of Cuba, for the Period from December 20, 1899 to December 21, 1900* (Washington, D.C.: U.S. Government Printing Office, 1900), vol. 7.

landscape featured new mills with productive capacities of over 50,000 tons. The industry had recovered and by far surpassed its pre-1895 output. The mills were owned by native Cubans and by United States corporations and businessmen.[58]

Although the available sources make it difficult to measure with precision the process of polarization of the planter class between 1886 and 1900, it is possible to obtain an adequate impression of that process by contrasting the production figures for the province of Matanzas in 1878 and 1913. This permits observation of long-term changes, while keeping in mind the fantastic recovery after 1886 and the equally formidable destruction of the Cuban-Spanish war of 1895–98. In 1878, 426 mills ground the cane production of 311,841 acres of land in Matanzas. In 1913, the area cultivated in cane had increased slightly to 343,929 acres, an increase of 10.3 percent relative to 1878. Thirty-nine centrales, or about 9 percent as many cane-grinding units as in 1878, ground all the cane of the province. On average, an ingenio of 1878 processed the cane of 739 acres of land, whereas the average central of 1913 ground cane from 8,803 acres of land. The remarkable increase in the scale of operations of the sugar mills was accompanied by a correlative decrease in the number of enterprises, turning the overwhelming majority of ingenio owners and their descendants into colonos. In Matanzas, the total land area under cultivation increased by only 10.3 percent between 1877 and 1913, but the area of land planted in cane from which the average mill drew its cane increased tenfold. Nine out of every ten mills disappeared as industrial units between 1877 and 1913.[59]

Centrales used cane from colonos, and also cane produced under the management of the sugar mill itself. A distinction emerged between tierras de administración and *tierras de colonos*. In the former, the administration of the sugar mill hired

Area of Mills in Production	Area of Average Mill in Production	Tons of Sugar Produced by Average Mill
19,270	2,753	690
33,096	3,310	982
106,911	2,889	2,920
161,456	3,295	3,128
6,048	3,024	3,686
n.a.	n.a.	n.a.
326,973	3,125	2,698

[a]Statistics for the province of Santiago (Oriente) were unavailable at the time of publication of Wood's report.

workers and managed the planting and harvesting of sugarcane. In the latter, colonos were in charge of the operation of the farms. The cane was delivered to the mill and the colono was paid by the weight of the cane, usually the price of approximately one-half of the sugar contained in the cane. Dependent colonos were sometimes tenants of the mills and in some cases owned lands that were mortgaged to the mills. In either case, the dependence of the colono translated into lower prices paid for the cane, and the terms of delivery of sugarcane were more favorable to the sugar mill (see Table 7.4). This type of cane farmer was sometimes called *colono de administración*, *colono financiado*, or *colono controlado*.[60]

Twentieth-century sugar mills were complex entities which combined wage labor, landlord-tenant relations, relations between independent and dependent farmers on the one hand and the mill on the other. In short, the social relations of production in the agricultural phase of the complex were heterogeneous, and the distribution of land between the mills and colonos was geographically differentiated according to the previous development—or lack of development—of ingenios in each locality. The area of land from which the cane was derived was larger than the area directly owned by the sugar mill. This larger area of the sugar mill complex also contained fallow lands, grazing lands, and sometimes forest lands. In 1913, the aggregate area of the sugar mill complexes of Cuba amounted to 2,940,000 acres. Of these, 1,592,573 acres were not planted in cane, leaving an aggregate cane area of 1,347,427 acres. The cane area in turn was subdivided into 605,674 acres planted by independent colonos and 743,433 acres planted by the sugar mills and their tenants. The sugar mills and their dependent tenants planted and harvested 55 percent of the cane lands, while independent colonos harvested the remaining 45 percent.

Table 7.4. Mills and Sugar Production in Cuba, 1900 and 1913

Province	1900 Number of Mills	1913 Number of Mills	% Change	1900 Sugar Produced (tons)	1913 Sugar Produced (tons)	% Change
Pinar del Río	7	7	0%	4,393	57,801	1216%
Havana	10	19	90%	8,931	330,149	3597%
Matanzas	37	39	5%	98,217	633,000	544%
Santa Clara	49	69	41%	139,319	906,879	551%
Puerto Príncipe	2	7	250%	6,704	225,863	3269%
Santiago	n.a.	31	n.a.	n.a.	611,785	n.a.
Cuba	105	172	64	257,564	2,765,477	974%

Sources: Leonard Wood, *Civil Report of Brigadier General Leonard Wood, Military Governor of Cuba, for the Period from December 20, 1899 to December 21, 1900* (Washington, D.C.: U.S. Government Printing Office, 1900) vol. 7; Secretaría de Agricultura, Comercio y Trabajo de Cuba, *Portfolio azucarero: Industria azucarera de Cuba, 1912–1914* (Havana: La Moderna Poesía, 1914).

The system of centrales was quite diverse in that some of the units had emerged historically as a result of the conversion of ingenios into centrales, while others had been established on virgin lands. In the former case, a large ingenio was modernized in a district. Surrounding ingenios were transformed into colonias. Surrounded by a belt of cane farms owned by colonos who had previously been owners of ingenios, these sugar mills relied extensively on the provision of cane by independent farmers (colonos independientes). The partition of the land that had existed under the regime of slavery did not easily lend itself to consolidation. The converted ingenio had to operate under the constraints created by an anterior plantation system in which the sugar mills were smaller and the existing property areas were smaller than required by the scale of operations of the central. It was practically impossible for a central to expand its landownership without coming up against the existing partition of land inherited from the period of slavery. Downwardly mobile plantations became colonias; upwardly mobile plantations became centrales. The representative converted ingenio ground more cane from colono lands than from lands under its direct ownership. In 1913, the fifty-four sugar mills that had been established before the abolition of slavery but had been transformed into centrales ground more cane from colonos than from their own lands. By contrast, in the central mills erected between 1880 and 1898, that is, between the start of the process of abolition but before 1898, independent colonos produced only 35 percent of the cane. In the mills erected after 1898, independent colonos harvested only 14 percent of the cane (see Table 7.5).

The colono system represented an attempt to preserve the plantation through the establishment of a division of labor between agriculture and industry. In this

Table 7.5. Land Use in Cuban Sugar Mills, by Date of Foundation of Mill, 1913

	Mills Erected before 1880	Mills Erected 1880–98	Mills Erected after 1898
Number of mills[a]	54	12	14
Acres planted in cane by estates[a]	203,078	51,979	179,659
Acres planted in cane by independent colonos	241,382	28,526	28,963
Total area planted in cane	444,461	80,506	208,622
Acres planted in cane by estate: average mill[b]	3,761	4,331	12,833
Acres planted in cane by independent colonos: average mill	4,469	2,377	2,069
Percentage of the cane area planted by the estate[a]	46	65	86
Percentage of the cane area planted by independent colonos	54	35	14
Area not planted in cane	378,067	129,696	497,011
Percentage of land not planted in cane	46	62	70
Average tons of sugar produced by mill	15,900	14,403	38,452
Yield of cane: tons per acre	18	19	23

Source: Secretaria de Agricultura de Cuba, *Portfolio azucarero industria azucarera de Cuba, 1912–1914* (Havana: La Moderna Poesía, 1914).

[a]Data include 80 mills with known dates of foundation out of a total of 172 mills.

[b]Includes land owned by mill and planted by tenant growers (dependent colonos).

sense it responded to the conditions of scarcity of capital and of labor in post-emancipation Cuba. In another sense, the colonato was an outgrowth of the property relations existing within the planter class of Cuba. Lands already fragmented by the ingenio system were refashioned to fulfill the purposes of the central sugar mills. The polarization of the planter class into industrialists and landowners was accompanied by a redivision of the properties of the landowners for parcelization to smaller colonos.

Land use varied according to the antiquity of the sugar mill in question. As might be expected, agricultural yields were lower in the lands surrounding the older mills, probably because of the soil exhaustion typical of plantation economies. The allocation of land between mills and colonos varied according to the date of foundation of the mills. Ownership of larger amounts of land by the newer mills permitted them to avoid the independent farmers typical of the older regions of sugar culture. Typically, the newest sugar mills built by U.S. corporations were established on virgin lands. These precursors of modern agribusiness usually owned all the lands in their vicinity. All lands were considered tierras de administración, including the lands leased to dependent colonos. In the U.S.-owned mills established after 1898, the independent cane farmers were much less significant than in the older areas of sugar culture. In Cuba the distinction between the older and the newer areas of sugar culture is drawn along an east-west axis. Matanzas in the west was the heartland of the ingenio economy until the abolition of slavery. Camagüey and Oriente in the east were the sites of the newest, U.S.-owned corporate mills. The changes observed point to the decline of the independent cane farmer, not necessarily to the decline of cane farmers dependent on the mill, whether they were known as financiados, controlados or de administración. As the modern U.S. corporation advanced in Cuban soil it abolished the independent colonato.

In 1913, 10 mills crushed cane exclusively from colono lands, 51 mills crushed cane exclusively from tierras de administración, and 111 mills crushed both administration and colono cane. In Camagüey, a region that had been characterized by the absence of plantation development in the nineteenth century and by de facto abolition and elimination of the plantations during the Ten Years' War of 1868–78, 6 of the 7 mills operating in 1913 used exclusively administration cane. The mills of Camagüey were of recent construction and were owned principally by U.S. corporations. In Cuba as a whole, the largest mills crushed cane exclusively from administration lands or dependent colonos. The corporate mill was typically established on virgin lands, had access to investment capital, links with the railroads, and was very often integrated vertically with the sugar refining industry of the United States. It was a unitary enterprise. The greater availability of capital to the new agribusiness corporations eliminated the need for the division of labor which the planters of Cuba had considered the panacea for the scarcity of capital that plagued the industry after abolition.

The Chaparra and Delicias mills of the Cuban American Sugar Company produced 77,246 and 68,413 tons of sugar, respectively, but did not grind any cane from independent colonos. The Stewart mill in Camagüey produced 53,625 tons of sugar without the assistance of independent colonos. All the lands of the Boston mill of the United Fruit Company, which produced an impressive 61,350 tons of sugar, were tierras de administración. The Preston mill owned 29,232 acres of land but did not use cane from independent farmers in the production of its 68,505 tons of sugar in 1913. In 1860, on average a Cuban ingenio produced around 400 tons of sugar, and a unit producing 2,000 tons was considered very large.[61] Together, the Chaparra, Delicias, Preston, Boston and Stewart mills produced over 300,000 tons, which is as much sugar as was produced in the entire island of Cuba in 1900 and more than the entire production of the neighboring Dominican Republic in 1913. These levels of output were achieved without any independent colonos. A second transition to a distinctly new type of sugar-producing enterprise, different in scale and structure from the pre-1898 centrales, advanced as U.S. capital poured into Cuba.

A great variety of enterprises, therefore, claimed the title of ingenio central in 1913. Some had been established before the abolition of slavery and had transformed themselves, modernized their milling operations, and entered into contractual agreements with surrounding cane farmers. Others had been established after abolition and had fomented immigration of colonos in a process of settlement of new lands. The mills of most recent construction were built by U.S. corporations in eastern Cuba. They typically owned all the lands in their vicinity and hired immigrant labor from the eastern Caribbean, Jamaica and Haiti, especially after 1912.

In 1913, the center of gravity of the sugar industry had already shifted from Matanzas, where it had been located in the nineteenth century, toward the east. Cuba's east-west counterpoint has been am important theme in its history. Revolutions begin in the east but culminate or are defeated in the west. Antonio Maceo's invasion of the west was the high point of the war of 1895–98.[62] The revolutionary war spread from the marginal areas of the east to the center of the sugar economy in the west. In 1956–59, the 26th of July movement was able to wage a revolutionary war, beginning from a base in a marginal zone of the east and spreading to the west. The east-west dynamic is important for understanding Cuba's revolutions, as well as the underlying socioeconomic terrain on which they have unfolded. It seems appropriate, therefore, to view the landscape of mills in Cuba in 1913 while keeping the east-west dynamic in mind.[63]

Moving west to east in the year 1913, the westernmost province, Pinar del Río, was a place of few and relatively small mills. Only seven centrales operated there in that year, and they produced 57,820 tons of sugar. We may get a sense of scale by pointing out that Central Chaparra, of the Cuban American Sugar Company, produced in eastern Cuba 77,246 tons of sugar that year, more than all the mills of Pinar del Río combined. The average mill in Pinar del Río produced 8,260 tons of sugar from an average of 3,675 acres of land planted in cane. The Cuban American Sugar Company's Chaparra mill, by contrast, ground cane from 23,273 acres of land.

The province of Havana had nineteen mills in operation and produced 330,247 tons of cane in 1913. Havana had a complex distribution of large and small mills. Without forgetting this nuance, it is worth pointing out that the average mill of Havana province was considerably larger than that of Pinar de Río, producing 17,381 tons of cane. On the average, the typical mill of Havana ground cane from an area of 6,071 acres of cane. East of Havana, the province of Matanzas was the heartland of the nineteenth-century ingenio. In 1913, there were forty-one centrales in operation producing an aggregate of 642,662 tons of sugar, that is, more than the Dominican Republic and Puerto Rico combined. Average mill production for that season stood a bit lower than that of Havana at 17,381 tons. Like Havana, Matanzas had a complex distribution of mill sizes. The largest six mills produced 35 percent of the output of the province at one extreme, and at the other the smallest six mills produced 3.6 percent. Santa Clara was the province with the highest aggregate output. It produced 907,199 tons of sugar in sixty-nine mills. Santa Clara had both the highest number of mills and the highest output of all six Cuban provinces. The average mill produced 13,148 tons of sugar, less than the centrales of Havana and Matanzas. Thus Santa Clara was a province of many relatively small mills, but this does not mean that the large central had not been established in Santa Clara. Centrales Caracas, Washington, Andreita, Hormiguero, Santa Teresa, Lequeito, and Tuinucú each produced over 25,000 tons of sugar. At the other extreme, Centrales Ramona, Natividad, Gratitud, Mapos, San Cristóbal, Carolina, Carmita, Luisa y Antonia, and Nuestra Señora de Regla each produced less than 5,000 tons. The typical mill ground cane from an area of 5,512 acres of land.

The province of Camagüey offers a striking contrast with Santa Clara. Camagüey had been historically a land of cattle ranches. In 1913 there were only seven mills in Camagüey, as in Pinar del Río in the west, but the four largest mills produced over 30,000 tons of sugar each. The seven mills of Camagüey produced four times as much sugar as the seven mills of Pinar del Río in the west. The Stewart mill produced 53,625 tons of sugar, more than any of the western mills. Central Jatibonico produced 45,529, about as much as the largest of the west, the Gómez Mena mill in Matanzas. Central Francisco produced 41,834 tons, Jagüeyal 34,476, and Senado 26,624. The other two mills produced 14,110 and 12,665 tons of sugar. In contrast to the western provinces, there were no mills producing less than 12,000 tons in Camagüey. Thus Camagüey was a land of few, new, and large mills.

The largest mills were located in the eastern province of Cuba, the province of Oriente. Central Chaparra of the Cuban American Sugar Company was located there. In 1913 it produced 77,246 tons of sugar. Central Preston of the United Fruit Company produced 52,212. Central Delicias, also of the Cuban American Sugar Company, produced 68,412, and Boston, of the United Fruit Company, produced 61,350. They were the four largest mills in Cuba. Santa Lucía produced

41,000 tons. In Oriente, another five centrales produced beyond 20,000 tons. These ten large mills produced 70 percent of the sugar of Oriente. Twenty-one smaller mills produced the remaining 30 percent. Thus, like Camagüey, Oriente was a province of very large mills, but unlike Camagüey, it did have a large cluster of smaller mills.[64] As large mills were built in the eastern provinces of Camagüey and Oriente, the center of gravity of the Cuban sugar economy shifted from west to east, away from the heartland of the ingenio system into new frontiers of sugar cultivation. During the world war, the process of construction of large mills in the east accelerated and by the mid-1920s the two eastern provinces of Cuba, Camagüey and Oriente, surpassed the other four provinces in total production of sugar.

The movement from west to east represents a parallel movement from the small central to the large one, from the heartland of the slave ingenios of the ancien regime to the new economic order established by U.S. sugar agribusiness, from the central based on independent colonos to the central that relied on cane from its own lands (tierras de administración) and from cane by colonos financiados. As we travel toward the east of Cuba, we move away from the benedictions of Adam Smith's division of labor which the planters of Cuba had suddenly discovered at the time of emancipation. If emancipation had made the centralistas turn toward Smith's division of labor because they did not have sufficient capital to take on the modernization process of the mills and the planting of all the cane at the same time, the gigantic corporate central of the east reminded them that the golden age of competition and family-based enterprise was coming to a close. A new age of corporate capital was emerging on the Cuban landscape. The new corporate U.S.-owned centrales were gigantic complexes owned by joint stock companies. Sidney Mintz called their corporate counterparts in Puerto Rico "company towns without the towns."[65]

The correspondence between size of the central and the strength of the independent colonos can be appreciated by contrasting the situation of the centrales of Cuba which produced over 40,000 tons of sugar with the average Cuban central. In Centrales Chaparra, Preston, Delicias, and Boston, all corporate and all located in Oriente, independent farmers produced none of the cane. Whereas in Cuba as a whole 56 percent of the lands in cane were planted by the estate or financed colonos, in the ten largest mills the corresponding figure was 82 percent. In other words, independent colonos harvested 44 percent of all the cane of Cuba but only 18 percent of the cane of the ten largest mills. The advance of the large central paralleled the demise of the independent colonos. Table 7.6 displays land use in Cuban sugar mills according to the nationality of the owner. Table 7.7 shows

Table 7.6. Land Use in Cuban Sugar Mills, by Nationality of Mill Owner, 1913

	British	Cuban	French	Spanish
Number of mills	7	67	5	41
Percentage of mills	4	39	3	24
Area planted in cane by estates[a]	29,702	245,448	27,989	133,997
Area planted in cane by independent colonos	23,957	228,648	7,459	150,394
Total area planted in cane	53,659	474,096	35,448	284,390
Percentage of the cane area planted by the estate[a]	55	52	79	47
Percentage of the cane area planted by colonos	45	48	21	53
Area not planted in cane	18,816	522,715	47,611	208,152
Percentage of land not planted in cane	26	52	57	42
Percentage of Cuban production	4	33	2	18
Aggregate tons of sugar produced	106,133	918,342	66,852	510,357
Yield of cane: tons per acre	18	18	18	18

Source: Secretaría de Agricultura, Comercio y Trabajo de Cuba, *Portfolio azucarero: Industria azucarera de Cuba, 1912–1914* (Havana: La Moderna Poesía, 1914).

[a]Includes lands owned by the mill but planted by tenants (dependent colonos). All areas are in acres.

the increase in provincial output of sugar from 1914 to 1918. Older sugar mills ground proportionately more cane from independent colonos that the younger mills of the twentieth century.

United States capitalists achieved control of more than half of the Cuban sugar crop only after 1914 as a result of two distinct processes. The first was the expansion caused by World War I and the second the contraction caused by the recovery of the beet crops in Europe. The expectation of increasing sugar prices during the war induced investment. U.S. capitalists purchased and built new sugar mills. After the war, the fall in sugar prices caused the bankruptcy of many Cuban-owned mills that had overextended their borrowing during the sugar fever. Through a process of foreclosures, U.S. banks and corporations achieved control of an additional 15 percent of the Cuban crop. From 1920 to 1924, the U.S. share of Cuba's principal export crop increased from 48 to 63 percent.[66] Both the process of erection of new mills during the boom and the process of foreclosure after it increased the share of Cuban mills owned by U.S. corporations. Five foreign-owned corporations owning multiple mills augmented the sugar production of the island in sixteen very large mills which produced nearly a million tons of sugar by the end of the 1920s. The majority of these mills were located on lands untouched by sugar monoculture in the nineteenth century, in the provinces of Camagüey and Oriente. The average production of sugar per mill was slightly over fifty-seven thousand tons, well above the average of twenty-six thousand tons for Cuban mills in 1913. Other mills were built by Cubans during the war.

United States	Other Foreign	Unknown	All Mills
39	2	11	172
23	1	6	100
272,462	1,008	32,827	743,434
153,922	6,552	34,742	605,674
426,384	7,560	67,570	1,349,107
64	13	49	55
36	87	51	45
724,382	6,317	64,579	1,592,573
63	46	49	54
37	0	5	100
1,013,265	11,338	139,205	2,765,492
21	15	18	19

The east-west division in Cuban agriculture is best exemplified by the case of the Cuba Cane Sugar Corporation, the largest enterprise created during World War I. In contrast to the other concerns established during the war, which typically were new mills in frontier regions, the banker-financed corporation purchased mills in the western part of the island. By the end of the world war, the management of the Cuba Cane discovered the disparity of conditions prevailing in the sugar mills of the older region of sugar culture in the west and the mills of the virgin regions of the east. In the west, the corporation encountered two problems: difficulties in buying and consolidating land from a multiplicity of owners and the power of the already established independent colonos. The first problem is evident in the reports on the cane lands of the corporation.[67]

The corporation purchased the lands of the mills and attempted to purchase surrounding lands where possible, leasing lands where necessary. In Central San Ignacio, a tract of land of 2,251 acres called San Francisco del Sinú did not appear in the local registrar's office and was still under contention in 1919. At Ingenio Feliz, the registration of the deed of conveyance of land to the corporation was suspended because a piece of land called San Antonio of eight acres did not appear as the property of the vendor. At Central Mercedes the title of the corporation had to be written "without prejudice to the rights that may be in the children and grandchildren of Mrs. Celia Hugartey y Smith in the finca Pedernales No. 1, which is one seventh of the tract of 19,992 acres, forming the plantation called Central Mercedes." At Central Lugareño a strip of land marked with a "K" in the deed was

Table 7.7. Sugar Production in Cuba, by Province, 1914 and 1918

Province	1914 Sugar Production in Tons	1918 Sugar Production in Tons	Percentage Change
Havana	344,013	450,938	31
Matanzas	591,988	810,550	37
Santa Clara	841,100	1,154,725	37
Camagüey	335,238	689,813	106
Oriente	733,850	1,092,163	49
Cuba total	2,846,188	4,198,188	48

Source: National City Bank of New York, *Cuba: Review of Commercial, Industrial and Economic Conditions in 1919* (New York: National City Bank of New York, 1919).

used as a right-of-way for the railroad and did not appear as the property of the vendor. In Central Socorro the original purchase of land was satisfactory, but a subsequent attempt to consolidate land from surrounding owners led to the suspension of the registration of the land "for the reason that it appears to be registered in favor of another person." In western Cuba the corporation encountered a pattern of land fragmentation which corresponded to the evolution of sugar production after the abolition of slavery. Sugar mills in the west were surrounded by independent cane farmers. The task of land consolidation was difficult. The allocation of land to sugar mills and to farmers had occurred according to the technological and productive imperatives of an earlier age in which the scale of production was more limited. The Cuba Cane Sugar Corporation wanted to purchase mills and sufficient lands to produce all the cane that the mills might need. Instead, it encountered the formidable obstacle of an entrenched class of independent colonos.

In other regions the corporation encountered a different obstacle to the acquisition of land. The deed to Central Lequeito was not yet executed in 1919. Half of the land of the Lequeito estate was situated on lands of haciendas comuneras. Under the Spanish colonial regime, this form of land title had been used in cattle ranching regions. The deeds of grant were circular and stipulated ownership of land up to a specified radius around a central point. The haciendas comuneras were a "corporate" or "communal" sort of land ownership prevalent in sparsely populated regions. In some instances, this led to considerable litigation over the boundaries of the estates. The expansion of the sugar estates in the eastern provinces proceeded in large measure as a function of the conversion of haciendas comuneras into delimited private property allotments. In 1914, Benito Celorio published a book complaining about the scandal of the transfers of hacienda comunera lands to "land eating interests" (*intereses geófagos*) at the service of U.S.

corporations in the eastern part of the island.[68] A sharp contrast emerged between the partitioned land of the west and the immense contiguous blocks of land available in the east, representing the contrast between the conversion of the older sugar mills and the establishment of new ones on virgin lands.

With the exception of the Cuba Cane, U.S. corporations established their newest mills in the eastern provinces, primarily in Camagüey and Oriente. The eastern areas had not experienced an expansion of the ingenio system in the nineteenth century comparable to that of Matanzas. The system of landed property in eastern Cuba was, as a result, different from that of western Cuba. Lower population densities and availability of land had permitted the development there, as in the Dominican Republic, of haciendas comuneras. As in the Dominican Republic, the haciendas comuneras were a communal system of landholding in which individuals possessed pesos (shares) to a title of land and enjoyed the right to use the land without holding a particular, delimited allotment in private property. The delimitation of land into private parcels was problematic and gave rise to many legal litigations over the titles. It seems that this system of pesos comuneros, or haciendas comuneras, as they were known in Cuba, allowed the transfer of large tracts of land to private interests after successful litigation in the courts. Benito Celorio's contemporary work on the haciendas comuneras in Cuba condemned the "dubious" acquisition of land by "*land eating interests*" in eastern Cuba.

> For some time now, and in coincidence with the fast increase in the value of lands, greed has arisen among certain elements, always open to any source of profit, even if it means taking recourse to doubtful means of questionable morality.
>
> The press has recorded the fact daily, reflecting the distress and the more or less noisy protests, and has branded the authors *geófagos*. They seated their operations in the eastern province in which, as we exposed, the original distribution of land and the uncertainty of the land areas and figures allows fabulous increments.[69]

Celorio pointed out that a process of transfer of land in large tracts was taking place in the east at a rapid pace. "It may be said that the phenomenon of the scandalous transactions of land delimitations is thoroughly eastern and is due to the absence of accurate facts in the original titles."[70]

The haciendas comuneras existed east of Sancti Spiritus, and their permanence in a region was a sign of the absence of a preestablished plantation economy. Although more prevalent in Camagüey and Oriente, haciendas comuneras existed in the provinces of Santa Clara, where Central Lequeito was located. Although this type of landed institution was an obstacle to the attempt of the Cuba Cane Sugar Corporation to obtain the land titles of Central Lequeito, in general the existence of haciendas comuneras permitted the expansion of immense U.S. corporate sugar mills in eastern Cuba.

The price boom of World War I allowed U.S. corporations such as the Cuba Cane to increase production in the western mills without much concern for cost efficiency. As the war drew to a close in 1918 and lower prices loomed on the horizon, however, the profitability of the western mills became a cause for concern. The Cuba Cane Sugar Corporation discovered that it was unable to control the price of the cane delivered in the western mills. An audit report of 1919 complained that "nearly all the cane used by the Cuba Cane Corporation *is Colono cane.*" Thirteen of the seventeen mills of the corporation were located in the western part of the island, and only four of the sugar mills were in the eastern part.[71] The strength of the independent colonato in the west was formidable, inasmuch as it represented a congealed structure left behind by the transition and conversion from ingenio to central in the two decades after abolition. When the unitary ingenios, which produced their own cane were replaced by centrales, the new expanded cane-grinding units entered into competition with each other for the cane grown by surrounding cane farmers. The differentiation of the hacendados into colonos and centralistas entailed the emergence of a new competitive structure in the Cuban countryside. An internal audit of the Cuba Cane Sugar Corporation complained in 1919 that "many colonos grow cane on land not under the control of the central, and where favorably located with respect to a number of centrals, they are able, through competition, to receive higher prices than the general average in the locality. The control by centrals of sufficient cane to work the mills to full capacity is, therefore, an important factor."[72] In 1919, an independent audit of the operations of the Cuba Cane Sugar Corporation questioned the wisdom of the purchase of mills in the western part of the island, indicating once again that the new prototype of North American central was based not on scarcities of capital and of labor and the consequent need to divide the industrial and agricultural operations, but on an abundance of capital and a desire to control through ownership if possible the land surrounding the sugar mills: "The cane situation for the Corporation's western centrals is not so favorable. The number of independent colonos is greater and there is a larger number of mills, so that in some localities the competition is very keen."[73] High prices of sugar during the war attenuated the impact of the independent colonato on the sugar mills of the Cuba Cane. It was possible to make sugar at almost any cost and still register a profit because of the acute shortage created by the collapse of the beet crops. But the price of cane was not the only factor pushing the costs of production upward. The prices of coal, oil, sacks, and labor power also increased during the war. This led the auditors of the Cuba Cane to question whether the western mills could resume production at profitable rates once world competition was restored at the end of the war. The North American corporate interests pursued the unitary type of enterprise in which mill and cane lands were owned by the same interest. The division of labor had been a useful expedient in the industry in the context of abolition, scarcity of labor, scarcity of capital, and the conversion of ingenios to centrales. The social system of the centrales of the east after 1898, and particularly after 1914, was different. It did not rely on the independent colonos.

The new mills owned by North American corporate capital were considerably larger than the average Cuban mill and considerably larger than the other new mills built in the period 1914–34. E. F. Atkins's Punta Alegre Sugar Company owned six of the new mills. The average Punta Alegre mill produced 55,000 tons of sugar in 1928–29. Cuba Cane's Violeta mill produced 63,000 tons that year. The American Sugar Refining Company owned two of the new mills: the Cunagua, with production of 75,534 tons, and the Jaronú, with production of 104,940 tons. The mills belonging to the Rionda interests independent of the Cuba Cane Sugar Corporation, Elia and Céspedes, produced 53,000 and 40,000 tons of sugar respectively. The General Sugars Company owned four of the new mills, with average production of 48,000 tons per mill. All of these mills were located in Camagüey or in Oriente. Thus World War I induced an expansion of the large North American central in eastern Cuba (see Table 7.8).

Altogether, four groups linked to the House of Morgan, one group linked to City Bank, plus the Hershey Corporation, owned sixteen of the post-1914 mills in Cuba. Combined, these new North American mills produced almost a million tons of sugar in 1929. The contrast with the smaller centrales of the pre-1914 period is great. But in addition, the contrast with the post-1914 mills in Cuba not owned by large North American concerns is great. Between 1916 and 1934, twenty-one new mills not owned by these five groups started operations. On average, the new mill not owned by U.S. capital produced nineteen thousand tons of sugar, as opposed to fifty-seven thousand for the corporate North American centrales. A new type of industrial colossus invaded the Cuban landscape during World War I and its immediate aftermath (see Map 7.1). The new central was, in the words of Rafael Bernabe, "an integrated chemical-industrial plant, containing a complex 'vascular system' through which the object of labor moved continuously, without the intervention of hand or hand-tools."[74]

The sugar boom of World War I induced an expansion of the railroad network

Table 7.8. U.S. Corporate Mills Built in Cuba during World War I

Company	Mill	Location (province)	Year of Foundation	Output in 1925 (tons)
Punta Alegre Sugar Company	1 Baragua	Camagüey	1916	98,406
Punta Alegre Sugar Company	2 Florida	Camagüey	1916	61,463
Punta Alegre Sugar Company	3 Punta Alegre	Camagüey	1917	87,862
Punta Alegre Sugar Company	4 Baguano	Oriente	1918	41,493
Punta Alegre Sugar Company	5 San German	Oriente	1919	28,458
Punta Alegre Sugar Company	6 Tacajó	Oriente	1916	41,945
Cuba Cane Sugar Corporation	7 Violeta	Camagüey	1918	79,338
American Sugar Refining Company	8 Cunagua	Camagüey	1918	97,684
American Sugar Refining Company	9 Jaronú	Camagüey	1921	97,554
General Sugars Company	10 San Cristóbal	P. del Río	1920	29,344
General Sugars Company	11 Agramonte	Camagüey	1916	64,591
General Sugars Company	12 Estrella	Camagüey	1918	52,585
General Sugars Company	13 Vertiente	Camagüey	1921	57,005
Manuel Rionda	14 Elia	Camagüey	1916	67,770
Manuel Rionda	15 Céspedes	Camagüey	1916	57,564
Hershey Corporation	16 Hershey	Havana	1919	33,808
Total output in 1928				997,143
Output of average mill				62,321

Source: Oscar Zanneti, "Centrales de propiedad yanqui en Cuba," (Havana: Instituto de Historia de Cuba, 1988); Farr & Co., *Manual of Sugar Companies* (New York: Farr & Co., 1926).

of Cuba and of the total carrying capacity. The development of the Cuba Railroad made the interior accessible to the sea.[75] In the period 1913–20, the four largest railroad concerns expanded the total number of railroad wagons in operation from 10,618 to 16,572.[76] Changes introduced by the war also include the vertical expansion of interests using sugar as an input in an attempt to control sources of raw material in a context of increasing prices for the raw product. Such is the case of the Hires & Company (Hires Root Beer), the Armour Corporation, and the Hershey Corporation (chocolate manufacturers). Hershey Corporation was an independent enterprise not linked to the refining establishment or to the Wall Street interests. It did not have any linkages to railroad or other sugar enterprises in Cuba.[77] These processes of vertical integration parallelled the further integration of the Cuban economy to the economy of the United States. In 1915, the Peninsular and Occidental Steamship Line opened a railway ferry service between Key West and Havana. The ferries were able to carry thirty standard railroad cars. According to a contemporary report, this phenomenal infrastructural integration meant that "sugar and molasses may be loaded at the Cuban mills and forwarded through to destination in the United States without transfer; while the heavy

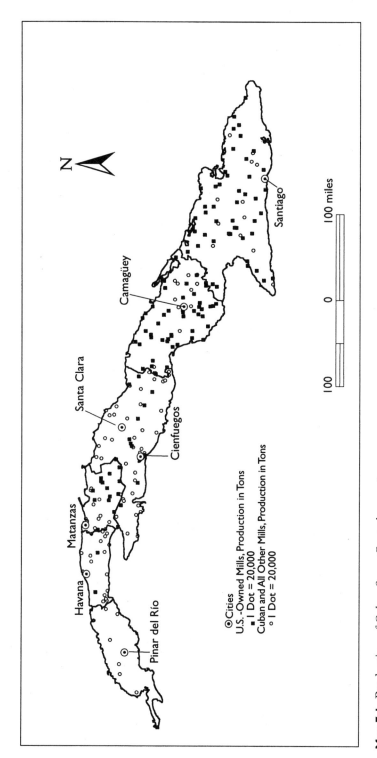

Map 7.1. Production of Cuban Sugar Centrales, 1928

Table 7.9. Number and Production of Sugar Mills in Cuba, by Province

Province	1901–2			1913–14			1923–24		
	No. Mills	Tons of Sugar	% of Cuban Output	No. Mills	Tons of Sugar	% of Cuban Output	No. Mills	Tons of Sugar	% of Cuban Output
Pinar del Río	8	26,264	3	7	57,818	2	10	149,469	3
Havana	17	96,675	11	19	330,147	12	18	375,046	8
Matanzas	56	331,648	38	39	633,000	23	32	562,438	12
Santa Clara	46	300,786	34	69	906,879	33	61	998,194	22
Camagüey	2	22,541	3	7	225,863	8	26	1,250,279	28
Oriente	16	101,785	12	31	611,785	22	47	1,199,727	26
Cuba total	145	879,699	100	172	2,765,492	100	194	4,535,153	100

Sources: José Huguet y Balanzo, *Ingenios que han hecho zafra en el año de 1901 a 1902 en cada una de las provincias de que se compone la isla de Cuba* (Havana: Imprenta Mercantil, 1902); Secretaría de Agricultura, Comercio y Trabajo de Cuba, *Portfolio azucarero: industria azucarera de Cuba, 1912–1914* (Havana: La Moderna Poesía, 1915); Farr & Co., *Manual of Sugar Companies* (New York: Farr & Co., 1924).

machinery from the United States can be loaded at place of manufacture and carried through to its Cuban destination without transfer."[78]

The centuries-old contrast between east and west in Cuban history continued into the twentieth century and took new forms. The construction of new mills in Camagüey and Oriente during the world war inclined the productive balance between the regions. In 1923, the eastern provinces of Camagüey and Oriente surpassed the western region in sugar production. The virgin east finally became the center of twentieth-century sugar monoculture. The province of Oriente produced 12 percent of the island's sugar in 1902, 22 percent in 1914, and 26 percent in 1924. The expansion of sugar production in Camagüey relative to the other provinces was even more drastic, rising from 2 percent of the island's output in 1902 to 8 percent in 1914 and 28 percent in 1924. Of the six provinces, Camagüey accounted for the smallest share of sugar production in 1902 and for the largest share in 1924. Nowhere in Cuba was the expansion caused by the world war more dramatic. Combined, Camagüey and Oriente produced 54 percent of Cuba's sugar in 1924, up from 15 percent in 1902.

The significance of uneven regional development lies in the changing social structure of sugar plantations as one moves from west to east in the Cuban landscape. The independent colonato lost weight in the island as a whole because of the great expansion of sugar production in the eastern provinces under a new system controlled principally by great U.S. agribusiness enterprises that leased lands to colonos instead of buying cane from independent farmers. The expansion in the eastern provinces was also accompanied by an increase of the share of sugar production under the control of United States corporations (see Table 7.9).

The Centrales of Colonial Puerto Rico

In the island of Puerto Rico the expansion of U.S. corporate agribusiness took place immediately after the occupation of 1898. The Aguirre, Fajardo, and South Porto Rico companies were all established in the first years of U.S. colonial rule. In 1926 a fourth corporation, the United Porto Rico Sugar Company, purchased existing mills in a process similar to the establishment of the General Sugars Company in Cuba. Lacking extensions of land comparable to those of Cuba, the U.S.-owned mills of Puerto Rico generally owned less land than their counterparts in Cuba or the Dominican Republic, even when the largest mills, such as the South Porto Rico Sugar Company's Guánica mill, had cane-crushing capacities on the same scale. In addition to the modern centrales owned by U.S. corporations and native entrepreneurs, there also existed in Puerto Rico many small enterprises that continued to supply local markets. Of 212 sugar-producing properties listed in the tax rolls of the U.S. colonial authorities in 1910, 45 were classified as centrales, 23 as haciendas, 30 as trapiches. The majority of the units (114) were listed without classification. The centrales had the largest output of sugar per unit at 7,920 tons per unit. The gap between the units classified as centrales and the next type of enterprise, ranked by size, was dramatic. The sugar-producing enterprises classified as haciendas had a mean output of 99 tons of sugar, followed by the unclassified units at 24.5 tons. The smallest enterprises, classified as trapiches, averaged 17 tons of sugar per unit. From the evidence, it appears that the unclassified units were located in a position intermediary between the haciendas and the trapiches but much closer in average output per unit to the trapiches than to the haciendas. For all practical purposes, we may consider them trapiches. The 45 units classified as centrales represented 21 percent of the sugar-producing units but produced 98 percent of the sugar. In other words, the 80 percent of the enterprises that were not classified as centrales produced barely 2 percent of the sugar of Puerto Rico in 1910. Evidently, the tax rolls kept accounts of radically different enterprises.[79]

The list of sugar-producing enterprises included very small units located in the mountainous interior of Puerto Rico, where the lands are not suitable for efficient sugarcane cultivation. There are records of the Rábanos, Perseverancia, Cuchilla

Table 7.10. Sugar-Producing Enterprises of Puerto Rico, 1910

Type of Unit	No. of Units	% of Units	Aggregate Output (tons)	Average Output (tons)	% of Puerto Rico's Production
Centrales	45	21.23	356,403	7,920	98.46
Haciendas	23	10.85	2,287	99	0.63
Unclassified	114	53.77	2,790	24	0.77
Trapiches	30	14.15	504	17	0.14
All units	212	100.00	361,984	1,707	100.00

Source: "Government of Porto Rico, Treasury Department, Bureau of Property Taxes: Comparative Statistical Report of Sugar Manufactured in Porto Rico from the Crops of 1907, 1908, 1909, and 1910," Records of the Bureau of Insular Affairs, Record Group 350, File 422, National Archives, Washington, D.C.

Grande, and Constancia mills of Lares, which had a small production of sugar and were classified as trapiches. Tomás Pietri, A. Anziani Franchi, F. Bianchi Ursini, Francisco Oliver, and Salomón Bartolomey are listed as owners of small sugar-producing properties in the municipality of Adjuntas. Their units were also classified as trapiches. The units classified as centrales and haciendas, by contrast, were located principally in coastal towns. The trapiches listed were small units that produced low-grade sugars for local markets in the interior highlands.

The haciendas exported 480 tons of sugar in 1910 and sold 1,807 tons locally. Only 21 percent of the sugar produced by the haciendas was exported. The unclassified units exported 865 tons of sugar and sold 1,925 locally. Only 31 percent of their output was exported. The trapiches, at the bottom of the scale, exported 6 tons of sugar and sold 498 tons locally. Only 1 percent of their production was exported. Thus the haciendas, unclassified units, and trapiches sold most of their sugar in the local market. The centrales, by contrast, produced vastly superior amounts of sugar and exported 96 percent of their production (see Table 7.10).

The 167 enterprises not classified as centrales exported less than one-third of their minute output. The 15,478 tons of sugar produced in the central mills for local consumption represented only 4 percent of the production of the 45 modern units. But even this small share of the output of the centrales was larger than the 4,230 tons of sugar produced by the remaining 167 smaller enterprises for the local market and represented 78 percent of local consumption. The production of the 167 haciendas, trapiches, and unclassified units did not supply even a fourth of the island's consumption and accounted for less than 2 percent of exports. The haciendas and trapiches were marginal enterprises of little significance for the sugar economy of the island as a whole. The Guánica mill of the South Porto Rico Sugar Company alone produced more sugar than these 167 outdated mills combined.

Table 7.11. Centrales of Puerto Rico, 1910

Output of Sugar in Tons	No. of Mills	% of Mills	Sugar Production (tons)	% of Production
Under 1,000	5	11%	459	0%
to 5,000	15	33%	54,336	15%
to 10,000	16	36%	113,161	32%
to 20,000	6	13%	80,544	23%
Over 20,000	3	7%	107,903	30%
All centrales	45	100%	356,403	100%

Source: "Government of Porto Rico, Treasury Department, Bureau of Property Taxes: Comparative Statistical Report of Sugar Manufactured in Porto Rico from the Crops of 1907, 1908, 1909, and 1910," Records of the Bureau of Insular Affairs, Record Group 350, File 422, National Archives, Washington, D.C.

The group of modern mills that produced for export was in turn stratified. A small number of large units owned by U.S. capital produced a large share of the output of the centrales, with the Guánica mill producing over 57,000 tons. The top 20 percent of the centrales (9 units) produced 53 percent of the sugar. The second quintile produced 20 percent of the sugar, the third quintile 14 percent, and the fourth quintile 10 percent. The bottom quintile produced a mere 2 percent of the product. The range in the output of sugar stretched from units like Central Barahona in Morovis, which produced 90 tons of sugar in 1910, or Central Soller in Camuy (250 tons), to Centrales Aguirre, Fajardo, and Guánica, with production of over 25,000 tons of sugar each (see Table 7.11 and Map 7.2).

Puerto Rican sugar production did not increase as fast during World War I as did the production of Cuba or the Dominican Republic. Total output increased from 347,000 tons in 1914 to 407,000 tons in 1920, an increase of 17 percent (in contrast to a 54 percent increase in Cuba and a 50 percent increase in the Dominican Republic in the same period). Sugar production could not be augmented through the creation of large sugar mills with extensive lands for cultivation of the type that developed in eastern Cuba or in Barahona and La Romana in the Dominican Republic. Nevertheless, sugar production continued to increase steadily. In the 1920s, the Puerto Rican landscape can be conceptualized as having two zones. The rectangular shape of the island contains, in the middle, a range of mountains called the Cordillera Central, which is located along an east-west axis and occupies most of the municipios. Surrounding this cordillera, along the coast there is a belt of flat land. The interior mountainous region was the site of the coffee industry. The coastal belt of land was the site of sugar production. A division of the quasi-rectangular island along a diagonal, from Boquerón in the Southwest to Loíza in

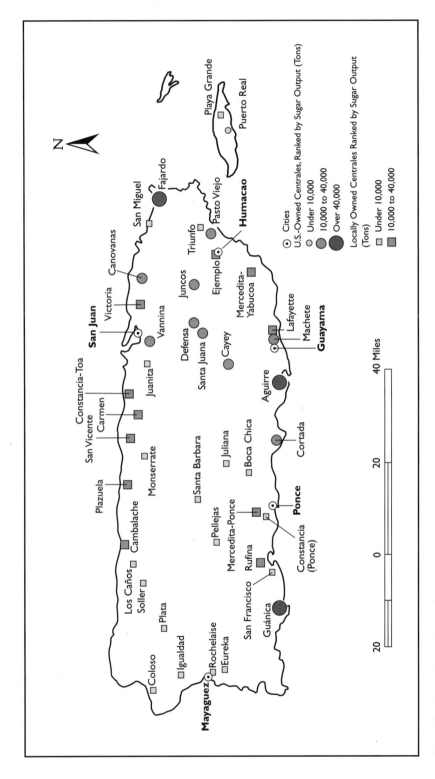

Map 7.2. Centrales of Puerto Rico, 1927

the northeast, separates the island into the zone of the large and the small centrales. The southern and eastern coastal plains were the site of the U.S.-owned centrales and some smaller locally owned centrales. The northern and western coastal plains contained only locally owned centrales.[80]

With the exception of the South Porto Rico Sugar Company, which owned Central Guánica, one of the largest of the world, the centrales of Puerto Rico were smaller than those of Cuba. Puerto Rico's inclusion within the tariff system of the United States, however, rendered the sugar industry there extremely profitable. The *Manual of Sugar Companies* of 1927 remarked that "whereas Cuban raw sugar pays the United States a duty of 1.7648 cents per pound, Porto Rican raws are admitted duty free, but sell here at a price usually on a parity with Cuban raws duty paid."[81] Despite the relatively smaller sizes of the corporations, the *Manual* advised investors that "satisfactory earnings and dividend records have been established and maintained, while a substantial proportion of excess earnings has been applied to further expansion of the business. . . . In this connection we direct attention to the descriptive and statistical information on Central Aguirre Sugar Co., Fajardo Sugar Co., and South Porto Rico Sugar Co."[82]

Beginning in the southwestern extreme of the island and moving east along the southern coast, we find the first central to be the Guánica Mill of the South Porto Rico Sugar Company. This was the largest on the island and one of the largest in the world. Guánica produced 93,031 tons of sugar in 1926–27, but unlike the eastern Cuban mills, Guánica Central relied extensively on colono cane. While Central Guánica owned 21,273 acres of land, 56 percent of the cane crushed was grown by colonos.[83] Central Guánica was built in 1905. In 1911, its grinding capacity exceeded the local output of cane by such a big factor that Central Guánica purchased twenty thousand acres of land in La Romana and began to import cane from the Dominican Republic. The cane was grown in La Romana and shipped overnight across the Mona Passage to be ground in Guánica the next day.[84] The company's *Fiftieth Anniversary Report* stated:

A unique feature of the Dominican operation was that for several years all of the cane was cut, shipped by rail to the pier, loaded on steamers, shipped overnight to the Guánica factory and unloaded in the morning in time to be ground that day. This required careful scheduling to prevent deterioration of the cane, which must be processed within twenty four to forty eight hours after it has been cut. In 1917, when 7,300 acres were under cultivation, the officers authorized the construction of a factory at La Romana, but some Dominican cane continued to be ground in Puerto Rico.[85]

The expansion into La Romana occurred after the U.S. occupation of the Dominican Republic at a time of rising sugar prices during World War I. Unlike the mills of Oriente, which were able to acquire vast tracts of virgin land in Cuba, the South Porto Rico operated under the constraints of limited land in the densely populated island of Puerto Rico. For this reason, even though the Guánica was until World War I one of the largest, if not the largest, mill in the world, it is somewhat different from the eastern centrales of Cuba in that it relied on colono canes to a greater extent. The Guánica mill was an early giant in the industry. Central Romana was more in tune with the movement of expansion during World War I.

Further east along the southern coast, in the municipality of Salinas, was the Aguirre Sugar Company. Aguirre was the second largest central in Puerto Rico, and the Aguirre Sugar Company owned another two centrales in the nearby towns of Santa Isabel (Central Cortada) and Guayama (Central Machete). Aguirre produced in 1926 61,786 tons of sugar, Cortada produced 13,652, and Machete 19,129. In combination, three centrales located near each other and connected by the railroad of the company produced 92,267 tons of sugar. The Aguirre mills owned 24,134 acres of land, and only 10 percent of the cane they ground was grown by colonos.[86] It therefore seems to fit the pattern that the larger the central, the smaller the share of land planted by independent colonos.

In the coastal belt that lies between Guánica and Salinas, between the Guánica and Aguirre mills, there were five mills: the San Francisco, Rufina, Constancia, Mercedita, and Bocachica. The last two were owned by the local Serallés family and produced 20,327 and 9,280 tons of sugar respectively. The San Francisco, Rufina, and Constancia produced 4,035, 14,175, and 3,928 tons of sugar respectively.

Moving along the southern coast from Salinas to Fajardo, the site of the next large U.S. concern, we find six mills: the Lafayette (17,777 tons), the Columbia (5,860 tons), the Mercedita of Yabucoa (19,679 tons), El Ejemplo (10,614), Pasto Viejo (13,037 tons), and Triunfo (4,750 tons). The Fajardo Sugar Company, the third U.S. concern, owned the large Fajardo Mill (43,927 tons) and one smaller mill (Canóvanas, 23,951 tons).[87]

The United Porto Rico Sugar Company was organized in 1926. In the zafra of 1927–28, the company had five mills in operation. These were located in the east-central region, within the boundaries of the imaginary line from Central Guánica to Central Canóvanas of the Fajardo Sugar Company, which delimit the area of foreign ownership. The five centrales of the United Porto Rico—Pasto Viejo,

Juncos, Defensa, Cayey and Santa Juana—produced 86,641 tons of sugar in 1926. The coastal belt of land from Guánica to Loíza was the site of the four U.S. concerns operating in Puerto Rico and the site of two of three local concerns that owned more than one central: the Serallés interests (Mercedita and Boca Chica) and the Roig interests (Roig and El Ejemplo).[88]

West of Loiza, moving along the perimeter of the island from Central Victoria in Carolina to Central Eureka in Hormigueros, we find only locally owned mills: Victoria, Vannina, Juanita, Constancia, Carmen, San Vicente, Monserrate, Plazuela, Cambalache, Los Caños, Coloso, Igualdad, Rochelaise, and Eureka. Average production for these mills was 12,685 tons of sugar. Inland we find four centrales: Soller, Pellejas, Santa Bárbara, and Juliana. Average production for these mills was 1,043 tons of sugar. Vieques had two mills: the Puerto Real (6,504 tons) and the Playa Grande (8,115 tons).

The exceptional profitability of sugar mills in Puerto Rico because of its inclusion in the U.S. customs area explains the interest of the United Porto Rico in these smaller mills. Puerto Rico did not experience a boom of construction of centrales during World War I. There was no phenomenon comparable to the expansion of the Cuba Cane or the Punta Alegre companies in Cuba. The only concern that expanded during the war boom, the South Porto Rico Sugar Company, expanded into the Dominican Republic. The large mills of Puerto Rico (Guánica, Aguirre, Fajardo) were built in the years immediately following the U.S. occupation of 1898. The United Porto Rico, which expanded in the mid-1920s, did so by acquiring five mills which on average produced 13,066 tons of cane each. The six mills of the Punta Alegre in Cuba, all new and all built after 1914, by contrast, produced 50,169 tons of sugar each.[89] If anything, the expansion of the United Porto Rico is comparable to that of its counterpart in Cuba, the General Sugars Company of City Bank, which acquired mills that went bankrupt during the sugar price slump of the 1920s.

In 1934, when the system of sugar quotas was established in an attempt to regulate the problem of overproduction, Puerto Rico received a favorable quota relative to Cuba. In 1935, Puerto Rico produced 43 percent as much sugar as Cuba, up from approximately 10 percent in 1920 and 1921. Direct colonial rule benefited the U.S. concerns operating there, as well as the class of local centralistas. The tariff, and under the Costigan Jones system, the quota, were the cement that bonded the Puerto Rican centralistas and the U.S. concerns into a single interest. Formal colonial rule gave producers in Puerto Rico an advantage in the U.S. market over Cuba and the Dominican Republic.

The Centrales of the Dominican Republic

At the opposite end of the spectrum, the sugar industry of the Dominican Republic received no special tariff advantage in the U.S. market. The Dominican sugar industry had undergone a limited process of expansion from 1890 to 1910. San Pedro de Macorís had become the center of the sugar industry during the late nineteenth century, but this development did not yet turn the Dominican Republic into the plantation regime. The expansion of the sugar industry occurred during the U.S. occupation of 1916–24. In the early 1930s, the sugar industry was geographically situated along the southern coast of the island, in what Dominicans refer to as "the south" (the southern coast west of Santo Domingo) and "the east" (the southern coast east of Santo Domingo) while extensive peasant farming survived in El Cibao. There were in 1933 two ingenios in Puerto Plata, the port city of El Cibao. Of these, the Amistad was a very small mill (751 tons) while the Monte Llano produced 12,000 tons. San Pedro de Macorís had six ingenios, Santo Domingo had two. The largest ingenios belonged to the South Porto Rico Sugar Company (La Romana in La Romana, 93,000 tons; the Santa Fe in Santa Fe, 50,288 tons) and to the West India Sugar/Cuban Dominican companies (B. H. Howell–James H. Post–National Sugar group), which owned the Barahona (43,316 tons), the Consuelo (57,720 tons), and the Quisqueya (30,427 tons), plus two smaller mills, the San Isidro and Las Pajas.[90] Combined, the seven mills of the West India and the South Porto Rico produced 309,436 tons. These two corporations controlled 77 percent of sugar production. Sugar was the principal export of the Dominican Republic in 1929 (see Map 7.3).

The *Manual of Sugar Companies* referred to the "progress" of the industry and associated it with the introduction of American capital, without, however, mentioning the "facilitating" events of 1916–24.

> There has been a steady upward trend in sugar production during recent years, as shown by comparing the crop of 47,000 long tons in 1903–04 with the record crop of 427,621 long tons in 1931–32. This progress has been chiefly due to the introduction of American capital, notably through the South Porto Rico Sugar Co., and the Cuban Dominican Sugar Corporation, the latter now succeeded by the West India Sugar Corporation. The mills operated by these two companies in the Dominican Republic during 1932–33 were alone responsible for over 70% of the country's entire crop.[91]

The Dominican industry differed from the Cuban and the Puerto Rican in that it did not enjoy the benefits of imperial preference. Unlike Cuban sugars, which

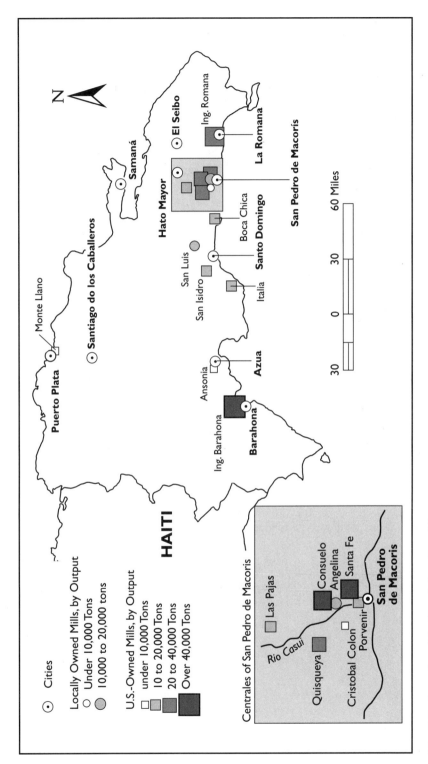

Map 7.3. Centrales of the Dominican Republic, 1930

entered the U.S. market at a 20 percent reduction of the full tariff, or Puerto Rican sugars, which entered free, the Dominican sugar industry paid the full tariff in the U.S. market. As a consequence, the Dominican sugar industry found its market primarily in Europe and Canada, even though the main producers were North American concerns.

> The full duty on foreign sugar, amounting to 2.50 cents a pound, is imposed upon all sugars entering the United States from the Dominican Republic. As this prevents selling upon a basis equal to Cuban raws which enjoy a 20% preferential tariff, most of this country's sugar is exported to other countries, principally the United Kingdom, which in 1932 purchased 70% of the crop. Sugar is the chief Dominican product for export, having constituted 61.44 per cent of all exports in 1932.[92]

Of the three cases, the Dominican shows the highest degree of industrial concentration, with two concerns owning three-quarters of the industry. Of the three locations, the Dominican Republic had the lowest output. This compact, highly centralized industry did not subject the Dominican Republic to the convulsions experienced in Cuba with the problems in the sugar market in the 1920s. The industry was concentrated in the south and relied principally on immigrant labor. Because it was outside the U.S. customs area and oriented toward Europe and Canada, the convulsions experienced by the industry during the Great Depression were not of the magnitude experienced by the Cuban industry. National production stood at 400,000 tons of sugar and could be disposed of more easily than the immense Cuban surpluses. Cuban production had reached the five-million-ton landmark in 1925, leading producers in that island to limit output in an attempt to cause a rise in price, with disastrous consequences.

By the end of the 1920s overproduction was afflicting the American Sugar Kingdom. The immense investments of U.S. corporations had reconfigured the insular economies of Cuba, Puerto Rico, and the Dominican Republic, strengthening sugar monoculture in the first and forcing a turn toward sugar in the other two. Everywhere the increase in the scale of operations was dramatic, while the transformation of the social structure of cane agriculture was swift, permitting the characterization of 1898–1934 as a totally new period in the history of sugar monoculture in the Caribbean. After World War I, few mills were built in any of the islands. The productive structure was in place. The construction of new mills practically ceased during the Great Depression of the 1930s.

Economic Collapse
and Revolution

World War I increased the demand for Caribbean sugar in Europe and drove up its international price. Before the war, the European allies of the United States were either self-sufficient in sugar or had drawn their supplies from continental Europe. The outbreak of war with Germany cut off the United Kingdom's sources of sugar in central Europe. The beet-growing areas of France were overrun by the invading German army. The principal alternative sources of sugar were Java and Cuba. The scarcity of shipping during the war impeded the importation of Javanese sugar, forcing the allies to turn for their supply to Cuba, whose sugar had been sent mostly to the United States since 1902. The Sugar Division of the United States Food Administration undertook the organization of sugar supply during the war through several committees: the Louisiana Sugar Committee, the (Beet) Sugar Distributing Committee, and the International Sugar Committee, which arranged for the purchase of foreign sugars in cooperation with England, France, and Italy. A government corporation known as the United States Sugar Equalization Board was created to buy the 1918–19 Cuban crop. At its meeting on November 1, 1917, the board decided that all purchases of sugar from Cuba, Santo Domingo, Puerto Rico, and St. Croix would be handled by the International Sugar Committee, and all purchases from Mauritius and the British West Indies would be handled by the British

Royal Commission on the Sugar Supply. The sugars of Brazil, Peru and Java continued to sell on the open market. Louisiana, Hawaii, and U.S. domestic beet sugars were sold exclusively in the United States through an arrangement between the U.S. Food Administration, the sugar growers, and the U.S. sugar refiners. Philippine sugars sold on the open market with the understanding that British and Canadian purchases from that source would be deducted from their allotment elsewhere.[1]

The Sugar Equalization Board organized what was in effect a purchaser's cartel to keep down the price of Cuban sugar. Herbert Hoover, United States food administrator, considered that the increasing price of sugar was not the result of increased demand but rather of collusion among Cuban producers: "Certain Cuban sugar producers (who are out of our reach), have combined to force up the price of the remaining 1917 Cuban crop, prior to the new crop in December and have lifted the price of raw sugar in New York from 5.9 cents in June to 7.5 cents, duty paid, on August 16th, and this against a 3 year pre-war average of 4.2 cents."[2] But keeping the price of Cuban sugar down required a combination of buyers, which could be in violation of the Sherman Antitrust Act. Hoover therefore sought the approval of President Woodrow Wilson to set up the buyers' cartel. Wilson replied: "Personally, I entirely approve of a 'combination' such as the one here proposed, for it is *not* in restraint of trade."[3] The International Sugar Committee consisted of Sir White-Todd and John Ramsey Drake, both of London, Earl D. Babst, president of the American Sugar Refining Company, William A. Jameson of Arbuckle Brothers, and George M. Rolph of the Sugar Division of the Food Administration. Shipping of sugar was also subjected to controls. Alfred Gilbert of the New York and Cuba Mail Steamship Company served as chair of the Joint Committee on West Indies Transportation, which was charged with coordinating the transportation of sugar at regulated prices. Frank C. Munson of the Munson Steamship Line, B. R. Stoddard, president of the West India Steamship Company, Ernest M. Bull of Bull Insular Line, and Franklyn D. Mooney of the New York and Porto Rico Steamship Company were the other members of the transportation committee. The steamship barons were charged with coordinating the shipment of Cuban sugars with the Cuban Producers Committee, composed of Hannibal J. DeMesa, Ernesto Longo, Miguel Mendoza, Coronel Tarafa, and the Cuban minister to the United States, Carlos Manuel de Céspedes. A second committee composed of Robert B. Hawley, president of the Cuban American Sugar Company, and Manuel Rionda, president of the Cuba Cane Sugar Corporation, was appointed by the Cuban government. A committee of U.S. refiners was also created. Its members were Claus A. Spreckels, of New York, president of the

Federal Sugar Refining Company, James H. Post, of New York, president of the National Sugar Refining Company, Charles M. Warner, of New York, president of the Warner Sugar Refining Company, George H. Earle Jr., of Philadelphia, president of the Pennsylvania Sugar Refining Company, and Dwight P. Thomas, of Boston, president of the Revere Refining Company. The state relied on the great barons of sugar refining, shipping, and colonial sugar plantations to organize the war economy. It also fomented the cartelization of the industry under war conditions, a seemingly paradoxical event since the sugar industry was one of the principal targets of government antitrust prosecutions from the 1890s to the 1920s.

Hoover estimated in August 1917 that an increase of 1.6 cents per pound in the price of Cuban sugar would represent "an added tax upon the American people of over $30,000,000 by the end of December."[4] The imperatives of the U.S. war economy thus prevented Cuban producers from realizing the full price of sugar determined by open supply and demand. Instead of a tax on the American people, the U.S. Sugar Equalization Board passed some of the cost of the war economy to the producers of sugar in Cuba. It would be impossible to determine what the real prices would have been in the absence of state regulation, that is, the exact amount of this Cuban subsidy to the United States. Cuban producers were palliated by the fact that prices nevertheless rose significantly during the war. Controls lasted beyond the signing of the armistice and continued until January 1920. When sugar prices were freed to operate on the basis of supply and demand, sugar futures skyrocketed from 9 cents per pound to 23.57 cents. In December 1920, prices plummeted to 4.63 cents, and the Cuban "dance of the millions" ended abruptly.

Despite state controls on the price of sugar, U.S. investments in the Cuban sugar industry soared during the war, increasing the number of large sugar mills. Some of these mills were in the midst of a process of expansion in 1919–20. The plummeting of sugar prices to prewar levels in 1920–21 caused the failure of many Cuban-owned mills and of practically all of the Spanish and Cuban banks in Havana. The debt acquired during the period of fabulous prices could not be repaid on the basis of post-1920 prices, resulting in transfers of sugar mills to United States interests. Under these conditions, large mills attempted to overcome the crisis by increasing output to realize the full potential of their economies of scale. All enterprises attempted to compensate the decline in profitability per pound of sugar with an increase in total output. This strategy logically accentuated the problem of overproduction, which plagued the sugar industry continuously after 1920. Seeking relief from plummeting prices, domestic sugar producers in the United States were able to persuade Congress to raise the sugar tariff. For Cuba, the problem of overproduction was compounded by the tariff increase of

1921, which raised the duty on Cuban sugar to 1.6 cents per pound, and by another increase to 1.7648 cents in 1922. Britain, the second largest purchaser of Cuban sugar, introduced imperial preferences in 1919 and established a subsidy for domestic beet consumption in 1924.[5] The crisis of overproduction of the sugar industry began in the early 1920s. When the New York stock market crashed in 1929 and the entire world economy entered into depression, the already acute problem of overproduction in the sugar industry was accentuated and became unbearable.

Before the onset of generalized crisis, the Cuban government intervened in 1926 to restrict output in an attempt to restore international sugar prices. In 1926, the Verdeja Act stipulated that all mills in Cuba should reduce output by 10 percent. The act also made provision to guarantee that all the cane of Cuban colonos be ground before that of administration lands, and some protections were enacted for the smallest farmers. This voluntary restriction of Cuban sugar output failed to boost international sugar prices, and the harvest of 1929 was carried out without quantitative restrictions. In 1930, a "gentleman's agreement" known as the Chadbourne plan supposedly committed representatives from Cuba, Puerto Rico, the Philippines, and the United States to a voluntary reduction of output for the years 1931–34.[6] Each region would limit its production to the levels reached in 1930 in an attempt to restore prices. The Hawley-Smoot Tariff in 1930 raised tariffs on Cuban sugar to 2 cents per pound. Average prices for sugar in New York declined from 3.77 cents per pound in 1930 to 2.92 cents in 1932. With a tariff of 2 cents per pound on their sugar, producers in Cuba received only 0.92 cents per pound in 1932. In the meantime, beet sugar production in the United States increased by 59 percent between 1930 and 1933, and Philippine production increased by 49 percent, in open violation of the gentleman's agreement of the Chadbourne plan.

The restrictive policy of the Verdeja Act and Chadbourne plan caused a dramatic decline in total Cuban sugar production. The two other zones of the American Sugar Kingdom, Puerto Rico and the Dominican Republic, experienced a continuing increase in sugar output from 1925 to 1934. In 1933, Cuban sugar output was only 39 percent of what it had been in 1925 (see Table 8.1). Some Cuban sugar producers, notably Julio Lobo, had expressed sharp opposition to the restrictive policies of the Chadbourne plan, but they did not prevail.[7]

The combination of declining prices in the international market, increasing tariffs in the United States, and a voluntary restriction of output on the part of producers in Cuba, which was not matched by the producers in the U.S. customs area, particularly by the beet-growing states or the Philippines, devastated the Cuban industry. Prices rose slightly in 1933, to 3.2 cents, leaving producers in

Table 8.1. Index of Sugar Production in Cuba, the Dominican
Republic, and Puerto Rico, 1925–1934 (1925 = 100)

Year	Cuba	Dominican Republic	Puerto Rico
1925	100	100	100
1926	95	114	92
1927	88	97	95
1928	78	119	114
1929	101	114	90
1930	91	116	131
1931	61	117	119
1932	51	138	150
1933	39	116	126
1934	45	123	148

Sources: Production series for Cuba and Puerto Rico are from *Sugar: Report to the
President of the United States* (Washington, D.C.: U.S. Government Printing Office, 1934),
144. Figures for the Dominican Republic are from Food and Agriculture Organization of
the United Nations, *The World Sugar Economy in Figures, 1880–1959* (Geneva: FAO-UN, 1961).

Cuba the net price of 1.2 cents after paying duty. The crisis had different effects on
the various sectors of the sugar industry. The owners of the vertically integrated
sugar mills were able to cushion the fall in the price of raw sugar through the
increase in the spread with the price on refined sugar. Inexpensive raw sugar
represented a reduction in costs for the refineries because prices on refined did
not fall as sharply as prices on raw sugar. The losses at the plantations translated
into gains at the refineries. Cuban mill owners who sold on the open market could
not compensate their losses in the raw sugar business with gains in refining. Cuban
sugar production declined from 5,775,000 tons in 1929 to 2,234,000 in 1933.

The absolute decline in physical output combined with a decline in the price of
sugar drastically reduced revenue from sugar sales. The Cuban crop of 1929 sold
for $231,485,100. The crop of 1933 brought in $53,973,000. Credit for centrales
and colonos was curtailed, and some workers were not paid or had their wages
slashed. Small colonos fared worse than large ones, while wages, according to the
U.S. Department of Labor, reached their lowest level since the abolition of slavery.[8] The number of sugar mills, which had increased from 174 in 1913–14 to 195
at the end of World War I, began to decline. In the zafra of 1933, only 125 mills
ground cane. Sugar mills reduced the length of the harvest from 145 days in 1925
to 67 days in 1933. Because construction of new mills ceased around 1925 and
hardly any improvements in physical plant took place after that date, idle construction workers swelled the ranks of the unemployed, adding to the generalized
misery caused by the lengthened tiempo muerto.

In 1933, the Cuban polity exploded in revolution, the dictator Gerardo Machado was overthrown, and anti-imperialist sentiment soared throughout the island. Massive rural and urban workers' strikes accompanied the political changes of the revolution. In August, September, and October of 1933, workers seized several dozen mills and declared the establishment of "soviets," or workers' councils. The demands of the workers influenced the radical nationalist government of Ramón Grau San Martín, which governed Cuba from September 10, 1933, until January 1934, when a coup of army sergeants led by Fulgencio Batista, with backing from Sumner Welles, the U.S. ambassador, forced Grau's resignation.

In August to October 1933, workers occupied and seized many sugar mills in Cuba in a wave of industrial unrest without precedent in the history of the island. The overthrow of the Machado regime and the revolt of the sergeants led by Batista broke the discipline of the armed forces. Soldiers refused to obey officers. Workers fraternized with soldiers. In Havana, an urban general strike of August 1–12 forced the resignation of Machado and sparked the occupations of the rural mills by literally thousands of workers. In Santa Clara province by the end of the month fifteen mills were in the hands of sixty thousand workers. On September 5, the manager of the Chaparra and Delicias mills of the Cuban American Sugar Company had to take refuge in a British freighter. Workers in the Jaronú, Boston, Preston, Cunagua, and Vertientes mills were on strike. Ten mills in Santa Clara, six in Camagüey, and thirteen in Oriente as well as most mills in Havana and Pinar del Río were on strike by September. By the end of September, thirty-six mills were occupied. In some mills organized by the unions most closely affiliated with the Cuban Communist Party, the Sindicato Nacional de Obreros de la Industria Azucarera and the Confederación Nacional de Obreros Cubanos, workers declared the establishment of soviets.[9] In one form or another, up to two hundred thousand workers participated in the strikes and mill occupations of August to October 1933.[10]

Although recent Cuban historiography has privileged the role of the Communist Party and the soviets of 1933, mill occupations were a broader phenomenon, involving unions of diverse political affiliation, such as Unión Obrera de Oriente, the Sindicato Regional de Obreros de la Industria Azucarera de Guantánamo and local initiatives led by anarchist and Trotskyist organizations and by the secretive Cuban revolutionary organization ABC. Communist Party influence was paramount, however, and it imprinted on the movement two contradictory features. The Third Period policies of the Comintern, which in Europe were characterized by a sharp rupture and open antagonism to Social Democratic unions and parties, were translated into Cuban politics as a sharp break with other anti-imperialist movements and organizations. This approach tended to isolate the Cuban Communist Party from other workers' organizations, who were derided as "reformist," or, in the terminology of the time, "social-fascist." In some instances Third Period politics stood in the way of collaboration with other organizations of workers, whether allied with some broader political current or independent. The Communist Party, however, vehemently insisted on internationalist working-class politics by organizing Jamaican, Haitian, Spanish, and British West Indian workers. This policy was bravely defended by Communist organizers everywhere, despite the fact that the onset of economic crisis had caused a surge of antiforeign feeling among certain layers of the Cuban population in general and among segments of the working class that competed in the labor market with the immigrant braceros.

Despite the diversity of the organizations involved in this massive wave of strikes and occupations, everywhere the demands of the workers reflected the fundamental characteristics of the plantation economy. Workers wanted recognition of their unions, a return to the wage levels of 1930, an eight-hour day with double pay for overtime, withdrawal of the Rural Guard from the plantations, recognition of the right to strike, cancellation of the debt owed to the company stores, no expulsions of workers or their families from the colonias, living quarters during the tiempo muerto, and dismissal of abusive managers.[11] Everywhere workers sought assurances that the mills would not shut down and demanded guarantees of employment in the next zafra.

Concerned about the revolutionary situation in Cuba, the sugar barons of Puerto Rico, who had historically struggled against union recognition, proposed to the Federación Libre del Trabajo the signing of an industry-wide agreement for the zafra of 1933–34. The offer also reflected local conditions. During the tiempo muerto in 1933, there was strike after strike in the tobacco, needlework, and transportation industries of Puerto Rico.[12] The offer by the employers revealed their deep concern about the possibility of strikes in Puerto Rico and sought to guarantee preemptively the uninterrupted progress of the harvest by granting certain concessions before labor struggles could interrupt it. On November 8, the mill workers of Central Plazuela in Barceloneta went on strike before the start of the harvest and stayed out until December 5. Local shopkeepers supported the strikers' demands for an end of payment in scrip redeemable only at the company store. On December 6, 1933, on the first day of the harvest, cane fires erupted in Central Coloso and twelve hundred workers went on strike. The next day eight thousand workers were on strike. Central Guánica of the South Porto Rico Sugar Company went on strike on December 31. By mid-January, the entire sugar industry of Puerto Rico was on strike, and in one town after another the police repressed assemblies of workers who had gathered to discuss the industry-wide agreement proposed by the sugar barons and signed by the labor leaders of the Free Federation of Workers (Federación Libre del Trabajo, or FLT) without consulting the rank and file.

By the early 1930s, the Free Federation of Workers which was linked to the Socialist Party of Puerto Rico, had become a bureaucratized union. Its leaders were co-opted into important positions in government. The secretary of labor, Prudencio Rivera Martínez, was a prominent leader of the Free Federation of Workers and of the Socialist Party (SP) while the most prominent historical leader of the FLT, Santiago Iglesias Pantín, was Puerto Rico's resident commissioner in Washington. The wildcat strikes represented the spontaneous, widespread refusal of the workers to accept the terms of the industry-wide agreement. But because the labor leaders were entrenched in the government, the strike had to be carried out against the employers and the labor leaders simultaneously and against the Department of Labor, whose resources were used by the FLT-SP's Prudencio Rivera Martínez to subdue the strike. Instead of withdrawing the industry-wide agreement and submitting the contract to the approval of the membership, the Socialist Party leadership used the paid employees of the Department of Labor and all of the organizers of the union to explain the contract to the workers, who refused to accept it. On January 11, 1934, workers in Guayama issued a call to Pedro Albizu Campos, leader of the Puerto Rican Nationalist Party, to address an assembly of six thousand people the next day.[13] Albizu spoke in Guayama and the workers constituted a new union, the Asociación de Trabajadores de Puerto Rico. Thereafter Albizu and the Nationalist Party contributed to the organization of the strike and served as negotiators representing the demands of the workers to the employers and the government. Nationalist organizers and Albizu personally spoke in many towns, including Bayamón, Arecibo, Fajardo, Río Piedras, Humacao, Yabucoa, and Salinas. Everywhere the workers demanded the abolition of payment in company scrip and the eight-hour day. Nevertheless, the combination of police repression, pressure from the employers, the use of all the resources of the FLT and Department of Labor to impose the agreement on the workers, the threat by the Socialist leadership to bring strikebreakers to mills that did not accept the contract, and finally, hunger, caused the defeat of the strikers. The general strike of 1934 represents a brief but explosive alliance between the working class of the sugar mills and colonias and the principal anti-imperialist organization of Puerto Rico. The defeat of the strike caused the steady decline of the bureaucratized Free Federation of Workers and the Socialist Party. The convergence of the working class and the Nationalists shook the stability of the

Puerto Rican political system in 1934 and set the stage for the dramatic changes that took place in the rest of the decade.[14]

The Great Depression was a convulsive epoch in the entire Spanish Caribbean. Dependence on the price of one crop subjected the plantation economies of the Spanish islands to the vicissitudes of the international sugar market. Cuba had become so dependent on the sugar industry that by the end of the decade some Cubans could not imagine the future of their country without sugar monoculture. "Without sugar, there is no nation."[15] Other Cubans questioned the extreme dependence of the island on sugar and sought an alternative course of development. "Because of sugar, there is no nation."[16] In Puerto Rico the sugar industry occupied the best coastal lands and displaced local food production. The island became dependent on imported food, particularly on rice from the United States. As the subsistence component of agriculture declined and local food production was unable to meet the needs of the population, the ability to buy food became ever more dependent on the wages paid by the sugar industry, the largest employer in the island. Despite the tariff advantage enjoyed by producers of sugar in Puerto Rico, the availability of surplus of workers drove down the price of labor power and prevented the high income of the sugar industry from trickling down to the population. In the Dominican Republic, a derided and immiserated immigrant proletariat worked in an enclave economy isolated from the rest of the national economy, which continued to be characterized by the predominance of a small, entrenched peasantry that produced some tobacco and cocoa for export and enough food to feed itself and the towns of the republic. The fate of most Dominican farmers was independent of that of the sugar industry, while the majority of the workers in the cane were foreigners who limited their consumption so as to assemble their petty savings for their return to Haiti. The sugar mills were concentrated in foreign hands, and the profits from the industry were repatriated to the parent corporations. Overall, the sugar industry contributed little to national development.

Imperial regulation of the sugar industry soon followed the explosive crises of 1933 in Cuba and 1934 in Puerto Rico. The Jones-Costigan Act of the U.S. Congress introduced a system whereby the United States assigned sugar quotas at specified minimum prices from each supplying region. The Jones-Costigan system revealed the international scope of the entire sugar complex. Each sugar-producing region (Cuba, Puerto Rico, the Philippines, Hawaii, domestic beet, domestic cane) received a sugar quota allocation. The system of graded imperial preference meant that some regions were affected more than others by the Jones-Costigan Act. The quotas were based on the existing levels of production in each region. The restriction of the Cuban crop caused by the Verdeja Act and the Chadbourne plan resulted in allocation of Cuban quotas far below the level of production reached in 1925. Before World War I, Puerto Rico produced in a typical year about 10 percent as much sugar as Cuba, after 1934, about 40 percent. The Cuban economist Oscar Pino Santos has identified the crisis of the 1930s and the system of sugar quotas as one of the long-term economic causes of the revolution of 1959. In the five years preceding 1959, Cuban production averaged no more than five million tons of sugar, that is, about as much as in 1925. The system of sugar quotas limited the development of Cuba's productive capacity over a period of thirty years during which the population of the island doubled.[17] The crisis also caused increased xenophobic persecution of immigrant workers. Public discussion in the newspapers addressed the question of whether Cuba was becoming "africanized," attacked the Haitian immigrants, and lamented the shifting racial composition of Camagüey, which had 31,992 Haitians, and 11,088 Jamaicans and other British West Indians.[18] Between 1934 and 1938 Haitians were persecuted and expelled from Cuba.[19] In 1935, the Commission on Cuban Affairs estimated that of the 514,000 available field workers in Cuba, as many as 100,000 were Haitians or Jamaicans.[20]

In the Dominican Republic, the dictator Rafael Leonidas Trujillo ordered a massacre of Haitians. Conservative estimates are that at least twelve thousand Haitians were killed during a week of army butchery in October 1937. In the words of Eric Roorda, "The army did not target those Haitians resident in the sugar colonies, but all those found outside the cane fields, even Haitians who were Dominican citizens by birth and those who had lived in the country for many years, were seized and killed."[21] While the complexities of Trujillo's dictatorship and of his expressed desire to "whiten" the Dominican Republic through immigration of whites and the expulsion of Haitians are not reducible to the economic crisis and reflect a long history of border conflicts with the neighboring republic, the massacre surely contributed to the further degradation of Haitian laborers trapped in the lands of the sugar mills.

The high period of sugar monoculture in the Caribbean and the crisis of the 1930s produced multiple responses. The effects of the imperial tariff and sugar quota systems with which the United States sought to regulate its sugar empire affected the livelihood of entire populations. As John Dalton concludes, "The tariff became the method for the determination of the sources of supply for the American market and, in turn, under the peculiar circumstances surrounding the economy of one-crop islands, sugar became the basis of the livelihood of over 15,000,000 people."[22] In 1933, the radical Grau government passed a law requiring all enterprises to draw at least 50 percent of their labor force from the native Cuban population.[23] After the Cuban revolution of 1933, the Platt Amendment was abrogated and the Roosevelt administration inaugurated its Good Neighbor Policy toward Latin America. In 1937, the *Ley de coordinación azucarera* biased the supply of cane in favor of the colonos and set minimum quotas for grinding the cane of small colonos. Land rents were lowered and a moratorium on the debt of colonos acquired during the worst years of the Depression was imposed. The law set a minimum guaranteed proportion of the price of sugar to be received by the colonos. The big winners of the revolution of 1933 were the colonos.[24] The accumulation of these institutional checks on the power of the U.S. sugar corporations stopped the transfer of Cuban mills to U.S. interests. After 1934 no Cuban sugar mills passed into foreign ownership. Instead, mills were repatriated to Cuban hands. Between 1929 and 1951, the number of U.S.-owned mills declined from seventy to forty-one.[25]

In Puerto Rico, the Great Depression led to the formation of the Popular Democratic Party in 1938 on a program based on the redistribution of the sugar latifundia and to the search for alternatives to sugar monoculture. The Chardón Plan drafted by the rector of the University of Puerto Rico in 1934 served as the founding economic program of the Populares, which was based on agrarian reform, the diversification of the economy of Puerto Rico, and a vague proposal for the industrialization of the island. A highly modified version of this program was implemented after World War II, within the framework of continuation of Puerto Rico's colonial relation to the United States. After World War II, the Populares recovered and actually implemented the famous five-hundred-acre law, an old statute instituted by the U.S. Congress at the behest of the protectionist beet farmers at the beginning of the century.[26] The law stipulated that no individual or corporation in the island could own more than five hundred acres of land. To replace the collapsing sugar economy, the Populares created an industrial incentives program to attract foreign industrial capital for factory production.[27] This course of development was radically different from the one produced by the Cuban Revolution of 1959, which, for all its changes and nationalizations, retained the sugar industry as a centerpiece of the national economic strategy.

What, if anything, can the example of the American Sugar Kingdom tell us about underdevelopment in the world economy and the processes that produce it? How does the plantation economy of the Spanish Caribbean in the twentieth century compare to previous plantation systems in the region? What can it tell us about the nature of the imperial economic relations imposed by the United States on this region? Is it an example of a plantation economy along the lines suggested by the plantation school? How does the American Sugar Kingdom fit the model of a pure plantation economy?

There is no question that the American Sugar Kingdom had common elements with previous plantation systems in the Caribbean. Monocultural production for export, lack of agrarian diversification, domination by foreign capital, the metropolitan exchange standard, control of all shipping by the metropolis, and an international tariff system that reproduced a colonial division of labor were no doubt present in the American Sugar Kingdom. These features would lead us to believe that the American Sugar Kingdom was merely one more instance of the plantation economy that has been so persistent in the Caribbean since the European conquest in the late fifteenth century. By the criteria of the plantation school, the American Sugar Kingdom was nothing short of a pure case of plantation economy.

Focusing exclusively on aspects common to all plantation economies, however, leaves many questions about the functioning of this plantation system not only unanswered but unformulated. It is not sufficient, in the study of underdevelopment, to emphasize the incorporation of a region into the world economy, the exclusive economic relations imposed by the conquering power, the colonial division of labor, and the predominance of metropolitan financial and shipping interests. Although these characteristics are unquestionably common to all plantation systems, certainly of all plantation systems in the Caribbean, focusing exclusively on these external relations does not allow us to query many important aspects of the functioning of colonialism and the process of underdevelopment. The answers as well as the questions about the nature of underdevelopment have to be historical and specific. In the model of the plantation school, it would seem that there is an entity called "plantation economy" which is the basic historical reality and of which the American Sugar Kingdom is merely one manifestation among many others in the last five hundred years. "Plantation economy" becomes such a general category that, like in so many other variants of dependency or world-system analysis, atemporal theoretical categories acquire a life of their own and impose on the social reality they were meant to explain. The categories now "make that reality fit their own a priori selves."[28] By focusing on external relations, the theory of plantation economy selects what we see, but it also omits important aspects of social reality. What is left out?

Most of the important concrete historical components of this particular plantation economy are not considered by the plantation school. That is, the specific, empirical substance of the social reality of the American Sugar Kingdom is replaced by general reified categories and teleological arguments about the unfolding of the plantation economy. Most important, the specific classes and class relations that constituted the plantation economy are left out of sight or compressed together and classified in the same category as coercive labor relations. An analysis of the historical development of the American Sugar Kingdom requires looking at what was specific to it, that is, at the differences from previous plantation economies. It is by understanding these differences that one can actually observe the specific class actors that formed this twentieth-century plantation economy. For it was not an abstractly conceived world market or an abstract metropolitan interest that created this plantation system. A specific segment of the capitalist class of the United States, the oligopolistic sugar refiners, were at the forefront of the development of the American Sugar Kingdom and were aided significantly by the intervention of the metropolitan state and its troops in Cuba, Puerto Rico, and the Dominican Republic. Local planters accommodated themselves to the realities of U.S. colonialism and struggled to achieve the best conditions possible within the colonial framework.

The specific class interests in the metropolis that benefited from the process of colonial expansion initiated in 1898 are the object of my analysis in Chapters 2 and 4. The peculiarities of this segment of the capitalist class, which deployed massive resources for expansion in the Caribbean, are crucial to understanding this plantation system. The principal owners of the plantations were no ordinary capitalists. They were, instead, one of the pioneering sectors of the corporate revolution that changed forever the structure of capitalist enterprise in the United States. This peculiarity explains the immense success and the thoroughly modern character of the sugar mills created in the Spanish Caribbean in the early twentieth century. The fact that the refiners had consolidated horizontally and that the corporate mechanisms they created allowed them to create colonial enterprises using metropolitan holding companies explains the preponderance of direct investment in vertically integrated enterprises in the colonies. While foreign ownership has been one of the characteristics of plantation economies through the ages, the specific form of foreign ownership that characterized the American Sugar Kingdom sets it apart and helps to explain the magnitude of the expansion of production in what became the principal sugar-producing region of the world.

The state that enabled the process of expansion of the sugar refiners had its own historically specific traits which need to be accounted for in an analysis of the process of underdevelopment in the Caribbean. The United States built a small empire in the Caribbean, but it had no central state agency (e.g., a colonial office) to administer the colonial territories or a single formula for colonial intervention everywhere. Cuban independence and the imposition of the Platt Amendment in 1903 turned that island into a semicolony of the United States while Puerto Rico remained under formal U.S. colonial rule. In the Dominican Republic, U.S. intervention in the customs receivership of 1905 and eventually in the occupation of 1916 led to another semicolonial formula after U.S. troops pulled out in 1924. Formal colonial rule in Puerto Rico gave that island's sugar industry an immense advantage in the U.S. market thanks to free trade. U.S. colonial policy was formulated by a Congress in which protectionist agrarian interests were a powerful force. The battle in the U.S. Congress around Cuban reciprocity ended in a victory for the protectionist cane and beet farmers of the United States in 1903 and created a long-lasting framework that regulated U.S.-Cuba commercial relations. Reciprocity was defeated and the Cuban sugar industry was forced to pay 80 percent of the U.S. sugar tariff throughout the entire period from 1903 to the Great Depression. The tariff itself changed in response to protectionist interests, increasing significantly after 1920. But the essential fact that Cuba paid most of the duty, and the Dominican Republic the full duty, regulated competition between the sugar industry of Puerto Rico and those two islands throughout this entire historical period. These historical specificities had enormous consequences. The sugar industry expanded disproportionately in Puerto Rico, thanks to this tariff advantage. The country most dominated by the sugar industry was not Cuba but Puerto Rico, in the weight of the industry relative to the other sectors of the economy. The imperial tariff system treated each region differently. Some of the subsequent turns in the colonial economies, particularly the Puerto Rican insistence on dismantling the sugar industry in the 1950s, reflect the disproportionately large place which the sugar industry occupied in the economy of that island during the first three decades of the century.

A third determinant of the process of underdevelopment has to do with the transformation of local class relations before the U.S. invasion of 1898. The capitalist farmers who produced most of the cane, the colonos, did not emerge out of nowhere. They were the product of a social transformation after the abolition of slavery, in which the planter class became differentiated into industrialists/centralistas on the one hand and colonos on the other. This local class transformation allowed the sugar industry to survive in the aftermath of abolition by separating the industrial and agrarian components of the sugar industry in a time of scarcity of capital. In the process of expansion of U.S. sugar refining interests in the Caribbean, refiners had to enter into alliances and contend with a class of capitalist cane farmers, which in Cuba had owned slaves barely twelve years before the U.S. invasion. The dynamic of class transformation and transition to wage labor had been initiated under the Spanish colonial regime, when Cuba was already oriented to the U.S. market under the domination of a Creole planter class. In Puerto Rico the weaker Creole planter class made a less successful transition to the system of sugar centrales based on wage labor. The Dominican Republic had the weakest sugar industry and no previous ingenio economy because slavery had been abolished in 1822 by the Haitians. Everywhere these local class relations conditioned the expansion of U.S. capital. In the west of Cuba, they prevented the successful penetration of U.S. capital into agriculture. Sugar mills had to adapt to the power of an entrenched class of colonos. It was easier to create a new plantation economy in the east than to overhaul the plantation economy of the west to fit the needs of U.S. capital. The development of the sugar industry in regions of colono entrenchment shows the weight of local class relations inherited and transformed from a previous stage of incorporation into the world market. These local class relations shaped the way metropolitan capital interacted with the local economic environments of the Caribbean.

What distinguished the American Sugar Kingdom most from all previous plantation systems in the region was the prevalence of wage labor. Capitalist cane farmers who employed wage workers produced most of the cane of the American Sugar Kingdom. The transition to wage labor and capitalist relations of production in the countryside had begun before the United States occupation of Cuba and Puerto Rico in 1898, more successfully in Cuba, less successfully in Puerto Rico. Under U.S. colonial rule, this transition to capitalist agriculture accelerated. The process of dispossession of rural producers and proletarianization was most acute in Puerto Rico, least acute in the Dominican Republic. Under U.S. colonial rule, international migration of workers accelerated, particularly to the most dynamic regions of expansion of the plantations in eastern Cuba. Jamaican, Haitian, British West Indian, Spanish, and Puerto Rican workers migrated to the plantations of Cuba and the Dominican Republic. Perhaps the issue of proletarianization and labor migration is where the example of the American Sugar Kingdom diverges most from the model of the plantation school. First, this is because extraeconomic coercion disappeared and was replaced by purely economic coercion, with the possible exception of Haitian cane cutters in the mills of the Dominican Republic. The separation of the direct producers from the means of production was not a continuation of the policies of extraeconomic coercion but rather a classic instance of the process of proletarianization typical wherever capitalist relations of production have taken hold. In other words, the emergence of wage labor needs to be explained historically and concretely, not written off a priori by a theoretical construct, in the fashion of the plantation school. A free labor market was created, not blocked, through emancipation without indemnification. Workers were free in the double sense in which all wage workers are free: they are juridically free and able to enter into contracts, and they are free from ownership of means of production capable of guaranteeing subsistence without having to sell their labor power.

Variations in the process of proletarianization in each island and in each region were the product of specific histories, not of a uniform process of incorporation into the world economy. Specification of these historical processes is required, that is, the processes need to be explained concretely. The plantation school would categorize all the labor arrangements of plantations as extraeconomic a priori, thus preventing us from seeing the enormous social transformation that took place after abolition and that should be at the center of our attention. The development of a local class of rural wage workers and the evolution of the planters into capitalist cane farmers, particularly in Cuba, are specific historical processes that conditioned the development of the plantation economy after 1898, once U.S. capital started flowing in. The existence of an entrenched peasantry in the Dominican Republic with access to land and the capability of subsisting based on independent household production explains the absence of a numerous rural proletariat in that country. The plantations had to rely on the importation of wage workers from the British West Indies and Haiti. These historical differences between islands and regions had enormous social consequences locally. In Puerto Rico, the sugar industry was the principal employer of native workers and the sugar proletariat was an important force in the political life of the colony. The Free Federation of Workers and the Socialist Party affiliated to it were important political forces in Puerto Rico. In the Dominican Republic, the sugar industry was practically a foreign enclave in which both the owners of the mills and the workers were foreigners. Workers' organizations were weak in the sugar industry and had a minimal impact on national life. Thus specific historical circumstances had important consequences for the development of the plantation economy. These consequences cannot be analyzed by simply declaring that in plantation economies all labor is coerced extraeconomically.

Capitalism is a worldwide economic system built on international *and local* class relations. Colonialism cannot function without local allies. Not all classes in the plantation economy experienced imperial rule and the domination of metropolitan capital in the same way. The study of underdevelopment has to grasp the specifics of both the metropolitan economy and the colonial regions. For the actual functioning of the plantation economy did not depend only on the centralized drive imposed by metropolitan capital. Inherited local class structures, class conflicts, and political structures determined the evolution of the plantation economy in each region. The imperial tariff system, which treated each of the islands differently, had immense repercussions on the development of the sugar industry everywhere. Direct U.S. colonial rule gave investors in Puerto Rico guarantees they did not enjoy in Cuba or the Dominican Republic. The development of underdevelopment in this Caribbean region was not determined merely by the expansion of U.S. colonial power in the region and the incorporation of the plantation economy into the U.S. colonial sphere. Instead, the process of incorporation into the imperial economic structure was conditioned by preexisting patterns of class relations, class conflicts, and previously established forms of colonial domination. Understanding how much of the stuff of empires is made of local class relations is important to understanding how, and how much, it can be transformed locally.

Epilogue

Sugar production is practically nonexis-
tent today in Puerto Rico. Between 1950 and 1960 the Constancia mill in Ponce,
Central San José, Pasto Viejo in Humacao, and Centrales Rochelaise and Victoria
closed. In the first half of the 1960s El Ejemplo, Guamaní, Juanita, and Plazuela
shut down. Centrales Canóvanas, Cayey, Machete, Río Llano, Rufina, San Vicente,
Santa Juana, and Soller all closed between 1965 and 1970. Cortada, Juncos, Lafayette, Los Caños, and Monserrate closed between 1970 and 1975. The giants of
the industry, which were established in the first decade after the U.S. occupation of
the island and controlled much of the wealth of the insular economy for decades,
collapsed in the late 1970s and 1980s. Central Fajardo of the Fajardo Sugar Company closed in 1978. Central Guánica, which in the first decade of the century had
been the largest sugar mill in the world, closed in 1982. Central Aguirre, whose
yearly dividends of 30 percent to its owners earned it the title of "Drake's Treasure" in the 1930s, stopped grinding in 1991.[1]

In Cuba, most mills were renamed after the revolution of 1959. Central Chaparra of the Cuban American Sugar Company became Jesús Menéndez, after the
famed Cuban labor leader. Delicias of the same company became Antonio Gui-
teras, the Punta Alegre was renamed Máximo Gómez, while the Boston and
Preston mills of the United Fruit Company became Centrales Nicaragua and
Guatemala, respectively. Central Zaza, which once belonged to a Cuban slave-
owning baron, became Central Benito Juárez, the Stewart mill was renamed Cen-

tral Venezuela, and Central Conchita in Matanzas became the Puerto Rico Libre mill.[2] In the Dominican Republic, the sugar industry has a much smaller weight in the economy than it had in the 1930s. Trujillo built the Catarey mill in 1949 and Central Río Haina. Soon thereafter he began acquiring most of the mills in the republic.[3] The majority of the mills owned by the Cuban Dominican–West India interests were acquired by the Trujillista state in the early 1950s, while the properties of the South Porto Rico Sugar Company were acquired by Gulf and Western in 1967.[4]

Legacies from the period of the American Sugar Kingdom still remain. It is not difficult for an inhabitant of New York today to perceive the remnants of this world, or rather of the two poles of the plantation economy, alive and well in the archaeology of the city from which the American Sugar Kingdom was administered. Around the corner from Wall Street, 29 Front Street, from which James Howell Post once administered an immense empire of sugar plantations in the Caribbean, is still there. The sugar refinery that initiated the National Sugar Refining Company is still in Yonkers, near the Ludlow train station. The Department of Chemistry of a prominent New York university is still called Havemeyer Hall.

The other extreme of the plantation economy is equally alive in the cultural archaeology of New York. Every Sunday afternoon during the summer, antillanos gather together near the south shore of the 72d Street lake in Central Park to play tumbadoras, sing, and dance Cuban rumba. Bobé, a Puerto Rican musician from Brooklyn, usually starts the sessions, singing and prodding the drummers, implying that they are out of sync and should concentrate on the clave, the wood sticks that guide the rhythmical pattern of the three drums of Afro-Cuban rumba. With great skill he gets the drummers into sync in a rhythmical pattern from Matanzas called *columbia*. He starts by fusing verses from an old *décima* from the mountainous region of Puerto Rico with the rhythm from Matanzas:

los veo desde aquí	I can see from here
los cañaverales	the canefields
y los cafetales	and the coffee fields
donde yo nací . . .	where I was born

After several décimas, Bobé is unhappy about the quality of the drumming, which he considers to be out of synchrony. With the determination of a foreman in the cane, Bobé appeals to an old chant that mentions the Rochelaise and Igualdad mills in western Puerto Rico, prodding the drummers and surrounding public to join in the chorus and get the rumba really started.

echa el molino	set the mill
a caminar	in motion
que hay que moler	we have to grind
en la central	in the central

A crowd of Cubans, Puerto Ricans, Dominicans, and other assorted New Yorkers gathers around the drummers to answer Bobé's improvisation and repeat the chorus from central Rochelaise: "*echa el molino a caminar, que hay que moler, en la central*." The rumba has picked up momentum, and everybody is well synchronized: *clave, cáscara, quinto, tres golpes, tumbadora*, singer, and chorus.

Pedro, a Cuban from Matanzas, soon steps in. Columbia is the typical form of rumba in his region, and he refuses to yield the spotlight to a Puerto Rican, in the typical competitive spirit of Afro-Caribbean rumberos. Pedro is a skilled Cuban troubadour, as knowledgeable about Afro-Cuban columbia as he is dexterous in the art of *punto guajiro*, a poetic form similar to Bobé's *décima jíbara*. He begins to improvise in the form of punto guajiro, something about Arsenio Martínez Campos, a Spanish general of the war of 1895, Antonio Maceo, his Cuban opponent and a symbol of Afro-Cuban pride, with images of *la tea*, the torch used by the insurgents to set cane fields afire. On the common ground of their shared poetic form of décima, the two troubadours will battle for the approval of the surrounding public. The rules of this poetic *controversia* require that Pedro stay on the theme initiated by Bobé, and, if possible, that he subvert it. In response to the theme of his rival, which concerned the beginning of work at the sugar mill, Pedro concludes his improvisation. He turns the rumba in a new direction, launching his *montuno*, aggressively facing his rival as he sings, chiding him for his authoritarian stance toward the drummers, and turning his entire poetic construction, and the world it invokes, upside down:

¡corre corre mayoral!	run, foreman, run!
¡la caña se quema!	the cane is burning!
¡la caña se quema!	the cane is burning!
¡la caña se quema!	the cane is burning!

Notes

Chapter 1

1. Williams, *Capitalism and Slavery*, originally published in 1944. Williams coined the term "American Sugar Kingdom" to refer to the plantation economy of Cuba, Puerto Rico, and the Dominican Republic in *From Columbus to Castro*, 428–42.

Ramiro Guerra y Sánchez *Azúcar y población en las Antillas*, originally published in 1927, occupies a similar seminal position in the Spanish Caribbean.

2. Sidney Mintz provocatively addressed the issue of coerced and free labor in "Was the Plantation Slave a Proletarian?"

3. Frank, *Latin America*, 23.

4. De Janvry, *Agrarian Question in Latin America*, 8.

5. "The most extreme—but also the most important—expression of the first silver age of the Spanish empire was Potosí, the silver mountain where the phrase 'worth a Potosí' sometimes 'worth a Perú' was coined. This hill, over 3,000 meters above sea level, was discovered by a Bolivian Indian in 1545. Not long after, it was to have consumed the lives of an estimated eight million of his brothers. The Spanish king and emperor of the Habsburgs, Charles V, designated the town that mushroomed there an imperial city. He inscribed on its shield: 'I am rich Potosí, treasure of the world, the king of the mountains, envy of kings.' By 1573 the census recorded 120,000 inhabitants, the same number as London and more than Madrid, Paris, or Rome. By 1650 the number had risen to 160,000. In the meantime the privileged among the residents enjoyed thirty-six highly ornamental churches, another thirty-six gambling casinos, fourteen academies of dance, and all the world's luxuries imported from Flanders, Venice, Arabia, India, Ceylon, China, and of course metropolitan Spain. Nearby, the city later named after Sucre was built to permit the enjoyment of the same luxuries at lower and more comfortable altitudes. Today a nostalgic descendant of the imperial Potosí observes: 'The city that gave the world the most and has the least.' Indeed, even the impoverished population it has today is no more than a third of the number it had four centuries ago" (Frank, *World Accumulation*, 48).

6. Gabriel García Márquez captures this aspect of the Caribbean when he writes, of the mythical village of Macondo, that "the world was so recent that many things lacked a name, and to mention them one had to point with the finger" (*Cien años de soledad*, 9).

7. Knight, *The Caribbean*, 3–22.

8. Greaves, "Plantations in World Economy," 16.

9. See Magnus Morner, "Hacienda hispanoamericana." Frank, *World Accumulation*, 92–93,

argues that the involution actually represented a shift to "inter-colonial" trade as opposed to trade with the metropolis. "This development of the hacienda and the growth of the latifundium are not simply an involution into the quiet of rural life as mining fell off. They represented the development of an alternative economic or productive base during the long seventeenth-century depression; and they were intimately related to the development of a trading and manufacturing economy, relatively independent of Spain, but nonetheless dependent on trade with the Spanish American colonies."

10. Smith, "Social Stratification," 227.

11. Frank, *World Accumulation*, 99, believes this represents a seventeenth-century transformation leading to the ascendancy of Britain to hegemony in the world market. "Thus, this seventeenth-century transition is also reflected in the changed commodity composition of international trade, from the spice and luxury trade of the sixteenth century to sugar (for increasingly widespread popular consumption) and new textile trade of the eighteenth century."

12. Mintz, *Sweetness and Power*, xx.

13. Smith, "Social Stratification," 232. In strictly Marxist categories, plantation slaves were not separated from the means of production but were instead means of production themselves. Yet the association of plantation labor with modern industrial labor has been persistent even among Marxist writers. C. L. R. James, *Black Jacobins*, 85–86, says of the slaves who carried out the Haitian Revolution: "The slaves worked on the land, and like revolutionary peasants everywhere, they aimed at the extermination of their oppressors. But working and living together in gangs of hundreds in the huge sugar-factories which covered the North Plain, they were closer to a modern proletariat than any group of workers in existence at the time, and the rising was, therefore, a thoroughly prepared and organized mass movement." In a similar vein, Du Bois, *Black Reconstruction in America*, 55–84, refers to the slave uprisings in the South of the United States during the Civil War as the "general strike."

14. It should be stressed that this position is by no means universal. Many critics, particularly class analysts, have emphasized the precapitalist character of the slave plantation. De Janvry presents one among many examples of a differing position: "The plantation system was established in those areas with potential for intensive, large-scale monoculture of a high-value tropical product for export. Sugarcane was the most important such crop for the first three centuries of colonization. Its cultivation spread quickly throughout the West Indies, north-eastern Brazil, the Veracruz coast in Mexico, and Peruvian coast. The motivation for plantation production was profit, and the operations were quite efficient and commercially oriented. However, since the importation of African slaves was necessary to provide the basis for cheap labor and since plantation management relied on paternalistic relations characteristic of feudalism, the plantations certainly could not be characterized as capitalist enterprises" (*Agrarian Question*, 62).

15. Some studies share that approach for the events of the recent pasts, such as Wells, *Modernization of Puerto Rico*, a study of Operation Bootstrap in Puerto Rico.

16. Gunder Frank's analysis was criticized by Laclau for its oversight of the importance of production relations. Subsequently, Frank incorporated these criticisms in *Lumpenbourgeoisie, Lumpendevelopment* and other works so that the two positions have come closer together. The position of Laclau, best expounded in "Feudalism and Capitalism in Latin America," errs in the

opposite direction. In identifying underdevelopment with the survival of precapitalist relations, Laclau's argument is incapable of explaining underdevelopment in those areas of the world where wage labor prevails, that is, increasingly in the world as a whole. My own position on this issue is that the capitalist world economy is a complex of capitalist, semicapitalist, and precapitalist relations of production articulated through the *capitalist* world market. See Mandel, *Late Capitalism*, 48–49, and Wolf, *Europe and the People without History*, 296–98.

The logical conclusion of Laclau's position is that of Warren, *Imperialism*. For a critique of Warren, see McMichael, Petras, Rhodes, "Industrialization in the Third World."

17. The concept "plantation" has embedded within it the idea of continuity. By contrast, scholars who have focused on problems such as slavery end up with completely different notions of *discontinuity* in Caribbean development.

18. A good concise statement of many of these problems may be found in Guerra y Sánchez, *Sugar and Society in the Caribbean* (the English translation of *Azúcar y población en las Antillas*).

19. Properly speaking, the "plantation school," also known as the Caribbean New World Group, included Lloyd Best, George Beckford, Norman Girvan, Clive Y. Thomas, H. R. Brewster, and Owen Jefferson. See Benn, "Theory of Plantation Economy and Society."

20. Best, "Mechanism of Plantation Type Societies."

21. Wagley, "Plantation America."

22. Best, "Mechanism of Plantation Type Societies."

23. Beckford, *Persistent Poverty*, 12.

24. Smith, Beckford, and Best derive this notion from Goffman, *Asylums*. Scott, *Slave Emancipation in Cuba*, 103, writes: "Evidence of the use of convicts in plantations is abundant. In the personal histories of the prisoners of the 1870s and early 1880s, plantations appear as places to which one is condemned, from which one escapes, or in which one dies." I find this feature absent in some kinds of plantations. For example, Sidney Mintz and Eric Wolf argue in "Haciendas and Plantations in Middle America and the Antilles," 402, that, in what they consider a "typical" plantation, "the labourer retains no relationship with the enterprise other than through intermittent sale of his labor power."

25. Mandle, "Plantation Economy," 57.

26. Ibid., 60.

27. Eric Wolf does something similar when he conflates most forms of extraeconomic coercion (including slavery and serfdom) under the notion "tributary mode of production." See Wolf, *Europe and the People without History*, 73–100.

28. Mandle, *Patterns of Caribbean Development*, 38.

29. Ibid.

30. Ibid., 43.

31. Mintz, "The Plantation as a Socio-Cultural Type," 43–44.

32. Thomas, *Plantations, Peasants, and the State*, seeks to define the "colonial-slave mode of production" on the basis of immediate relations of production (slavery) and the political relations obtaining in society (colonialism).

33. Thomas, *Plantations, Peasants, and the State*, 9–10.

34. Ibid., 10.

35. The standard works on the history of sugar are Lippman, *Historia do açucar*, and Deerr, *History of Sugar*. Galloway, *Sugar Cane Industry*, is an excellent survey of sugarcane agriculture throughout the centuries; Mintz, *Sweetness and Power*, is a fascinating and innovative work which incorporates the study of sugar consumption in the core of the world economy into the analysis of the development of plantation agriculture.

36. Watson, "Arab Agricultural Revolution," 8–35.

37. Galloway, "Mediterranean Sugar Industry," 177–94.

38. Ibid., 33.

39. Verlinden, *Beginnings of Modern Colonization*, 17–26.

40. Galloway, "Mediterranean Sugar Industry," 190. For Morocco, see Berthier, *Un épisode de l'histoire de la canne à sucre*.

41. Malowist, "Debuts du système de plantations," 28–29.

42. Ratekin, "Early Sugar Industry in Española"; Moya Pons, *Manual de historia dominicana*, 31–38; Cassá, *Historia social*, 1:65–71.

43. Schwartz, *Sugar Plantations in the Formation of Brazilian Society*.

44. Dunn, *Sugar and Slaves*.

45. James, *Black Jacobins*.

46. Sheridan, "Plantation Revolution," 25.

47. Abbé Raynal, *A Philosophical History of the East and West Indies*, 6:412–14, quoted in Sheridan, "Plantation Revolution," 22.

48. Williams, *From Columbus to Castro*, 361.

49. Scarano, *Sugar and Slavery in Puerto Rico*.

50. Slavery was abolished in Santo Domingo in 1822, in the British Caribbean in 1833, in Martinique and Guadeloupe during the revolutions of 1848, in the Dutch colonies in 1863, in Puerto Rico in 1873, and in Cuba in 1880–86. See Blackburn, *Overthrow of Colonial Slavery*. For the aboliton of slavery in Santo Domingo under the Haitian government of Boyer in 1822, see Cassá, *Historia social*, 1:174, and Moya Pons, *Manual de historia dominicana*, 223–24; for Puerto Rico, see Díaz Soler, *Historia de la esclavitud negra en Puerto Rico*; for Cuba, see Scott, *Slave Emancipation in Cuba*.

51. Williams, *Capitalism and Slavery*, 176.

52. See Tomich, " "Second Slavery,' " 103–17.

53. Mintz, *Sweetness and Power*, 148–49.

54. Langley, *Struggle for the American Mediterranean*.

55. Roy, *Socializing Capital*.

Chapter 2

1. Roy, *Socializing Capital*, 220.

2. See Landes, *Unbound Prometheus*.

3. For Japan, see Norman, *Japan's Emergence as a Modern State*; for the concept of "bourgeois revolution from above" see Zeitlin, *The Civil Wars in Chile*.

4. Harry Magdoff, *Imperialism*, 34–67.

5. See Barraclough, *Introduction to Contemporary History*.

6. Roy, *Socializing Capital*, 21–40, shows conclusively that size and capital intensity are associated with the emergence of corporations in industrial branches of production, but gains in productivity are not.

7. Ibid., 40–79.

8. This is true of the sugar factories but not necessarily of the agricultural phase of cane cultivation or the harvesting of cane, where the machete continued to be the essential tool and still is in some regions today.

9. An excellent discussion of these processes can be found in Murray, *Development of Capitalism in Colonial Indochina*.

10. Vogt, *Sugar Refining Industry*, 14.

11. Ibid., 17.

12. Chalmin, "Important Trends in Sugar Diplomacy before 1914," 12; "Copia mecanografiada del informe económico de la liga de las naciones sobre la situación azucarera mundial: julio 4, 1929," Secretaría de la Presidencia, Legajo 51, No. 76, Archivo Nacional de Cuba.

13. Galloway, *Sugar Cane Industry*, 8–9.

14. Vogt, *Sugar Refining Industry*, 17.

15. Ibid., v.

16. Eichner, *Emergence of Oligopoly*, 339–42.

17. Ibid., 42–43.

18. Mullins, "Sugar Trust," 29.

19. Vogt, *Sugar Refining Industry*, 33; Mullins, "Sugar Trust," 29, expresses the same idea: "The impending struggle foreshadowed large losses to all refiners, for the business was highly organized, with gigantic interests at stake."

20. Eichner, *Emergence of Oligopoly*, 67.

21. Mullins, "Sugar Trust," 28.

22. Zerbe, "American Sugar Refinery Company," 345.

23. Ibid., 339. Eichner argues that the debates about the conditions of the formation of the trust are subjective in that they involve an estimation of what constitutes a "reasonable" profit (*Emergence of Oligopoly*, 7). "This argument, that businessmen agreed to consolidation in order to avoid ruinous competition, keep production levels steady, and maintain reasonable profit margins, has much in common with the explanation, rhetoric aside, that the consolidation movement was fostered by a desire for monopoly profits. Ignoring for a moment the question of whether or not monopoly results in certain economies, one should realize that the only difference between these two views is the difference of opinion as to what constitutes a '*reasonable*' profit" (ibid., 7, emphasis added). The real issue, however, does not resolve around "reasonable" but around average or above average profits. The formation of trusts and the merger movement of the turn of the century should be seen as part of a secular trend of industrial concentration, not as a reaction to an economic conjuncture. The trusts were formed, depending on specific circumstances, to protect, maintain, or increase the rate of profit.

24. Ibid., 76.

25. Hilferding, *Finance Capital*, 418.

26. Mullins, "Sugar Trust," 30–35.

27. Eichner, *Emergence of Oligopoly*, 86.

28. The negotiations were interrupted when the Havemeyer Sugar Refining Company at Greenpoint burned down. The fire was believed to have been set by some workers in the refinery in response to the crushing of a strike eight months earlier. A cooperage factory also owned by the Havemeyers had been set on fire some weeks earlier. See ibid., 83; *New York Times*, June 15, 1887.

29. Mullins, "Sugar Trust," 31; Eichner, *Emergence of Oligopoly*, 65–66. In the 1870s there had been a struggle over the tariff between refiners who could process low-grade sugars and refiners who could not. The former wanted a tariff that discriminated against high-grade sugars, the latter one that discriminated against low grades.

30. Zerbe, "American Sugar Refinery Company," 347.

31. Eichner, *Emergence of Oligopoly*, 91.

32. Adler, *Claus Spreckels*, 24.

33. Ibid., 33–102.

34. "At Spreckels' Mercy: The Great Sugar King Squeezing the Trust," *New York Times*, August 9, 1888.

35. Eichner, *Emergence of Oligopoly*, 154; "At Spreckels' Mercy."

36. Eichner, *Emergence of Oligopoly*, 155; Cordray, "Claus Spreckels of California," 83, 90, 251–53, 268–71. See also Kent, *Hawaii*, 35–63.

37. Eichner, *Emergence of Oligopoly*, 157; Adler, *Claus Spreckels*, 24–25; *New York Times*, May 22, 1888, September 8, November 28, December 10, 1889.

38. *New York Times*, November 28, 1889.

39. Eichner, *Emergence of Oligopoly*, 157.

40. Pino Santos, *El asalto a Cuba*, 110; Allen, *Story of the Growth of E. Atkins & Co.*, 27.

41. Eichner, *Emergence of Oligopoly*, 166. The Havemeyer brothers Henry and Theodore, together with John Searles, sold their Spreckels Sugar Refining Company of Philadelphia stock to the trust for $5,400,000 whereas they had just bought it for $2,250,000, thus realizing a profit of $3,150,000. See Zerbe, "American Sugar Refinery Company," 354.

42. Taussig, "Sugar," 336.

43. Eichner, *Emergence of Oligopoly*, 170–71.

44. Mullins, "Sugar Trust," 85; Eichner, *Emergence of Oligopoly*, 173.

45. Eichner, *Emergence of Oligopoly*, 140.

46. Havemeyer answered a question about the significance of the change in the legal form as follows: "Well, from being illegal as we were, we are now legal as we are. Change enough, isn't it?" (Mullins, "Sugar Trust," 73, from *Louisiana Planter*, November 4, 1905, 301).

47. Eichner, *Emergence of Oligopoly*, 151.

48. Carosso, *More Than a Century of Investment Banking*, 30; Navin and Sears, "Rise of a Market for Industrial Securities," 120, 125; Mullins, "Sugar Trust," 70; *New York Times*, July 31, 1890, 8.

49. Kolko, *Triumph of Conservatism*, 31, 62, 181. Roy, *Socializing Capital*, 220, assesses the

importance of this case: "The E. C. Knight case was one of the decisive points of the process . . . by which there arose an organizational option that would soon be institutionalized. The large corporations that followed were not pioneers like American Cotton Oil or American Sugar Refining. Industrialists seeking to govern their industries, financiers hunting for alternatives to the saturated railroads, and states searching for a judicial and statutory resolution to the question of how to conceive of collective actors within a jurisprudence that recognized only individuals created a new form of property that socialized capital across the capitalist class."

50. Navin and Sears, "Rise of a Market for Industrial Securities," 116.

51. Eichner, *Emergence of Oligopoly*, 152–87.

52. Nelson, *Merger Movements in American Industry*; Kolko, *Triumph of Conservatism*, 26–57.

53. Eichner, *Emergence of Oligopoly*, 194; Norcross, "Rebate Conspiracy," 66–73.

54. Mullins, "Sugar Trust," 95–96.

55. Eichner, *Emergence of Oligopoly*, 209; *New York Times*, October 5, 1892, 5; also Mullins, "Sugar Trust," 96; Vogt, *Sugar Refining Industry*, 49.

56. Pino Santos, *La oligarquía yanqui en Cuba*. In this otherwise excellent book, Pino Santos underestimates the links between the National and the American sugar refining companies. The links, however, strengthen Pino Santos's argument about the U.S. financial oligarchy in Cuba.

57. Eichner, *Emergence of Oligopoly*, 294.

58. Ibid., 212–22; Mullins, "Sugar Trust," 113–49.

59. Mullins, "Sugar Trust," 100.

60. Ibid., 103–4.

61. Ibid.; Weigle, "Sugar Interests," 297.

62. Weigle, "Sugar Interests," 297; Eichner, *Emergence of Oligopoly*, 224.

63. Weigle, "Sugar Interests," 297.

64. Mullins, "Sugar Trust," 108.

65. Ibid., 113, extends the duration of the price war to 1903, which seems highly unlikely given the increase in the price margin between raw and refined sugar in the years 1901–2 (1.003 and 0.903 cents respectively).

66. Eichner, *Emergence of Oligopoly*, 261. Havemeyer once testified to the Ways and Means Committee of the United States House of Representatives as follows:

Q: "When you sell in this country you control the price?"

A: "Yes Sir."

Q: "And it was organized [the trust, C.A.], as I understand it, with a view of controlling the price and output to the people of this country?"

A: "That was one of the objects of the consolidation."

Q: "That was the principal object in organizing the American Sugar Refining Company?"

A: "It may be said that was the principal object."

Quoted in Zerbe, "American Sugar Refinery," 349.

67. For an interesting argument about intercommodity competition (cane sugar, beet sugar, corn syrup), see Timoshenko and Swerling, *World's Sugar*.

68. Eichner, *Emergence of Oligopoly*, 229–59. By 1910 beet sugar represented only 13 percent of

U.S. domestic consumption. On the role of the trust in developing and controlling the beet sugar industry, see Mullins, "Sugar Trust," 186–238; Norcross, "Beet Sugar Round-Up"; Welliver, "The Mormon Church and the Sugar Trust."

69. Moody, *Truth about the Trusts*, 453. The "seven greater industrial trusts" were, ranked by capitalization, United States Steel, Consolidated Tobacco, American Smelting and Refining, Amalgamated Copper, International Mercantile Marine, American Sugar Refining Company, and Standard Oil.

70. Eichner, *Emergence of Oligopoly*, 302–8.

71. Ibid., 308.

72. *National Cyclopaedia of American Biography*, vol. 25, 424. For the relation between the Guaranty and Morton Trust companies with the House of Morgan, see Corey, *House of Morgan*. Carosso, *Investment Banking*, tries to minimize the concentration of banking discovered by the Pujo Committee in 1912.

73. Among the important members of the Sugar Equalization Board, which organized the supply of sugar during the war, were James H. Post representing the U.S. refiners, Manuel Rionda representing the "Cuban" planters, and F. A. Dillingham of the South Porto Rico Sugar Company representing the "Porto Rican" planters. The chairman of the Sugar Equalization Board was Herbert Hoover. See Bernhardt, *Sugar Industry*, 52; Needham, "Control of the Sugar Market during World War I," U.S. Department of Labor, Bureau of Labor Statistics, Division of Historical Studies of Wartime Problems, March 1942 (available in Hoover Library, Stanford University).

74. Kolko, *Main Currents in Modern American History*, 6.

75. Kolko, *Triumph of Conservatism*.

76. Eichner, *Emergence of Oligopoly*, 324.

77. See the euphoric reports in Guaranty Trust Company of New York, *Cuba*, and National City Bank of New York, *Cuba*.

Chapter 3

1. Chalmin, "Important Trends in Sugar Diplomacy," 18–19.

2. "It is impossible to point to a particular year in which the policy shifted from one objective to another, but it is reasonably clear that between 1789, when a sugar tariff was first imposed, and 1891, the year of the inauguration of the subsidy system under the McKinley Tariff (1890), the major objective of the tariff was to raise revenue for the Federal Treasury.

"It should be recalled that in the nineteenth century the government did not tap individual revenue and corporate incomes as a major source of tax revenue. Government receipts were derived largely from import duties and domestic excise taxes, total ordinary receipts of the government approximating $300,000,000 a year, and of this amount import duties totaled roughly $200,000,000. About 20 percent of these duties were obtained from the duty on sugar" (Dalton, *Sugar*, 21).

3. Taussig, *Some Aspects of the Tariff Question*, 100.

4. Ibid., 57.

5. Weigle, "Sugar Interests," 293.

6. "The uneasiness and discontent of this period (1891–1892) led, in large measure, to the revolution of the American settlers against the monarchy of Queen Liliuokalani, and the establishment of the Republic of Hawaii (1892). As has subsequently occurred in other areas, e.g., Cuba and the Philippine Islands, *the economics of sugar accelerated the speed of political events*" (Dalton, *Sugar*, 25, emphasis added).

7. Taussig, *Some Aspects of the Tariff Question*, 70–79.

8. Benjamin, *The United States and Cuba*, 6. U.S. farmers were never able to impose the exclusion of raw sugar that the refiners imposed on refined sugar, so that the power of the latter on this score was significantly greater.

9. Weigle, "Sugar Interests," 38, 43.

10. Cordray, "Claus Spreckels of California," 32.

11. Ibid., 33–34.

12. Adler, *Claus Spreckels*, 3.

13. Ibid., 12.

14. Dozer, "Opposition to Hawaiian Reciprocity," 157, emphasis added.

15. Detailed accounts of the struggle over Hawaiian reciprocity are found in Weigle, "Sugar Interests," 1–160; Dozer, "Opposition to Hawaiian Reciprocity."

16. Taussig, *Some Aspects of the Tariff Question*, 56.

17. Taussig's analysis reflects his bias against the reciprocity treaty with Hawaii. He opposed the inclusion of Hawaii in the U.S. market structure. See Taussig, "Sugar," and Taussig, "Burden of the Sugar Duty." Dalton, *Sugar*, 24–25, recognized the impact on Hawaii. "For the first time, Congress juggled the interests of the various sugar-producing groups. In this case, Louisiana, with her direct bounty, and Cuba, with free sugar, were aided whereas Hawaii suffered the rude shock of the withdrawal of tariff protection." Weigle, "Sugar Interests," 9, cites Taussig favorably, but then argues that the McKinley Tariff had the effect of undoing reciprocity.

18. Weigle, "Sugar Interests," 51.

19. "It is true that many, even the majority, of the leaders of the revolution owned sugar stocks, the standard form of wealth in the islands. It is also true, however, that the majority of the big Hawaiian sugar planters are on record as opposed to annexation. Fear of the interruption of the contract labor system caused them to take this position" (ibid., 90).

20. Pratt, "Hawaiian Revolution," 274. The role of sugar was so prominent that some observers characterize the events as a "planters' revolution." James Geschwender argues, in "Hawaiian Transformation," 207: "The place of Hawaiian sugar in the American market was threatened in 1890 when Congress passed the McKinley Act, repealing the sugar tariff. Hawaiian sugar producers no longer gained from the reciprocity treaty. That the Hawaiian state acted in their interest was no longer sufficient to ensure the continuation of capital accumulation. They concluded that their future depended on Hawaii being annexed to the United States. . . . So in 1893 they launched a planter's revolution, overthrew the Hawaiian monarchy and when denied immediate annexation, established the Republic of Hawaii. Hawaii was finally annexed as a territory of the United States in 1898."

21. Weigle, "Sugar Interests," 122.

22. Welliver, "Annexation of Cuba by the Sugar Trust," 382.

23. See Zanetti, "En busca de la reciprocidad."

24. Ibid., 202–3. Zanetti points out (203–4) that José Martí was quick to notice the implications of the McKinley Tariff in advancing Cuban economic and political dependence on the United States: "Economic union means political union. The people who buy, command. The people who sell, serve. To assure liberty, commerce must be balanced. A people who want to die sell only to one buyer, whereas a people who want to be saved sell to more than one. The excessive influence of one country over the commerce of another turns into political influence." Martí, *Obras completas*, 6:160.

25. Atkins, *Sixty Years in Cuba*, 121.

26. Weigle, "Sugar Interests," 189–91. In Hawaii, the negative impact of the McKinley Tariff forced planters to modernize their mills and increase productivity: "The McKinley Act ushered in a period of intense competition for the American sugar market and motivated the Hawaiian sugar producers to improve methods of cultivation and increase their level of mutual cooperation" (Geschwender, "Hawaiian Transformation," 207).

27. Weigle, "Sugar Interests," 195–200, contains detailed estimates of these holdings based on the Spanish Treaty Claim Commission under which planters sough relief from the U.S. government for the destruction caused by the Cuban revolution of 1895–98.

28. For accounts of the pressure brought to bear to bear on the senators by the Sugar Trust to pass the Wilson Tariff, see Taussig, *Tariff History of the United States*, 314–15, and Weigle, "Sugar Interests," 201.

29. The petition of the commercial interests was signed, among others, by B. H. Howell Son & Company (sugar brokers) National Sugar Refining Company, Hugh Kelly, Czarnikow Mac-Dougall & Company (sugar brokers), Bartram Bros., Mollenhauer Sugar Refining Company, Munson Steamship Company, Arbucke Brothers (sugar refiners), and A. W. Colwell (sugar machinery). A delegation met with President McKinley on February 9, 1898. See Weigle, "Sugar Interests," 237–38.

30. Adler, *Claus Spreckels*, 55.

31. Weigle, "Sugar Interests," 12–16.

32. Roosevelt to Wood, May 14, 1901, quoted ibid., 255.

33. Weigle, "Sugar Interests," 275–79.

34. Ibid., 292.

35. Ibid., 340–47.

36. Dalton, *Sugar*, 32.

37. Best, "Mechanism of Plantation Type Societies."

38. "The tariff of 1897 was passed when already there were threatenings of war with Spain, Cuba being the cause. Cuba is the greatest sugar territory in the world. It could supply the world with sugar, and not be closely cultivated. If there should be war, Havemeyer realized it would assuredly end in Cuba being wrested from Spain, American capital would pour into the island, which would become part of the United States. There would no longer be a tariff barrier to keep its sugar out. The enterprise of Americans would soon discover that they could make more money on their sugar by refining it themselves, and sending the refined article to the United

States, than by selling it raw to the Trust for refining. And that would spell ruin to the Trust. Cuba must be kept out of the United States. If war could not be prevented, there must be assurance that Cuba must not be annexed."

"If Cuba had been annexed to the United States, following the War of 1898, and if the constitution's guarantee of unrestricted free trade among the various parts of the country had been extended to her, that would have been the deathblow to the Trust. For the Trust's life depends on maintaining a tariff adjusted delicately and skillfully to the purpose of keeping out all refined sugars, and giving the Trust special privileges in the importation of raw sugars."

"The Trust did not want Cuba given free trade with the United States. To that extent its interest was identical with the interest of the beet sugar industry. But the Trust did want the Cuban tariff so adjusted as to give the Trust a large advantage in importing raw sugar from Cuba. In this the Trust and the beet separated" (Welliver, "Annexation of Cuba," 381).

39. Weigle, "Sugar Interests," 135.

40. Eichner, *Emergence of Oligopoly*, 253.

41. Adler, *Claus Spreckels*, 105; Eichner, *Emergence of Oligopoly*, 270–71.

42. Timoshenko and Swerling, *World's Sugar*, 25.

43. Kent, *Hawaii*, 52.

44. Welliver, "Annexation of Cuba," 387.

45. "Transcript of Record, Supreme Court of the United States, October Term, 1914, No. 280, Allan H. Richardson, as Treasurer of Porto Rico, Plaintiff in Error, vs. The Fajardo Sugar Company, In Error for the District Court of the United States for Porto Rico" (filed November 10, 1914), 23–24.

46. Gayer et al., *Sugar Economy of Puerto Rico*, 35.

47. Dalton, *Sugar*, 28.

48. "It is a question of whether we are in the business to produce quantity or to produce profits. In that connection I gave you an interesting comparison last week, where South Porto Rico on an output of less than a million bags earned $3,970,000 before charges, and Cuba Cane on an amount of four million, five hundred thousand bags earned $4,800,000" (Horace Havemeyer to Manuel Rionda, November 10, 1925, Record Group IV, Series 96, Braga Brothers Collection, University of Florida, Gainesville).

Chapter 4

1. The basic facts of absentee ownership were stressed by a collection of studies on American imperialism in the Caribbean published in 1928–31: Knight, *Americans in Santo Domingo* (1928); Jenks, *Our Cuban Colony* (1929); Diffie and Diffie, *Porto Rico* (1931). The series of books was edited by Harry Elmer Barnes and includes a study of U.S. imperialism in Central America: Kepner and Soothill, *Banana Empire* (1935).

More recent studies on foreign ownership for the same period include Pino Santos, *El asalto a Cuba* (1973); Vázquez Galego, *Consolidación de los monopolios en Camagüey en la década del veinte* (1975); Lozano, *Dominación imperialista en la República Dominicana* (1976); Zanetti and García,

United Fruit Company (1976); Uz, ed., *Monopolios extranjeros en Cuba* (1984); Zanetti, "Cuestiones metodológicas de la investigacion de los monopolios imperialistas" (1983); Córdova Iturregui, "El Trust del Azúcar y el Trust del Tabaco en Puerto Rico," (1987).

2. Zeitlin, "Corporate Ownership and Control."

3. Williams, *From Columbus to Castro*, 428–42.

4. Hilferding's famous study, *Finance Capital* (1910), is replete with examples from the U.S. sugar refining industry and the American Sugar Refining Company.

5. Benjamin, *United States and Cuba*, 13.

6. Ibid., 95.

7. Lewis, *America's Stake in International Investments*, 606; Faulkner, *Decline of Laissez Faire*, 74.

8. Pérez, *Cuba*, 162.

9. Ibid., 158, 192–95.

10. Zanetti and García, *Caminos para el azúcar*.

11. See Oscar Pino Santos, *El asalto a Cuba*, 48.

12. Secretaría de Agricultura, Comercio y Trabajo de Cuba, *Portfolio azucarero*. This source contains mill-by-mill statistics on the 174 centrales in Cuba in 1913. One mill owned by joint Anglo-American interests was counted as North American, and four mills of joint Cuban-Spanish ownership were counted as Spanish.

13. Farr & Co., *Manual of Sugar Companies* (1948), 33.

14. Welliver, "Annexation of Cuba," 386. Welliver counts the American Sugar Refining Company and the National Sugar Refining Company as a single "interest group" which he collectively called the "Sugar Trust."

The Cuban American was a holding company which controlled the Chaparra, San Manuel, Delicias, Tinguaro, Nueva Luisa, Constancia, Unidad, and Mercedita mills, the Cuban Sugar Refinery at Cárdenas, and the Granmercy Refinery, at Granmercy, Louisiana. See "Documentos Relacionados con la solicitud de autorización de la administración de los Centrales Chaparra y Delicias para traer a Cuba por Puerto Padre 2,000 immigrantes procedentes de las Islas inglesas para la zafra de 1923–24," Secretaría de Agricultura, Industria, y Comercio, Fondo 3012, Legajo 4, Expediente 45, Archivo Nacional de Cuba.

15. Mullins, "Sugar Trust," 185.

16. The list is located in "Expediente relativo a la escritura y estatutos relativos a la compañía azucarera 'the Cuban American Sugar Company,'" Secretaría de Hacienda, Legajo 147, Expediente 211, Archivo Nacional de Cuba.

17. Ibid. contains the following distribution of stock certificates: Thomas A. Howell, 137; Albert Bunker, 133; George Bunker, 133; John Farr, 302; Charles H. Howell, 39; Elizabeth Howell and James Howell Post, Trustees of Frederick H. Howell, 110; Frederick H. Howell, 687; Helen A. Howell, 51; Mary A. Howell, 56; J. Adolph Mollenhauer, 133; Abrain A. Post, 262; James Howell Post, 2,299.5; Corine H. Wiley, Thomas A. Howell, James H. Post, Trustees of Corine H. Wile, 81, for a total of the B. H. Howell Group of 4,423.5.

18. Zeitlin and Ratcliff argue in *Landlords and Capitalists*, 54–55, that "a term is needed not merely for a group of interrelated kindred, but in particular for one forming a *more complex social unit in which economic interests and kinship bonds are inextricably intertwined*. We thus use the term

'kinecon group' to designate the type of effective kinship units controlling the top corporations. The concept of the kinecon group is class-specific; that is to say, it applies only where the ownership of stock in the large corporation is the characteristic and preponderant form of capital ownership and where the connection between stock ownership and corporate control has become attenuated, if not historically problematic. The corporation is the characteristic juridical unit of ownership of the means of production under contemporary capitalism, and the set of interrelated kindred who control it through their combined ownership interests and strategic representation in management constitutes the kinecon group. Ordinarily, the kinecon group consists of the primary, secondary, and other relatives among the officers, directors, and principal shareholders, whose combined individual and indirect (institutional) shareholdings constitute the dominant proprietary interest in the corporation."

I have included the Bunker and Mollenhauer interests in this group because they represent refining interests which, together with Post and Howell, established the National Sugar Refining Company.

19. Farr & Co., *Manual of Sugar Companies* (1926), 46.

20. Ibid., 20–21; Cf. Oscar Pino Santos, *El asalto a Cuba*, 99–100.

21. Farr & Co., *Manual of Sugar Companies* (1926).

22. Pino Santos, *El asalto a Cuba*, 43–44. Manuel Rionda argued along the same lines that the reconstruction of the Cuban sugar crop from 1900 to 1913 was "done without any outside assistance for Cuba had no outside financial support. Those Americans who went there during the American occupation entered the Eastern section; their capital did not go towards rebuilding the old section" (Rionda, "Resume of Cuba Cane Sugar Corporation Matters," July 29, 1919, Series 127, Braga Brothers Collection, University of Florida, Gainesville.

23. Pino Santos, *El asalto a Cuba*, 73–135.

24. Soref, "Finance Capitalists."

25. "Expediente relativo a la escritura y estatutos relativos a la compañía azucarera 'the Cuban American Sugar Company,'" Secretaría de Hacienda, Legajo 147, Expediente 211, Archivo Nacional de Cuba.

26. Córdova Iturregui, "El Trust del azúcar," 15.

27. *New York Times*, March 6, 1938, sec. 2, 9, 1; Córdova Iturregui, "El Trust del azúcar," 16–17.

28. Citibank was founded in 1812 and failed in 1837. Moses Taylor entered the bank originally as a representative of John Jacob Astor in 1837. Taylor's fortune was made as a trader in Cuban sugars: "Like other nineteenth century merchants, Taylor began his business career as an apprentice. He started at the age of fifteen in the firm of G. G. and S. S. Howland, the leading merchant house in the Latin American trade. In 1832, at the age of twenty-six, he went into business for himself, opening a firm specializing in importing Cuban sugar. The firm was successful from the outset. Although the great fire of 1835 destroyed Taylor's warehouse, the firm quickly recovered. It began trading in other commodities and invested in ships to carry goods to and from Havana and other Latin American ports. By the time of the 1837 panic and his appointment as a director of City Bank, Taylor was one of New York's leading merchants. By 1855, his firm was reported to be paying more customs duties than any other firm in the United

States except A. T. Stewart and Company, the famed dry goods merchants" (Cleveland and Huertas, *Citibank*, 17). For a history of Moses Taylor and Company's activities in the Cuban trade, see Ely, "Old Cuba Trade."

29. "Biographical Sketch of Moses Taylor," Moses Taylor Collection, New York Public Library.

30. Cleveland and Huertas, *Citibank*, 41.

31. See Hilferding, *Finance Capital*.

32. Cleveland and Huertas, *Citibank*, 16–31, 41, 107.

33. Jenks, *Our Cuban Colony*, 176–77.

34. National City Bank of New York, *Cuba*, 3–5.

35. Jenks, *Our Cuban Colony*, 177–78.

36. Between 1922 and 1927, six mills were built. After that date, the construction of sugar mills in Cuba practically came to a standstill.

37. See Jenks, *Our Cuban Colony*, 178: "The immediate consequence of the sugar boom was the development of new enterprises. By the beginning of 1918, 39 mills had been newly built, reconstructed, or were being installed. Ten commenced operations in 1916; 12 the following year. At least 25 of these mills were put up on the initiative of Cubans, who found the capital among their friends and connections.

"A handful of them were built outright by Americans. Edwin F. Atkins took the lead, combining two new mills, Florida and Punta Alegre, with Trinidad in 1916 under the control of the Punta Alegre Sugar Company. Rival refiners followed quickly. The Warner Sugar Refining Company erected Central Miranda in Oriente Province. The West India Sugar Finance Corporation, organized by Thomas A. Howell of B. H. Howell and Son (National Sugar Refining Company), financed and undertook the management of Alto Cedro, Cupey, and Palma, also at the eastern end of the island."

38. Braga Brothers Collection, "Report by George W. Goethals and Company, Inc., on the Cuba Cane Sugar Corporation, July 11, 1919," 2, Series 127 (36), University of Florida Archives, Gainesville.

39. Jaretzki was born in New York in 1861 and graduated from Harvard in 1881 and from Columbia Law School in 1884. He joined Sullivan & Cromwell in 1881 and became a member in 1894. A specialist in corporation law, he was also a director of the Manatí Sugar Company (*New York Times*, March 15, 1925, 26, 5).

40. Alfred Strauss was born in New York in 1864, left City College of New York before graduation, and joined the banking house of J. & W. Seligman & Company in 1882. In 1901 he was admitted as partner and eventually became the leading partner. In 1918–21 he served as vice-chairman of the Federal Reserve Board, resigning from the Seligman firm during the tenure. Strauss went to Paris with President Wilson as adviser on financial questions (*National Cyclopaedia of American Biography*, 22:246).

41. Charles Sabin was born in Massachusetts in 1868, became a clerk in Albany Bank, and stayed there from 1891 to 1908. In 1907 he became vice-president of the National Copper Bank in New York City and president of Guaranty Trust Company in 1915 (*New York Times*, October 12, 1933, 25,1).

42. Manuel Rionda to Lagemann, December 27, 1915, Record Group II, ser. 2, Braga Brothers Collection, University of Florida, Gainesville; McAvoy-Weissman, "Manuel Rionda and the Formation," 5.

43. Dalton, *Sugar*, 28.

44. Benjamin, *United States and Cuba*, 195.

45. "The Busines of the Czarnikov-Rionda Company, of which Rionda was managing partner in New York, was that of sugar merchants. It was really a world-wide business. C. Czarnikov, Ltd., of London, was the leading dealer in European beet and other sugars which were marketed in Great Britain. Congressional investigations and federal suits against the Sugar Trust had dealt respectfully with the Czarnikov partners as the most powerful personalities in the sugar market" (Jenks, *Our Cuban Colony*, 179).

46. Manuel Rionda, "Resume of Cuba Cane Sugar Corporation Matters, Prepared by Mr. Manuel Rionda, at White Sulphur Springs before the Publication of General Goethal's report, revised as to certain figures, July 29, 1919," Series (127), 2, Braga Brothers Collection, University of Florida, Gainesville.

47. William J. McCahan of the prominent Philadeplphia sugar refining family participated with Manuel Rionda in the founding of the Francisco Sugar Company. In the first meeting of the board of directors, McCahan voted his shares "by proxy to Manuel Rionda" (Minute Book of the Francisco Sugar Company, 1,3, Braga Brothers Collection, University of Florida, Gainesville).

Cf. Jenks, *Our Cuban Colony*, 179: "The Rionda family were concerned in the W. J. McCahan Sugar Refining Company of Philadelphia, and in several sugar estates in Cuba, in addition to the those which the firm represented as an agent."

48. "The Stewart was organized in 1906. It was one of the first new Cuban plantations to be erected in the middle of the Island. The organizers of the enterprise came to grief before the factory was started. Sullivan & Cromwell were the lawyers of that firm and made financial arrangements by which my chief, Mr. Czarnikow, joined to finish the factory. I was made president in 1907 and remained as such during the entire period of construction and uplifting, but resigned in 1911 when the Company had become prosperous and was out of all its financial difficulties. Our house continued to finance the company and sell its sugars" (Rionda, "Resume of Cuba Cane Sugar Corporation Matters," 3–5).

49. McAvoy, "Manuel Rionda," 5. All of these firms were part of the Morgan empire. The Bankers Trust was the commercial bank of the group, DeLamar was a big stock owner in the International Banking Company, a Morgan-promoted trust. Sullivan & Cromwell was a firm of attorneys historically identified with the House of Morgan. In October 1912, J. & W. Seligman & Company joined in underwriting the Manatí.

50. Manuel Rionda to Lagemann, December 27, 1915, Record Group II, Ser. 2, Braga Brothers Collection, University of Florida, Gainesville, quoted in McAvoy, "Manuel Rionda," 11, 17.

51. La Julia and Jobo in Havana Province; Socorro, Mercedes, Conchita, Soledad, Feliz, Alava, San Ignacio, and Santa Gertrudis in Matanzas; Lequeitio, María Victoria, and Perseverancia in Santa Clara; Jagüeyal, Lugareño, and Morón and Stewart in Camagüey.

52. McAvoy, "Manuel Rionda," 12–13.

53. Ibid., 11.

54. Marwick, Mitchell, Peat & Co. to the Directors of the Czarnikow-Rionda Company, April 29, 1919, Series 127, Braga Brothers Collection, University of Florida, Gainesville.

55. Allen, *Story of the Growth of E. Atkins & Co.*, 13.

56. Ibid., 21.

57. Mullins, "Sugar Trust," 176; Allen, *Story of the Growth of E. Atkins & Co.*, 23.

58. Pino Santos, *El asalto a Cuba*, 110; Allen, *Story of the Growth of E. Atkins & Co.*, 27.

59. Allen, *Story of the Growth of E. Atkins & Co.*, 27.

60. Ibid., 29–30.

61. Farr & Co., *Manual of Sugar Companies* (1934).

62. Allen, *Story of the Growth of E. Atkins & Co.*, 32–33.

63. Ibid., 34.

64. Ibid., 35.

65. Ibid.

66. "Obituary of Eugene Van Rensselaer Thayer," *New York Times*, January 2, 1937, 11, 5.

67. Allen, *Story of the Growth of E. Atkins & Co.*, 41.

68. I follow Soref's definition of a "finance capitalist" as someone who sits on the board of directors of a bank and an industrial enterprise. See Soref, "Finance Capitalists"; Zeitlin and Soref, "Finance Capital," 67.

69. The following directors of the Punta Alegre Sugar Company were also on the boards of directors of banks: Charles D. Armstrong (Union National Bank of Pittsburgh); Edwin F. Atkins (Belmont Savings Bank, vice-president, Guaranty Company of North America, Second National Bank of Boston); Robert W. Atkins (Merchant's National Bank of Boston); Ernest B. Dane (Provident Institution for Savings, Merchant's National Bank of Boston); Clifton H. Dwinnel (First National Bank of Boston, first vice-president); Henry Horblower (Arlington Cents Savings Bank, First National Corporation); Louis K. Liggett (American Trust Company, National Bank of Roxbury, New Netherland Bank, National Shawmut Bank of Boston, Rockland Bank of Roxbury); Charles Spencer (First National Bank of Boston, vice-president); Galen L. Stone (First National Bank of Boston, Old Colony Tust Company). See Directory of Directors Company, *Directory of Directors of the City of Boston and Vicinity*, 1914 and 1921.

70. Secretaría de Agricultura, Comercio y Trabajo de Cuba, *Portfolio azucarero*; Pino Santos, *El asalto a Cuba*, 75.

71. Directory of Directors Company, *Directory of Directors of the City of New York* (1921–22).

72. Ibid.

73. Benjamin, *United States and Cuba*, 196.

74. Bernabe, "Prehistory of the Partido Popular Democrático," 34.

75. The General Sugars Company was a holding company whose stock was held by the National City company, the stock of which, in turn, was held by the National City Bank. "The National City Bank denied being in the sugar business since the bank held no direct shares in the sugar company" (Smith, *United States and Cuba*, 30, 194).

76. Ibid.

77. Ibid., 30.

78. Ibid., 16. Benjamin's contention that the National City "came into possession of sixty mills as a result of the crisis, which properties it organized under the General Sugar Company" seems inflated. The bank may have come into possession of sixty large properties, including colonias. National City foreclosed many properties, fused them, reorganized the industry, and retained in operation only the largest mills. See Benjamin, *United States and Cuba*, 16.

79. Cleveland and Huertas, *Citibank*, 107.

80. *Gaceta Oficial, Edición Extraordinaria No. 43, Decreto 1583*, October 10, 1920, leg. 12, no. 1, Secretaría de la Presidencia, Archivo Nacional de Cuba.

81. "República de Cuba, Secretaría de Hacienda, Sección de Acuñación de Monedas, Havana, Noviembre 3 de 1920, Numerario Recibido de los Estados Unidos desde el día 12 de Octubre por los bancos y compañías que se expresan," caja 12, no. 1, f. 35, Secretaría de la Presidencia, Archivo Nacional de Cuba.

82. José Gómez Mena to Mario Menocal, President of the Republic of Cuba, November 22, 1920, Secretaría de la Presidencia, leg. 12, no. 2, Archivo Nacional de Cuba.

83. Mario Menocal to Hawley-CUBANACO, November 22, 1920, leg. 12, no. 2, Secretaría de la Presidencia, Archivo Nacional de Cuba.

84. Central Chaparra, *Album de vistas del gran Central Chaparra*.

85. "Confluente Sugar Company to Srs. de la Comisión de Liquidación Bancaria," June 27, 1922, Donativos y Remisiones, leg 449, no. 5, Archivo Nacional de Cuba.

86. R. Egaña, Confluente Sugar Company, to Presidente de la Junta Liquidadora del Banco Nacional, February 25, 1925, Donativos y Remisiones, leg 449, no. 5, Archivo Nacional de Cuba.

87. Ibid.

88. Farr & Co., *Manual of Sugar Companies* (1924), 18.

89. Benjamin, *United States and Cuba*, 30.

90. Calder, *Impact of Intervention*, 92.

91. Lozano, *Dominación imperialista en la República Dominicana*, 154.

92. Ibid., 26.

93. Calder, *Impact of Intervention*, 92.

94. Lozano, *Dominación imperialista en la República Dominicana*, 158.

95. Muto, "La economía de exportación de la República Dominicana, 1900–1930," *EME-EME Estudios Dominicanos*, 33 (November–December 1974): 80, quoted in Cordero and del Castillo, *Economía dominicana*, 21.

96. Cordero and del Castillo, *Economía dominicana*, 21.

97. Ibid., 21–22, citing William L. Bass, *Reciprocidad* (Santo Domingo: Imprenta La Cuna de América, 1902), 39–40.

98. Cordero and del Castillo, *Economía dominicana*, 22–25.

99. Ibid., 31.

100. The haciendas comuneras were also common in Cuba east of Sancti Spiritus. They were important in Camagüey and Oriente, which in the twentieth century became the seats of the largest U.S. sugar mills. See Celorio, *Haciendas comuneras*, 16–17.

101. Calder, *Impact of Intervention*, 104.

102. Ibid., 104–5.

103. Ibid., 98.

104. Lozano, *Dominación imperialiste en la República Dominicana*, 157; Knight, *Americans in Santo Domingo*, 139.

105. Knight, *Americans in Santo Domingo*, 137.

106. Ibid., 130.

107. Ibid., 131.

108. Ibid.

109. Pino Santos, *El asalto a Cuba*, 103–4.

110. South Porto Rico Sugar Company, *Fiftieth Anniversary Report*, 4–5.

111. Cordero and del Castillo, *La economía dominicana . . .* , 42.

112. South Porto Rico Sugar Company, *Fiftieth Anniversary Report*, 5.

113. "Mr. Schall, chairman of the South Porto Rico Board of Directors, is President of the American Colonial Bank in San Juan, Porto Rico. Mr. Dillingham, President of South Porto Rico, is also of the above bank. Mr. Welty, another Director of the sugar concern, is a member of Mr. Schall's firm in New York. Mr. Tilney is of the Bankers Trust Company [House of Morgan, C.A.] and Mr. Horace Havemeyer is also a director of both, besides being a member of Havemeyer and Elder, Inc., and thus a representative of the vague central organization of Sugardom" (Knight, *Americans in Santo Domingo*, 137).

114. Gilmore, *Porto Rico Sugar Manual*, 249–80.

115. On May 1, 1900, the U.S. Congress imposed a duty of 15 percent of the normal rate on goods exchanged between Puerto Rico and the United States. On July 25, 1900, in accordance with the provisions of the Foraker Law, a presidential decree placed Puerto Rico fully within the United States tariff system. After 1901, trade between the United States and Puerto Rico was free of duty. See Medina Mercado, "El proceso de acumulación de tierras," 14; Smith, *La tarifa*.

116. In Cuba, United States rule had to contend with the remnants of the Partido Revolucionario Cubano and the revolutionary polity that had gathered around the cry of Cuba Libre since 1895. The Magoon Intervention of 1906, the uprising of the Partido Independiente de Color in 1912, and the "Liberal" revolution of 1917 challenged the stability of Cuba under the Platt Ammendment. In the Dominican Republic, the U.S. occupation of 1916 elicited a decentralized guerrilla response that made the continuation of a U.S. presence in that island very difficult. By comparison with these two examples, colonial Puerto Rico was a haven of stability for U.S. capital. For Cuba, see Pérez, *Cuba under the Platt Amendment*, and for the Dominican Republic, Calder, *Impact of Intervention*.

117. South Porto Rico Sugar Company, *Fiftieth Anniversary Report*, 2; Cf. J. D. H. Luce, founder of the Aguirre Sugar Company, to U.S. senator Henry Cabot Lodge, July 15, 1898, quoted in McAvoy, "Brotherly Love," 99: "As an imperialist, you may not be surprised that I wish to be in the front row of colonial expansion! In short, I am very anxious to go to Porto Rico."

118. Aguirre Sugar Company, *Fiftieth Anniversary Report*, 15; McAvoy, "Early United States Investors," 2.

119. McAvoy, "Early United States Investors," 4.

120. Aguirre Sugar Company, *Fiftieth Anniversary Report*, 16.

121. Palmer, "Interpreting Corporate Interlocks."

122. The other Boston representatives on the board of directors were Charles Francis Adams II, Louis Bacon, George Wigglesworth, Robert Frederick Herrick, and Robert Treat Paine II. Adams was nephew by marriage of Luce. Bacon was the brother-in-law of Sturgis Lothrop and presumably replaced him to oversee family investments. Wigglesworth was president of the Amoskeag textile mills and chairman of the board of the New England Trust Company. Herrick was a rising corporation lawyer, director of the First National Bank of Boston and of the United Fruit Company. Paine was, among other things, on the board of General Electric. See McAvoy, "Early United States Investors," 6.

George Cabot Lee was a member of the investment banking firm of Lee, Higginson and Company until 1940. Charles Grey Bancroft was first vice-president and treasurer of the United Shoe Machinery Corporation and thereafter president of the International Trust Company until it merged with the First National Bank of Boston. Robert T. Paine II left the board of Aguirre in 1916 and was replaced by New York real estate man Charles G. Meyer.

Unless otherwise stated, information about company directors is from Directory of Directors Company, *Directory of Directors in the City of New York*. This directory lists individuals in alphabetical order. Therefore, I have not cited page numbers.

123. McAvoy, "Early United States Investors," 7.

124. Quoted ibid., 10.

125. The *Fiftieth Anniversary Report* of the Aguirre Sugar Company provides the following list of directors: Charles Francis Adams (1905–), Louis Bacon (1905–37), Charles L. Crehore (1905–25), John Farr (1905–33), Robert F. Herrick (1905–42), J. D. H. Luce (1905–21), Robert T. Paine II (1905–16), James H. Post (1905–38), George Wigglesworth (1905–30), George C. Lee (1910–), Thomas A. Howell (1911–30), Charles G. Meyer (1916–), Charles G. Bancroft (1919–44), Charles L. Carpenter (1919–29), Charles Hartzell (1919–28), J. Brooks Keyes (1921–).

I have added after each name the years for which they were members of the board of Aguirre. If no end year appears, the individuals were still directors of the company as of 1949, the year of the *Fiftieth Anniversary Report*.

126. *National Cyclopaedia of American Biography*, 53:11–12.

127. See Roy, *Socializing Capital*, 265–73.

128. Fajardo Sugar Company, *Fiftieth Anniversary Report*, 3.

129. Eichner, *Emergence of Oligopoly*, 309.

130. Soref, "Finance Capitalists"; Zeitlin and Soref, "Finance Capital."

131. Sweezy, "Interest Groups in the American Economy," 161.

132. Ibid., 164.

133. Sweezy, "Decline of the Investment Banker."

134. See Ayala, "Theories of Big Business."

135. The Bankers Trust and the Guaranty Trust were the commercial banks of the Morgan group, which in addition consisted of J. P. Morgan and Company, Drexel and Company, as

investment banks, and the Prudential and New York Life insurance companies. See Corey, *House of Morgan*; Perlo, *Empire of High Finance*, 61–91; Menshikov, *Millionaires and Managers*, 228–58.

136. South Porto Rico Sugar Company, *Fiftieth Anniversary Report*, 2.

137. Herzig-Shannon, "El American Colonial Bank," 2–3.

138. McAvoy, "Early United States Investors," 12.

139. Ibid., 14.

140. Of the founders of the South Porto Rico Sugar Company, William Schall was a partner of the house of Muller and Schall and president of the recently founded American Colonial Bank of Porto Rico; Frank Dillingham was a member of the legal firm that represented Muller and Schall; Percy Chubb was founder and president of the Federal Insurance Company and head of Chubb & Son, maritime underwriters, firms in which Schall was a director; Fritze was the German vice-consul in Ponce and partner of banking firms associated with Muller and Schall (Fritze and Lundt, Banco Crédito y Ahorro Ponceño); Rudolph Keppler was a German who migrated to the United States as a boy, joined the New York Stock Exchange in 1875, and became its president from 1898 to 1902; Edmund Pavenstedt was a partner in Muller and Schall and had managed his father's plantation in Puerto Rico in the 1880s. The other founders were Julius A. Stursberg, W. C. Cushman, C. M. Russell, and John E. Berwind. Stursberg was involved in insurance companies and various other ventures, Cushman and Russell are of unknown origin, and John E. Berwind was a Pennsylvania coal magnate whose fortune in 1924 was estimated at $150 million. Berwind was the outstanding capitalist of the group, but he does not appear to have been the center of it. In addition to numerous coal companies, Berwind was president of the Puerto Rico Coal Company, vice-president of the Havana Coal Company, and director of the New York and Porto Rico Steamship Company.

141. McAvoy, "Early United States Investors," 17.

142. Knight, *Americans in Santo Domingo*, 137.

143. "The Tax Case of the Guanica Central," January 2, 1926, Record Group 350, File 27229/6, Insular Bureau, War Department, National Archives, Washington, D.C.

144. United States Circuit Court of Appeals for the First Circuit. No. 2479, *Manuel V. Domenech, Treasurer, Plaintiff, Appellant, v. Horace Havemeyer et al. (Russell & Co., Sucesores S. en C.), Defendant, Appellee; No. 2480, Same v. South Porto Rico Sugar Company (of Porto Rico).; No. 2481, Same v. South Porto Rico Sugar Company (of New Jersey) Opinion of the Court, April 28, 1931* (Boston: L. H. Lane, 1931), 5, in Record Group 350, File 27229/30, National Archives, Washington, D.C.

145. The emphasis on power and the critique of the functionalist argument are especially prominent in Roy, *Socializing Capital*.

Chapter 5

1. In varying degrees, this generalization is true of the three great classics on the sugar economy of the late 1920s and early 1930s: Knight, *Americans in Santo Domingo* (1928); Jenks, *Our Cuban Colony* (1929); Diffie and Diffie, *Porto Rico* (1931).

2. Davis, "Capitalist Agricultural Development."

3. Guerra y Sánchez, *Industria azucarera de Cuba*, 114–15.

4. An arroba is equal to twenty-five pounds.

5. Guerra y Sánchez, *Industria azucarera de Cuba*, 124.

6. Ibid., 125.

7. Ibid., 126, emphasis added.

8. Ibid., 127.

9. Mann, *Agrarian Capitalism*, 29.

10. Ibid.

11. In the South of the United States, sharecropping persisted until the agricultural reforms of the New Deal introduced subsidies and crop restrictions. See ibid.

12. Bergad, *Cuban Rural Society*, 277–78.

13. Venegas Delgado, "Acerca del proceso de concentración y centralización de la industria azucarera."

14. Iglesias García, "Del ingenio al central," chap. 8, "Agriculture."

15. Bergad, *Cuban Rural Society*, 279, 285.

16. Secretaría de Agricultura, Comercio y Trabajo de Cuba, *Portfolio azucarero*.

17. Bird, *Report on the Sugar Industry*, 51. The yearly cycle of tiempo muerto was essentially the same in Cuba and Puerto Rico. See U.S. Tariff Commission, *Sugar* (1934).

18. Cabrera Pérez, *Memoria explicativa*.

19. See Ibarra, "Mecanismos económicos del capital financiero."

20. Cabrera Pérez, *Memoria explicativa*, passim.

21. Hoernel, "Sugar and Social Change in Oriente."

22. Francisco Sugar Company, *Minute Book*, February 14, 1900.

23. Ibid., April 25, 1902.

24. Ibid., October 1, 1902.

25. Ibid., October 7, 1912.

26. Francisco Sugar Company, "Manager's Report," 1917, 5.

27. Benn, "Theory of Plantation Economy and Society."

28. Cf. Mandle, *Patterns of Caribbean Development*, 38. In his essay "Plantation Economy," 57, Mandle argues that "for analytic reasons . . . we will refer to the economies of the New World where plantations were dominant as 'plantation economies' by which we mean regimes which can be considered neither capitalist nor feudal and which have their own dynamic pattern based upon technology and social relations which inhere in the plantation as the dominant unit of output."

In a similar vein, Eric Williams had earlier generalized in his characterization of the plantation economy as "an unstable economy based on a single crop which combined the vices of feudalism and capitalism with the virtues of neither" (*Negro in the Caribbean*, 13).

29. For "flexible production" see Smith, *Lean Production*; Harrison, *Lean and Mean*. The overemphasis on "Fordist" industrial conditions has led some proponents of the so-called regulation school to overlook the historical antecedents of current so-called post-Fordist industrial organization. As shown here, there are older forms of flexible subcontracting and just-in-

time delivery. For a critique of the regulation school, see Brenner and Glick, "Regulation Approach."

30. "All the expenses of planting, cultivating, and harvesting the cane are met by the grower. However, the mill is stated to be 'an interested party' in his plantations, 'with all the rights and privileges accorded by the law.' Any lapse on the part of the grower in the planting, cultivating, or harvesting of his cane, it is agreed, 'will cause great and irreparable damage to the *central* (mill).'

"The mill may prescribe the type of fertilizer the grower is to use, and—in irrigated districts— the time when irrigation of cane must cease before cutting. Special supervision by the mill is usually provided for in the case of *gran cultura* cane grown by the grower."

"The mill may determine the rate of cutting and deliveries for grinding" (Gayer et al., *Sugar Economy of Puerto Rico*, 134–35).

31. Cuba Cane Sugar Corporation, "Report of Frank Feuille on the Landed Properties of the Cuba Cane Sugar Corporation."

32. The Julia, Jobo, Conchita, Feliz, Socorro, San Ignacio, Soledad, Santa Gertrudis, Alava, Mercedes, Marie Victoria, Perseverancia, and Lequeito mills were located in the west. The Lugareño, Morón, Jagüeyal, and Stewart mills were located in the east.

33. Goethals & Company, "Report by George W. Goethals and Company, Inc., on the Cuba Cane Sugar Corporation."

34. Ibid., 8.

35. Ibid., 28.

36. Dye, "Cane Contracting and Renegotiation."

37. U.S. Tariff Commission, *Sugar* (1926), 74.

38. The nineteenth-century figures are from Curbelo, *Proyecto para fomentar*, 11; Montoro, *Discursos*, 292; Moreno Fraginals, *El Ingenio*, 1:190–91; Bergad, *Cuban Rural Society*, 327–28. The figures for 1913 are from Secretaría de Agricultura, Comercio y Trabajo, *Portfolio azucarero*.

39. Bergad, *Cuban Rural Society*, 328.

40. The decline in agricultural yields may be related to a reduction in the intensity of work after emancipation. The data presented here, however, only measure yields of cane per unit of land. They do not offer a direct measure of yields of cane per worker or per unit of labor input.

41. These figures can be easily converted into tons per acre, the measure used in Puerto Rico and in U.S. reports. A caballería is equal to 33.6 acres, and an arroba is equal to 25 pounds, a short ton is equal to 2,000 pounds, and a long ton is equal to 2,240 pounds. I have retained arrobas and caballerías for ease of comparison with nineteenth-century Cuban figures.

42. Bergad, *Cuban Rural Society*, 328.

43. Moreno Fraginals, *El ingenio*, 1:190–91. Moreno's figures are possibly overestimations.

44. A sample of Cuban mills studied by the U.S. Tariff Commission in Cuba averaged 18.26 tons of cane per acre in 1931–32. About 80 percent of the sample was colono cane. In Puerto Rico, colono farms averaged 28 tons per acre in 1931–32, while company farms averaged 37 tons per acre, which is more than double the Cuban average (U.S. Tariff Commission, *Sugar* [1934], 67, 118).

For the development of the irrigation systems in Puerto Rico and their effect on yields relative to Cuba, see de Abad, *Azúcar y caña de azúcar*, 65–68.

45. Bergad, *Cuban Rural Society*, 327.

46. Curbelo, *Proyecto ara fomentar*, 11, estimated that a caballería of good land would yield one hundred thousand arrobas of cane. The cane, in turn, would yield 8 percent *azúcar de guarapo*, 2 percent *azúcar de miel*, and 1.75 percent *miel para aguardiente*.

Montoro, *Discursos*, 292, published in 1894, mentions that in Germany, Austria, and France, beet farmers were extracting yields of 13 percent while in Cuba the cane yields were below 8 percent.

47. Bernabe, "Prehistory of the Partido Popular Democrático," 70.

48. Junta de Salario Mínimo de Puerto Rico, *La industria del azúcar en Puerto Rico*, 20.

49. Bergad, *Coffee and the Growth of Agrarian Capitalism*.

50. Bernabe, "Prehistory of the Partido Popular Democrático," 57, 70.

51. Bird, *Report on the Sugar Industry*, 67.

52. U.S. Tariff Commission, *Sugar* (1934), 67, 118.

53. Scarano, "El colonato azucarero," 157.

54. Bird, *Report on the Sugar Industry*, 73.

55. U.S. Tariff Commission, *Sugar* (1934), 119, 192.

56. Medina Mercado, "El proceso de acumulación de tierras."

57. Fajardo Sugar Company, "Memorandum concerning bill to provide Civil Government for Porto Rico, 8.

58. Ibid., 18.

59. Medina Mercado, "El proceso de acumulación de tierras," 42.

60. Bernabe, "Prehistory of the Partido Popular Democrático," 55–72.

61. Shipping costs of sugar to the United States markets were 0.0587 cents per pound higher for Cuba than for Puerto Rico in the period 1918–23. This is a very small difference. For practical purposes, shipping costs may be considered equivalent. See U.S. Tariff Commission, *Sugar* (1926), 58. By the late 1920s and early 1930s, shipping costs were higher from Puerto Rico but the tariff advantage was so much greater than the difference in shipping costs that it made the latter insignificant. Puerto Rican sugar was shipped to U.S. ports at an average cost of 0.163 cents per pound in 1929, 0.162 in 1930, and 0.156 in 1931. For those same years Cuban shipping costs were, in cents per pound, 0.145, 0.126, and 0.124. Puerto Rico enjoyed a tariff advantage of 1.7648 cents per pound in 1928 and 2 cents per pound in 1930 and 1931. Subtracting the Cuban advantage in shipping costs, Puerto Rican sugar still enjoyed a price advantage of 1.7288 cents per pound in 1929, 1.964 in 1930, and 1.968 in 1931. See U.S. Tariff Commission, *Sugar* (1934), 74, 124.

62. Gilmore, *Porto Rico Sugar Manual*, 249–80.

Chapter 6

1. For a critique of "world systems theory" and "dependency theory," which argue that underdevelopment is fundamentally an expression of "external relations," that is, of the way in which countries are "inserted" into the capitalist world economy, see Zeitlin, *Civil Wars in Chile*, 3–20.

2. Moya Pons, *Manual de historia dominicana*, 225. The abolition of slavery was the first public decree of President Jean Pierre Boyer once the island of Hispaniola was unified under his government in 1822.

3. See, for example, Mandle, "Plantation Economy"; Mandle, *Patterns of Caribbean Development*.

4. Giusti-Cordero, "Labor, Ecology and History," 1051.

5. This is one of the central arguments of Giusti's exhaustive research in "Labor, Ecology and History."

6. Mintz, "From Plantations to Peasants," 127–53. A full discussion can be found in Giusti, "Labor, Ecology and History," 112–236.

7. Weyl, "Labor Conditions in Puerto Rico," 724.

8. Scott, *Slave Emancipation in Cuba*, 87.

9. The slave population of Camagüey declined from 14,807 in 1862 to 2,290 in 1877; that of Oriente declined from 50,863 to 13,061 in the same period. See Scott, "Explaining Abolition," 88.

10. Scott, *Slave Emancipation in Cuba*, 87–88.

11. Ibid., 139–40.

12. Scott, "Defining the Boundaries of Freedom," 82.

13. Ayala, "Social and Economic Aspects of Sugar Production," 96; U.S. War Department, *Report on the Census of Cuba*, 558–59.

14. Du Bois, *Black Reconstruction in America*, and Foner, *Reconstruction*.

15. Bergad, *Cuban Rural Society*, 285.

16. Scott, "Defining the Boundaries of Freedom," 86.

17. Ibid.

18. Scott, *Slave Emancipation in Cuba*, 259.

19. The complex movements of population are analyzed in ibid., 247–54. The concept of "reconstituted peasantry" is developed by Mintz in "From Plantations to Peasants in the Caribbean," 127–53, and in "Slavery and the Rise of Peasantries."

20. Hoernel, "Sugar and Social Change," 220–21.

21. Scott, *Slave Emancipation in Cuba*, 250; Hoernel, "Sugar and Social Change," 222.

22. The dual social nature of the semipeasant and semiproletarian precaristas of eastern Cuba in the 1950s produced a complex debate about the social bases of the Cuban revolution, which one pole characterized as a "peasant war" and another as a "proletarian insurrection." Giusti in "Labor, Ecology and History" argues that this dual character of agricultural workers may be an almost universal characteristic of Caribbean peasants/proletarians.

23. Hoernel, "Sugar and Social Change," 222.

24. Iglesias García, "Del ingenio al central," 44–46.

25. Pérez de la Riva, "Cuba y la migración antillana, 1900–1931," 5.

26. Iglesias García, "Del ingenio al central," 47.

27. Bergad, *Cuban Rural Society*, 285.

28. Ibid., 288.

29. Iglesias García, "Características de la inmigración española," 82.

30. Scott, *Slave Emancipation in Cuba*, 289.

31. Ibid., 290.

32. Moya Pons, *Manual de historia dominicana*, 225.

33. Cassá, *Historia social y económica*, 2:13–37. See also Domínguez, *Economía y política de la República Dominicana*, for the period between independence and the annexation to Spain; Mejía Ricart, ed., *Sociedad dominicana durante la primera República*; Moya Pons, *Manual de historia dominicana*; and Gleijeses, *Dominican Crisis*, chap. 1.

34. "El Cibao was the only region of the country which did not have a *caudillo* in the period 1844–1865. Quite to the contrary, the tobacco and commercial petty bourgoisies became the enemies of the *caudillos* and the defenders of public liberties" (Domínguez, "Economía dominicana durante la primera república," 87).

35. Moya Pons, *Manual de historia dominicana*, 407; Calder, *Impact of Intervention*, 92.

36. Cassá, *Historia social y económica*, 2:82.

37. Del Castillo, "Azúcar y braceros."

38. Moya Pons, *Manual de historia dominicana*, 403–12.

39. Bryan, "Transition to Plantation Agriculture," 96.

40. De Hostos, "Falsa alarma, crísis agrícola," 159–76.

41. Bryan, "Transition to Plantation Agriculture," 103.

42. Del Castillo, "Azúcar y braceros," 6–13; Martínez, "La fuerza de trabajo en el proceso de modernización."

43. Baud, "Origins of Capitalist Agriculture," 144.

44. Bryan, "Transition to Plantation Agriculture," 99.

45. Baud, "Origins of Capitalist Agriculture," 145.

46. "During the zafra, it is true that many come from all parts of the Republic looking for work . . . when the newcomer stays, if he is a hard working man, he gets married right away with great advantages, and finds that his wife has very good lands, because all the women have them, and there you have the immigrant turned into a proprietor" (*El Eco de la Opinión*, October 1892, cited in Martínez, "La fuerza de trabajo en el proceso de modernización," 112–13).

47. Del Castillo, *Inmigración de braceros azucareros*, 32.

48. Del Castillo, "Azúcar y braceros," 15.

49. Ibid., 13–15.

50. Calder, "Dominican Turn towards Sugar," 18.

51. Dietz, *Economic History of Puerto Rico*, 20.

52. Bergad, "Recent Research on Slavery in Puerto Rico," 102.

53. Scarano, *Sugar and Slavery in Puerto Rico*, 33.

54. Bergad, *Coffee and the Growth of Agrarian Capitalism*; Picó, *Libertad y servidumbre en el Puerto Rico*; Picó, *Amargo café*.

55. Bergad, "Coffee and Rural Proletarianization."

56. Ramos Mattei, *Sociedad del azúcar*, 21. There is some debate about the extent of rural proletarianization in nineteenth-century Puerto Rico. Different assessments of the degree to which proletarianization advanced in the nineteenth century depend on the point of reference of the author in question. When the point of reference is the first half of the nineteenth century, the second half was evidently characterized by a widening process of proletarianization, espe-

cially in the coffee region. When the optic is shifted to the twentieth century, the nineteenth century process of proletarianization seems paltry by comparison. See Bergad, "Agrarian History of Puerto Rico," and Bergad, *Coffee and the Growth of Agrarian Capitalism*; Brass, "Free and Unfree Rural Labour in Puerto Rico." In an essay based on secondary literature which suffers from an excessive association between tropical agriculture and unfree labor similar to that of the plantation school, Brass questions Bergad's estimates of the scope of free labor in nineteenth-century Puerto Rico. Brass's postulate of the existence of unfree labor is based on the "bonding role of the estate store." The general strike of Puerto Rican cane cutters in 1934, in which the elimination of payment in scrip was one of the central demands, would figure as a movement of unfree labor, once one accepts this line of reasoning.

57. Del Castillo, *Inmigración de braceros azucareros*, 34.

58. "Months after the American flag was raised in Puerto Rico the cities of the country received the first waves of hungry ex-coffee farmers looking for refuge. . . . The ex-proprietors were followed by others. After them, thousands of ex-workers—half the population of the country made a living in the coffee region—from the coffee zone ran to the cities. Only a few months had passed since the American flag was first raised, when under its shadow there arose the sickening slums which distress us" (Corretjer, *La lucha por la independencia de Puerto Rico*, 41–42).

59. Allen, *Story of the Growth of E. Atkins & Co.*, 3.

60. Pérez de la Riva, "Cuba y la migración antillana."

61. Alvarez Estévez, *Azúcar e inmigración*, 34.

62. Pérez de la Riva, "Cuba y la migración antillana," 13. The United Fruit Company also organized the internal migration of 14,229 Cubans into colonization areas in the eastern part of the island, building 1,714 houses to accommodate the families. Each household was assigned six acres of land for subsistence farming during the tiempo muerto (Petras, *Jamaican Labor Migration*, 246).

63. Petras, *Jamaican Labor Migration*, 238.

64. Ibid., 240.

65. Pérez de la Riva, "Inmigración antillana," 85.

66. Central Chaparra, *Album de vistas del gran Central Chaparra*.

67. Dr. Eugenio Molinet (Chaparra Sugar Company) to Secretario de Agricultura, Comercio y Trabajo de Cuba, November 12, 1924, fondo 302, leg. 4, exp. 45, Secretaría de Agricultura, Industria y Comercio, Archivo Nacional de Cuba.

68. Guy Morrison Walker to Manuel Rionda, February 8, 1919; Manuel Rionda to Guy Morrison Walker, March 14, 1919, Series 10 A (9), Braga Brothers Collection, University of Florida, Gainesville.

69. Francisco Sugar Company, "Minute Book," February 14, 1900, 14.

70. Ibid., June 30, 1907, 127.

71. Ibid., 128.

72. Ibid., June 30, 1907, 143.

73. Alvarez Estévez, *Azúcar e inmigración*, 48–49, 198–99.

74. Ibid., 46.

75. Ibid., 191.

76. Loveira, "Labour in the Cuban Sugar Industry," 426.

77. These figures are the simple averages of the wages reported by each of the 174 centrales of Cuba in Secretaría de Agricultura, Comercio y Trabajo de Cuba, *Portfolio azucarero*.

78. Marcus, *Labor Conditions in Puerto Rico*, 19.

79. Loveira, "Labour in the Cuban Sugar Industry," 426.

80. Ibid., 427. After the deepest slump in Cuba's sugar industry and the revolution of 1933, the U.S. Foreign Policy Association reported that "representative" daily wages for cane cutters dropped from $1.20 in 1920 to 80 cents in 1925, 60 cents in 1930, and reached an all-time low of 20 cents in 1933. Daily wages for hauling cane dropped from 60 cents in 1920 to 25 cents in 1925, 15 cents in 1930, and reached an all-time low of 5 cents in 1933. These figures show some discrepancies from those given by Loveira and seem excessively low, but they may nevertheless be considered useful as an indicator of the trend in wages over time. See Commission on Cuban Affairs, *Problems of the New Cuba*, 287; Petras, *Jamaican Labor Migration*, 242.

81. Alvarez Estévez, *Azúcar e inmigración*, 59.

82. Pérez de la Riva, "Cuba y la migración antillana, 1900–1931."

83. Cordero and del Castillo, *Economía dominicana*, 23–24.

84. Ibid., 24.

85. Sidney Mintz, "Foreword" to Guerra y Sánchez, *Sugar and Society in the Caribbean*, xiv.

86. Calder, *Impact of Intervention*, 98.

87. Ibid.

88. Lozano, *Dominación imperialista*, 158.

89. Del Castillo, *Inmigración de braceros azucareros*, 6.

90. William L. Bass, *Reciprocidad* (Santo Domingo: Imprenta la Cuna de América, 1902), 76, quoted in del Castillo, *Inmigración de braceros*, 34.

91. Del Castillo, *La inmigración de braceros*, 53.

92. Hernández, *Inmigración haitiana*, 55–60.

93. Roorda, "Genocide Next Door." The use of the Haitian and Dominican armed forces to coerce laborers to work and stay in the plantations has led many analysts to question whether Haitian labor can be considered "free." As late as the 1980s, Maurice Lemoine used the term "slavery" to refer to the condition of Haitian workers in the Dominican Republic. Paul Latortue used the term "neo-slavery." Roger Plant's study of the condition of Haitian workers in the *bateyes* of the Dominican Republic in the early 1980s was undertaken at the behest of the Anti-Slavery Society and was inspired by the United Nations Working Group on Slavery. See Lemoine, *Azúcar amargo*; Latortue, "Neo-Slavery in the Canefields," 18–20; Plant, *Sugar and Modern Slavery*.

Glenn Peruser argues that the disparity of conditions in Haiti and in the countries that receive its migrants are so great at all times that even drastic changes in conditions, such as wages, fail to stem the flow of migrants. Haiti's position as the most backward country in the Western Hemisphere leads to "immutable flows" from the country. See Peruser, "Haitian Emigration in the Early Twentieth Century."

Although this topic is beyond the time frame of this investigation, the extreme conditions under which these workers have labored throughout the twentieth century in the Dominican harvest raises an important question for researchers. Instead of the debated incompatibility of slavery and capitalism at the time of abolition, Haitian labor in the Dominican Republic raises the question of the compatibility of extreme forms of extra-economic coercion and modern corporate agribusiness.

94. Ames, "Labor Conditions in Porto Rico," 378. In 1900 Puerto Rico had a population density of 271 persons per square mile, while Cuba and the Dominican Republic had a population density of 37 persons per square mile. This immense difference is a basic starting point in understanding the lack of open land resources in Puerto Rico and the differences in agrarian social structure from the Dominican Republic and Cuba. While the evolution of class relations is not reducible simply to demographic factors, the latter are the terrain on which the former evolve.

95. "Report of the Commissioner of Labor in Hawaii," *Bulletin of the Department of Labor* (Washington, D.C., 1903), No. 47, 702, reprinted in Centro de Estudios Puertorriqueños (City University of New York), *Documentos de la migración puertorriqueña*.

96. See Maldonado Denis, *Puerto Rico y Estados Unidos*.

97. Córdova Iturregui, "Una explicación," 41–61. The treasurer of Puerto Rico, William Franklin Willoughby, justified centralized control of tax assessments as follows in his book *Territories and Dependencies of the United States*, 9: "The administration of the [property] tax, it should be said, is entirely in the hands of the insular government, the treasury of Porto Rico making the assessment of property and taking charge of the collection of the tax. The reasons for this arrangement, instead of one by which the tax is collected by the local authorities, as usually prevails in the United States, are to secure economy of administration, on the one hand, and on the other, to avoid the inequitable action in respect to both the assessment of property and the collection of the taxes that would result if these matters were left to the local authorities."

98. Jacob Hollander, the author of the law, was a distinguished economist from Johns Hopkins University with a vast publishing record, including works on David Ricardo. Hollander occupied many important positions in imperial administration. President McKinley appointed him in 1897 secretary of the Bimetallic Commission in charge of negotiating monetary agreements with European industrialized nations. In 1904 Hollander was appointed to write a tax law, this time in Indian Territory in Oklahoma. In 1905 he was sent by President Roosevelt as special commissioner plenipotentiary to the Dominican Republic (1905–6), as an agent of the State Department with respect to Dominican affairs (1906–7), and as a financial adviser to the Dominican Republic (1908–10), where he reorganized the readjustment of the public debt of that country. The customs receivership over the Dominican Republic, of which Hollander was in charge, forcefully reoriented the debt of that island from European to U.S. creditors. See Córdova Iturregui, "Una Explicación," 42–43. On the Dominican customs receivership see Rippy, "Initiation of the Customs Receivership."

99. Córdova Iturregui, "Una explicación," 74.

100. Mintz, *Caribbean Transformations*, 118.

101. Córdova Iturregui, "Una explicación," 76.

102. For the curious cultural patterns generated by the migration from the highlands to the coast, see Mintz, *Caribbean Transformations*, 118–23: "When I came here in 1907, the colored

people lived on the Colonia. I got work with the woodcutting crew that was clearing the land here, and they let me put up my house here near the beach. At first, I stayed mainly with my crew. But there was a group of white slaves [agregados] living on the Colonia, and I got to know some of them. They told me not to be bothered by the colored people. You know that in the highland we say the colored folks are witches. I soon found out they are all right. The white slaves, some of them lived here with their whole lives and they got along fine with the Negroes.

"When we came here from the highland (*altura*), we settled near the Rillieux family [a large Oriente family descended from the slaves of a French hacendado]. There would be bomba dances each weekend, and I would go to watch and dance. Well, my father would get furious because I was dancing with negroes, and he would blame my mother, who was not so white as he" (ibid., 119).

Mintz's rendering of agregados as "white slaves" is an extreme interpretation of their situation, which was characterized by exchange of usufruct rights for labor services or was used instead to keep a resident labor force on the land to guarantee a supply of workers who were paid wages during the harvest.

103. Ames, "Labor Conditions in Porto Rico," 380.

104. Pérez Velasco, "La condición obrera en Puerto Rico," 161; Secretaría de Agricultura, Comercio y Trabajo de Cuba, *Portfolio azucarero*.

105. Marcus, *Labor Conditions in Porto Rico*, 19.

106. Ibid., 32.

107. Ibid.

108. Ibid., 19.

109. See Ayala, "Collapse of the Plantation Economy."

110. Bernabe, "Prehistory of the Partido Popular Democrático," 64–70, 73–75.

111. Manning, "Employment of Women in Puerto Rico"; González, "Industria de la aguja en Puerto Rico"; Hernández Angueira, "El trabajo femenino."

112. For example, Rodríguez, *A Report on Wages and Working Hours in Various Industries and on the Cost of Living in the Island of Puerto Rico During the Year 1933*; Pérez, "Health and Socio-Economic Conditions on a Sugar Cane Plantation," and Pérez, *Living Conditions among Small Farmers in Puerto Rico*.

113. Bird, *Report on the Sugar Industry*, 43.

Chapter 7

1. See Langley, *Struggle for the American Mediterranean*.

2. Rippy, "Initiation of the Customs Receivership."

3. These figures are meant to give a sense of scale, not an exact account. In 1935, the 1-million-ton crop of Puerto Rico employed in its production 100,880 workers, of which 92,398 were field workers, according to Gayer et al., *Sugar Economy of Puerto Rico*, 163. I thus derive these figures assuming that 100,195 workers produce a million tons of sugar, and that of these, 90,000 are field workers. I believe this is a very conservative estimate of the number of workers, since

productivity, especially in Puerto Rico, had experienced a drastic increase with the favorable sugar quotas the country received in 1934.

4. Pérez, *Cuba under the Platt Amendment, 1902–1934*, 187.

5. Weigle, "Sugar Interests," 214–17, 260.

6. South Porto Rico Sugar Company, *Fiftieth Anniversary Report*, 2.

7. The argument has been put forward for the Puerto Rican case by Ramos Mattei, *Sociedad del azúcar*, and by Martínez Vergne, *Capitalism in Colonial Puerto Rico*.

8. "The inferiority of beet disappeared when, obeying the economic principle of the division of labor, cultivation was separated from milling" (Reed, Ruiz y Compañía, *Memoria de un ingenio central*, 9).

9. Manuel Moreno-Fraginals argues that the term "central" derives from the French "des usines centrales," a term used as early as 1844 in Martinique to refer to sugar factories designed to centralize the cane milling of several ingenios. See Moreno Fraginals, "Plantaciones en el Caribe," 58. In Cuba "el central" is a derivation of "el ingenio central." In Puerto Rico "la central" is a derivation of "la hacienda central."

10. Zanetti, "En busca de la reciprocidad," 165–205.

11. In the region of Remedios in the province of Santa Clara massive immigration of Canary Islanders permitted the expansion of sugar culture during and after abolition. Julián Zulueta, one of the great barons of slavery in Cuban history, built Central Zaza and eventually a railroad to the port of Caibarién. A frontier of sugar culture in the 1880s and the 1890s, Remedios experienced a process of concentration which generated differentiation within the planter class. The number of sugar mills in the region declined from forty in 1878 to seventeen in 1894 while sugar production more than doubled. The frequent trips of the ships *Juan Forgas* and *Martín Saenz* from Caibarién to the Canary Islands brought colonos who worked principally with their families but hired wage labor during the zafra. See Venegas Delgado, "Acerca del proceso de concentración y centralización de la industria azucarera en la región remediana."

12. Scott, *Slave Emancipation in Cuba*, 227–54.

13. U.S. War Department, *Report on the Census of Cuba, 1899*, 558–59.

14. Un colono de Las Villas, *Esclavitud blanca*.

15. Professor Fe Iglesias García of the Instituto de Historia de Cuba generously allowed me to consult the manuscript of her forthcoming book *Del ingenio al central*. I was also able to consult the following articles and manuscripts: "El censo cubano de 1877 y sus diferentes versiones"; "Changes in Cane Cultivation in Cuba, 1860–1900"; "Azúcar y crédito durante la segunda mitad del siglo xix en Cuba"; "Algunos aspectos de la distribución de la tierra en 1899"; "El movimiento de pasajeros entre España y Cuba, 1882–1900." I also consulted Santos Víctores and Venegas Delgado, "Un siglo de historia local"; Scott, "Class Relations"; Venegas Delgado, "Acerca del proceso de concentración."

16. Reed, Ruiz y Compañía, *Memoria de un ingenio central*, 4–6.

17. Guerra y Sánchez et al., *Historia de la nación cubana*, 7:151–64.

18. Reed, Ruiz y Compañía, *Memoria de un ingenio central*, 9.

19. Ibid.

20. Scott, *Slave Emancipation in Cuba*, 217. There was, however, itinerant and permanent migration of Canary Islanders. See García, "El movimiento de pasajeros entre España y Cuba."

21. *"Ingenio* Central en Puerto Príncipe," *Diario de la Marina*, May 13, 1880; *"Ingenios* Centrales," *La Discusión*, May 14, 1880; "El *Ingenio* Central de Puerto Príncipe," *La Correspondencia de Cuba*, May 14, 1880, all reprinted in Ruiz, Reed y Compañía, *Memoria de un ingenio central*, n.p.

22. Bryan, "Transition to Plantation Agriculture," 82.

23. Baud, "Origins of Capitalist Agriculture," 136.

24. Ibid., 138–39.

25. Ibid., 141–42. Cf. Bryan, "Transition to Plantation Agriculture," 86–87: "Singled out for their efforts to teach Dominicans the art of growing sugar were Joaquín Delgado, Evaristo Lamar, Francisco Savinón, and A. Abreu. In fact, Abreu built the first Cuban steam mill in 1874 (La Esperanza) in the environs of the capital; Enrique Lamar built La Caridad, and to complete in some form the trinity of faith, hope and charity, Salvador Ros, a Cuban who took out North American Papers of Citizenship, built Santa Fe. Another Cuban emigré, Juan Amechazurra, built La Angelina."

26. Cassá, *Historia social y económica*, 2:130, citing *Gaceta Oficial*, no. 418, June 17, 1882.

27. Ibid., 2:132.

28. Del Castillo, "Formation of the Dominican Sugar Industry," 217–18.

29. Muto, "Illusory Promise," 35–36.

30. Cassá, *Historia social y económica*, 2:136; Dietz, *Economic History of Puerto Rico*, 19.

31. Dietz, *Economic History of Puerto Rico*, 101.

32. Curet, *De la esclavitud a la abolicion*.

33. Ramos Mattei, *Sociedad del azúcar*, 26.

34. Martínez Vergne, *Capitalism in Colonial Puerto Rico*, 31–32.

35. It seems that the absence of a division of labor between mill and farm which characterized San Vicente was typical in Puerto Rico. Rosich and Rosich, *Fabricación de azúcar de moscabado en relación con las factorías centrales*, 7, argue that "the hacendados being at the same time farmers and industrialists they have not been able to devote all their attention to bettering the work on the land or intensive cane cultivation."

Medina Mercado, "El proceso de acumulación de tierras," traces thirty-four cane haciendas in the municipalities of Fajardo, Luquillo, and Ceiba, beginning in 1886. By 1901, only seventeen were functioning as sugar producers (117). The process of differentiation into mill owners and colonos in the area occurred after the foundation of the Fajardo Sugar Company in 1905: "In this new arrangement most hacendados became colonos dedicated to planting and producing sugar cane. Faced with the impossibility of maintaining both facets of production, they chose the productive phase which was most feasible at the time." (52).

36. Martínez Vergne, *Capitalism in Colonial Puerto Rico*, xii, 12, 39, 76, 107.

37. Ramos Mattei, *Sociedad del azúcar*, 18, 26, 27.

38. Governor to the President of the Diputación Provincial, Obras Públicas, Carreteras, Construcción, Leg. 161, Exp. 193, Archivo General de Puerto Rico, quoted in Giusti-Cordero, "Labor, Ecology and History," 440.

39. Ramos Mattei, *Sociedad del azúcar*, 28.

40. Ibid., 26.; Ramos Mattei, *Hacienda azucarera*; and Ramos Mattei, *Azúcar y esclavitud*.

41. Martínez Vergne, *Capitalism in Colonial Puerto Rico*, ix.

42. Giusti-Cordero, "Labor, Ecology and History," 522.

43. Davis, *Report of Brigadier General Geo. W. Davis*, 34.

44. Food and Agriculture Organization of the United Nations, *World Sugar Economy in Figures*; Gayer et al., *Sugar Economy*, 80.

45. Giusti-Cordero, "Labor, Ecology and History," 456.

46. Clark et al., *Porto Rico and Its Problems*, 14.

47. Taller de Formación Política, *¡Huelga en la caña!*

48. Bergad, *Coffee and the Growth of Agrarian Capitalism*.

49. Zeitlin, *Civil Wars in Chile*.

50. See Pérez, *Cuba between Empires*.

51. There is an interesting discussion about the Cuban Revolutionary Party and its artisan base, with a personal emphasis on Sotero Figueroa, the Puerto Rican printer who edited the newspaper of the Party (*Patria*) in New York, in Meléndez, *Puerto Rico en "Patria."* Julio Ramos's introduction to the writings of Luisa Capetillo (1879–1922), a Puerto Rican feminist who worked as a reader in the workshops of the cigar makers, analyzes the political culture of the Cuban and Puerto Rican cigar makers in the United States (Ramos, ed., *Amor y anarquía*).

52. Zeitlin, *Civil Wars in Chile*, 19.

53. Pérez, *Cuba between Empires*; Foner, *Spanish-Cuban-American War*.

54. Pérez, "Insurrection, Intervention, and the Transformation of Land Tenure Systems." For the destruction of the sugar industry of Matanzas, see Bergad, *Cuban Rural Society*, 305–34. The situation in 1898–1902 is described in Hitchman, "U.S. Control over Sugar Production"; Huguet y Balanzo, *Ingenios que han hecho zafra*.

55. Wood, *Civil Report of Brigadier General Leonard Wood*.

56. Cuban sugar output was typically measured in sacks of 325 pounds or in tons of 2,000 pounds. Cane production was measured in arrobas and land areas in caballerías.

57. An excellent history of Cuba between 1898 and the revolution of 1933 is Pérez, *Cuba under the Platt Amendment*.

58. The following analysis is based on Secretaría de Agricultura de Cuba, *Portfolio azucarero*. The *Portfolio* contains descriptions, histories of ownership, and photographs of the 172 centrales operating in Cuba in the harvest of 1912–13 and an appendix with mill-by-mill agricultural and industrial statistics. I have processed these figures using the Statstical Package for the Social Sciences. The *Portfolio* has information for each of the 172 sugar mills on the following variables: Agricultural data: (1) area planted with cane by estate or financed colonos, (2) area planted with cane by independent farmers, (3) total area planted, (4) area of land not cultivated for cane, (5) predominant class of soil, (6) number of Cuban colonos, (7) number of foreign colonos, (8) yield of cane: arrobas per caballería, (9) yield of cane: tons per hectare, (10) yield of cane: tons per acre, (11) yield of sugar obtained by the factory: arrobas per caballería, (12) yield of sugar obtained by the factory: tons per hectare, (13) yield of sugar obtained by the factory: tons per acre, (14) distance of planting: varas, (15) distance of planting: meters, (16) distance of planting:

feet, (17) dominant variety of cultivated cane, (18) fertilizers used, (19) irrigation used, (20) railway lines: standard gauge: kilometers, (21) railway lines: narrow gauge: kilometers, (22) number of sugar and cane cars, (23) number of locomotives, (24) public railway service, (25) average wages of men in the fields.

Factory data: (26) average wages of men in the factory, (27) cane ground per diem: arrobas, (28) cane ground per diem: tons, (29) total grinding capacity: tons, (30) capacity actually used: percent, (31) total cane ground in the season: arrobas, (32) total cane ground in the season: tons, (33) mill extraction, (34) sugar in the cane: percent, (35) sugar in the juice: percent, (36) average purity of juice, (37) total bags of sugar produced, (38) tons of sugar produced, (39) first sugar produced: percent of cane, (40) second sugar produced: percent of cane, (41) total sugar produced: percent of cane, (42) polariscope test of first sugar, (43) polariscope test of second sugar, (44) molasses: gallons, (45) horsepower capacity of the boiler plant, (46) tons of coal burned, (47) tons of wood burned, (48) cost of sugar transportation per bag, (49) cost of sugar transportation per ton, (50) chemists employed: Cubans, (51) chemists employed: foreigners.

In addition, the *Portfolio* indicates the date of foundation and the name and nationality of the founder for many but not all of the mills. It lists the nationality and name of the owner in 1913 for all mills.

I would like to thank Zoila Lapique of the Biblioteca Nacional José Martí in Havana for directing me to this invaluable source.

59. The number of mills and land areas for 1878 are from Bergad, *Cuban Rural Society*, 158; for 1913, the figures are from Secretaría de Agricultura de Cuba, *Portfolio azucarero*.

60. Secretaría de Agricultura de Cuba, *Portfolio azucarero*, uses the term "colono financiado"; Guerra y Sánchez, *La industria azucarera de Cuba*, refers to "colonos controlados."

61. Moreno Fraginals, *El ingenio*, 1:173.

62. Foner, *Antonio Maceo*, 201–23.

63. "Havana and Santiago, the western and eastern population centers of Cuba, lie, of course, on the same island but, historically, they might almost have been islands themselves. Both areas developed and grew almost independently of each other, each with its own character. Separated by almost 700 miles of thickly vegetated but thinly populated terrain, the only practical link throughout the colonial period remained by sea" (Hoernel, "Sugar and Social Change," 217).

64. All the data on mill sizes is from Secretaría de Agricultura de Cuba, *Portfolio azucarero*. I have processed the data in a spreadsheet and calculated the figures mentioned above. All figures are in tons of 2,000 pounds.

65. Mintz, "Cañamelar," 321.

66. Farr & Co., *Manual of Sugar Companies* (1924), 18.

67. "Report of Frank Feuille on the Landed Properties of the Cuba Cane Sugar Corporation (New York: May 15, 1919)," Ser. 127 (43), Braga Brothers Collection, University of Florida, Gainesville.

68. Celorio, *Haciendas comuneras*.

69. Ibid., 212.

70. Ibid., 213.

71. The Julia, Jobo, Conchita, Feliz, Socorro, San Ignacio, Soledad, Santa Gertrudis, Alava,

Mercedes, Marie Victoria, Perseverancia, and Lequeito mills were located in the west. The Lugareño, Morón, Jagüeyal, and Stewart mills were located in the east.

72. Cuba Cane Sugar Corporation, "Report by George W. Goethals," 8.

73. Ibid.

74. Bernabe, "Prehistory of the Partido Popular Democrático," 22.

75. Jenks, *Our Cuban Colony*, 181.

76. The United Railways of Havana expanded from 5,913 wagons in 1913 to 7,129 in 1920. The Havana Central expanded from 291 to 568, the Cuban Central from 2,378 to 3,334, and the Cuba Railroad from 2,036 to 5,541 (Zanetti and García, *Caminos para el azúcar*, 254).

77. Ibid., 255.

78. Guaranty Trust Company of New York, *Cuba*, 54.

79. "Government of Porto Rico, Treasury Department, Bureau of Property Taxes: Comparative Statistical Report of Sugar Manufactured in Porto Rico from the Crops of 1907, 1908, 1909, and 1910," Records of the Bureau of Insular Affairs, Record Group 350, File 422, National Archives, Washington, D.C.

80. A more nuanced division of the island into "six economic regions" may be found in Bernabe, "Prehistory of the Partido Popular Democrático," 56–79.

81. Farr & Co., *Manual of Sugar Companies* (1927), 71.

82. Ibid., 71. John Farr was a director of the Aguirre and the Fajardo Sugar Companies.

83. All data on the output of the centrales is from Farr & Co., *Manual of Sugar Companies* (1927); the data on acreage and colonos for Guánica is from Bernabe, "Prehistory of the Partido Popular Democrático," 70.

84. South Porto Rico Sugar Company, *Fiftieth Anniversary Report*, 5.

85. Ibid.

86. Farr & Co., *Manual of Sugar Companies* (1927); Bernabe, "Prehistory of the Partido Popular Democrático," 57.

87. Pasto Viejo was acquired by the United Porto Rico Sugar Company in 1926.

88. The other local interests owning more than one central were the two Georgetti mills (Los Caños and Plazuela) and the mills of the "Grupo Fabian" (San Vicente, Carmen, and Constancia). See Bernabe, "Prehistory of the Partido Popular Democrático," 76.

89. The Punta Alegre mills produced in aggregate as much as the output of the Dominican Republic in 1927.

90. Farr & Co., *Manual of Sugar Companies* (1933). The figures are for the zafra of 1929–30.

91. Ibid., 108.

92. Ibid.

Chapter 8

1. Needham, "Control of the Sugar Market during World War I," 1–5, U.S. Department of Labor, Bureau of Labor Statistics, Division of Historical Studies of Wartime Problems, March 1942, Hoover Library, Stanford University.

2. Herbert Hoover to Woodrow Wilson, August 22, 1917, cited ibid., 10.

3. FA 10H-A7-Case 5278 (sugar file), National Archives, quoted ibid., 10–12.

4. Hoover to Wilson, August 22, 1917, ibid., 10.

5. Pollitt, "Cuban Sugar Economy," 9.

6. Thomas Chadbourne, the author of the plan, was a New York corporate lawyer with interests in Cuban sugar mills and ties to the Chase National Bank.

7. "Copia de carta mecanografiada dirigida a José López Oña por Julio Lobo manifestándole su oposición a una restricción en el azúcar, para Cuba exclusivamente y también al control de venta, nov. 17, 1930," Secretaría de la Presidencia, Caja 36, No. 16, Archivo Nacional de Cuba.

8. "General Survey of Wages in Cuba, 1931 and 1932," *Monthly Labor Review* 32 (December 1935): 1405, quoted in Carr, "Mill Occupations and Soviets," 131.

9. Carr, "Mill Occupations and Soviets," 138–42.

10. Alvarez Estévez, *Azúcar e inmigración*, 213–14.

11. Carr, "Mill Occupations and Soviets," 155.

12. Bernabe, "Prehistory of the Partido Popular Democratico," 190–204; Archivo General de Puerto Rico, Fondo de los Gobernadores, Huelgas, Box 675, contains the governor's files on the following events: "Huelga Agrícola (Arroyo, Patillas, Maunabo) 1933"; "Huelga Despalilladoras (Caguas) 1933"; "Huelga de la Aguja (Lares) 1933"; "Huelga Trabajadores de la United Porto Rico Sugar Company (Las Piedras y Gurabo) 1933"; Box 676 contains the governor's files on the strikes: "Despalilladoras de Cayey (1933)"; "Utuado-Huelga de la Aguja (1933)"; "Daily Report on Strikes throughout the Island—Sept. 1933–Dec. 1933" [town-by-town reports of the chief of police of Puerto Rico, Colonel Elisha Riggs, which began shortly after the general strike which overthrew Machado in Cuba, C.A.]; "Porto Rican American Tobacco Strike—Sept. 1933"; "Huelga Asociación de Choferes por aumento de la gasolina"; "Huelga Panaderos—Gremio Vendedores de Pan (1933)"; "Huelga de Trabajadores de la United Porto Rico Sugar Company en Gurabo (1933)"; "Huelga Universidad de Puerto Rico (1933) Estudiantes."

13. "Telegrama a Don Pedro Albizu Campos pidiendo ponerse al frente del Movimiento en Guayama (January, 1934)." Fondo de los Gobernadores, Huelgas, Box 676, Archivo General de Puerto Rico.

14. Taller de Formación Política, *¡Huelga en la Caña!*; Bernabe, "Prehistory of the Partido Popular Democrático," 190–203.

15. José Manuel Casanova, Sugar Mill Owner's Association, 1940, quoted in Pérez Stable, *Cuban Revolution*, 14.

16. Raul Cepero Bonilla, Cuban economist, 1940, quoted ibid., 14. Cf. Portell Vilá, "Industria azucarera y su futuro," 161–79.

17. Pino Santos, *Oligarquía yanqui en Cuba.*

18. Rogelio Piña, "Sin un jornal decoroso, el cubano no desplazará nunca al haitiano de los ingenios," *Diario de la Marina*, July 8, 1934.

19. Alvarez Estévez, *Azúcar e inmigración*, 229–41.

20. Elizabeth Mclean Petras, *Jamaican Labor Migration*, 248; Commission on Cuban Affairs, *Problems of the New Cuba*, 285.

21. Roorda, "Genocide Next Door," 306.

22. Dalton, *Sugar*, 33.

23. Alvarez Estévez, *Azúcar e inmigración*, 237.

24. Pollit, "Cuban Sugar Economy," 20.

25. Ibid., 21.

26. Similar legislation was enacted for the Philippines. The Public Land Act of 1902 prohibited the acquisition by corporations of public lands greater than 1,024 hectares (2,500 acres). This legislation represented the interests of the protectionist sugar-producing regions of the United States, and it was advanced in Congress by representatives of the beet-producing states. This limitation had been designed by the beet sugar interests, "who wished to keep out Philippine sugar at all hazards and had shrewdly figured that the simplest way to do this would be to prevent its production on a commercial scale." Dean C. Worcester, *The Philippines Past and Present* (New York: 1914), 2:838–39, quoted in Quirino, *History of the Philippine Sugar Industry*, 50.

27. Pantojas García, *Development Strategies*.

28. Zeitlin, *Civil Wars in Chile*, 227.

Epilogue

1. Commonwealth of Puerto Rico, Department of Agriculture, Office of Agricultural Statistics, *Facts and Figures*, 37–38; Estado Libre Asociado de Puerto Rico, Departamento de Agricultura, *Anuario de Estadísticas Agrícolas de Puerto Rico, 1990/91*.

2. González Medina, *Manual azucarero de Cuba*.

3. Moya Pons, *Manual de Historia Dominicana*, 517.

4. Del Castillo et al., *La Gulf & Western en la República Dominicana*, 201.

Bibliography

Abad, José Ramón. *Puerto Rico en la feria de exposiciones de Ponce en 1882.* 1885. Reprint. San Juan, Puerto Rico: Editorial Coquí, 1967.

Abelarde, Pedro E. *American Tariff Policies toward the Philippines.* New York: Kings Crown Press, 1947.

Adler, Jacob. *Claus Spreckels: The Sugar King in Hawaii.* Honolulu: University of Hawaii Press, 1966.

Aguilar, Luis E. *Cuba 1933: Prologue to Revolution.* Ithaca: Cornell University Press, 1972.

Aguirre Sugar Company. *Fiftieth Anniversary Report.* New York: Aguirre Sugar Company, 1949.

Albert, Bill, and Adrian Graves, eds. *Crisis and Social Change in the International Sugar Economy, 1860–1914.* Edinburgh: ISC Press, 1984.

——. *The World Sugar Economy in War and Depression, 1914–1940.* London: Routledge, 1988.

Allen, Benjamin. *A Story of the Growth of E. Atkins & Co. and the Sugar Industry in Cuba.* Boston: N.p., 1926.

Allen, M. P. "Economic Interest Groups and the Corporate Elite Structure." *Social Science Quarterly* 58 (1958): 597–615.

Alvarez Estévez, Rolando. *Azúcar e inmigración, 1900–1940.* Havana: Editorial de Ciencias Sociales, 1988.

Ames, Azel. "Labor Conditions in Puerto Rico." *Bulletin of the Department of Labor* (Washington, D.C.) 34 (1901): 377–99.

Ashtor, E. "Levantine Sugar Industry in the Late Middle Ages: A Case of Technological Decline." In *The Islamic Middle East, 700–1900: Studies in Economic and Social History*, edited by A. L. Udovitch. Princeton: Princeton University Press, 1981.

Atkins, Edwin Farnsworth. *Sixty Years in Cuba: Reminiscences of Edwin F. Atkins.* Cambridge, Mass.: Privately Printed at the Riverside Press, 1926.

Ayala, César. "The Collapse of the Plantation Economy and the Puerto Rican Migration of the 1950s." *Latino Studies Journal* 7 (Winter 1996): 62–90.

——. "Industrial Oligopoly and Vertical Integration: The Origins of the American Sugar Kingdom in the Caribbean, 1881–1921." Ph.D. diss., State University of New York at Binghamton, 1991.

——. "Social and Economic Aspects of Sugar Production in Cuba, 1880–1930." *Latin American Research Review* 30 (1995): 95–124.

——. "Theories of Big Business in American Society." *Critical Sociology* 16 (Summer–Fall 1989): 91–119.

Báez Evertsz, Franc. *Azúcar y dependencia en la República Dominicana.* Santo Domingo: Editorial de la Universidad Autónoma de Santo Domingo, 1978.

——. *Braceros haitianos en la República Dominicana.* Santo Domingo: Instituto Dominicano de Investigaciones Sociales, 1986.

Banaji, Jairus. "For a Theory of Colonial Modes of Production." *Economic and Political Weekly*, December 23, 1972, 2498–2502.

Baralt, Guillermo A. *Esclavos rebeldes: Conspiraciones y sublevaciones de esclavos en Puerto Rico, 1795–1873*. Río Piedras, Puerto Rico: Huracán, 1981.

Baran, Paul, and Paul Sweezy. *Monopoly Capital*. New York: Monthly Review Press, 1966.

Barbour, Jeffrey, and David Bunting. "Interlocking Directorates in Large American Corporations, 1896–1964." *Business History Review* 45 (Autumn 1971): 317–35.

Barraclough, Geoffrey. *An Introduction to Contemporary History*. Harmondsworth: Penguin Books, 1967.

Baud, Michiel. "The Origins of Capitalist Agriculture in the Dominican Republic." *Latin American Research Review* 22 (1987): 135–53.

———. "Sugar and Unfree Labour: Reflections on Labour Control in the Dominican Republic, 1870–1935." *Journal of Peasant Studies* 19 (1992): 301–25.

Bearden, J., and B. Mintz. "Regionality and Integration in the United States Interlock Network." In *Networks of Corporate Power: A Comparative Study of Ten Countries*, edited by Frans N. Stokman, Rolf Ziegler, and John Scott. Cambridge, Eng.: Polity Press, 1985.

Beckford, George. *Persistent Poverty: Underdevelopment in the Plantation Economies of the Third World*. Oxford: Oxford University Press, 1970.

Benjamin, Jules Robert. *The United States and Cuba: Hegemony and Dependent Development, 1880–1934*. Pittsburgh: University of Pittsburgh Press, 1974.

Benn, Denis M. "The Theory of Plantation Economy and Society: A Methodological Critique." *Journal of Commonwealth and Comparative Politics* 12 (1977): 249–60.

Berbuse, Edward J. *The United States in Puerto Rico, 1898–1900*. Chapel Hill: University of North Carolina Press, 1966.

Bergad, Laird. "Agrarian History of Puerto Rico, 1870–1930." *Latin American Research Review* 13 (1978): 63–94.

———. "Coffee and Rural Proletarianization in Nineteenth Century Puerto Rico, 1840–1898." *Journal of Latin American Studies* 15 (1983): 83–100.

———. *Coffee and the Growth of Agrarian Capitalism in Nineteenth Century Puerto Rico*. Princeton: Princeton University Press, 1983.

———. *Cuban Rural Society in the Nineteenth Century: The Social and Economic History of Sugar Monoculture in Matanzas*. Princeton: Princeton University Press, 1992.

———. "Recent Research on Slavery in Puerto Rico." *Plantation Society* 2 (April 1983): 99–109.

Berle, Adolf A. "The Impact of the Corporation on Classic Economic Theory." *Quarterly Journal of Economics* 79 (1965): 25–40.

Berle, Adolf, and Gardiner C. Means. *The Modern Corporation and Private Property*. New York: Macmillan, 1932.

Bernabe, Rafael. "Prehistory of the Partido Popular Democrático: Muñoz Marín, the Partido Liberal, and the Crisis of Sugar in Puerto Rico, 1930–1935." Ph.D. diss., State University of New York at Binghamton, 1988.

Bernhardt, Joshua. *The Sugar Industry and the Federal Government: A Thirty Year Record (1917–1947)*. Washington, D.C.: Sugar Statistics Service, 1948.

Berthier, Paul. *Un épisode de l'histoire de la canne à sucre: Les anciennes sucreries du Maroc et leurs réseaux hydrauliques*. Rabat: Imprimeries Françaises et Marocaines, 1966.

Best, Lloyd. "The Mechanism of Plantation Type Societies: Outlines of a Model of Pure Plantation Economy." *Social and Economic Studies* 17 (1968): 283–326.

Bird, Esteban. *Report on the Sugar Industry in Relation to the Social and Economic System of Puerto Rico*. San Juan: Government Office of Supplies, Printing and Transportation, 1941.

Blackburn, Robin. *The Overthrow of Colonial Slavery, 1776–1848*. London: Verso, 1988.

Brandeis, Louis D. *Other People's Money and How the Bankers Use It*. New York: Frederick A. Stokes, 1914.

Brass, Tom. "Free and Unfree Rural Labour in Puerto Rico during the Nineteenth Century." *Journal of Latin American Studies* 18 (1986): 181–93.

Bravo, Juan Alfonso. "Azúcar y clases sociales en Cuba, 1511–1959." *Revista Mexicana de Sociología* 43 (1989): 1189–1228.

Brenner, Robert. "The Origins of Capitalist Development: A Critique of Neo-Smithian Marxism." *New Left Review* 104 (1977): 25–92.

Brenner, Robert, and Mark Glick. "The Regulation Approach: Theory and History." *New Left Review* no. 188 (July–August 1991): 45–120.

Bryan, Patrick. "The Transition of Plantation Agriculture in the Dominican Republic, 1870–84." *Journal of Caribbean History* 10–11 (1978): 82–105.

Buitrago Ortiz, Carlos. *Los orígenes históricos de la sociedad precapitalista en Puerto Rico*. Río Piedras, Puerto Rico: Huracán, 1976.

Bullock, Charles J. "The Concentration of Banking Interests in the United States." *Atlantic Monthly* 92 (1903): 182–92.

Cabrera Pérez, José Ramón. *Memoria explicativa e ilustrada de varios centrales del término municipal de Ciego de Ávila, Provincia de Camagüey*. Havana: Montalvo, Cárdenas, 1919.

Calder, Bruce J. "The Dominican Turn toward Sugar." *Caribbean Review* 10, no. 3 (1981): 18–21, 44–45.

———. *The Impact of Intervention: The Dominican Republic during the U.S. Occupation of 1916–1924*. Austin: University of Texas Press, 1984.

———. "Varieties of Resistance to the United States Occupation of the Dominican Republic, 1916–1924." *South Eastern Conference on Latin America, Annals* 11 (1980): 103–19.

Carosso, Vincent P. *Investment Banking in America: A History*. Cambridge, Mass.: Harvard University Press, 1970.

———. *More Than a Century of Investment Banking: The Kidder, Peabody and Company Story*. New York: McGraw-Hill, 1979.

Carr, Barry. "Mill Occupations and Soviets: The Mobilisation of Sugar Workers in Cuba, 1917–1933." *Journal of Latin American Studies* 28 (1996): 129–58.

Carr, E. H. *The Twenty Years' Crisis, 1919–1939*. London: Macmillan, 1946.

Cassá, Roberto. *Historia social y económica de la República Dominicana*. 2 vols. Santo Domingo: Editorial Alfa y Omega, 1986.

———, ed. *La sociedad dominicana durante la Primera República*. Santo Domingo: Alfa y Omega, 1977.

Castor, Suzy. *La ocupación norteamericana de Haití y sus consecuencias*. México City: Siglo Veintiuno, 1971.

Celorio, Benito. *Las haciendas comuneras*. Havana: Imprenta Rambla-Bouza, 1914.

Central Chaparra. *Album de vistas del gran Central Chaparra*. N.p. (ca. 1916), Folleto 917.2916, Biblioteca Nacional José Martí, Havana.

Centro de Estudios Puertorriqueños (City University of New York). *Documentos de la migración puertorriqueña, 1879–1901*. New York: Center for Puerto Rican Studies, 1977.

Cepero Bonilla, Raúl. *Azúcar y abolición*. Barcelona: Editorial Crítica, 1976.

Chalmin, Philip G. "The Important Trends in Sugar Diplomacy before 1914." In *Crisis and Change in the International Sugar Economy, 1860–1914*, edited by Bill Albert and Adrian Graves. Edinburgh: I.S.C. Press, 1984.

Chandler, Alfred D. *Strategy and Structure*. Cambridge, Mass.: MIT Press, 1962.

———. *The Visible Hand: The Managerial Revolution in American Business*. Cambridge, Mass.: Harvard University Press, 1977.

Charles, Gerard Pierre. *Génesis de la revolución cubana*. Mexico City: Siglo Veintiuno, 1976.

Chevalier, Jean Marie. *La structure financière de l'industrie Americaine*. Paris: Cujas, 1970.

Clark, Truman. *Puerto Rico and the United States, 1917–1933*. Pittsburgh: University of Pittsburgh Press, 1975.

Clark, Victor S., et al. *Porto Rico and Its Problems*. Washington, D.C.: Brookings Institution, 1930.

Cleveland, Harold van B., and T. Huertas. *Citibank: 1812–1970*. Cambridge, Mass.: Harvard University Press, 1985.

Commission on Cuban Afffairs. *Problems of the New Cuba*. New York: Foreign Policy Association, 1935.

Commonwealth of Puerto Rico, Department of Agriculture. *Facts and Figures on Puerto Rico's Agriculture, 1978/79–1979/80*. Santurce, Puerto Rico: Department of Agriculture, 1980.

Constantino, Renato. *A History of the Philippines: From the Spanish Colonization to World War Two*. New York: Monthly Review Press, 1976.

Corbitt, Duvon C. "Immigration in Cuba." *Hispanic American Historical Review* 2 (1942): 280–307.

Cordero, Walter, and José del Castillo. *La economía dominicana durante el primer cuarto del siglo XX*. Santo Domingo: Fundación García Arévalo, 1979.

Córdova Iturregui, Félix. "El Trust del azúcar y el Trust del tabaco en Puerto Rico." University of Puerto Rico, 1987.

———. "Una explicación sintomática de la Leyenda de El Dorado: El Bill Hollander." TMs, University of Puerto Rico, 1988.

Cordray, William W. "Claus Spreckels of California." Ph.D. diss., University of Southern California, 1955.

Corey, Lewis. *The House of Morgan: A Social Biography of the Masters of Money*. New York: G. Howard Watt, 1930.

Corretjer, Juan Antonio. *La lucha por la independencia de Puerto Rico*. Guaynabo, Puerto Rico: Cooperativa de Artes Gráficas, 1974.

Corwin, Arthur F. *Spain and the Abolition of Slavery in Cuba, 1817–1886*. Austin: University of Texas Press, 1967.

Crist, Raymond E. "Sugar Cane and Coffee in Puerto Rico." *American Journal of Economics and Sociology* 7 (January, April, and July 1948): 173–94, 321–27, 469–74.

Cuba Cane Sugar Corporation. "Report by George W. Goethals and Company, Inc., on the Cuba Cane Sugar Corporation, July 11, 1919." Series 127 (36), Braga Brothers Collection, University of Florida, Gainesville.

———. "Report of Frank Feuille on the Landed Properties of the Cuba Cane Sugar Corporation." Series 127 (43), Braga Brothers Collection, University of Florida, Gainesville.

Curbelo, José. *Proyecto ara fomentar y poner en estado de producción seis Ingenios Centrales de 1,000,000 arrobas cada uno, con Alambique, para trabajar las mieles que resultan de la elaboración*. Havana: La Propaganda Literaria, 1882.

Curet, José. *De la esclavitud a la abolicion: Transiciones económicas en las haciendas azucareras de Ponce, 1845–1873*. Río Piedras: CEREP, 1979.

Dalton, John Edward. *Sugar: A Case Study of Government Control*. New York: Macmillan, 1937.

Davis, George W. *Report of Brigadier General Geo. W. Davis, U.S.V., on Civil Affairs of Porto Rico*. Washington, D.C.: U.S. Government Printing Office, 1900.

Davis, John Emmeus. "Capitalist Agricultural Development and the Exploitation of the Propertied Laborer." In *The Rural Sociology of Advanced Societies: Critical Perspectives*, edited by Frederick H. Buttel and Howard Newby. Montclair, N.J.: Allanheld, Osmun, 1980.

De Abad y Bohigas, Luis Víctor. *Azúcar y caña de azúcar: Ensayo de orientación cubana*. Havana: Editorial Mercantil, 1945.

Debouzy, Marianne. *Le capitalisme sauvage aux Etats Unis*. Paris: Cujas, 1970.

Deerr, Noel. *The History of Sugar*. 2 vols. London: Chapman and Hall, 1949–50.

De Golia, Darwin. *The Tariff of Puerto Rico*. San Juan: Puerto Rico Emergency Relief Administration, 1935.

De Hostos, Eugenio María. "Falsa Alarma, Crísis Agrícola (1884)." In *Hostos en Santo Domingo*, edited by Emilio Rodríguez Demorizi. Ciudad Trujillo: Imp. J. R. vda. García, 1939, vol. 1:159–176.

De Janvry, Alain. *The Agrarian Question in Latin America*. Baltimore: Johns Hopkins University Press, 1981.

De la Uz, Féliz. ed. *Los monopolios extranjeros en Cuba*. Havana: Editorial de Ciencias Sociales, 1984.

Del Castillo, José. "Azúcar y braceros: Historia de un problema." *EME-EME Estudios Dominicanos* 10 (58): 3–19.

———. "The Formation of the Dominican Sugar Industry: From Competition to Monopoly, from National Semi-Proletariat to Foreign Proletariat." In *Between Slavery and Free Labor: The Spanish-Speaking Caribbean in the Nineteenth Century*, edited by Stanley L. Engerman, Manuel Moreno Fraginals, and Frank Moya Pons. Baltimore: Johns Hopkins University Press, 1985.

———. *La inmigración de braceros azucareros en la República Dominicana, 1900–1930*. Santo Domingo: Centro Dominicano de Investigaciones Antropológicas, 1978.

Del Castillo, José, et al. *La Gulf & Western en la República Dominicana*. Santo Domingo: Editorial de la Universidad Autónoma de Santo Domingo, 1974.

Departamento de Agricultura, Estado Libre Asociado de Puerto Rico. *Anuario de Estadísticas Agrícolas de Puerto Rico, 1990/91*. Santurce, Puerto Rico: Departamento de Agricultura, 1991.

Descamps, Gastón. *La crisis azucarera y la isla de Cuba*. Havana: La Propaganda Literaria, 1885.

Descartes, Sol Luis. *Organization and Earnings on 130 Sugar Cane Farms in Puerto Rico, 1934–35*. San Juan: Bureau of Supplies, Printing and Transportation, 1938.

———. "La situación hipotecaria rural en Puerto Rico." *Universidad de Puerto Rico, Estación Experimental Agrícola, Boletín* 42 (1936): 1–29.

De Vroey, Michael. "The Separation of Ownership and Control in Large Corporations." *Review of Radical Political Economy* 7, no. 2 (1975): 1–10.

Díaz Quiñones, Arcadio. "Isla de quimeras: Pedreira, Palés, Albizu (El intelectual, el poeta, el profeta)." *Revista de Crítica Literaria Latinoamericana* 23 (1997): 229–46.

Díaz Santana, Arizmendi. "The Role of Haitian Sugar Braceros in Dominican Sugar Production." *Latin American Perspectives* 3 (1976): 120–32.

Díaz Soler, Luis M. *Historia de la esclavitud negra en Puerto Rico*. Río Piedras, Puerto Rico: Editorial Universidad de Puerto Rico, 1981.

Dietz, James L. *Economic History of Puerto Rico: Institutional Change and Capitalist Development*. Princeton: Princeton University Press, 1986.

Diffie, Bailey W., and Justine W. Diffie. *Porto Rico: A Broken Pledge*. New York: Vanguard Press, 1931.

Directory of Directors Company. *Directory of Directors in the City of New York*. New York: Directory of Directors Company, 1905–25.

Domenech v. South Porto Rico Sugar Company. *United States Circuit Court of Appeals for the First Circuit. No. 2479, Manuel V. Domenech, Treasurer, Plaintiff, Appellant, v. Horace Havemeyer et al. (Russell & Co., Sucesores S. en C.), Defendant, Appellee; No. 2480, Same v. South Porto Rico Sugar Company (of Porto Rico).; No. 2481, Same v. South Porto Rico Sugar Company (of New Jersey) Opinion of the Court, April 28, 1931*, Boston: L. H. Lane. In Record Group 350, File 27229/30, National Archives, Washington, D.C.

Domhoff, G. William. *Power Structure Research*. Beverly Hills: Sage, 1980.

——. *Powers That Be: Processes of Ruling Class Domination in America*. New York: Random House, 1978.

——. "Rockefeller Economic Power—an Overview." *International Socialist Review* 36 (1975): 6–9.

——. *Who Rules America?* Englewood Cliffs, N.J.: Prentice-Hall, 1967.

——. *Who Rules America Now? A View for the '80s*. Englewood Cliffs, N.J.: Prentice-Hall, 1983.

Domínguez, Jaime. "La economía dominicana durante la Primera República." In *La sociedad dominicana durante la Primera República, 1844–1861*, edited by Tirso Mejía Ricart. Santo Domingo: Editora de la Universidad Autónoma de Santo Domingo, 1977.

——. *Economía y política de la República Dominicana, 1844–1861*. Santo Domingo: Alfa y Omega, 1976.

Dooley, Peter C. "The Interlocking Directorate." *American Economic Review* 59 (1969): 314–23.

Dozer, Donald Marquand. "The Opposition to Hawaiian Reciprocity, 1876–1888." *Pacific Historical Review* 14 (1945): 157–83.

Drinnon, Richard. *Facing West: The Metaphysics of Indian Hating and Empire Building*. Minneapolis: University of Minnesota Press, 1980.

Du Bois, W. E. B. *Black Reconstruction in America: An Essay toward a History of the Part Which Black Folk Played in the Attempt to Reconstruct Democracy in America, 1860–1880*. 1962. Reprint. New York: Atheneum, 1977.

Dumoulin, John. "El movimiento obrero en Cruces, 1902–1925." *ISLAS* (Universidad de Santa Clara, Cuba) 62 (January-April 1979): 83–121.

Dunn, Richard S. *Sugar and Slaves: The Rise of the Planter Class in the British West Indies, 1624–1713*. New York: Norton, 1972.

Dye, Alan. "Cane Contracting and Renegotiation: A Fixed Effects Analysis of the Adoption of New Technologies in the Cuban Sugar Industry, 1899–1929." *Explorations in Economic History* 31 (April 1994): 141–75.

——. "Tropical Technology and Mass Production: The Expansion of Cuban Sugar Mills, 1899–1929." *Journal of Economic History* 53 (June 1993): 396–99.

Eblen, Jack Ericson. *The First and Second United States Empires: Governors and Territorial Government, 1784–1912*. Pittsburgh: University of Pittsburgh Press, 1968.

Eichner, Alfred S. *The Emergence of Oligopoly: Sugar Refining as a Case Study*. Baltimore: Johns Hopkins University Press, 1969.

——. *Megacorp and Oligopoly*. Cambridge, Eng.: Cambridge University Press, 1976.

Ellis, Ellen Deborah. *An Introduction to the History of Sugar as a Commodity*. Philadelphia: J. C. Winston, 1905.

Ely, Roland T. "The Old Cuba Trade: Highlights and Case Studies of Cuban-American Interdependence during the Nineteenth Century." *Business History Review* 38 (1964): 456–78.

Estado Libre Asociado de Puerto Rico, Departamento de Agricultura. *Anuario de estadísticas agrícolas de Puerto Rico, 1990/91*. San Juan, Puerto Rico: Departamento de Agricultura, 1991.

Fajardo Sugar Company. *Annual Report to the Stockholders*. New York: Fajardo Sugar Company, 1921.

——. *Fiftieth Anniversary Report to the Stockholders*, New York: Fajardo Sugar Company, 1955.

——. "Memorandum concerning bill to provide Civil Government for Porto Rico, introduced in the House of Representatives, March Fifteenth, Nineteen Hundred and Ten, being No. 23,000." Record Group 350, File 422 (1910), National Archives, Washington, D.C.

Farr & Co. *Manual of Sugar Companies*. New York: Farr & Co., 1924–48.

Fast, Jonathan, and Luzviminda Francisco. "Philippine Historiography and the De-Mystification of Imperialism: A Review Essay." *Journal of Contemporary Asia* 4 (1974): 344–58.

Faulkner, Harold Underwood. *The Decline of Laissez Faire*. New York: Rinehart, 1953.

Feagin, Joe R. *The Urban Real Estate Game: Playing Monopoly with Real Money*. Englewood Cliffs, N.J.: Prentice-Hall, 1983.

Filler, Louis. *The Muckrakers*. University Park: Pennsylvania State University Press, 1976.

Fitch, Robert. "Sweezy and Corporate Fetishism." *Socialist Revolution* 2, no. 6 (1971): 93–127.

Fitch, Robert, and Mary Oppenheimer. "Who Rules the Corporations?" Part I, *Socialist Revolution* 1, no. 4 (1970): 73–108; Part II, *Socialist Revolution* 1, no. 5 (1970): 61–114; Part III, *Socialist Revolution* 1, no. 6 (1970): 33–94.

Florescano, Enrique, ed. *Haciendas, latifundios, y plantaciones en América Latina*. Mexico City: Siglo Veintiuno, 1978.

Foner, Eric. *Reconstruction: America's Unfinished Revolution, 1863–1877*. New York: Harper & Row, 1988.

Foner, Philip Sheldon. *Antonio Maceo: The "Bronze Titan" of Cuba's Struggle for Independence*. New York: Monthly Review Press, 1977.

——. *A History of Cuba and Its Relations with the United States*. 2 vols. New York: International Publishers, 1962.

——. *The Spanish-Cuban-American War and the Birth of American Imperialism*. 2 vols. New York: Monthly Review Press, 1972.

Food and Agriculture Organization of the United Nations. *The World Sugar Economy in Figures, 1880–1959*. Geneva: FAO-UN, 1961.

Francisco Sugar Company. "Manager's Report of the Francisco Sugar Company, 1917–1921." Record Group IV, Series 96, Braga Brothers Collection, University of Florida, Gainesville.

——. Minute Book of the Francisco Sugar Company. Series 90, box 1, Braga Brothers Collection, University of Florida, Gainesville.

Frank, André Gunder. *Latin America: Underdevelopment or Revolution?* New York: Monthly Review Press, 1969.

——. *Lumpenbourgeoisie, Lumpendevelopment*. New York: Monthly Review Press, 1972.

——. *World Accumulation, 1492–1789*. New York: Monthly Review Press, 1978.

Gage, Charles E. "The Tobacco Industry in Puerto Rico." *Circular No. 519, United Sates Department of Agriculture*. Washington, D.C.: U.S. Department of Agriculture, March 1939, 1–53.

Galbraith, John Kenneth. *The New Industrial State*. Boston: Beacon, 1967.

———. "A Review of a Review." *Public Interest* 9 (1967): 109–18.

Galloway, J. H. "The Mediterranean Sugar Industry." *Geographic Review* 67 (1977): 177–94.

———. *The Sugar Cane Industry: A Historical Geography from Its Origins to 1914*. Cambridge, Eng.: Cambridge University Press, 1989.

García Márquez, Gabriel. *Cien años de soledad*. Bogotá: Editorial Oveja Negra, 1985.

Gayer, Arthur D., et al. *The Sugar Economy of Puerto Rico*. New York: Columbia University Press, 1938.

Gellman, Irwin. *Roosevelt and Batista: Good Neighbor Policy in Cuba, 1933–1945*. Albuquerque: University of New Mexico Press, 1972.

Genovese, Elizabeth Fox, and Eugene D. Genovese. *Fruits of Merchant Capital: Slavery and Bourgeois Property in the Rise and Expansion of Capitalism*. New York: Oxford University Press, 1983.

Geschwender, James. "The Hawaiian Transformation: Class, Submerged Nation, and National Minorities." In *Ascent and Decline in the World System*, edited by Edward Friedman. Beverly Hills: Sage, 1982.

Gibb, George S., and Evelyn H. Knowlton. *History of the Standard Oil Company (New Jersey): The Resurgent Years, 1911–1927*. New York: Harper & Brothers, 1957.

Gilmore, A. B. *The Porto Rico Sugar Manual, Including Data on Santo Domingo Mills*. New Orleans: A. B. Gilmore, 1930.

Ginger, Roy. *Eugene V. Debs*. New York: Collier, 1962.

Giusti-Cordero, Juan A. "Labor, Ecology and History in a Caribbean Sugar Plantation Region: Piñones (Loíza), Puerto Rico 1770–1950." Ph.D. diss., State University of New York at Binghamton, 1994.

Gleijeses, Piero. *The Dominican Crisis*. Baltimore: Johns Hopkins University Press, 1976.

Goethals & Company. "Report by George W. Goethals and Company, Inc., on the Cuba Cane Sugar Corporation (July 11, 1919)." Series 127 (36), Braga Brothers Collection, University of Florida, Gainesville.

Goffman, Erving. *Asylums*. New York: Doubleday, 1961.

Goldsmith, R. W., and R. C. Pamerlee. *The Distribution of Ownership in the 200 Largest Non-Financial Corporations*. Washington, D.C.: U.S. Government Printing Office, 1940.

Gómez Acevedo, Labor. *Organización y reglamantación del trabajo en el Puerto Rico del siglo XIX*. San Juan: Instituto de Cultura Puertorriqueña, 1970.

González, Lydia Milagros. "La industria de la aguja en Puerto Rico y sus orígenes en los Estados Unidos." In *Género y trabajo: La industria de la aguja en Puerto Rico y el Caribe Hispano*, edited by María del Carmen Baerga. Río Piedras, Puerto Rico: Editorial de la Universidad de Puerto Rico, 1993.

González Medina, Gonzalo. *Manual azucarero de Cuba*. Havana: Editorial de Ciencia y Técnica, Instituto Cubano del Libro, 1971.

Gordon, Robert Aaron. *Business Leadership in the Large Corporation*. Berkeley: University of California Press, 1961.

Graham, Richard. "Slavery and Economic Development: Brazil and the United States in the Nineteenth Century." *Comparative Studies in Society and History* 23 (1981): 620–55.

Grasmuck, Sherry. "Migration within the Periphery: Haitian Labor in the Dominican Sugar and Coffee Industries." *International Migration Review* 16 (Summer 1982): 365–77.

Greaves, Ida C. "Plantations in World Economy." In Pan American Union, *Plantation Systems of the New World*. Washington, D.C.: General Secretariat of the Organization of American States, 1959.

Greenfield, S. "Plantations, Sugar Cane, and Slavery." In *Roots and Branches: Current Directions in Slave Studies*, edited by Michael Craton. Toronto: Pergamon, 1979.

Guaranty Trust Company of New York. *Cuba*. New York: Guaranty Trust Company of New York, 1916.

Guerra y Sánchez, Ramiro. *Azúcar y población en las Antillas*. 1927. 3d ed. Havana: Editorial Cultural, 1944. Translated into English as Guerra y Sánchez, *Sugar and Society in the Caribbean: An Economic History of Cuban Agriculture*. New Haven: Yale University Press, 1964.

——. *La industria azucarera de Cuba: Su importancia nacional, su organización, su situación actual*. Havana: Editorial Cultural, 1940.

——, et al. *Historia de la nación cubana*. Vol. 7. Havana: Editorial Historia de la Nación Cubana, 1952.

Harrison, Bennett. *Lean and Mean: The Changing Landscape of Corporate Power in the Age of Flexibility*. New York: Basic Books, 1994.

Herman, Edward S. *Corporate Control: Corporate Power*. New York: Cambridge University Press, 1981.

——. "Do Bankers Control Corporations?" *Monthly Review* 25 (1973): 12–29.

Hernández Angueira, Luisa. "El trabajo femenino a domicilio y la industria de la aguja en Puerto Rico, 1914–1940." In *Género y Trabajo: La industria de la aguja en Puerto Rico y el Caribe Hispano*, edited by María del Carmen Baerga. Río Piedras, Puerto Rico: Editorial de la Universidad de Puerto Rico, 1993.

Hernández, Frank Marino. *La inmigración Haitiana*. Santo Domingo: Ediciones Sargazo, 1973.

——. "La inmigracion haitiana en la República Dominicana." *EME-EME Estudios Dominicanos* 1, no. 5 (1973): 24–56.

Herzig-Shannon, Nacy. "El American Colonial Bank y sus directores." Graduate History Department, University of Puerto Rico, 1994.

Hicks, Frederic. "Making a Living during the Dead Season in Sugar-Producing Regions of the Caribbean." *Human Organization* 31 (1972): 73–81.

Hidy, Muriel E., and Ralph W. Hidy. *History of the Standard Oil Company (New Jersey): Pioneering in Big Business, 1882–1911*. New York: Harper & Brothers, 1955.

Hilferding, Rudolf. *Finance Capital: A Study of the Latest Phase of Capitalist Development*. 1910. Reprint. London: Routledge & Kegan Paul, 1981.

Hindley, Brian. "Separation of Ownership and Control in the Modern Corporation." *Journal of Law and Economics* 13 (1970): 185–221.

History Task Force, Centro de Estudios Puertorriqueños, City University of New York. *Labor Migration under Capitalism*. New York: Monthly Review Press, 1979.

Hitchman, James H. "U.S. Control over Sugar Production, 1898–1902." *Journal of Inter-American Studies and World Affairs* 12 (January 1970): 90–106.

Hobson, John. *Imperialism: A Study*. Ann Arbor: University of Michigan Press, 1965.

Hoernel, Robert B. "Sugar and Social Change in Oriente, Cuba, 1898–1946." *Journal of Latin American Studies* 8 (1976): 215–49.

Hollander, Jacob H. "The Readjustment of San Domingo's Finances." *Quarterly Journal of Economics* 21 (1903): 405–26.

Huguet y Balanzo, José. *Ingenios que han hecho zafra en el año de 1901 a 1902 en cada una de las provincias de que se compone la isla de Cuba*. Havana: Imprenta Mercantil, 1902.

Ibarra, Jorge. "Los mecanismos económicos del capital financiero obstaculizan la formación de la burguesía doméstica cubana, 1898–1930." *Islas* (Santa Clara, Cuba) 79 (September–December 1984): 71–92.

Iglesias García, Fe. "Algunos aspectos de la distribución de la tierra en 1899." *Santiago* (Universidad de Santiago de Cuba) 40 (1980): 119–78.

———. "Azúcar y crédito durante la segunda mitad del siglo XIX en Cuba." *Santiago* 52 (1983): 119–44.

———. "Carácteristicas de la imigración española a Cuba (1904–1930." *Economía y desarrollo* (Havana) 18 (March–April 1988): 76–101.

———. "El censo cubano de 1877 y sus diferentes versiones." *Santiago* 34 (June 1979): 167–214.

———. "Changes in Cane Cultivation in Cuba, 1860–1900." *Social and Economic Studies* 37 (March–June 1988): 341–63.

———. "Contratados peninsulares para Cuba." *Anuario de Estudios Americanos* (Spain) 51, no. 2 (1994): 93–112.

———. "Del ingenio al central." Instituto de Historia de Cuba. Havana, 1995.

———. "El movimiento de pasajeros entre España y Cuba, 1882–1900." Instituto de Historia de Cuba, 1995.

James, C. L. R. *The Black Jacobins: Toussaint L'Ouverture and the San Domingo Revolution*. New York: Random House, 1963.

James, David R., and Michael Soref. "Profit Constraints and Managerial Autonomy: Managerial Theory, Unmaking the Corporation President." *American Sociological Review* 46 (February 1981): 1–18.

Jenks, Leland H. *Our Cuban Colony*. New York: Vanguard Press, 1929.

Josephson, Matthew. *The Robber Barons: The Great American Capitalists, 1861–1901*. New York: Harcourt Brace, 1934.

Junta de Planificación de Puerto Rico. *Serie histórica del empleo, desempleo, y grupo trabajador en Puerto Rico*. San Juan: Junta de Planificación de Puerto Rico, 1985.

Junta de Salario Mínimo de Puerto Rico. *La industria del azúcar en Puerto Rico*. San Juan: Junta de Salario Mínimo, 1942.

Kaysen, Carl. "Another View of Corporate Capitalism." *Quarterly Journal of Economics* 79 (February 1965): 41–51.

———. "The Social Significance of the Modern Corporation." *American Economic Review* 47 (1957): 311–19.

Kent, Noel J. *Hawaii: Islands under the Influence*. New York: Monthly Review Press, 1983.

Kepner, Charles D., and Jay H. Soothill. *The Banana Empire*. New York: Vanguard Press, 1935.

Kerr, James E. *The Insular Cases: The Role of the Judiciary in American Expansionism*. Port Washington, N.Y.: Kennikat Press, 1982.

Kindleberger, Charles. *The World in Depression, 1929–1939*. Berkeley: University of California Press, 1973.

Kirk, Grayson L. *Philippine Independence*. New York: Farrar and Rienhart, 1936.

Kirkendall, Richard S. *Social Scientists and Farm Policies in the Age of Roosevelt*. Columbia: University of Missouri Press, 1966.

Kirkland, Edward. "The Robber Barons Revisited." *American Historical Review* 66 (1960): 68–84.

Knight, Franklin W. *The Caribbean: The Genesis of Fragmented Nationalism*. New York, Oxford University Press, 1978.

——. *Slave Society in Cuba during the Nineteenth Century*. Madison: University of Wisconsin Press, 1970.

Knight, Melvin K. *The Americans in Santo Domingo*. New York: Vanguard Press, 1928.

Koenig, Thomas, Robert Gogel, and John Sonquist. "Models of the Significance of the Interlocking Corporate Directorates." *American Journal of Economics and Sociology* 38 (1979): 173–86.

Kolko, Gabriel. "Brahmins of Business, 1870–1914: A Hypothesis on the Social Basis of Success in American History." In *The Critical Spirit*, edited by Kurt H. Wolf and Barrington Moore. Boston: Beacon, 1967.

——. *Main Currents in Modern American History*. New York: Pantheon Books, 1984.

——. "The Premises of Business Revisionism." *Business History Review* 33 (1959): 330–44.

——. *The Triumph of Conservatism*. New York: Free Press, 1963.

Kotz, David M. *Bank Control of Large Corporations in the United States*. Berkeley: University of California Press, 1978.

Laclau, Ernesto. "Feudalism and Capitalism in Latin America." In Ernesto Laclau, *Politics and Ideology in Marxist Theory*. London: Verso, 1977.

LaFeber, Walter. *The New Empire: An Interpretation of American Expansion, 1860–1898*. Ithaca: Cornell University Press, 1963.

Landes, David S. *The Unbound Prometheus*. Cambridge, Eng.: Cambridge University Press, 1969.

Langley, Lester D. *Struggle for the American Mediterranean: United States–European Rivalry in the Gulf-Caribbean, 1776–1904*. Athens: University of Georgia Press, 1985.

——. *The U.S. and the Caribbean in the 20th Century*. Athens: University of Georgia Press, 1985.

Larner, Robert J. *Management Control of the Large Corporation*. New York: Dunellen, 1970.

——. "Ownership and Control of the 200 Largest Non-Financial Corporations." *American Economic Review* 56 (1966): 777–87.

Latortue, Paul. "Neo-Slavery in the Canefields: Haitians in the Dominican Republic." *Caribbean Review* 14, no. 4 (1985): 18–20.

Lemoine, Maurice. *Azúcar amargo: Hay esclavos en el Caribe*. Santo Domingo: CEPAE, 1987.

Leuchtenburg, William E. *Franklin D. Roosevelt and the New Deal*. New York: Harper & Row, 1963.

Lewis, Cleona. *America's Stake in International Investments*. Washington, D.C.: Brookings Institution, 1938.

Lewis, S., and T. G. Matthews, eds. *Caribbean Integration*. Río Piedras, Puerto Rico: Institute for Caribbean Studies of the University of Puerto Rico, 1967.

Lippman, Edmund Oscar von. *Historia do açúcar, desde a época mais remota até o começo da fabricaçao do açúcar de beterraba*. 2 vols. Translated from the German to the Portuguese by Rodolfo Countinho. Rio de Janeiro: Ediçao do Instituto do Açúcar e do Alcool, 1941–42.

López, Adalberto, and James Petras. *Puerto Rico and the Puerto Ricans*. Cambridge, Mass.: Schenkman, 1974.

López Domínguez, Francisco A. "Origen y desarollo de la industria del azúcar en Puerto Rico." *Revista de Agricultura de Puerto Rico* 19 (August 1927): 49–55; (September 1927): 103–6; (October 1927): 167–72; (November 1927): 287–89.

López Segrera, Francisco. *Cuba, capitalismo dependiente y subdesarollo (1510–1959)*. Mexico City: Diógenes, 1973.

Loveira, Carlos. "Labour in the Cuban Sugar Industry." *International Labour Review* 20 (1929): 424–29.

Lozano, Wilfredo. *La dominación imperialista en la República Dominicana, 1900–1930: Estudio de la primera ocupación norteamericana de Santo Domingo.* Santo Domingo: Editora de la Universidad Autónoma de Santo Domingo, 1976.

Lundberg, Ferdinand. *America's 60 Families.* New York: Vanguard Press, 1937.

———. *The Rich and the Super Rich.* New York: Bantam Books, 1968.

Magdoff, Harry. *Imperialism: From the Colonial Age to the Present.* New York: Monthly Review Press, 1978.

Majka, Linda C., and Theo J. Majka. *Farm Workers, Agribusiness, and the State.* Philadelphia: Temple University Press, 1982.

Maldonado Denis, Manuel. *Puerto Rico y Estados Unidos: Emigración y colonialismo.* Mexico City: Siglo XXI, 1976.

Malowist, Marian. "Les debuts du système de plantations dans la période des grandes découvertes." *Africana Bulletin* 1 (1968): 9–30.

Mandel, Ernest. *Late Capitalism.* London: Verso, 1978.

———. *Marxist Economic Theory.* London: Pluto Press, 1977.

Mandle, Jay R. *Patterns of Caribbean Development: An Interpretive Essay on Economic Change.* New York: Gordon and Breach Science Publishers, 1982.

———. "The Plantation Economy: An Essay in Definition." *Science and Society* 34 (1972): 49–62.

Mann, Susan Archer. *Agrarian Capitalism in Theory and Practice.* Chapel Hill: University of North Carolina Press, 1990.

Manning, Caroline. "The Employment of Women in Puerto Rico: Home Work in the Needle Trades." *Bulletin of the Women's Bureau, United States Department of Labor.* Washington, D.C.: U.S. Government Printing Office, 1934.

Marcus, Joseph. *Labor Conditions in Puerto Rico.* Washington, D.C.: U.S. Government Printing Office, 1919.

Mariolis, Peter. "Interlocking Directorates and Control of Corporations: The Theory of Bank Control." *Social Science Quarterly* 56 (1975): 425–39.

Martí, José. *Obras Completas.* Vol. 6. Havana: Editorial de Ciencias Sociales, 1975.

Martínez Fernández, Luis. "The Sweet and the Bitter: Cuban and Puerto Rican Responses to the Mid-Nineteenth Century Sugar Challenge." *New West Indian Guide* 67 nos. 1 and 2 (1993): 47–67.

Martínez, Héctor Luis. "La fuerza de trabajo en el proceso de modernización de la industria azucarera dominicana: caso de San Pedro de Macorís." *ECOS* (Universidad Autónoma de Santo Domingo) 2, no. 3 (1994): 111–26.

Martínez Vergne, Teresita. *Capitalism in Colonial Puerto Rico: Central San Vicente in the Late Nineteenth Century.* Gainesville: University of Florida Press, 1992.

Mathews, Thomas. *La política puertorriqueña y el Nuevo Trato.* Río Piedras, Puerto Rico: Editorial Universitaria, 1975.

May, Robert E. *The Southern Dream of Caribbean Empire, 1854–1861.* Baton Rouge: Louisiana State University Press, 1973.

McAvoy, Muriel. "Brotherly Love: The Correspondence of Henry Cabot Lodge and J. D. H. Luce, 1898–1913." *Historia y Sociedad* (Río Piedras, Puerto Rico) 1 (1988): 99–102.

———. "Early United States Investors in Puerto Rican Sugar." Paper presented at the Fourteenth Conference of the Association of Caribbean Historians, San Juan, Puerto Rico, April 16–21, 1982.

———. "Officers and Directors of United States Companies Investing in Cuban Sugar: A Listing with Brief Biographical Data." Paper presented at the Twenty-first Colloque de l'Association des Historiens da la Caraibe, Basse-Terre, Guadeloupe, March 19–24, 1989.

McAvoy Weissman, Muriel. "Manuel Rionda and the Formation of the Cuba Cane Sugar Corporation." Paper presented at the Twenty-first Colloque de l'Association des Historiens de la Caraibe, Basse-Terre, Guadeloupe, March 19–24, 1989.

McMichael, Philip, James Petras, and Robert Rhodes. "Industrialization in the Third World." In *Critical Perspectives on Imperialism and Social Class in the Third World*, edited by James Petras. New York: Monthly Review Press, 1978.

McWilliams, Carey. *Factories in the Field*. Boston: Little, Brown, 1939.

Medina Mercado, Luis. "El proceso de acumulación de tierras ocasionado por el desarrollo del capital industrial azucarero: El caso de la Fajardo Sugar." Thesis, University of Puerto Rico, 1987.

Mejía Ricart, Tirso, ed. *La sociedad dominicana durante la Primera República, 1844–1861*. Santo Domingo: Universidad Autónoma de Santo Domingo, 1977.

Meléndez, Edgardo. *Puerto Rico en "Patria."* Río Piedras, Puerto Rico: Decanato de Estudios Graduados e Investigación, Universidad de Puerto Rico, 1996.

Menshikov, S. *Millionaires and Managers: Structure of the U.S. Financial Oligarchy*. Moscow: Progress Publishers, 1973.

Mills, C. Wright. *The Power Elite*. New York: Oxford University Press, 1956.

———. *The Sociological Imagination*. New York: Oxford University Press, 1959.

Mintz, Beth, and Michael Schwartz. "Financial Interest Groups and Interlocking Directorates." *Social Science History* 7 (1983): 183–204.

———. "Interlocking Directorates and Interest Group Formation." *American Sociological Review* 46 (1981): 851–69.

———. "The Structure of Intercorporate Unity in American Business." *Social Problems* 29 (1981): 87–103.

Mintz, Sidney W. "Cañamelar." in Julian Steward et al. *The People of Puerto Rico*. Urbana: University of Illinois Press, 1953.

———. *Caribbean Transformations*. Baltimore: Johns Hopkins University Press, 1974.

———. "From Plantations to Peasants in the Caribbean." In *Caribbean Contours*, edited by Sidney Mintz and Sally Price. Baltimore: Johns Hopkins University Press, 1985.

———. "The Plantation as a Socio-Cultural Type." In Pan American Union, *Plantation Systems of the New World*. Washington, D.C.: General Secretariat of the Organization of American States, 1959.

———. "The Rural Proletariat and the Problem of Rural Proletarian Consciousness." In *Peasants and Proletarians: The Struggles of Third World Workers*, edited by Robin Cohen, Peter Gutkind, and Phyllis Brazier. New York: Monthly Review Press, 1979.

———. "Slavery and the Rise of Peasantries." In *Roots and Branches: Current Directions in Slave Studies*, edited by Michael Craton. Toronto: Pergamon Press, 1979.

———. *Sweetness and Power: The Place of Sugar in World History*. New York: Viking, 1985.

———. "Was the Plantation Slave a Proletarian?" *Review—Fernand Braudel Center for the Study of Economics, Historical Systems, and Civilizations* 2, no. 1 (1978): 81–98.

——. *Worker in the Cane: A Puerto Rican Life History*. New York: Norton, 1974.

Mintz, Sidney, and Eric Wolf. "Haciendas and Plantations in Middle America and the Antilles." *Social and Economic Studies* 6 (September 1957): 380–412.

Mizruchi, Mark S. *The American Corporate Network, 1900–1970*. Beverly Hills: Sage, 1982.

——. "Relations among Large American Corporations, 1904–74." *Social Science History* 7 (1983): 165–83.

Mizruchi, Mark S., and Michael Schwartz, eds. *Intercorporate Relations: The Structural Analysis of Business*. Cambridge, Eng.: Cambridge University Press, 1987.

Montoro, Rafael. *Discursos políticos y parlamentarios*. Philadelphia: La Compañía Lévytype, Impresores y Grabadores, 1894.

Moody, John. *Masters of Capital*. New Haven: Moody, 1919.

——. *The Truth about the Trusts*. New York: Moody, 1904.

Morales Carrión, Arturo. *Puerto Rico and the Non-Hispanic Caribbean: A Study in the Decline of Spanish Exclusivism*. Río Piedras, Puerto Rico: University of Puerto Rico Press, 1952.

Moreno Fraginals, Manuel. *El Ingenio: Complejo económico social cubano del azúcar*. 3 vols. Havana: Editorial de Ciencias Sociales, 1977.

——. "Plantaciones en el Caribe: El caso Cuba–Puerto Rico–Santo Domingo (1860–1940)." In *La historia como arma y otros ensayos sobre esclavos, ingenios, y plantaciones*. Barcelona: Editorial Crítica, 1983.

Morner, Magnus. "La hacienda hispanoamericana: Examen de las investigaciones y debates recientes." In *Haciendas, latifundios y plantaciones en América Latina*, edited by Enrique Florescano. Mexico City: Siglo XXI, 1978.

Moya Pons, Frank. *La dominación haitiana*. Santiago de los Caballeros: Universidad Católica Madre y Maestra, 1972.

——. *Manual de historia dominicana*. Santiago de los Caballeros: Universidad Católica Madre y Maestra, 1984.

Mullins, Jack Simpson. "The Sugar Trust: Henry O. Havemeyer and the American Sugar Refining Company." Ph.D. diss., University of South Carolina, 1964.

Muñiz Varela, Miriam. "El capital monopólico en la transición al capitalismo en Puerto Rico." *Revista de Ciencias Sociales de la Universidad de Puerto Rico* 23 (1981): 445–94.

Murray, Martin J. *The Development of Capitalism in Colonial Indochina (1870–1940)*. Berkeley: University of California Press, 1980.

Muto, H. Paul. "The Illusory Promise: The Dominican Republic and the Process of Economic Development, 1900–1930." Ph.D. diss., University of Washington, 1976.

Myers, Gustavus. *History of the Great American Fortunes*. New York: Modern Library, 1936.

National City Bank of New York. *Cuba: Review of Commercial, Industrial and Economic Conditions in 1919*. New York: National City Bank of New York, 1919.

Navin, Thomas R., and Marian V. Sears. "The Rise of a Market for Industrial Securities, 1877–1902." *Business History Review* 29 (1955): 105–38.

Nelson, Ralph L. *Merger Movements in American Industry*. Princeton: Princeton University Press, 1956.

Norcross, Charles P. "The Beet Sugar Round-Up." *Cosmopolitan* 47 (November 1909): 713–21.

——. "The Rebate Conspiracy." *Cosmopolitan* 47 (December 1909), 65–73.

——. "The Trail of the Hunger Tax." *Cosmopolitan* 47 (October 1909): 588–97.

Norich, Samuel. "Interlocking Directorates, the Control of Large Corporations, and Patterns of Accumulation in the Capitalist Class." In *Classes, Class Conflict, and the State: Empirical Studies in Class Analysis*, edited by Maurice Zeitlin. Boston: Winthrop, 1980.

Norman, E. H. *Japan's Emergence as a Modern State: Problems of the Meiji Period*. New York: International Secretariat, Institute of Pacific Relations, 1940.

O'Connor, James F. *Accumulation Crisis*. New York: Basil Blackwell, 1984.

Palmer, Donald. "Interpreting Corporate Interlocks from Broken Ties." *Social Science History* 7 (Spring 1983): 217–31.

Pantojas García, Emilio. *Development Strategies as Ideology: Puerto Rico's Export-Led Industrialization Experience*. Boulder: Lynne Rienner, 1990.

Pérez, Louis A. Jr. *Cuba between Empires, 1878–1902*. Pittsburgh: University of Pittsburgh Press, 1987.

———. *Cuba between Reform and Revolution*. New York: Oxford University Press, 1988.

———. "Cuba Materials in the Bureau of Insular Affairs Library." *Latin American Research Review* 13, no. 3 (1978): 182–88.

———. *Cuba under the Platt Amendment, 1902–1934*. Pittsburgh: University of Pittsburgh Press, 1987.

———. "Insurrection, Intervention, and the Transformation of Land Tenure Systems in Cuba, 1895–1902." *Hispanic American Historical Review* 65 (1985): 229–54.

———. *Intervention, Revolution and Politics in Cuba, 1913–1921*. Pittsburgh: University of Pittsburgh Press, 1987.

Pérez, Manuel A. *Living Conditions among Small Farmers in Puerto Rico (Research Bulletins on Agriculture and Livestock 2)*. San Juan: Bureau of Supplies, Printing and Transportation, 1942.

———, et. al. "Health and Socio Economic Conditions on a Sugar Cane Plantation." *Puerto Rico Journal of Public Health and Tropical Medicine* 12, no. 4 (June 1937): 405–90.

Pérez de la Riva, Juan. "Cuba y la migración antillana, 1900–1931." In Juan Pérez de la Riva et al., *La república neocolonial*, Vol. 2. Havana: Editorial de Ciencias Sociales, 1979.

———. "La inmigración antillana a Cuba durante el primer tercio del siglo XX." *Revista de la Biblioteca Nacional José Martí* 6, no. 2 (May–August 1975): 75–87.

Pérez Stable, Marifeli. *The Cuban Revolution: Origins, Course, and Legacy*. Oxford: Oxford University Press, 1993.

Pérez Velasco, Erick. "La condición obrera en Puerto Rico (1898–1920)." *Plural* (Revista de la Administración de Colegios Regionales, Puerto Rico) 3, nos. 1–2 (1984): 157–70.

Perkins, Van L. *Crisis in Agriculture: The Agricultural Adjustment Administration and the New Deal, 1933*. Berkeley: University of California Press, 1969.

Perlo, Victor. *The Empire of High Finance*. New York: International Publishers, 1957.

———. "People's Capitalism and Stock Ownership." *American Economic Review* 48 (1958): 333–47.

Peruser, Glenn. "Haitian Emigration in the Early Twentieth Century." *International Migration Review* 18 (Spring 1984): 4–18.

Peterson, Shorey. "Corporate Control and Capitalism." *Quarterly Journal of Economics* 79 (1965): 1–24.

———. "Corporate Control and Capitalism: Reply." *Quarterly Journal of Economics* 79 (1965): 492–99.

Petras, Elizabeth McLean. *Jamaican Labor Migration: White Capital and Black Labor, 1850–1930*. Boulder: Westview Press, 1988.

Petras, James, ed. *Critical Perspectives on Imperialism and Social Class in the Third World*. New York: Monthly Review Press, 1978.

Pichardo, Hortensia. *Documentos para la historia de Cuba*. Vol 2. Havana: Editorial de Ciencias Sociales, 1973.

Picó, Fernando. *Amargo café: Los pequeños y medianos caficultores en Utuado en la segunda mitad del siglo XIX*. Río Piedras, Puerto Rico: Huracán, 1981.

———. *Libertad y servidumbre en el Puerto Rico del siglo XIX: Los jornaleros utuadeños en las vísperas del auge del café*. Río Piedras, Puerto Rico: Huracán, 1979.

Pierre, Guy. "The Frustrated Development of the Haitian Sugar Industry between 1915/18 and 1938/39: International Financial and Commercial Rivalries." In *The World Sugar Economy in War and Depression, 1914–1940*, edited by Bill Albert and Adrian Graves. London: Routledge, 1988.

Pino Santos, Oscar. *El asalto a Cuba por la oligarquía financiera yanqui*. Havana: Casa de las Américas, 1973.

———. *El imperialismo norteamericano en la economía de Cuba*. Havana: Editorial de Ciencias Sociales, 1973.

———. *La oligarquía yanqui en Cuba*. Mexico City: Editorial Nuestro Tiempo, 1975.

Plant, Roger. *Sugar and Modern Slavery: A Tale of Two Countries*. London: Zed Books, 1987.

Pollitt, Brian H. "The Cuban Sugar Economy and the Great Depression." *Bulletin of Latin American Research* 3, no. 2 (1984): 3–28.

———. "The Cuban Sugar Economy in the 1930s." In *The World Sugar Economy in War and Depression, 1914–1940*, edited by Bill Albert and Adrian Graves. London: Routledge, 1988.

Pomeroy, William J. *American Neo-Colonialism: Its Emergence in the Philippines and Asia*. New York: International Publishers, 1970.

Portell Vilá, Herminio. "La industria azucarera y su futuro." *Revista Bimestre Cubana* 50 (1942): 161–79.

Porto Rico, Commissioner of Agriculture and Labor. *Report of the Commissioner of Agriculture and Labor of Porto Rico, 1920*. Washington, U.S. Government Printing Office, 1920.

Pratt, Julius W. *America's Colonial Experiment*. New York: Prentice-Hall, 1950.

———. *Expansionists of 1898: The Acquisition of Hawaii and the Spanish Islands*. New York: Quadrangle Books, 1964.

———. "The Hawaiian Revolution: A Re-interpretation." *Pacific Historical Review* 1 (September 1932): 273–94.

Puerto Rico, Departamento del Trabajo, Beneficencia y Corrección. *Cuarto informe anual del Negociado del Trabajo dirigido a la Asamblea Legislativa de Puerto Rico*. San Juan: Bureau of Supplies, Printing and Transportation, 1916.

Puerto Rico Reconstruction Administration. *Census of Puerto Rico, 1935: Population and Agriculture*. Washington, D.C.: U.S. Government Printing Office, 1938.

Quintero Rivera, Angel G. "Background to the Emergence of Imperialist Capitalism in Puerto Rico." *Caribbean Studies* 3, no. 3 (1973): 31–63.

Quirino, Carlos. *History of the Philippine Sugar Industry*. Manila: Kalayaan Publishing Company, 1974.

Ramos Mattei, Andrés. *Azúcar y esclavitud*. Río Piedras, Puerto Rico: Universidad de Puerto Rico, 1982.

———. *La hacienda azucarera: Su crecimiento y crisis en Puerto Rico (siglo XIX)*. Río Piedras, Puerto Rico: Huracán, 1986.

———. "Las inversiones norteamericanas en Puerto Rico y la ley Foraker, 1898–1900." *Caribbean Studies* 14 (October 1974): 53–69.

———. *La sociedad del azúcar en Puerto Rico, 1870–1910*. Rio Piedras: Decanato de Asuntos Académicos del Recinto de Río Piedras de la Universidad de Puerto Rico, 1988.

Ramos, Julio, ed. *Amor y anarquía: Los escritos de Luisa Capetillo*. Río Piedras, Puerto Rico: Ediciones Huracán, 1992.

Rand McNally & Co. *Rand McNally Cosmopolitan World Atlas*. Chicago: Rand McNally, 1987.

Ratekin, Mervyn. "The Early Sugar Industry in Española." *Hispanic American Historical Review* 34 (February 1954): 1–19.

Reed, Ruiz y Compañía. *Memoria de un ingenio central en Puerto Príncipe*. Havana: La Propaganda Literaria, 1880.

Richardson v. Fajardo Sugar Company, 1915. *Allan H. Richardson, Treasurer of Puerto Rico, v. Fajardo Sugar Company*, U.S. Circuit Court of Appeals, 1st Circuit (Transcript of Record) October 15, 1915, Record Group 350, File 26604/5, National Archives, Washington, D.C.

Rippy, J. Fred. "The Initiation of the Customs Receivership in the Dominican Republic." *Hispanic American Historical Review* 17 (1937): 419–57.

Rochester, Anna. *Rulers of America: A Study of Finance Capital*. New York: International Publishers, 1937.

Rodríguez, Artemio P. *A Report on Wages and Working Hours in Various Industries and on the Cost of Living, in the Island of Puerto Rico during the Year 1933*. San Juan: Bureau of Supplies, Printing and Transportation, 1934.

Rodríguez, Manuel Angel. "La emigración agrícola puertorriqueña: ¿Solución a nuestro problema?" *El Caribe Contemporáneo* (UNAM-Mexico) 8 (June 1984): 79–91.

Rodríguez, P. P. "La pensée nationale bourgeoise pendant les premières années de la République: Le cas José Comallonga." In Centre Interuniversitaire d'Etudes Cubaines, *Les années trente à Cuba*. Paris: Editions L'Harmattan, 1982.

Roorda, Eric Paul. "Genocide Next Door: The Good Neighbor Policy, the Trujillo Regime, and the Haitian Massacre of 1937." *Diplomatic History* 20 (Summer 1996): 301–19.

Rosich, M., and J. Rosich. *Fabricación de azúcar de moscabado en relación con las factorías centrales*. Ponce, Puerto Rico: Tipografía Baldorioty, Marina y Aurora, 1902.

Ross, David F. *The Long Uphill Path: A Historical Study of Puerto Rico's Program of Economic Development*. San Juan: Editorial Edil, 1976.

Roy, William G. "Interlocking Directorates and the Corporate Revolution." *Social Science History* 7 (1983): 143–64.

———. *Socializing Capital: The Rise of the Large Industrial Corporation in America*. Princeton: Princeton University Press, 1997.

Salmi-Bianchi, Jeanne Marie. "Les anciennes sucreries du Maroc." *Annales: Economies, Societés, Civilisations* 24 (1969): 1176–80.

Sánchez-Albornoz, Nicolás. *The Population of Latin America: A History*. Berkeley: University of California Press, 1974.

Santiago, Kelvin Antonio. "La concentración y la centralización de la propiedad en Puerto Rico (1898–1929)." *Hómines* (Universidad Interamericana de Puerto Rico) 6, no. 2 (1983): 15–43.

———. "El Puerto Rico del siglo XIX: Apuntes para su análisis." *Hómines* (Universidad Interamericana de Puerto Rico) 5, nos. 1–2 (1981): 7–23.

Santos Víctores, Iván, and Hernán Venegas Delgado. "Un siglo de historia local: El barrio de Arango (1825–1933)." *Islas* (Universidad de Santa Clara, Cuba) 63 (1979): 13–64.

Scarano, Francisco. "El colonato azucarero en Puerto Rico, 1873–1934: Problemas para su estudio." *Historia y Sociedad* 3 (1990): 143–67.

——. *Sugar and Slavery in Puerto Rico: The Plantation Economy of Ponce, 1800–1850*. Madison: University of Wisconsin Press, 1984.

——, ed., *Inmigración y clases sociales en el Puerto Rico del siglo XIX*. Río Piedras, Puerto Rico: Huracán, 1981.

Schroeder, Susan. *Cuba: A Handbook of Historical Statistics*. Boston: G. K. Hall, 1982.

Schumpeter, Joseph. *Capitalism, Socialism, and Democracy*. New York: George Allen & Unwin, 1976.

Schwartz, Michael. "What the Rockefeller Family Owns." *International Socialist Review* 36 (1975): 10–15.

Schwartz, Stuart B. *Sugar Plantations in the Formation of Brazilian Society, 1550–1835*. London: Cambridge University Press, 1985.

Scott, Christopher. "Peasants, Proletarianization and the Articulation of Modes of Production: The Case of Sugar Cane Cutters in Northern Peru, 1940–1969." *Journal of Peasant Studies* 3 (1976): 321–42.

Scott, John. *Capitalist Property and Financial Power: A Comparative Study of Britain, the United States, and Japan*. New York: New York University Press, 1986.

——. *Corporations, Classes, and Capitalism*. London: Hutchinson, 1985.

Scott, Rebecca J. "Class Relations in Sugar and Political Mobilization in Cuba, 1868–1899." *Cuban Studies* 15 (Winter 1985): 15–28.

——. "Defining the Boundaries of Freedom in the World of Cane: Cuba, Brazil and Louisiana after Emancipation." *American Historical Review* 99 (1994): 70–102.

——. "Explaining Abolition: Contradiction, Adaptation and Challenge in Cuban Slave Society, 1860–1886," *Comparative Studies in Society and History* 26 (January 1984): 83–111.

——. "Exploring the Meaning of Freedom: Post-Emancipation Societies in Comparative Perspective," *Hispanic American Historical Review* 68 (August 1988): 407–28.

——. *Slave Emancipation in Cuba: The Transition to Free Labor, 1860–1899*. Princeton: Princeton University Press, 1985.

Secretaría de Agricultura, Comercio y Trabajo de Cuba. *Portfolio azucarero: Industria azucarera de Cuba, 1912–1914*. Havana: La Moderna Poesía, 1914.

Sheridan, Richard B. "The Plantation Revolution and the Industrial Revolution." *Caribbean Studies* 9, no. 3 (1969): 5–25.

Silva, Arnaldo. *Cuba y el mercado mundial azucarero*. Havana: Editorial de Ciencias Sociales, 1971.

Sitterson, J. Carlyle. *Sugar Country: The Cane Sugar Industry in the South, 1753–1950*. Frankfort: University of Kentucky Press, 1953.

Smith, Adam. *The Wealth of Nations*. Chicago: Chicago University Press, 1976.

Smith, Dudley. *La tarifa*. San Juan: Cámara de Comercio, 1938.

Smith, Raymond T. "Social Stratification, Cultural Pluralism, and Integration in West Indian Societies." In S. Lewis and T. G. Matthews, eds., *Caribbean Integration*. Río Piedras, Puerto Rico: Institute for Caribbean Studies of the University of Puerto Rico, 1967.

Smith, Robert Freeman. *The United States and Cuba: Business and Diplomacy, 1917–1960*. New York: Bookman Associates, 1960.

Smith, Tony. *Lean Production: A Capitalist Utopia?* Amsterdam: International Institute for Research and Education, 1995.

Sonquist, John, and Thomas Koenig. "Interlocking Directorates in the Top U.S. Corporations: A Graph Theory Approach." *Insurgent Sociologist* 5, no. 3 (1975): 196–229.

Soref, Michael. "The Finance Capitalists." In *Classes, Class Conflict, and the State: Empirical Studies in Class Analysis*, edited by Maurice Zeitlin. Boston: Winthrop, 1980.

South Porto Rico Sugar Company. *Fiftieth Anniversary Report*. New York: South Porto Rico Sugar Company, 1951.

Sternsher, Bernard. *Rexford Tugwell and the New Deal*. New Brunswick: Rutgers University Press, 1969.

Steward, Julian, et al. *The People of Puerto Rico*. Urbana: University of Illinois Press, 1953.

Stocking, George W., and Myron Watkins. *Cartels in Action*. New York: Twentieth Century Fund, 1946.

———. *Cartels or Competition?* New York: Twentieth Century Fund, 1948.

———. *Monopoly and Free Enterprise*. New York: Twentieth Century Fund, 1951.

Stoler, Ann Laura. *Capitalism and Confrontation in Sumatra's Plantation Belt*. New Haven: Yale University Press, 1985.

Strong, Leonard Alfred George. *The Story of Sugar*. London: Weidenfeld and Nicolson, 1954.

Sweezy, Paul. "Corporations, the State, and Imperialism." *Monthly Review* 30 (1978): 1–11.

———. "The Decline of the Investment Banker." In *The Present as History*, edited by Paul Sweezy. New York: Monthly Review Press, 1953.

———. "Interest Groups in the American Economy." In *The Present as History*, edited by Paul Sweezy. New York: Monthly Review Press, 1953.

———. *Monopoly and Competition in the English Coal Trade, 1550–1850*. Cambridge, Mass.: Harvard University Press, 1938.

———. "Resurgence of Finance Capital: Fact or Fancy?" *Socialist Revolution* 2 (1972): 157–90.

———. *The Theory of Capitalist Development*. New York: Monthly Review Press, 1976.

———, ed. *The Present as History*. New York: Monthly Review Press, 1953.

Swerling, Boris Cyril. *International Control of Sugar, 1918–41*. Palo Alto: Stanford University Press, 1949.

Taller de Formación Política. *La cuestión nacional: El Partido Nacionalista y el movimiento obrero puertorriqueño*. Río Piedras, Puerto Rico: Editorial Huracán, 1981.

———. *¡Huelga en la caña!* Río Piedras, Puerto Rico: Editorial Huracán, 1984.

Tate, Merze. *Hawaii: Reciprocity or Annexation*. East Lansing: Michigan State University Press, 1968.

———. *The United States and the Hawaiian Kingdom: A Political History*. New Haven: Yale University Press, 1965.

Taussig, Frank William. "The Burden of the Sugar Duty." *Quarterly Journal of Economics* 23 (May 1909): 548–53.

———. *Some Aspects of the Tariff Question: an Examination of the Development of American Industry under Protection*. Cambridge, Mass.: Harvard University Press, 1934.

———. "Sugar: A Lesson on Reciprocity and the Tariff." *Atlantic Monthly* 101 (March 1908): 334–44.

———. *The Tariff History of the United States (7th ed., revised, with additional material, including a consideration of the tariff of 1922)*. New York: G. P. Putnam's Sons, 1923.

Thomas, Clive Y. *Plantations, Peasants, and the State: A Study of the Mode of Sugar Production in Guyana*. Los Angeles: Center for Afro-American Studies of the University of California, 1984.

——. *The Rise of the Authoritarian State: An Essay on the State in the Capitalist Periphery*. New York: Monthly Review Press, 1985.

Timoshenko, V. P. *World Agriculture and the Depression*. New York: Garland, 1983.

Timoshenko, V. P., and B. C. Swerling. *The World's Sugar: Progress and Policy*. Palo Alto: Stanford University Press, 1957.

Tomich, Dale. "The 'Second Slavery': Bonded Labor and the Transformation of the Nineteenth Century World Economy." In Francisco O. Ramírez, ed., *Rethinking the Nineteenth Century: Contradictions and Movements*. New York: Greenwood Press, 1988.

——. *Slavery in the Circuit of Sugar: Martinique and the World Economy, 1830–1848*. Baltimore: Johns Hopkins University Press, 1990.

——. "Small Islands and Huge Comparisons: Caribbean Plantations, Historical Unevenness, and Capitalist Modernity." *Social Science History* 18 (Fall 1994): 339–58.

——. "Spaces of Slavery, Times of Freedom: Rethinking Caribbean History in World Perspective." *Comparative Studies on South Asia, Africa and the Middle East* 17 (1997): 67–80.

——. "World Slavery and Caribbean Capitalism: The Cuban Sugar Industry, 1760–1868." *Theory and Society* 20 (1991): 297–319.

Un colono de Las Villas. *La esclavitud blanca*. Havana: Imprenta de A. Alvarez y Compañía, 1893.

U.S. Tariff Commission. *Sugar: Report of the United States Tariff Commission to the President of the United States: Differences in Cost of Production of Sugar in the United States and Cuba, as Ascertained Pursuant to the Provisions of Section 315 of Title III of the Tariff Act of 1922*. Washington, D.C.: U.S. Government Printing Office, 1926.

——. *Sugar: Report to the President of the United States*. Washington, D.C.: U.S. Government Printing Office, 1934.

U.S. War Department. *Report on the Census of Cuba, 1899*. Washington, D.C.: U.S. Government Printing Office, 1900.

Unwalla, D. B., and W. L. Warner. "The System of Interlocking Directorates." In *The Emergent American Society*, edited by W. L. Warner. New Haven: Yale University Press, 1967.

Useem, Michael. *The Inner Circle: Large Corporations and the Rise of Business Political Activity in the U.S. and the U.K.* New York: Oxford University Press, 1984.

Uz, Félix de la, ed. *Los monopolios extranjeros en Cuba*. Havana: Editorial de Ciencias Sociales, 1984.

Vázquez Galego, Antonio. *La consolidación de los monopolios en Camagüey en la década del veinte*. Havana: Editorial Arte y Literatura, Instituto Cubano del Libro, 1975.

Veblen, Thorstein. *Absentee Ownership and Business Enterprise in Recent Years: The Case of America*. New York: Viking, 1945.

Venegas Delgado, Hernán. "Acerca del proceso de concentración y centralización de la industria azucarera en la región remediana a fines del siglo XIX." *Islas* (Universidad de Santa Clara, Cuba) 73 (1982): 65–121.

Veras, Ramon Antonio. *Migración caribeña: Un capítulo haitiano*. Santo Domingo: Editora Taller, 1985.

Verlinden, Charles. *The Beginnings of Modern Colonization*. Ithaca: Cornell University Press, 1970.

Villarejo, Don. *Stock Ownership and the Control of Corporations*. Ann Arbor: Radical Education Project, ca. 1962.

Vogt, Paul S. *The Sugar Refining Industry of the United States: Its Development and Present Condition*. Philadelphia: Publications of the University of Pennsylvania, 1908.

Wagley, Charles. "Plantation America, a Culture Sphere." In *Caribbean Studies, a Symposium*, edited by Vera Rubin. Seattle: University of Washington Press, 1957.

Wallerstein, Immanuel. *Historical Capitalism*. London: Verso, 1988.

Wallich, Henry C. *Monetary Problems of an Export Economy: The Cuban Experience, 1914–1947*. Cambridge, Mass.: Harvard University Press, 1950.

Warren, Bill. *Imperialism: Pioneer of Capitalism*. London: Verso, 1980.

Watson, Andrew M. "The Arab Agricultural Revolution and Its Diffusion, 700–1100." *Journal of Economic History* 34 (1974): 8–35.

Weigle, Richard Daniel. "The Sugar Interests and American Diplomacy in Hawaii and Cuba, 1893–1903." Ph.D. diss., Yale University, 1939.

Welliver, Judson C. "The Annexation of Cuba by the Sugar Trust." *Hampton's Magazine* 25 (May 1910): 375–88.

——. "The Mormon Church and the Sugar Trust." *Hampton's Magazine* 25 (January 1910): 82–93.

——. "The Secret of the Sugar Trust's Power." *Hampton's Magazine* 25 (May 1910): 717–22.

Wells, David A. *The Sugar Industry of the United States and the Tariff*. New York: N.p., 1878.

Wells, Henry. *The Modernization of Puerto Rico*. Cambridge, Mass.: Harvard University Press, 1969.

Wessman, James M. "Division of Labour, Capital Accumulation and Commodity Exchange on a Puerto Rican Sugar Cane Hacienda." *Social and Economic Studies* 27 (December 1978): 464–80.

Weyl, Walter E. "Labor Conditions in Porto Rico." *Bulletin of the Bureau of Labor* (Washington, D.C.) 61 (November 1905): 723–856.

Williams, Eric. *Capitalism and Slavery*. New York: Capricorn Books, 1966.

——. *From Columbus to Castro: The History of the Caribbean*. New York: Vintage, 1984.

——. *The Negro in the Caribbean*. Washington, D.C.: Associates in Negro Folk Education, 1942.

Willoughby, William Franklin. *Territories and Dependencies of the United States: Their Government and Administration*. New York: Century, 1905.

Wolf, Eric. *Europe and the People without History*. Berkeley: University of California Press, 1982.

——. *Peasant Wars of the Twentieth Century*. New York: Harper, 1969.

Wood, Leonard. *Civil Report of Brigadier General Leonard Wood, Military Governor of Cuba, for the Period from December 20, 1899 to December 21, 1900*. 12 vols. (Washington, D.C.: G.P.O., 1900): vol 7.

Wright, Irene. "The Commencement of the Sugar Cane Industry in America, 1519–1538 (1563)." *American Historical Review* 21 (July 1916): 755–80.

Youngman, Anna. "The Tendency of Modern Combination." *Journal of Political Economy* 15 (April 1907): 193–208, 284–98.

Zanetti, Oscar. "En busca de la reciprocidad." *Santiago* (Santiago de Cuba) 57 (March 1985): 165–205.

——. "Centrales construídos durante el período 1914–1934." Unpublished manuscript, Instituto de Historia de Cuba, Havana, 1989.

——. "Cuestiones metodológicas de la investigacion de los monopolios imperialistas: La experiencia cubana." Biblioteca Nacional José Martí, Havana, 1983.

——. "Producción de centrales yanquis, años 1912–1913 y 1927–28." Instituto de Historia de Cuba, 1989.

Zanetti, Oscar, and Alejandro García. *Caminos para el azúcar*. Havana: Editorial de Ciencias Sociales, 1987.

———. *United Fruit Company: Un caso de dominio imperialista en Cuba*. Havana: Editorial de Ciencias Sociales, 1976.

Zeitlin, Maurice. *The Civil Wars in Chile (or the Bourgeois Revolutions That Never Were)*. Princeton: Princeton University Press, 1984.

———. "Corporate Ownership and Control: The Large Corporation and the Capitalist Class." *American Journal of Sociology* 79 (1974): 1073–1119.

———. "On Class Theory of the Large Corporation." *American Journal of Sociology* 81 (1976): 894–903.

Zeitlin, Maurice, and Richard Earl Ratcliff. *Landlords and Capitalists: The Dominant Class of Chile*. Princeton: Princeton University Press, 1988.

Zeitlin, Maurice, and Michael Soref. "Finance Capital and the Internal Structure of the Capitalist Class in the United States." In *Intercorporate Relations: The Structural Analysis of Business*, edited by Mark S. Mizruchi and Michael Schwartz. Cambridge, Eng.: Cambridge University Press, 1987.

Zerbe, Richard. "The American Sugar Refinery Company, 1887–1914: The Story of a Monopoly." *Journal of Law and Economics* 12 (October 1969): 339–75.

Index